D1192949

WARBURTON

i.t.a.

DATE DUE			

i.t.a.:

An Independent Evaluation

This book
is the report of a study,
carried out for the Schools Council,
on the use of
the initial teaching alphabet
as a medium for
beginning reading with infants

i.t.a.:
An Independent Evaluation

F. W. WARBURTON, *Professor of Experimental Education, Department of Education, University of Manchester*

VERA SOUTHGATE, *Lecturer in Curriculum Development, School of Education, University of Manchester*

JOHN MURRAY and W. & R. CHAMBERS

550 20216 1 (Chambers)
7195 1935 7 (Murray)

Printed in Great Britain by
Newgate Press Limited, London EC1

Contents

Foreword

by Professor Sir Cyril Burt

Reading is by far the most important subject that the young child learns at school It is also the most difficult to teach. 'One in six of our boys and girls,' so a recent report assures us, 'leaves school unable to read as that phrase is ordinarily understood – a higher proportion than in any other civilised country'. Nor are the reasons far to seek. English, owing to its composite origin, partly Anglo-Saxon, partly Norman-French, with later literary borrowings from a dozen different tongues, has a more erratic orthography than any other contemporary language. As a result, 'the problem of the best reading method' has formed a scholastic battleground for generations – 'a field strewn with lost causes and littered with exploded ideas'. Of the many ingenious plans proposed to facilitate the tasks of both child and teacher, Sir James Pitman's 'initial teaching alphabet' is the most recent. No other device has aroused such widespread interest or provoked so many investigations into its merits and its limitations.

The aim of the joint enquiry carried out by Professor Warburton and Mrs Southgate has been to collect and sift the mass of evidence now available, and to supplement it by the practical testimony of teachers themselves. The thoroughness with which they have ransacked the literature, the succinct and systematic way in which they have analysed the problems involved and examined the conclusions put forward, above all the cautious and impartial spirit in which they have balanced the pros and cons and reached their own evaluation, deserve high praise. The information thus accumulated is set out in three main parts: first, replies received from local education authorities; secondly, the views of infant teachers and other first-hand observers; thirdly, the reports of investigators in various countries who have carried out and published experimental and statistical studies of the new procedure.

On one essential point the evidence from all three sources appears fairly conclusive. So long as the children are tested in the medium which they have used, those infants who have been taught by i.t.a. appear to make, on an average, more rapid progress than those in the control groups who have been taught with the older alphabet and spelling. Backward readers, bewildered by the difficulties presented by the traditional orthography, all too often develop a profound and permanent antipathy for anything to do with print. 'Few things,' wrote Matthew Arnold in one of his reports as Inspector of Schools, 'create so much unhappiness in the life of the school child as the way he is taught to read'. With the Pitman alphabet many of these difficulties are largely circumvented; and the child's eager interest in the content of his reading books is more readily preserved. Nevertheless, this is by no means the most important issue. What the teacher wants to know is, not whether children taught with a simplified style of printing can learn to read more speedily *in that particular style*, but whether their preliminary efforts with this novel medium will help them to read and spell with greater ease and accuracy when they have changed over to the ordinary style. Here the data so far obtained are less conclusive; and somewhat conflicting verdicts have been reached by different investigators and by different teachers. Part of the trouble arises from the fact that very few follow-up studies have been prolonged for more than a couple of years. As Professor Warburton puts it, 'the evidence is not compelling that i.t.a. is the superior medium *after the transition* to t.o., particularly as some closely controlled researches that have been pursued to the third year suggest that the t.o. groups catch up; we must await the findings of other researches'.

Sir James Pitman's printed alphabet, like Sir Isaac Pitman's shorthand, is based essentially on phonic principles: all words are spelt as they are pronounced. It is therefore not surprising to find that its benefits show up most clearly when children are tested for accuracy of pronunciation. In tests of speed those taught by i.t.a. seem a little slow, since phonic analysis is necessarily a slower business than the method of look-and-say. Nor do they (as judged by the averages in the tables) shine in tests of comprehension; and comprehension is after all the most vital part of reading. Few people in later life require to read aloud, but all are expected to understand what they read. In silent reading a different spelling for words or syllables with the same sound but a different meaning is often not a hindrance but a help: consider how quickly the eye distinguishes between such homonyms as 'eye' and 'I', 'hole' and 'whole', 'mist' and 'missed', 'by', 'bye' and 'buy', 'fizzing' and 'physical'. As regards spelling, says Professor Warburton, 'the evidence is completely mixed'. But a glance at the published tables makes one thing clear. Alike in reading and in spelling the average differences reported by various investigators, even when they seem to favour children taught by i.t.a., are so slight and so variable that no *over-all* advantage of any practical importance can reasonably be claimed for the new medium.

From my own experience I am tempted to suggest that the main reason for the frequent discrepancies in the results obtained is to be sought in the wide mental differences between individual pupils. Several investigators, we are told, have noted that i.t.a. seems more successful with the brighter pupils than with the dull. The self-consistent style of spelling which it adopts naturally favours those young readers who tackle unknown words by analysing the constituent letters in the printed syllables, and then re-synthesise the constituent sounds which make up the spoken phrase. This process of mental analysis and re-synthesis must of itself demand a relatively high measure of intelligence. But equally important, I believe, are the differences in children's imagery – a point that hitherto seems to have been largely overlooked. The effective use of phonic methods is scarcely possible without good auditory imagery. And the dull, for the most part, are predominantly visualisers. Their thoughts are couched in terms of what they see, not in terms of verbal soliloquies which they mentally hear or utter. They associate meanings chiefly with the visual impression produced by the word as a whole, when seen as a distinctive pattern, not by attending separately to the individual letters. In short, they learn, as the teacher says, by 'look-and-say'.

Accordingly, since children differ so widely in mental characteristics – not to mention the differences between the cultural backgrounds of their homes – it follows that there can be no one sovereign way of teaching every child to read. No *single* method or medium is likely to possess a general superiority over all other procedures ᶜor all types of children. To my mind, therefore, the real question is, not whether i.t.a. is definitely better than any of the other numerous devices that have previously been tried, but for what particular type of child it is the most appropriate.

Professor Warburton and Mrs Southgate conclude their evaluation by saying that 'the mainly favourable tone of this report should not be taken to imply that the use of i.t.a. is the final and only solution'. And some of the most valuable sections in their chapters are those that outline their own 'suggestions for further research'. One point which in my opinion calls for special study is the possible improvement on the 'augmented alphabet'. Many of the novel symbols present difficulties to the young writer; and for the reader one of the most obvious defects is the lack of any hint as to where the accent should fall. English speech abounds in unaccented syllables, usually containing what is called the 'indeterminate e', as in 'miserable' or 'literary'. Oddly enough, for this recurrent sound the new teaching alphabet includes no specific symbol. I should therefore like to see comparative trials made with the International Phonetic Alphabet, though without its drastic changes in orthography. It is now regularly used by phoneticians and linguists, and has been adopted by many training colleges as an aid to speech-training and the teaching of English. For the abler pupils it will prove indispensable when they come to learn foreign languages. Still more important, as our authors point out, there is a pressing need for improved techniques in the researches themselves – better criteria, more effective tests, and more up-to-date methods of statistical analysis.

Meanwhile, their book presents by far the most comprehensive and impartial study of this complex and urgent problem. It should prove of the utmost value, not only to practising teachers and students in training colleges and institutes of education, but also to academic psychologists engaged in child study or educational research, and to all who have at heart the welfare, happiness and intellectual progress of the child himself.

CYRIL BURT

Authors' Acknowledgements

THE authors wish to thank the very large number of people who, by their co-operation in the form of discussions, answers to queries, correspondence, research reports and clerical help, have made invaluable contributions to this report.

In particular, we should like to express our gratitude to the hundreds of teachers who, often at great inconvenience to themselves, so willingly expressed their views, frankly and at length, and to all the local education authority officials, members of H.M. Inspectorate, linguists and reading experts, lecturers, publishers, parents and others who provided us with valuable oral and written evidence.

Our thanks are also due to Sir James Pitman and members of the i.t.a. Foundations in this country and in the U.S.A. and to Dr John Downing and members of the Reading Research Unit, all of whom answered our many queries patiently and in detail.

We are equally indebted to the many researchers and experts, both at home and abroad, who provided us with their research reports and comments.

Finally, we wish to acknowledge the help given by Dr D. G. Lewis of the Department of Education, University of Manchester, who suggested improvements to the analysis of variance design set out in Chapter 16, and by Mr G. O'Halloran of the i.t.a. Foundation, who provided information about i.t.a. publications between 1967-9 on which the selected additional bibliography in Appendix G was based.

For permission to reproduce copyright material in Appendix B we are grateful to Professor Axel Wijk for an example of his 'Regularized Inglish', Professor E. Fry for an example of his Diacritical Marking System, Thomas Nelson & Sons Ltd for a page from *Colour Story Reading* by J. K. Jones, Educational Explorers Ltd for miniature word charts from *Reading with Words in Colour* by C. Gattegno, and Her Majesty's Stationery Office for an extract from *Children and their Primary Schools*.

F. W. WARBURTON
VERA SOUTHGATE

CHAPTER I

Introduction

I   i.t.a.*

SIR JAMES PITMAN designed what he originally termed the Augmented Roman Alphabet and which he later named the 'initial teaching alphabet' (usually abbreviated to 'i.t.a.') as a means of simplifying the early stages of learning to read. In its present form i.t.a. consists of 44 characters, 24 of which are retentions of letters from our traditional 26-letter alphabet and 20 are new characters. Pitman's aim was to produce an alphabet which closely approached a one-to-one relationship between spoken sound and written symbol, while at the same time endeavouring to ensure that children would experience little difficulty in transferring from reading materials printed in i.t.a. to reading materials printed in our traditional orthography (usually abbreviated to 't.o.'). A sample of prose printed in i.t.a. is given in Appendix B. Further details of the alphabet itself can be found in Pitman (1959) and (1961).

The first experiment in which i.t.a. was used in infant schools in England commenced in September 1961. It was undertaken by the Reading Research Unit of the Institute of Education of London University, under the supervision of John Downing and with the support of the Ministry of Education. Additional schools were drawn into the experiment during the next two years until, by September 1963, over 3,000 infants were using i.t.a. in experimental classes. Further details of this experiment are reported in Downing (1962), (1964a), (1964b), and (1967).

Interim research reports on the experiment, supplemented by comments from teachers who were using i.t.a., began to be published in 1962 and created a great deal of interest. At this time only those schools taking part in the Reading Research Unit's experiment had access to books printed in i.t.a. In June 1963, books printed in i.t.a. were made freely available and, as a result, schools other than the experimental ones began to use i.t.a. The indications were that the use of i.t.a. was spreading fairly rapidly in Great Britain, but accurate information on the extent of its use was not available.

Meanwhile the Reading Research Unit had inaugurated additional experiments with i.t.a. and its use had spread to other countries, notably the U.S.A., in which many different experiments had been set up and interim reports published.

II   Independent evaluations of current curriculum changes

In October 1964, the Schools Council was set up in response to 'a recognition by all branches of the education service that co-operative machinery was needed to organise

* The reader may find it helpful to examine Appendices A and B before reading the main body of this report.

a more rapid, and more effective, response to change' (The Schools Council (1965)). As part of its work the Schools Council recognised 'the need for evaluation of new developments in curriculum, courses and teaching methods'. Accordingly, their intention was that both their own and other important projects in these fields should each have 'an associated programme of evaluation which, using both measurement and judgement techniques, will attempt to answer the question: "Can the claims made for this new approach be substantiated?"'

The aim of these independent evaluations was to present teachers and other educationists with interim information about curriculum developments, while they are still in the formative stages, with a view to stimulating new thinking. Among current educational projects, the use of i.t.a. as a means of beginning reading was clearly one of great interest to teachers, particularly in primary schools. Accordingly, among the future research projects proposed by the Schools Council (1965) was 'a preliminary study towards an evaluation of the initial teaching alphabet'. This report is the result of that proposal.

III The scope of this evaluation

The brief for this research project was as follows. A preliminary, independent evaluation was to be made of the available evidence relating to the use of the initial teaching alphabet as a means of beginning reading with infants in schools. The evaluation was to be considered as a preliminary step to the setting up of a full-scale experiment, should this be deemed necessary. It was suggested that the investigation should incorporate the following three broad lines of approach:

1 An evaluation of all the published research evidence on i.t.a. at home and abroad, including an appraisal of the methodology behind the results of experiments which had been carried out in both Great Britain and the United States of America.

2 The collection and evaluation of the views of knowledgeable people, who had been closely connected with the use of i.t.a., in such a way that this verbal evidence would represent a swathe cut right through every stratum of people involved in any way with i.t.a.

3 Suggestions regarding future research projects on i.t.a. which might be considered necessary.

It was stressed that, as this was to be the first independent report of this nature to be commissioned by a Ministry, almost as important as the results of the evaluation were the methods which would be developed for carrying it out. The Schools Council (1965) themselves showed that they were aware of many of the difficulties which would be encountered, when they noted:

'It has to be recognised, however, that many of the new approaches now being developed have aims which made evaluation difficult. In the present state of knowledge, it is less easy to evaluate how far a new approach has encouraged the development of certain attitudes of mind, or methods of thought, than to say how far the pupils have acquired skills or factual knowledge. It follows that those responsible for evaluating current projects of curriculum development are likely to be involved in exploring methods of evaluation as much as, and perhaps more than, conducting an actual evaluation.'

2

IV Carrying out the brief

The collection of evidence took place during 1966 and the writing of the report continued into 1967. Accordingly, this report refers mainly to the evidence available in 1966, although it was found possible to take note of a few of the reports published early in 1967. (A selected list of later publications on i.t.a. is included in Appendix G.)

As the Schools Council had foreseen, to plan how the evidence should be collected and evaluated posed many problems. These were increased by limitations on both time and personnel, in the face of the enormous amount of both published and oral evidence. Thus the authors would not claim to be entirely satisfied with the methods they have evolved. What can be said is that they set out, with open minds, to collect as much evidence as possible and to evaluate and present it fairly.

Professor F. W. Warburton is responsible for Part Three of the report—'i.t.a. in Practice: Evidence From Research'; Mrs Vera Southgate is responsible for Part One—'A Brief Inquiry into the Extent of the Use of i.t.a.' and Part Two—'i.t.a. in Practice: Evidence from Interviews'; while the 'Introduction' and 'Final Conclusions' are the joint responsibility of the two authors.

PART ONE

A BRIEF INQUIRY INTO
THE EXTENT OF THE USE OF i.t.a.

CHAPTER 2

Information obtained from local education authorities in England and Wales

I   The need for information

As this preliminary independent evaluation of i.t.a. was concerned with its use in the initial stages of reading, the number of schools using it with infant pupils clearly represented one important piece of evidence. In January 1966, when this research project commenced, no such figures were available.

Certain figures, representing numbers of schools and children using i.t.a. in both Great Britain and the U.S.A. had been published but they could only be considered as estimates. The reason for the lack of precise information, as far as Britain was concerned, lay in the traditional freedom of headteachers to use any approach to reading which they might care to choose. Consequently, once books printed in i.t.a. were made freely available to all schools, as happened in June 1963, it was impossible for interested people to do more than guess at the number of schools using i.t.a. Furthermore, such figures as were quoted often referred to the whole of Great Britain and they included junior and secondary schools using i.t.a. with older pupils. Thus, the figures available, although they represented evidence of a fairly rapid spread in the use of the new alphabet, were not precisely relevant to this particular piece of research. The exact information required was the number of schools in England and Wales using i.t.a. with infant pupils. Such information could only be obtained by direct contact and close co-operation with local education authority officials.

II   Preparation of a questionnaire

It was decided that a very simple questionnaire, regarding the number of schools in the authority using i.t.a., would be sent to the Director of Education of every local education authority in England and Wales. A letter explaining the project and asking for the Director of Education's co-operation would accompany the questionnaire. A copy of the questionnaire is given in Appendix C.

Realising the burden which is often placed on local education authority officials by requests from researchers for the completion of lengthy and complicated questionnaires, this particular one was kept as short and simple as possible. An additional reason for brevity and simplicity was the certainty that, the more complicated and time-consuming the questionnaire, the lower the percentage of returns was likely to be.

The most important questions, relative to this particular enquiry, were the first three, concerning the number and percentage of schools containing infant pupils which were known either to be using i.t.a. or to have used it and discarded it. A request for more detailed information regarding the number of classes or children using i.t.a. in each school would have presented local authority officials with an impossible

6

task and would undoubtedly have led to a large percentage of non-return of questionnaires. Accordingly, the information received, and set out in the following tables, merely indicates that a school was making some use of i.t.a. The extent of its use in a school was not known; it could have been used with only one class or with all the classes in the school.

Question 4 on the questionnaire, relating to the use of i.t.a. in junior and secondary schools, other than as a continuation of work commenced in an infant school, and Question 5, referring to other uses of i.t.a., such as in special schools and classes and with adult illiterates, were not of direct relevance to this enquiry. These two questions were included because they would help to round out the total picture of the use of i.t.a. in England and Wales.

III   Return of the questionnaires

The questionnaires were sent out at the beginning of April 1966. The majority were completed and returned by June 1966. The outstanding questionnaires were mostly from those local education authorities who were experiencing the greatest difficulty in collecting the information, namely large counties and authorities in the London area.

It had been realised that while an adviser or inspector in a county borough was likely to know exactly which schools in his authority were using i.t.a., the same would not necessarily be true of large counties. In some cases, the county officials went to a great deal of trouble in sending out questionnaires to all their schools in order to obtain the information asked for. Such a procedure naturally delayed the return of the questionnaires. A few counties, when returning their completed questionnaires, included covering letters indicating that the figures might not be absolutely accurate. Such accuracy could only have been achieved by circulating all their schools, a course they were anxious not to take lest it should be interpreted by headteachers as an infringement of their freedom to choose how reading should be taught. One county authority declined to complete the questionnaire on account of hesitancy about asking for detailed information from its schools.

TABLE 2(a)

Return of questionnaires

Local Education Authorities	Total No.	Forms Completed	Forms Not Returned
Counties	60	58	2
County Boroughs	82	81	1
*London area	21	19	2
Totals	163	158	5

The Inner London Education Authority, the Outer London Boroughs and certain other county boroughs and counties, experienced additional difficulty in that local

* N.B. Throughout the tables in this chapter, the figures for 'London area' represent the combined figures for the Inner London Education Authority and the Outer London Boroughs Education Committees.

authority boundaries had been altered a short time previously. Delay in the return of completed questionnaires was inevitable in these circumstances.

During the summer and autumn of 1966 two reminders were sent to local education authorities who had not replied to the original letter. These, together with the retarded delays occasioned by special difficulties in collecting information, resulted in the last return arriving in December 1966. Hence, the majority of the information given referred to schools using i.t.a. in the Spring and Summer Terms of 1966. A very small proportion related to its use in the Autumn Term of 1966.

From the 163 local education authorities in England and Wales (excluding the Channel Islands), completed returns were received from 158, as set out in the following table. This represents a return of 97%.

IV   Results obtained from questionnaires

Unless otherwise stated, the results set out in the following tables refer to the combined figures received from 158 local education authorities in England and Wales.

A.   LOCAL EDUCATION AUTHORITIES USING i.t.a. WITH INFANTS

Of the 158 local education authorities which sent in completed forms, 140 were using i.t.a. in one or more schools containing infant pupils (see Table 2(b)). In some of these authorities, i.t.a. was also being used in schools containing older pupils and in other circumstances. In 18 local education authorities, i.t.a. was not being used at all.

TABLE 2(b)

Use of i.t.a. in 158 Local Education Authorities

Local Education Authorities	Total No.	Using i.t.a.	Not using i.t.a.
Counties	58	50	8
County Boroughs	81	72	9
London area	19	18	1
Totals	158	140	18

TABLE 2(c)

Numbers of Local Education Authorities with the lowest incidences of the use of i.t.a.

Local Education Authorities using i.t.a.	Total No.	No. of infant schools using i.t.a.					
		1	2	3	4	Less than 5	5 & over
Counties	50	7	–	2	2	11	39
County Boroughs	72	8	9	9	6	32	40
London area	18	5	4	3	2	14	4
Totals	140	20	13	14	10	57	83

8

Of the 140 local education authorities using i.t.a., some were using it to a very limited extent. For example, in 20 of these authorities only one school was using i.t.a. with infants and in a total of 57 authorities it was being used in four or less infant schools. Details of local education authorities making only slight use of i.t.a. are given in Table 2(c).

In contrast, in some local education authorities i.t.a. was being used in large numbers of schools, as can be seen from Table 2(d). It should be noted that the figures in this table represent six different local education authorities, in that the authority with the highest number of schools using i.t.a. was never identical with the authority having the highest percentage of its infant schools using i.t.a.

TABLE 2(d)

**The highest incidence of the use of i.t.a.
in schools containing infant pupils**

Local Education Authorities (all in England)	Schools using i.t.a.	
	Highest No.	Highest %
County	172	24
County Borough	41	100
London area	33	17·5

The total number of schools in England and Wales in which i.t.a. was being used with infant pupils in the summer of 1966 was 1,554. This figure represents 9·2% of the total number of infant schools in the 158 local education authorities from which completed questionnaires were received. Details are given in Table 2(e).

TABLE 2(e)

Use of i.t.a. in schools containing infant pupils

Local Education Authorities	Total No. of schools	Schools using i.t.a.	
		No.	%
Counties	12,094	869	7·2
County Boroughs	3,364	596	14·7
London area	1,410	89	6·3
Totals	16,868	1,554	9·2

Although information regarding schools proposing to use i.t.a. was not requested, the returns from seven authorities contained notes to the effect that additional infant schools were intending to introduce i.t.a. during the following term. The figures given were 37, 38, 4, 8, 1, 2 and 1; this represented a further 91 schools.

The three foregoing tables also give some indication that the use of i.t.a. was by no means evenly spread throughout the country. It will be noted that the highest incidence is to be found in the county boroughs. The percentage of schools using i.t.a. in

9

the counties was only half that of the county boroughs. The Inner London Education Authority and the Outer London Boroughs had a slightly lower percentage than the counties. This lower incidence in the London area is in line with a tendency, revealed by the figures, for schools in the South of England to have adopted i.t.a. less frequently than those in the North of England. Nevertheless, in two county boroughs in the South, the figures returned represented 66% and 50% of all infant schools in the respective authorities. The highest concentrations of the use of i.t.a., however, were found in the North Midlands and the North-West. The two county boroughs with the highest percentages of infant schools using i.t.a., namely 100% and 95% as well as the county with the lowest percentage, namely 24%, were all located in this area.

One further geographical trend which was most noticeable was the small proportion of Welsh schools using i.t.a., in comparison with English schools. The figures in Table 2(f) illustrate this trend very clearly.

TABLE 2(f)

Use of i.t.a. in schools containing infant pupils
(England and Wales separately)

	Total No. of Schools	Schools using i.t.a.	
		No.	%
England	15,243	1,499	9·7
Wales	1,625	55	3·4
England and Wales	16,868	1,554	9·2

The tendency for few Welsh schools to have used i.t.a. is further illustrated by the fact that out of 13 counties, five had no school using i.t.a., while three had one school each. Of the four county boroughs, one had no school using i.t.a. and two had one school each. In other words, of the 17 counties and county boroughs in Wales, only six had more than one school using i.t.a.

TABLE 2(g)

Schools containing infant pupils which have discarded i.t.a,

Local Education Authorities	No. of schools		%
	Using i.t.a.	Discarded i.t.a.	
Counties	869	16	1·9
County Boroughs	596	12	2
London area	89	4	4·5
Totals	1,554	32	2

Question 3a on the questionnaire asked each local education authority to give the number of infant schools which had begun to use i.t.a. and had later discontinued its use. Twenty local education authorities recorded small numbers of schools falling into this category; they amounted in all to 32 schools. These figures, which represent 2% of the total number of schools which had experimented with i.t.a. with infants are set out in Table 2(g).

At the time when the questionnaire was devised, it was not known whether a large or small proportion of those schools which had begun to use i.t.a. had later discontinued its use. Had the proportion of such schools been large, it was considered that it would have been extremely important to discover the reasons which had led head-teachers to take such decisions. Consequently, question 3b asked if local education authorities would be willing to supply details of schools which had discarded i.t.a., if further information should be required. The 20 local authorities concerned all indicated their willingness to co-operate further in this way. In the event, it was not found necessary to pursue this point further.

Five local authorities, representing nine schools which had discontinued using i.t.a., added footnotes to the questionnaire, explaining the course of action taken by the schools concerned. The exact remarks are quoted below; the figure in brackets preceding each remark represents the number of schools in the local education authority which had ceased to use i.t.a.:

(1) 'Discontinued because of expense.'

(1) 'Head abandoned limited use of i.t.a. for reasons arising from school organisa-tion – not from any dissatisfaction with results.'

(4) 'Two of these schools would use i.t.a. again if they had any pupils who would benefit. One other school ceased to use i.t.a. because of staffing difficulties.'

(1) 'Curtailment due to staffing difficulties.'

(2) 'Recently discontinued in both schools because of changes of headteachers.'

It will be noted that all these remarks, which were volunteered, were indicating that the abandonment of i.t.a. was not due to dissatisfaction with the results of using the alphabet.

The above explanations regarding 9 of the 32 schools left the actions of only 23 schools unexplained. Visits to local education authorities and discussions with local advisers and inspectors furnished reasons for this small number of schools discarding i.t.a. Some of the reasons followed the lines of the above quotations, while others indicated certain doubts concerning various aspects of the use of the alphabet itself. Nevertheless, at the end of 1966, it was quite clear that only a negligible number of schools had returned to the use of t.o. with infants after using i.t.a. for reasons other than administrative ones. Accordingly, it was deemed unnecessary to contact such schools with a view to obtaining further information.

B. L.E.A.S USING i.t.a. WITH OLDER PUPILS

By the summer of 1966, some junior schools were using i.t.a. with certain first- and second-year children as a continuation of the process of learning to read with i.t.a. begun in infant schools or classes. Question 4 on the questionnaire was not designed to discover the number of such schools but rather to show which junior and secondary modern schools were using i.t.a. as a remedial measure to aid non-readers or poor readers to make a new beginning. Table 2(h) sets out the relevant figures.

TABLE 2(h)

Use of i.t.a. in Junior and Secondary Schools

Local Education Authorities	No. of Schools		
	Junior	*Sec. Mod.*	*Total*
Counties	253	30	283
County Boroughs	139	30	169
London area	4	3	7
Totals	396	63	459

C. L.E.A.S USING i.t.a. IN OTHER CIRCUMSTANCES

Of the 140 local education authorities in which i.t.a. was being used in one or more infant schools, 78 gave details of its use other than in infant, junior or secondary modern schools (see Table 2(i)). None of the 18 local education authorities which did not use i.t.a. in infant schools, made use of it in other circumstances.

TABLE 2(i)

**Local Education Authorities using i.t.a.
in additional circumstances**

| | *No. of
Local Education
Authorities* |
|---|---|
| Counties | 28 |
| County Boroughs | 43 |
| London area | 7 |
| Total | 78 |

The replies to Question 5 on the questionnaire included mention of the use of i.t.a. in all the circumstances set out in Table 2(j). The number in the right-hand column merely indicates the number of returns which mentioned these particular circumstances. It was not possible to calculate, for example, the total number of E.S.N. schools experimenting with i.t.a. as, while some returns mentioned the exact number of schools, others wrote in general terms of 'experiments in E.S.N. schools'. Some local education authorities listed more than one of the categories in Table 2(j).

Two authorities volunteered comments indicating that the use of i.t.a. had been discontinued in the following circumstances:

'Three special schools have used the i.t.a. alphabet. Two have discontinued its use as it did not prove successful with their pupils.'

'One Remedial Reading Centre has discontinued its use.'

TABLE 2(j)

Additional circumstances in which i.t.a. was being used

Details	No. of Local Education Authorities
E.S.N. Schools	27
Schools for Maladjusted Children	1
Schools for Delicate and Physically Handicapped Children	6
Schools for Partially-Sighted Children	2
Schools or Classes for Deaf Children	2
Special Schools (type not specified)	13
Hospital Schools	2
Child Guidance Clinics and School Psychological Services	11
Diagnostic Unit	1
Remedial Centres and Remedial Services	14
Classes or Groups of Immigrant Children	7
Speech Defects Clinic	1
Junior Training Centres (Health Department)	2
Youth Club for former E.S.N. School Children	1
Army School of Preliminary Education – with semi-literates	1 1
Adult non-readers in prison	1
Classes for adult illiterates	2

PART TWO

i.t.a. IN PRACTICE:
EVIDENCE FROM INTERVIEWS

CHAPTER 3

Collecting the Evidence

I Introduction

A. THE BREADTH OF EVIDENCE REQUIRED

THE verbal evidence required in this section of the evaluation was intended to represent a swathe cut right through experience and informed opinion. It was obtained from knowledgeable or interested people who had direct experience with, or views on, i.t.a. and by observations in schools.

It was necessary that this evidence should represent the views of as many different categories of people as possible and that, within each category, there should be a diversity of views if such a diversity existed. The experiences of teachers who had used i.t.a. had necessarily to come high on the list of priorities, although the views of teachers who had considered using i.t.a. but refrained from doing so also needed to be sounded. Advisers and inspectors of primary education who had observed teachers and children using i.t.a. were in positions to give valuable evidence, as were other knowledgeable visitors to schools such as Her Majesty's Inspectors, University and College of Education lecturers, educational psychologists and remedial teachers.

Another important group of people with whom discussions had to be arranged included Sir James Pitman, the inventor of the alphabet, John Downing and other members of the Reading Research Unit of the Institute of Education of London University and members of the i.t.a. Foundations in both London and the U.S.A. Others who were in positions to make useful contributions to the enquiry included linguists, educational research workers and those who might be classified in general terms as 'educationists', many of whom were lecturers and, in some cases, writers on such subjects as reading, primary education or educational psychology.

The evidence on the use of i.t.a. as a means of beginning reading would clearly not be complete without the comments and reactions of the children who were involved, as well as the parents of the children who had used i.t.a. The views of parents could certainly be ascertained, whereas with children it seemed more likely that the evidence would consist of the reports by parents and teachers, on children's reactions.

Such was the broad field it was hoped to investigate, in a short space of time, with very limited resources.

B. SITUATIONS IN WHICH PEOPLE GAVE EVIDENCE

People's opinions on i.t.a. were collected in three main situations. First, in the course of visits to local education authorities, the views of local inspectors and teachers were invited. Secondly, evidence was taken from individuals, with whom appointments were made outside the setting of a local education authority, and with people who were met at conferences and lectures. Thirdly, towards the end of the enquiry, three group discussions were specially arranged, with a view to filling in discernible gaps in the verbal evidence. In addition, a certain amount of written evidence was received but this was small in comparison with the large amount of verbal evidence which was collected in face-to-face situations.

C. DANGERS OF BIAS

It was apparent that there could be two main sources of bias in this part of the evaluation: the first lay in the selection of schools to be visited and people to be interviewed; the second concerned the subjective nature of the assessment of the results of observations, discussions and interviews. In a preliminary evaluation of a current curriculum change, such as this one, there must necessarily be limiting factors of time, money and personnel, all of which may be likely to increase rather than decrease the bias. For example, the time factor prevented the use of sampling techniques for the selection of local education authorities or schools to be visited and of people to be interviewed. Similarly, the available research grant only permitted the employment of one interviewer. The number of visits and interviews which one investigator can arrange and undertake in different parts of the country, in a few months, is necessarily limited.

It might perhaps be suggested that a greater breadth of evidence could have been collected in the available time by sending out questionnaires to knowledgeable and experienced people and that, furthermore, such evidence would have been likely to be free from bias arising from the subjective nature of the interviews. Such a procedure was considered but rejected on the following grounds:

(i) It would have been necessary to send the questionnaires either to all local authorities and teachers using i.t.a. or to a representative or random sample of them. Yet the information necessary to follow any of these procedures was not available until almost the end of the enquiry, when the majority of the questionnaires, mentioned in Chapter 2, had been returned by local education authorities.

(ii) Most local officials and teachers have neither the time nor the interest to fill in lengthy questionnaires and many, in fact, are not willing to do so.

(iii) Even lengthy questionnaires can easily suffer from bias, not only in the manner in which the questions are framed, but also by the conscious or unconscious omission of certain questions.

(iv) In contrast, in face-to-face interviews, especially in relatively unstructured interviews, it is quite often the unexpected remarks or aspects of the subject, on which the interviewer or the compiler of the questionnaire would not have thought of posing questions, which are the most illuminating.

(v) In an interview, in contrast to information given on a questionnaire, interesting points which emerge can be followed up and enlarged on.

(vi) In personal interviews, especially when these take place in the schools in which curriculum changes are being experimented with, the opinions of the person being interviewed can be absorbed in the setting of his or her age, past experience, attitudes and beliefs and the climate of the teaching situation, in a way which no questionnaire, however detailed, could disclose.

Nevertheless, it was realised that, however fair an observer or interviewer tried to be, some bias arising from his or her past experience and present attitudes and beliefs was likely to creep in. In an attempt to prevent such bias, a very great effort was made by the interviewer to approach each interview with an open mind. The brief notes taken during an interview were expanded to form full notes immediately afterwards. In an effort to avoid a 'mental set' which would lead to certain expectations at interviews, these reports of interviews were filed as soon as they were written and were never looked at again until all the interviews had been completed. It followed that no broad conclusions were drawn during the course of visits and interviews; they only began to emerge clearly when all the records of interviews were reviewed together towards the end of the evaluation.

The foregoing dangers of bias, among others, were perceived and steps were taken to avoid them as far as was possible. Nevertheless, the procedures adopted to obtain a fair cross-section of the available evidence were not considered to be perfect. However, both the methods of selecting people to give verbal evidence and the interviewing techniques employed are described in detail so that the reader may judge for himself the extent to which possible bias in these directions has been avoided. In addition, in writing up reports of verbal evidence, particularly from teachers, their actual words have frequently been quoted, thus making direct evidence available to the reader of this report. Accordingly, it is hoped that the conclusions drawn from this collection of reports of verbal evidence and observations may represent a fair assessment of the use of i.t.a. in the early stages of reading.

II   Evidence from local education authorities visited

To ensure that none of the short available time was wasted, it was essential that visits to local education authorities should commence as early as possible in the evaluation. The limitation of time made it impractical to await the return of questionnaires regarding the number of schools using i.t.a. in each local authority, in order to draw a representative sample of local education authorities.

The first local authorities to experiment with i.t.a. were those which had participated in the Reading Research Unit's original experiment in 1961. They were mainly situated in the northwest of England and the Midlands. These authorities formed obvious starting points for immediate visits. Here were to be found not only teachers with the longest experience of i.t.a. but also the largest numbers of teachers with the widest range of experiences–that is experiences ranging from five years to less than one year with i.t.a., experiences as control schools and experiences both inside and outside experiments. Local authorities other than those which took part in the first experiment were visited at a later stage in the enquiry.

At the completion of the enquiry nine local authorities, extending from large counties to small county boroughs, had been visited. Seven of these authorities took part in the Reading Research Unit's first experiment, three joining in 1961 and the remaining four in 1962. One local authority had six schools carrying out their own experiments with i.t.a., while in another authority nearly all infant schools were using i.t.a. but were not involved in experiments of any kind. In these nine authorities the percentages of schools containing infant pupils using i.t.a. ranged from 100% to 6·6%.

It was originally hoped to cast the net much more widely by visiting local education authorities in many different parts of the country. Although the time factor prevented this, as more schools were visited it was realised that further visits would not necessarily have brought forward more information. In fact, it became apparent that a system of 'diminishing returns' was in operation, in that the more teachers who were interviewed, the less new information came to light. In other words, teachers in different schools and in different areas appeared to have a common range of experiences with, and ideas on, the use of i.t.a. About half-way through the enquiry, nearly all these experiences and ideas had been related to the interviewer. Later visits tended to produce the same range of information, albeit phrased differently by individual teachers; they therefore usually served to confirm earlier impressions rather than to alter or extend them.

These visits to local education authorities, which provided the bulk of the verbal evidence which was collected, revealed rich mines of first-hand experience and information about the use of i.t.a. They involved individual discussions with 12 local advisers, inspectors and administrators, supported by visits to 46 schools, in which discussions took place with 196 headteachers and members of their staffs. Further details regarding people who were interviewed on visits to local education authorities are given in Appendix D, Tables D/1–D/5.

III Evidence from individuals

A. ADDITIONAL ADVISERS AND INSPECTORS

The views of advisers and inspectors in primary education were considered to be particularly important, as they were the people likely to have had the greatest opportunity of observing and comparing both i.t.a. and t.o. classes. Accordingly, additional individual interviews were arranged with eight local inspectors, advisers and administrators from a further five authorities. In an attempt to achieve a balance, two of these local authorities were selected because it was known that few of their schools used i.t.a. In one of these authorities the inspectors did not know of any school which was using i.t.a. with infants and in the other only a very few schools were using it. Discussions with these inspectors and advisers disclosed a different point of view from that expressed by many officials from authorities in which the use of i.t.a. was widespread.

Individual discussions also took place with a few members of H.M. Inspectorate. In addition, private reports to which they had contributed in 1963 and 1965 were made available to the researchers and proved to be of great value in that they summarised the views of the many inspectors who had observed i.t.a. in use with infants.

B. OTHER INDIVIDUALS

As well as advisers and inspectors there were many other people who were able, and willing, to contribute valuable points of view relating to the use of i.t.a. The procedure adopted for discovering the views of these knowledgeable, well-informed and interested individuals can best be described as a system of collection. Two lists were made: the first consisting of named individuals whose views were considered to be essential to the evaluation, and the second comprising a list of categories of people likely to hold views which would add to the value of the enquiry. The named list included Sir James Pitman, research workers who had undertaken research in the use of i.t.a., and educationists who had, either by lecturing or writing, publicised their views on different aspects of i.t.a. both in Great Britain and abroad. Great care was taken that the named individuals covered the whole range of published views on i.t.a. Definite appointments were made to have discussions with those people on the list who lived in Great Britain. Correspondence was entered into with the people who lived abroad and quite a number of them were interviewed when they attended conferences in Europe in the summer of 1966.

Interviews with those on the second list, consisting of categories of relevant people, were arranged in a different manner. Keeping the list in mind, the interviewer, wherever she went in the course of the year and whenever she came into contact with a person who fell into one of the categories, asked for his or her views on i.t.a. In many cases the interviewer had no forewarning as to the direction which the views might take so that, in this sense, the collection of individuals' opinions could be said to be unbiased. Some of the situations in which people were met were as follows: at conferences, lectures, seminars and committee meetings; on visits to local education authority offices, schools, Colleges of Education and Universities; and on social occasions.

Lectures and conferences proved particularly useful occasions for collecting people's impressions of i.t.a. Often the lectures themselves were on the subject of i.t.a., but on other occasions they concerned different aspects of reading or other educational subjects. The audiences at many of these lectures and conferences contained a wide variety of people working in different branches of education. Consequently, they provided extremely fruitful ground for the accumulation of evidence of people's opinions. A list of lectures and conferences attended in the course of this investigation is given in Table D/6 in Appendix D.

Notes were taken at every lecture. In many cases, when the lecture was concerned specifically with i.t.a., the lecturer kindly gave the investigator a copy of the paper which had been read. Quite frequently, especially at residential conferences, a private discussion was arranged with the lecturer, following his lecture. In addition, residential conferences provided admirable opportunities for informal discussions, sometimes individually and sometimes in groups, with teachers and other educationists. For example, at the six-day i.t.a. Conference at Cambridge, the investigator usually tried to join unknown groups of conference members at lunch-time and during tea and coffee breaks in order to talk to them. By this means, discussions of varying lengths took place with literally scores of knowledgeable people. Many of them were teachers using i.t.a. in local education authorities scattered all over the country and some were teachers from abroad; they also included administrators, lecturers, researchers and reading counsellors (U.S.A.).

C. WRITTEN EVIDENCE

Correspondence, as well as discussions and lectures, often provided valuable evidence. Not only was there correspondence which had been invited from people abroad, as already mentioned, but other people both at home and abroad who heard of this enquiry frequently wrote letters setting forth their views on the matter. Some individuals whom the researcher would have liked to meet, but found it impossible to do so, went to the trouble of expressing their views in letters. Such correspondence gave a breadth to the evaluation which could not have been achieved, in the time, merely by face-to-face enquiries.

Another aspect of evidence by correspondence arose when brief summaries of research experiments or reports were printed in the national press or in educational journals. Requests to the people concerned for further details or full reports were almost invariably granted. In addition, certain people sent in unsolicited reports which they thought might prove helpful to the evaluation. In this way a pile of personal written evidence by correspondence was added to the large accumulation of written records of discussions and lectures.

IV   Group discussions

Throughout the enquiry, a record was kept of the number of persons in each category with whom individual discussions had taken place. As the enquiry proceeded, steps were taken to try to fill obvious gaps by means of arranging individual talks with additional people in the relevant categories. Towards the end of the period allowed for the evaluation, it became apparent that the available time was not sufficient to permit the rounding out of the evidence by means of further individual talks. Accordingly, group discussions were specially arranged for three categories of people from whom it was felt that further evidence should be obtained. They were local advisers and inspectors, College of Education lecturers and parents.

A. LOCAL AUTHORITY ADVISERS AND INSPECTORS

Two reasons led to the decision to try to arrange a group discussion with additional local advisers and inspectors of primary education. First, the fact that such people could give an overall view of both i.t.a. and t.o. in use in infant schools made it important to meet as many of them as possible. Secondly, in the views collected from local education authorities at that stage, the South of England was not well represented. Accordingly a date and time for a meeting in London was arranged and letters were sent to the Directors of Education of 23 local education authorities within reasonable travelling distance of London. The letter explained the nature of the project and invited the Director of Education to nominate an adviser or inspector of primary education, who had had the opportunity of visiting infant schools using i.t.a. and t.o. and who would attend the meeting in order to put forward his or her views.

A good response was made to this invitation. Fifteen people were present at the meeting, representing 14 local education authorities, of which 8 were counties and 6 were county boroughs or London boroughs. These local authorities ranged in size from large counties to small boroughs. The schools using i.t.a. with infants in the different counties ranged from 13% to 2%; the range for boroughs was 50% to 15%. The total number of schools containing infant pupils in the whole of the area covered by these 14 local authorities was 2,012, of which 167 (i.e. 8%) were using i.t.a. Further details of the schools in these local education authorities are set out in Table D/5 in Appendix D. It is clear that the 15 people present at this group discussion represented a considerable body of knowledge and experience regarding beginning reading with infants.

B. COLLEGE OF EDUCATION LECTURERS

In order to obtain the views of additional college lecturers who had had opportunities of visiting both t.o. and i.t.a. schools, an invitation similar to that distributed to local authorities was sent to the Colleges of Education within the area training organisation represented by the School of Education of the University of Manchester. Two consecutive dates were set for group discussions; five lecturers attended one meeting and three the other. These eight lecturers came from five different Colleges of Education.

C. PARENTS

Although the interviewer had talked to some parents of children who had used i.t.a., it was considered that additional evidence from parents was desirable. Consideration was given to the possibility of arranging meetings of parents in two schools, in a low socio-economic area and a high socio-economic area respectively. In the event, it did not prove possible to arrange the former, but a most successful meeting of 34 parents in a school in a high socio-economic area took place.

V Total numbers of people who contributed verbal evidence

The total number of people who contributed verbal evidence to this evaluation in the form of individual and group discussions approached 400. Of this number 57 took part in three group discussions and approximately 330 had individual talks with the interviewer. Details of how this total is made up are given in Table D/7 in Appendix D.

The largest group of people consists of 246 headteachers and members of their staff with whom the interviewer had personal discussions. The majority of them had used i.t.a. and many had taken part in the Reading Research Unit's experiments. A few had considered using i.t.a. and decided against it and a further few were in t.o. schools not concerned at all with i.t.a. Most of the teachers were from England but a small proportion were from Wales and Scotland, while others were from abroad. Details of the schools in which these teachers taught can be found in Table D/4 in Appendix D.

Discussions were arranged with 35 local education authority officials, mainly advisers and inspectors in primary education, who came from 28 local authorities, of which 13 were counties and 15 county boroughs, including London boroughs. Details regarding these local education authority officials are given in Tables D/1 and D/2 in Appendix D. The importance to be placed on the views of these 35 local inspectors and advisers can perhaps best be appreciated by considering a few details of the areas which they represented. Table D/5 in Appendix D sets out some details of the schools in these 28 local education authorities. The total area covered by these authorities contained 5,448 schools attended by infant pupils, representing 32% of all such schools in England and Wales. The percentage of schools using i.t.a. with infants in these particular authorities covered the widest possible range, from 100% to nil. The total number of schools using i.t.a. with infants in these 28 authorities was 636, which is approximately 41% of all schools using i.t.a. with infants in England and Wales.

The background of experience of the 35 officials in observing both i.t.a. and t.o. in use with infants is obviously formidable. While it would be fanciful to assume that an adviser in a large county had visited all the infant schools in the authority, nevertheless such a person must be credited with an extensive knowledge of the infant schools within the authority. In a county borough, on the other hand, the inspector or adviser is likely to be acquainted with all the schools. Accordingly, although time precluded the selection of a representative sample of local education authorities as regards their use of i.t.a., it is considered that the proportion of authorities with whom the investigators were in contact, the variety in their sizes, the range of their interest in i.t.a. and the large total number of infant schools using both t.o. and i.t.a. which they included, served to present a fairly complete range of representative opinions about i.t.a.

Other categories of people whose views on i.t.a. were obtained consisted of 28 further visitors to schools; 38 other knowledgeable or interested people, as for example visiting professors and educationists from abroad, linguists, writers and lecturers; and 41 parents of children who had used i.t.a. Complete details of the people interviewed are given in Table D/7 in Appendix D. Altogether, in a period of one year, one interviewer gathered opinions from some 388 people, whose views are described and summarised in the following chapters of this section of the report.

CHAPTER 4

Interviewing Procedures

I Procedures for individual interviews

To some extent discussions with different people followed different procedures depending on the person's experience and the situation in which they took place. Nevertheless, certain features were common to all individual interviews. Accordingly, repetition will be minimised by outlining these common features before details of the selection procedures and various patterns of interviews are noted. The majority of individual interviews consisted of the following five stages:

A. an explanation of the research project;

B. a request for general impressions of i.t.a.;

C. questions designed to extend the discussion on various points;

D. factual questions regarding background;

E. concluding questions designed to elicit summaries of general impressions.

The following descriptions of these five stages will help to clarify the most usual pattern of individual interviews.

A. EXPLANATION OF THE RESEARCH PROJECT

In order to gain the maximum co-operation from the people concerned, it was considered essential that they should understand exactly the nature of the enquiry and be convinced, not only of its value, but also of its impartiality. This aim was particularly important where headteachers and teachers were concerned, for many of them had become rather weary of researchers, officials and other visitors asking them endless questions about i.t.a. Unless they could be persuaded to accept that this project was of an essentially different nature from preceding pieces of research and that it would provide valuable information for other teachers, it was unlikely that worthwhile information would be obtained from the discussions. One further reason for taking great pains to clarify the purpose of the project lay in the fact that, as it was the first of the Schools Council's independent evaluations of current curriculum changes, any misunderstanding regarding its nature could well have had deleterious effects on later evaluations.

Consequently, in the initial stages of every discussion, the aims and methods of the enquiry were clearly stated. In certain cases when people were not familiar with the Schools Council, brief details of its purposes and the work in which it was already engaged were given. The absolute impartiality of the enquiry was next emphasised. It was indicated that although the Schools Council was responsible for this evaluation, it was in no way concerned that the outcome should be in any specific direction. The requirement was that all available evidence should be gathered together. Hence all experiences and all shades of opinion relating to the use of i.t.a. in the early stages of reading needed to be pooled in order to present a complete and fair picture.

The time and care expended at the beginning of discussions in explaining these points was considered to be amply repaid by the warmth and enthusiasm with which most people welcomed the idea and by the full co-operation which they gave. A very common response, from teachers and other educators, to the preceding sort of explanation was 'What a good idea!' In fact, the interviewer felt certain that those people being interviewed did all in their power to produce every possible shred of evidence or opinion relating to i.t.a.

B. REQUEST FOR GENERAL IMPRESSIONS

On very many occasions, when the person being interviewed had accepted and welcomed the nature of the enquiry, he would make the following sort of remark to the interviewer: 'You go ahead and ask me what you want to know and I'll do my best to answer your questions.' In fact, at the beginning of this evaluation, the possibility of gathering information in interviews by posing a prepared list of questions or by introducing a pre-selected series of topics had been considered. It had been discarded on the grounds that, however carefully the questions were phrased or the topics chosen, the mere presentation of certain subjects and the omission of others would be likely to structure the situation in such a way as to create or suggest a bias in one direction or the other. Accordingly, in reply to a person's invitation to ask questions, the interviewer replied that she would prefer to hear the person's general impressions of i.t.a., expressed in his own words. The point was invariably stressed that all experiences and views, whether these emphasised the advantages or disadvantages of i.t.a., or a mixture of both, were of equal value. Phrases such as, 'I am here to act as a sort of sponge or piece of blotting paper which will absorb whatever you have to say', were often used by the interviewer.

The interviewee's response to the invitation to give his or her general impressions of i.t.a. formed the major part of each interview. There was never any problem about encouraging people to talk freely. Indeed, most of those who were interviewed appeared to welcome the opportunity of formulating and communicating their ideas to an impartial yet interested outsider. In particular, many teachers seemed to appreciate the chance to talk absolutely freely without fear of offending, for example, administrators and research workers who were known, or thought to have, definite ideas either for or against the use of i.t.a.

The interviewer also felt that it was of help in establishing a high degree of rapport with teachers, when they realised that she herself was an experienced primary school teacher and was knowledgeable about the early stages of reading. Quite often infant teachers volunteered the information that some of their previous visitors to school (more often men than women) had not really understood the infant classroom situation. In consequence, these visitors had asked questions which the teachers considered foolish or which they found impossible to answer and thus the teacher had not felt it possible to talk freely to them.

It was evident that the subject of i.t.a. was one to which those whose opinions were invited had given great thought. Accordingly they nearly always responded fluently and at length. During this most important part of each interview, direct questions were rarely necessary, the odd non-committal comment being all that was required to keep the discourse flowing. While the interviewee talked, the interviewer made brief notes; these were expanded to form a full report immediately afterwards, while the points made were still fresh in mind.

The effect of inviting people to give their general ideas on i.t.a. also appeared to induce them to state their main conclusions first, before proceeding to elaborate minor points. Interesting comparisons were thus provided of those facets of i.t.a. to which various people gave priority of importance.

During all individual discussions, and equally in group discussions, the interviewer was at great pains to refrain from expressing her own points of view. Occasionally, when asked for her opinions, the kind of reply that was given was, 'I should prefer to know what *you* think. It's *your* experience and views which are important in this evaluation'.

C. EXTENSION QUESTIONS

The general impressions upon which people elaborated sometimes needed to be followed up by questions from the interviewer intended to extend, expand, amplify or clarify what had been said. For instance, while talking freely a person would, on occasions, briefly mention a point to which he had obviously given great thought, for example the effect of i.t.a. on dull or bright children. In this case, at the end of the general discussion, the interviewer would ask the person concerned to elaborate on this point. Certain people, for example headteachers of schools which had originally been control schools and had later begun to use i.t.a. or heads of schools running parallel classes in t.o. and i.t.a., clearly had valuable backgrounds of experience, likely to enable them to make assessments on particular aspects of i.t.a. If it was considered that the interviewee had failed to develop such issues in giving his or her general impressions, questions were framed to elicit more information. Examples of some of the extension questions posed on certain occasions to various categories of people are given in Table E/1 in Appendix E.

D. FACTUAL BACKGROUND QUESTIONS

In many of the interviews certain factual questions needed to be asked. The information required referred to the local education authority itself, the school in question or the interviewee's own background of experience. The latter was particularly important in order that people's comments could be viewed in relation to their previous experiences with, or observations of, children of various ages learning to read in different ways. These factual questions sometimes preceded, and on other occasions followed, the request for the person's general impressions of i.t.a.

A headteacher, for instance, was usually asked factual questions concerning the size of the school, the number of years they had been using i.t.a. and so on, near the beginning of an interview. Similarly, local officials were normally asked early in an interview, about the number of schools in the authority using i.t.a. On the other hand, information from teachers, concerning the ages of children whom they had previously taught to read by means of t.o. and the reading schemes which they had used, could be gleaned by questions at any stage in the interview if such information did not emerge spontaneously in the course of the discussion.

Examples of various factual questions relating to background factors concerning the local education authority, the school and the interviewee himself, are given in Table E/2 in Appendix E.

E. CONCLUDING QUESTIONS

The final stage of each interview consisted of the posing of certain questions designed to encourage the interviewee to sum up his or her main conclusions. At this point, teachers, advisers and inspectors were usually asked about the advantages and disadvantages they had perceived when i.t.a. was used. They were requested to enumerate their conclusions and to express their hopes or intentions regarding the future use of i.t.a. Examples of these concluding questions are given in Table E/3 in Appendix E.

II Procedure on l.e.a. visits

A. THE APPROACH TO LOCAL EDUCATION AUTHORITIES

The first approach to a local education authority was a letter to the Director of Education explaining the purpose of this evaluation project, setting out details of the information to be collected and requesting his co-operation. He was asked to nominate someone who had observed i.t.a. being used in schools and with whom the interviewer could have a preliminary discussion. In some cases it was the Director of Education himself who preferred to have this first discussion with the interviewer; in most cases it was a primary school adviser or inspector and in a few instances it was an adviser for remedial education.

Discussions with individual representatives of local education authorities followed the lines already described. In every single case the person concerned was extremely helpful about giving factual information, expressing his or her own views on i.t.a. and making the necessary arrangements for visits.

B. THE SELECTION OF SCHOOLS TO BE VISITED

In many cases when the discussion turned towards the selection of particular schools to be visited, the adviser stated that the interviewer would be welcome to visit any or all of the schools in the authority. However, in every case the interviewer left the choice of schools to the local representative, asking only that there should be a variety of schools which would give a fair cross-section of the work with i.t.a. in the area. It was suggested that schools falling into some of the following categories of schools might possibly be included in a representative sample: a school which had obtained very good results using i.t.a.; a school which had not found i.t.a. so successful; a school which the organiser considered an average i.t.a. school; a school which had begun to use i.t.a. and had abandoned it; a t.o. school which had considered using i.t.a. but had decided against it; a control school, if the authority had taken part in the Reading Research Unit's first experiment; and a junior school which had been fed by some infants taught by i.t.a. and some infants taught by t.o. In addition, a variety of factors such as large and small schools, schools in good residential areas as opposed to schools in very poor areas, infant schools and all-age primary schools, as well as schools working on both formal and informal lines were mentioned.

Following the lines of these suggestions, interesting and varied programmes of school visits were arranged in each local authority by the adviser or inspector. Everyone seemed to go out of his way to display every available aspect of the use of i.t.a. in beginning reading within the authority. In many cases the local inspector proposed extra visits to schools likely to be of special interest; for example, a school which was

27

carrying out an experiment with i.t.a. and t.o. on its own initiative or a school which had originally been highly 'anti-i.t.a.' but was now using i.t.a. with enthusiasm. The interviewer felt that, even had there been time to carry out a sampling procedure, no more varied or representative programme could have resulted.

The number of schools visited in different authorities ranged from nine to three. A summary of these schools set out in different categories is given in Table D/3 in Appendix D. Two examples of the programmes of visits arranged in two authorities will serve to illustrate the pattern of visits. One county borough, which took part in the Reading Research Unit's first experiment, arranged the following programme of four visits: one 'control' infant school; two i.t.a. experimental infant schools, of which one was the school most enthusiastic and the other the school least enthusiastic about i.t.a. within the borough; and one junior school taking children from both experimental and control classes. In one large county, nine schools were visited. Five of these schools had been experimental schools in the Reading Research Unit's first experiment; two were infant and three were primary schools; of these one had begun to use i.t.a. in 1961, two in 1962 and two in 1963. Three of the nine schools had contained control classes as part of the 1961 experiment. Of these, one had begun to use i.t.a. by 1962, a second began to use i.t.a. in 1964 and the third school was still continuing to use t.o. The ninth school in this series of visits was an infant school which had had both control and experimental classes in the Reading Research Unit's experiment and which also had classes taking part in the Reading Research Unit's experiment which began in 1963.

C. PROCEDURE ON SCHOOL VISITS

1 General procedure

The usual programme was for only two schools per day to be visited so that a complete morning or afternoon could be spent in each. Occasionally, when two schools were adjacent, two visits were arranged in one morning. In some areas the local inspector accompanied the interviewer to the school, but on only one or two occasions was he present during the interviewer's discussions with teachers.

Each school visit began with a private talk with the headteacher, in which an explanation of the project was made, followed by questions and discussion, as already described. This talk with the headteacher was, on some occasions, followed by group discussions with class-teachers at lunch-time or break-time. One advantage of such a meeting was that the interviewer only needed to give one explanation of the research to all the teachers. A second advantage was that many different facets of the use of i.t.a. were discussed and varied opinions emerged. Regardless of whether there was a staffroom discussion or not, a number of individual conversations with teachers took place in each school, although not necessarily with every teacher. Visits to classes and talks with children supplemented the discussions.

2 Selection of teachers to be interviewed

Within each school the decision as to classes to be visited and teachers with whom discussions should take place was left to the headteacher, following suggestions of various criteria of selection put forward by the observer. The procedure was similar to that employed when talking to local education authority officials about the selection of schools within an authority. First it was indicated that a broad view of the opinion within the school was required, and that this might perhaps be achieved by talking to the teacher who was most enthusiastic about i.t.a., a teacher who was less enthusiastic and one who took a middle view. (As it turned out many schools did not have so many divergent opinions.) With regard to the other teachers it was suggested that, in the main, experienced teachers were likely to produce more valuable opinions than newly-trained teachers as they would have backgrounds of experience of teaching in t.o. with which to compare their current experience of using i.t.a. On the other hand, discussions did take place with a few probationary teachers and with students on teaching practice. Married women who had returned to teaching after absences of a number of years also provided useful information about their reactions to the use of i.t.a., particularly as many of them were mothers of children of infant age.

Headteachers themselves frequently suggested members of the staff with whom they thought it would be particularly valuable for the interviewer to talk: for example, a teacher who had been in charge of a control class, and who had not been keen on the idea of i.t.a. at first, but who had later asked to use it because of the progress she had noted in the i.t.a. experimental classes. Neither did headteachers hesitate to suggest that the interviewer should talk to members of staff who were still not anxious to use i.t.a., even though the rest of the teachers in the school were converted to it. In other words, just as the local education authority officials had done, so did headteachers go out of their way to present to the interviewer every shade of opinion within their schools.

3 Individual talks with teachers

The interviewer never made a request to have private interviews with teachers, as it was felt that it was preferable for headteachers to propose arrangements for discussions which would prove most convenient, according to the circumstances of the school. Yet, when an explanation of the project had been given to headteachers, many of them proposed arrangements whereby the interviewer could have private discussions with individual members of staff. Such arrangements could most easily be made in those larger schools in which the headteacher was not in charge of a class. In certain schools the headteacher kindly looked after various teachers' classes, thus enabling a succession of teachers to have individual discussions with the interviewer in a staffroom or the headteacher's study. These opportunities for quiet, uninterrupted talks usually provided the most rewarding interviews.

In contrast, in those small infant schools in which headteachers were in charge of classes, a talk with a teacher had necessarily to take place in the classroom while the teacher was still in charge of the children. This was far from being the ideal situation for having an uninterrupted conversation, but in a proportion of schools it could not be avoided. In such schools a combined discussion with the headteacher and staff over lunch often helped to supplement the talks with individual teachers. Wherever the discussion with a teacher took place, it followed fairly closely the pattern already described, with the major portion of the time being devoted to the teacher expressing her own views on i.t.a. On only very rare occasions was the headteacher present when the teacher was talking to the interviewer.

4 Selection of classes to be visited

The selection of classes to be visited within a school was closely linked with the teachers who were interviewed. Children at every stage of learning to read, both with i.t.a. and with t.o., within the age-range of 4–10 years were observed. At the lowest age-level, children in the pre-reading stages were seen while at the upper level there were children who had made the transfer from i.t.a. two and three years previously. In some junior schools, classes originally taught by i.t.a. were contrasted with classes taught by t.o.; in other junior schools both these groups of children were found in the same classes. Every type of school organisation was seen including streamed schools, in which both upper and lower streams were observed, unstreamed schools and vertically grouped schools. Within the classrooms the range of timetabling was from rigid timetables to 'free days'; working groups of children extended from whole classes, through small groups to individuals; the teaching procedures employed covered a similar range from very formal to absolutely informal.

One important sidelight on observing so many children who had learned to read by i.t.a. should probably be mentioned at this point. It was fairly obvious that an observer who did not have an extensive background of teaching reading and observing reading being taught, could not be expected to make a reasonably objective assessment of the reading progress made by children who had used i.t.a. What was not so obvious, but became so during the enquiry, was that a continuous kaleidoscope of children learning to read by means of i.t.a. could achieve a mesmeric effect which seriously blunted judgement. Even seeing control classes of children using t.o. did not really serve to break the uninterrupted diet of i.t.a., as discussions with the teachers of such classes usually centred on i.t.a. Accordingly, at intervals, the interviewer found it imperative to visit infant schools which were not using i.t.a. and were not interested in it. Some were using well-known reading schemes; others were using quite new reading schemes. The interviewer talked to these teachers about the approaches they were using and observed the children. No mention of i.t.a. was made throughout a visit of this nature. Such visits were extremely interesting in themselves but, from the point of view of this enquiry, they performed an essential function in that they reminded the interviewer of the normal standards of children using t.o. and the views of teachers whose experiences and interests were limited to t.o.

As the evaluation of i.t.a. proceeded, more time in schools was devoted to discussions with teachers than to observation of classes and talks with children. Such a procedure did not spring from any lack of interest in the children and what they were doing; rather was it a result of the process of 'diminishing returns' mentioned earlier. The large number of classes of all kinds which were visited in the early stages of the research, as well as prior to it, brought to light certain trends and patterns of results which continued to be confirmed rather than contradicted by additional visits. In these circumstances, and bearing in mind that to be effective a visit to a class required a substantial length of time, it was considered that in the latter part of this enquiry the available time was most fruitfully expended in listening to the views of teachers and other educators.

5 Procedure on class visits

When visiting classes the observer relied on the teacher to present a fair cross-section of the children and their work. First the teacher was asked to choose a few children who were the best readers in the class. The observer listened to these children read, both from basic reading books and from book corner books, looked at some of their written work, and often some of their creative work, and talked to them. The same plan was followed with children whom the teacher chose from among the slowest reading group and an average group of children. In addition, the observer talked to scattered children in the class, as well as children working in corridors and halls. Observations of how children within the classes were working, as well as what they were actually working at, could be added to impressions of displays and exhibitions of children's work to form a fairly composite picture, not only of the reading and writing ability of a class, but also of the children's interests, attitudes and general standards of work and behaviour.

III Procedure at group discussions

The procedure adopted at the four group discussions, which were specially arranged towards the completion of this evaluation, varied somewhat according to the numbers present and the composition of the groups. The initial procedure was the same for each group in that the interviewer opened the proceedings with the usual explanations of the aims and scope of the enquiry.

In the two group discussions for College of Education lecturers, as the numbers were small, it was thought best to ask first for the lecturers' main impressions of the use of i.t.a. in the schools they had visited. This request led to general discussions in which everyone's views were put forward. The discussions were concluded by asking each member individually to try to sum up his or her views.

The group discussions which took place with parents and with local education authority advisers and inspectors were conducted on similar lines, in that the interviewer was anxious to obtain their views on certain specific aspects of i.t.a. on which only they could supply the evidence. Accordingly, the interviewer had prepared in advance a list of questions and topics for discussions. Topics intended for the meeting of local advisers and inspectors are set out in Table E/4 in Appendix E, while the questions posed to parents are given in Chapter 12. In both these groups, the members had plenty to say and were eager to say it. Accordingly, their replies to the questions were more often lengthy and qualified than brief and definite. Thus it came about that a great deal of general discussion was mingled with, and followed, the questions posed. At the end of each meeting, some attempt was made to encourage those present to sum up their views, but this proved rather difficult.

CHAPTER 5

Infant Teachers' General Impressions of i.t.a.

I Preliminary points

MOST of the verbal evidence described in this section of the report was gathered from class-teachers and headteachers in the schools that were visited in different parts of England. Discussions outside schools with other teachers from all over Great Britain and from abroad enriched and verified the evidence obtained within schools. It should be emphasised that the evidence cannot be attributed solely to experience with one type of child, teacher, school, reading scheme, method, class organisation, classroom procedure, or any other factor usually considered to have relevance in situations in which children learn to read. The comments made by teachers sprang from first-hand experiences with practically every possible combination of an exceedingly wide range of such factors.

One further point needs to be made. The discussions which took place with teachers in schools were necessarily linked with the investigator's observations in these schools. In an attempt to avoid, as far as possible, the latter colouring the former, two devices are employed in this description of teachers' views. Firstly, teachers' actual words are quoted as often as possible. Secondly, where the investigator's observations or ideas are given, this fact is made obvious in the text. Thus it is hoped that the reader can clearly differentiate the views of the teachers from the conclusions of the investigator and so be enabled, should he wish to do so, to draw from the mass of evidence provided by teachers, different conclusions from those which are set out.

Visits to schools in which i.t.a. was being used and talks with experienced teachers who had used i.t.a. and were able to compare it with their previous experiences with t.o., represent an extremely important part of this preliminary evaluation of i.t.a. Subjective appraisals of new curriculum developments, when such judgements are made by teachers with a breadth of practical experience in the subject concerned, must rank high in the list of available evidence.

Details of the range of these teachers' experiences with i.t.a. are summarised in Table D/4 in Appendix D. It might have been supposed that schools so different from each other as those visited would have yielded different information and that, for instance, the views of teachers in the following contrasting categories of schools might need to be presented separately in this report: schools in contrasting socio-economic areas; schools vertically grouped or grouped according to age; schools working on formal as opposed to informal lines and schools believing in an early beginning to reading in contrast to schools supporting the idea of a delayed start. In a similar manner, contrasting groupings of children, teachers, reading materials and methods which might have been expected to yield differing results could have been drawn up. In the event, when the entire written records of interviews were examined, it was found that the broad picture of the use of i.t.a., depicted by teachers in all the varying types of schools, did not show large variations. General patterns of beliefs and ideas emerged almost regardless of the schools which had fostered them. Consequently, to segment the verbal evidence given by teachers into divisions according to different criteria relating to schools, teachers, children, methods or procedures proved largely unnecessary. The areas of agreement among all teachers with experience of i.t.a. were so extensive that teachers' comments can be drawn together into broad conclusions without injustice to any group.

II Reasons for using i.t.a.

If headteachers did not mention the reasons which had first led them to use i.t.a., they were usually questioned on this point at the end of a discussion. The reasons given may best be summarised by dividing the schools visited into 'early users', who began to use i.t.a. in 1961 and 1962, and 'later users' who started to use it in September 1963 or later.

Three main reasons were given by the early users. Stated briefly they were: interest in new ideas; dissatisfaction with t.o.; and dissatisfaction with reading standards in the school. The first two reasons were sometimes linked together. Dissatisfaction with reading standards was given less frequently than the two preceding reasons.

Only two headteachers among the early users indicated that they had been asked to join the original experiments; the remainder had volunteered. One of the two said:

'I was hesitant at first. Then I thought that if no-one was willing to experiment, no progress would be made, so I agreed.'

A number of other headteachers who were doubtful at first stated that they had intended to discard i.t.a. after a year or so, if they were not satisfied with it. For instance, one headmaster of an all-age primary school answered the question in this way:

'My woman deputy-head was very keen and persuaded me. I meant to abandon it if it didn't work.'

The majority of headteachers, however, replied in similar vein to the following:

'I was interested in new ideas, particularly in reading, and didn't want to get into a rut.'

This sort of comment was often coupled with dissatisfaction with t.o. in respect of its difficulty for children, and the methods and reading schemes which are necessitated by its irregularity. Very many teachers spoke of the 'grind' of learning to read by t.o. and were willing to experiment with any approach which might simplify the task for children. Some said that i.t.a. sounded more logical for children, as they would not be faced with changing rules. Talking of t.o. reading schemes, two headteachers spoke as follows:

'I believe in change and in not getting into a rut. We had used the *Pilot Reading Scheme* and were just thinking of trying *Happy Trio* when we heard about i.t.a. and decided to try it.'

33

'We were sick of *Happy Venture* and wanted something new. We were not completely sure about i.t.a. at first. I looked on it as an experiment and meant to abandon it if it was not successful.'

One infant headteacher of a school which began to use i.t.a. in 1962 produced a different reason for her decision. She replied:

'I wanted something to help me to change the teachers' attitude to reading. They were very formal. i.t.a. has helped to change this.'

Those who began to use i.t.a. in 1963 or later often repeated the reasons given by the early users, while augmenting them with additional reasons. Some who had only recently begun to use i.t.a. volunteered information such as the following:

'In the early years I was prejudiced against i.t.a. I was put off by all the publicity and by what I considered to be extravagant claims.'

Others made this sort of remark:

'We waited until anyone could buy the books. We wouldn't have liked to be involved in the Reading Research Unit's experiments–far too much testing and too many visitors.'

On the other hand, most of the later users had decided to try i.t.a. because they had read articles about it, and/or because they had been impressed by visits to i.t.a. schools. The following represent a selection of such comments.

'I read about i.t.a. and thought it might be the answer to this school's reading problems.'

(Infant school in a slum area)
'Our reading was never very good. I visited an i.t.a. school in the same sort of area as this school and I was charmed by the free writing. There had never been anything like this in our school.'

'I had read about i.t.a. and was interested because there was so much "grind" about reading with t.o.'

'I visited many infant schools using i.t.a. I was impressed with what I saw, especially the feeling of confidence in the children–reading was their chief pleasure. These impressions were the same, even in schools that used different methods.'

Lest it should be thought that only schools with low reading standards were interested in i.t.a., the following reply from a headmaster of an all-age primary school, in a good socio-economic area, should be included.

'The teaching of reading in this school formerly was efficient (our standards were six months ahead of national norms), but the children didn't seem to me to enjoy reading as much as I'd have liked them to do. I felt that so much was happening in Primary Schools–expansion of the curriculum, the frontiers widening, children's knowledge expanding and so on–that reading was becoming even more of a necessary basic skill than formerly. So, I wanted reading to be more enjoyable and more understanding.'

III General impressions

In the vast majority of cases, infant headteachers and class teachers who had used i.t.a. were favourably impressed. Some of their comments denoted an approval which amounted to the utmost fervour. For example, remarks such as the following were fairly common: 'I find it absolutely marvellous'. 'I am a convert; I love it.' 'I'm sold on it, hook, line and sinker.' Other teachers expressed more moderately-worded approval and a few qualified their approval. The following are typical examples of comments made by headteachers and teachers:

'I thoroughly approve. The enthusiasm of the children never palled; it went on right through their reading and writing. The staff were soon so sure that it was good that all succeeding children who came into the school were put onto i.t.a.'

'Since using i.t.a., all the teachers in the school have been happy about it. I myself would be very unhappy if I had to move to a school where I couldn't use i.t.a., e.g. because the staff didn't want to.'

'The whole school is now using it, because I think it's a miracle.'

'I was not keen at first but now I am thoroughly converted and would hate to go back to t.o.'

'I have accepted i.t.a. so happily that I just cannot imagine teaching infants without it now. I am absolutely in favour of it. I only wish all schools would use it.'

This last opinion was expressed by many teachers who approved of i.t.a. They felt sorry for children in other schools who did not have the advantage of i.t.a. and could not think why other schools were taking so long to change over from t.o.

Among the many conversations with enthusiasts one final example may be given. One headmistress of an infant school, when asked to sum up her opinions about i.t.a., replied, 'I am very happy about i.t.a.' The interviewer, remembering that this headmistress had earlier mentioned using the Stern Apparatus in mathematics and trying out other new ideas, followed up the first question by asking how she rated i.t.a. in comparison with other new educational ideas which she had tried in the past. Her reply was, 'It rates very highly among all the things I have tried; in fact, it is the highlight of my teaching career'. These comments were all the more impressive in that they came, not from a young person overflowing with enthusiasm, but from an older, rather sedate and carefully controlled person who was quite clearly not given to emotional outpourings.

In addition to the majority of teachers who expressed their views along the lines already indicated, there was a smaller percentage of teachers who, although they approved of i.t.a., added notes of caution, such as the following: 'It is not all it's cracked up to be'. 'It is not the answer to all reading problems.' 'It's no use thinking it's the panacea for all ills.' These teachers thought that i.t.a. was preferable to t.o., but some were rather disappointed because their results were not as miraculous as, after reading early published results and hearing certain lectures, they had hoped it might be. 'Reading still has to be taught', some of them said. Nevertheless, nearly all these teachers preferred to continue to use i.t.a. than to return to t.o.

There was one smaller group of teachers who had not yet made up their minds whether their preference was for i.t.a. or t.o. They appeared to be thoughtful teachers who were giving careful consideration to the use of the two alphabets and who were determined not to be rushed into making hasty judgements. They could see some advantages in i.t.a. but they still had certain reservations or doubts which they felt might be dispelled or verified by another few years' experience with i.t.a. One such teacher summed up her attitude in this way: 'I am not yet sure in my own mind whether i.t.a. is of real help to the children, but one thing I am certain of is that it does no harm to them'. Of all the teachers involved in the use of i.t.a. whose opinions were asked, only one expressed outright disapproval. Her views are given later in this chapter.

The consensus of opinion of those teachers interviewed, who were experienced in using both i.t.a. and t.o., is quite clearly illustrated in their replies to the two specific questions which follow.

IV   Headteachers' intentions of continuing to use i.t.a.

Not every headteacher using i.t.a. was asked whether he or she would continue to use it. In certain cases, such as when a school was running its own experimental classes using t.o. and i.t.a., and the head had indicated that she had not yet come to definite conclusions, the question was not appropriate. The same applied to schools which had only been using i.t.a. one or two years. A total of 29 headteachers of infant schools and all-age primary schools, experienced in using i.t.a. with infants, were asked the following specific question at the conclusion of an interview: 'Will you continue to use i.t.a. or will you return to t.o.'? Their replies were as follows: 26 said 'i.t.a.'; two said 'i.t.a.', with certain qualifications; and one was doubtful but thought possibly 'i.t.a.' Not one replied 't.o.' Of the two replies qualifying the statement, one said, 'As long as the staff continue to be happy with it'. The second headmistress, although she basically approved of i.t.a., replied:

'I can't really be definite here. t.o. has a much greater wealth of books which makes me hesitate. I'll be quite happy with i.t.a. for the next two or three years but I'm not certain about ten years' time.'

The one doubtful person was a headmaster of an all-age primary school, who said:

'I am still doubtful, but perhaps I'll continue with i.t.a. for the sake of the six or so dull children and for the way the easier, earlier reading in i.t.a. helps the other subjects.'

In this particular school emphasis was laid on neat, correctly-spelt written work in the junior classes and the headmaster's main doubts concerned the transition in writing.

In connection with the question of the continued use of i.t.a., it would have been of interest to have talked to a few headteachers who had used i.t.a. and subsequently returned to t.o. In the event, no such school was encountered in the course of the visits. In one l.e.a. the interviewer was taken to a t.o. infant school in which a recently-appointed headmistress had come from an i.t.a. school. She would have liked to introduce i.t.a. in her present school but felt that the staff were not yet sufficiently favourably disposed towards the idea. A glance at Table 2(g) in Chapter 2 makes it clear that in June 1966 there were few such schools in the country which had discontinued the use of i.t.a. Notes which accompanied some of the completed questionnaires to local educational authorities disclosed that the reasons for a return to t.o. in these few schools were usually administrative rather than related to the alphabet itself.

V Key question to class teachers

Every discussion with a class teacher who had used i.t.a. and had previously had experience with t.o. terminated with the following 'key question': 'Suppose you were now appointed to be the head of a new infant school, you would have to set about ordering stocks of books. Consequently you would have to decide whether to use i.t.a. or t.o. Which would you choose?'

The following figures refer to teachers of i.t.a. classes in the schools visited, but additional teachers with whom discussions took place, other than in schools, gave replies in accordance with the pattern demonstrated below:

TABLE 5(a)

Teachers' choice of i.t.a. or t.o.

Choice	No. of teachers
i.t.a.	78
i.t.a. (with certain qualifications)	3
i.t.a. (in poorer districts only)	3
t.o.	2
uncertain	1
Total	90

Of the first 78, the majority either said 'i.t.a.' unconditionally or they added 'definitely' or some such emphatic word or phrase; the remainder added 'providing the staff agreed'. Of the next group of six teachers, five were in one school, and in a group discussion they plumped for i.t.a. with two qualifications: first, providing the staff agreed; and second, as long as it was certain that there would be continuity for children who had not transferred by the time they left the infant school. The sixth teacher in this category taught in a school which was running its own experiment. Her reply was that if a new school was a one-form entry she would use i.t.a., but that if it were a two-form entry, she would have one class using i.t.a. and one t.o., because such a situation is so stimulating for the teachers.

Two of three teachers in the next category came from the same school and the third from a different school. Both schools were in poor socio-economic areas. Their replies were as follows:

'I should choose i.t.a. for a school like this, but for a school of bright children I'd start with t.o. and later put those who hadn't got away onto i.t.a.'

'In a poor district – definitely i.t.a. In a better area – t.o. There would be no point in i.t.a. because their parents have books and the children see t.o. at home.'

'I'm not really certain. It would depend on the area. In an area like this, perhaps i.t.a.'

Only two teachers out of 90 replied that they would use t.o. if appointed as head-teachers of new infant schools. The first was the teacher mentioned earlier as the only one interviewed who expressed disapproval of i.t.a. Her current class of six-year-olds was her only experience of children who were using i.t.a. The children had been with her nearly a year. She said she had not liked the idea of i.t.a. at first and she was still not keen on it. She did not think any child in her current class was any better than he would have been with t.o. and she felt that the bright ones had been held back.

The second teacher was more experienced with both i.t.a. and t.o. She had begun to use it in 1961 and continued for three years. Then in 1964 and 1965 the school had begun its own experiment of one vertically grouped class using i.t.a. and one t.o. This particular teacher had been in charge of the t.o. class in the preceding year and the i.t.a. class in the current year. She said she had originally tried i.t.a. with an open mind. She had enjoyed teaching the classes with i.t.a. and equally the class with t.o. She had been interested in both. However, although she could see advantages in i.t.a. for free writing, she had come to the conclusion that 'i.t.a. is not all it's cracked up to be,' and that 'the transition stage is hard for the teacher'. Furthermore, after having had experience of the two experimental classes, she felt that her t.o. children were as good last year as her i.t.a. children this year.

VI   A note on teachers' reactions

Lest we should be tempted to wonder whether a selection of the views of teachers who have had experience of i.t.a., in which the majority are in favour, a few have doubts and reservations, while only one disapproves, is a biased selection, one might profitably reconsider the manner of the selection of schools and teachers. In particular it should be remembered that each local education authority was asked to suggest a fair sample of schools, including the one which was *least* enthusiastic about i.t.a. Similarly, in each school the headteacher was asked to introduce the interviewer to the teacher who was least enthusiastic as well as the one who was most enthusiastic. Moreover, certain headteachers invited the interviewer to talk to particular teachers who were known to be dubious about the value of i.t.a.

It is equally important in this respect to consider the framework within which the teacher's comments as set out in this report were made. During the past five years in which i.t.a. has been in use, countless records of teachers' comments on i.t.a. have been quoted both verbally and in print by such people as Pitman, research workers in this country and abroad, educationists who were known to be enthusiastic about i.t.a. and by participating headteachers, class teachers and remedial teachers. Many of the remarks are similar to those quoted in this report. Yet it might fairly be suggested that the comments quoted here should be given greater weight than other comments so far published.

Not that it is in any way suggested that the teachers who on previous occasions have expressed their opinions of i.t.a. were not speaking honestly. Nevertheless the setting of many previous reports of teachers' comments was entirely different from the present setting. The main differences are as follows:

(i)   Nearly all the earlier published accounts of teachers' comments came from early participants. The teachers who are willing to be the first to experiment with any innovation in education are usually lively, go-ahead people and there is a tendency for their reports to be ultra-enthusiastic. Thus many people's judgements on the favourable comments of the 'early users' of i.t.a. were to some extent suspended until they could be reinforced or contradicted by 'later users'.

(ii)   The comments collected in this enquiry came from 'later users' as well as from 'early users'. Many of the later users were taking i.t.a. in a much calmer fashion than the early enthusiasts. Furthermore, some of the later users of i.t.a. were those who were among the 'original doubters'.

(iii)   The early enthusiastic comments of teachers were generally made to people who were known to have, or thought to have, special interests in i.t.a. Consequently it was rather difficult for those who had not visited many schools which were using i.t.a. to assess how representative the views might be. It could well have been that, among the early users, those who had doubts refrained from expressing them to people with known interests in i.t.a. Such a restraint could well have sprung from feelings of kindliness and a desire not to hurt or offend an interested party.

(iv)   On the other hand, in this enquiry it is much more likely that the whole gamut of opinions was produced: firstly, because the impartiality of the evaluation was stressed; and secondly, because it was emphasised that all shades of opinion would be useful to the evaluation.

Accordingly, although many of the remarks quoted appear to mirror earlier comments, the circumstances in which they were made were such that they should merit serious consideration as a fair cross section of the views of a large variety of teachers.

CHAPTER 6

Infant Teachers' Comments on Reading

I Preliminary points

A. LINGUISTIC SKILLS

BEFORE considering teachers' comments on the reading progress of infants, attention should be directed to a number of relevant points. The first relates to the fact that the acquisition or improvement of the language skills–listening, speaking, reading and writing–represents a totality in which the sub-divisions are closely linked and inter-woven. Guidance, reinforcement and practice of all the sub-skills mentioned are occurring throughout the day in infant schools. To attempt to isolate the process of learning to read from the other linguistic skills is to institute an artificial division. Nevertheless, such a division has been adopted in this report in order to simplify and clarify the reporting of teachers' comments.

B. INFANT TEACHERS' ASSESSMENTS OF READING PROGRESS

The second important point to be borne in mind is that the use of objective tests of reading ability is not a common practice in British infant schools. Accordingly, the assessments made by headteachers and teachers of children's reading progress with i.t.a. were much more frequently subjective than objective. To merely collect, state and summarise the subjective judgements of teachers without attempting to relate these assessments to their beliefs, attitudes and previous experiences would prove a sterile exercise.

It was quite clear that teachers tended to judge the reading progress of i.t.a. classes against their recollections of the standards achieved by previous, similar classes in which t.o. had been used. In this context it was particularly important for the inter-viewer to ascertain whether each teacher interviewed had used t.o. with a class as nearly identical as possible to her current i.t.a. class. As already explained, within the selected schools discussions with experienced infant teachers were given priority over discussions with, for example, recently qualified teachers or those whose previous experiences were not with infants. Questions of fact had then to be posed to teachers, as well as certain subjective assessments made by the interviewer in order to build up useful frames of reference against which to view teachers' comments on reading progress.

C. TEACHERS' FRAMES OF REFERENCE

As it was considered to be of little value to view teachers' comments on reading progress in isolation, without reference to their criteria of judgement, the third important preliminary point to note is the extraordinarily large number of background features which contribute to the frame of reference of any one teacher or school. Among such factors the following could be listed: the teacher's age, training, teaching experience, ability, interest and attitude to reading; the age, intelligence and home backgrounds of the children whom she had previously taught and the socio-economic levels of the families of the children in different schools; the buildings themselves; the general beliefs about infant education which were in force in the schools and the internal organisation of the schools designed to exemplify these beliefs, as well as the specific attitude towards reading found among the staffs of the schools.

Information on certain of these background features could be obtained fairly accurately by asking questions or by making simple observations in the schools. Assessment of other relevant factors, however, called for subjective appraisals on the part of the observer. Examples of both methods of procedure are given.

Specific questions were put to the teachers interviewed on the more factual aspects of their experiences of teaching the early stages of reading, including questions on the ages and types of children taught, methods* and materials* used and classroom procedures* formerly adopted. Information about the reading schemes, books and apparatus which teachers had previously used could be reliably ascertained by questions. The same was true, to some extent, of the methods they had employed, even though, as Morris (1959) points out, close observation of teaching methods reveals that teachers do not always do exactly what they think or say they do.

Questions to teachers of i.t.a. classes, concerning the reading materials they had formerly used in t.o. with equivalent classes, led to mention of a majority of the reading schemes and sets of apparatus published in Great Britain, including *The Happy Venture Readers*, *Janet and John*, *The Beacon Readers*, *Vanguard Readers*, *Gay Way Readers*, *The Pilot Reading Scheme*, *The McKee Readers*, *The Royal Road Readers*, *John and Mary*, and *Mac and Tosh*. Some teachers had adhered closely to one basic scheme, while others had used a combination of two or more schemes. A minority of teachers had refrained from using basic schemes, but had utilised instead home-made materials and apparatus with a variety of simple supplementary reading books and larger story books. The methods used by these teachers in their experiences with t.o. ranged as widely as the reading books with which they were familiar.

Among those factors relating to reading progress, which required a subjective assessment on the part of the investigator, there was one of particular importance which had to be made in every school visited. It comprised the basic attitude of the teachers towards reading. Usually the attitudes of the staff reflect, although they do not necessarily mirror, the attitude of the headteacher.

The variations in this basic attitude in different infant schools is enormous. On the one hand there is the school whose attitude would be summed up in comments such as 'We consider reading to be very important'; 'We lay great emphasis on reading'; and 'We want children to acquire the skill as early as possible'. At the other extreme the attitude might be expressed as follows: 'We believe in a delayed start to reading'; 'We don't rush reading'; and 'There is no stress on children reading early, as we believe that reading is only one small part of the child's all-round development'. Every shade of attitude between these two extremes can be noted in infant schools and in the course of this enquiry, within both t.o. and i.t.a. schools, the entire range of

* Reference should be made to 'Terminology' in Appendix A.

41

attitudes to reading was encountered. Those supporting the first basic attitude may be described as 'early starters' and the second group as 'delayed starters'. It then becomes quite clear that if two teachers or two schools hold these utterly opposing beliefs, not only the reading progress of their pupils, but also the judgements of the teachers on this reading progress, cannot in any way be considered as directly comparable. It was essential for the interviewer to try to compare like with like.

II Progress in reading

A. GENERAL IMPRESSIONS

1 *A large measure of agreement*

When reports on children's reading progress with i.t.a. were reviewed in the light of the wide range of different relevant factors in the schools visited, one exceedingly interesting fact emerged. Despite the observed variety of background features relating to reading, the majority of teachers' comments were in the same direction–a favourable direction. The main pattern of opinions regarding reading progress was as follows: most teachers spoke of an improvement in reading progress; a few could see little difference; no-one suggested that less progress was made with i.t.a. than would have been achieved if t.o. had been used.

Among the large number of teachers who were favourably impressed by children's reading progress, certain variations of opinions were noticeable, but they represented differences of degree rather than of direction. If these minor divergences of opinions are noted first, the broad pattern of favourable reports on reading progress will emerge more clearly. Degree of enthusiasm appeared to the interviewer to be related to three main factors: age of children taught; length of teachers' experience with i.t.a.; and teachers' general attitude to reading.

Firstly, regarding the age of children taught, the discernible trend was that the younger the children the more enthusiastic was the teacher about the value of i.t.a. in helping children to read. Teachers of reception classes were almost unanimous in indicating that i.t.a. had effected a great improvement in reading. Teachers of older infants, even when favourably disposed towards i.t.a., as most of them were, were more inclined to temper their conclusions by reference to anxieties concerning the problems of transition in reading and spelling.

Secondly, the length of time that teachers had been using i.t.a., as well as when they had begun to use it, resulted in slight differences of opinion about children's reading progress. Some teachers with four and five years' experience of i.t.a. spoke of their awareness that the reading results of children in their classes were not as spectacular in succeeding years as in the first year in which they had used i.t.a. The observer likewise noticed that teachers who had only been using i.t.a. for a year or two, even when they were favourably impressed with it, were not making quite such enthusiastic claims about children's reading progress as did some teachers of the original i.t.a. classes. Yet, despite this small divergence, the majority of teachers who had used i.t.a., whether their experience was of one or five years' duration, were of the opinion that children's reading progress was better with i.t.a. than with t.o.

A third difference in degree of enthusiasm was noted between teachers who believed in an early start to reading and those who supported a delayed beginning. As might be expected, schools which did not lay great emphasis on reading even when the teachers thought that i.t.a. was a valuable aid to reading, did not report such rapid progress as schools in which teachers expressed strong beliefs about the importance of reading.

To turn to the few teachers who had noted little difference in children's progress in reading, whether i.t.a. or t.o. was used, it appeared to the interviewer that they were mostly to be found in two distinct categories of schools. The first group consisted of schools which believed in delaying the beginning of reading and laid greater emphasis on other aspects of the curriculum. Certain teachers in such schools, although not all of them, said that the use of i.t.a. had made little difference to reading progress. Even so, some of them still preferred i.t.a. to t.o. because of its effect on free writing.

Secondly, there were schools in which children had always attained very high reading standards. Most of these were schools in good socio-economic areas but a few were in much poorer areas. The probable common denominator was that the high standards of reading prevalent in these schools represented the high priority which the teachers attached to the acquisition of this skill. In other words, they were schools in which strong reading drives were permanently in force. It was in a porportion of such schools visited that a few teachers did not believe that i.t.a. had accelerated reading progress, although teachers in other schools in which equivalent attitudes to reading prevailed concluded that children did read more quickly and easily with i.t.a.

Nevertheless, despite the exceptions just noted, there was no doubt whatsoever in the minds of most teachers who had used i.t.a. that children's reading progress had thereby been improved. The preceding discussion of the situations in which certain teachers' views showed variations, albeit on the same theme, enables the majority of teachers' comments on reading progress with i.t.a. to be summarised in broad conclusions relating to one particular aspect of the process of children beginning to read.

2   A good beginning

Most teachers who had used i.t.a. with infants were in general agreement that it had enabled children to make a good beginning to reading. There were no doubts about their certainty on the following four points:
  (i)   i.t.a. makes beginning reading easier for children;
  (ii)   children are much happier using i.t.a.;
  (iii) children begin to read earlier with i.t.a.;
  (iv)   children learn to read more quickly with i.t.a.
The teachers' greatest pleasure came from their observations that i.t.a. made the task of learning to read much easier for children and consequently they found more enjoyment in the process than formerly. Most teachers laid greater stress on this aspect of enjoyment than on their belief that i.t.a. helped children to learn to read earlier and more quickly, although many such comments were made.

One headmaster said, 'I have no doubts whatsoever that a gain in reading has been made. The children achieve reading skill earlier with i.t.a.' One headmistress stated that 'Even dull children can begin to read at six with i.t.a.' Another headteacher pointed out how advantageous it is to teachers of large classes when children begin to read earlier. One teacher, referring to the decrease in the time now required to learn to read, said, 'The child picks up tremendous momentum in reading'. The fact that most children learned to read so quickly with i.t.a. was a source of amazement and pleasure to many teachers who had, as they now described it, 'struggled' so long with t.o. One teacher summed up for many when, she said, 'Children get off to a really good start with i.t.a.'

3 *A better attitude to reading*

The majority of the teachers interviewed appeared to consider the change in children's attitudes to reading to be at least as important, or even more important, than their increased progress in reading. Teachers' comments on children's attitudes can be summarised in this way. Children enjoy learning because of the simplicity and regularity of the alphabet; this gives them confidence so that they are eager to try; the regularity of the sound-symbol relationship means that their attempts are generally successful; and this in turn cuts out frustrations and gives them a sense of achievement. Not every teacher mentioned every one of these points but this was the general tenor of their thoughts concerning children's attitudes to reading with i.t.a.

Teachers' emphasis on children's enjoyment has already been mentioned. The younger the children concerned, the more the teachers stressed this happy attitude. It was also most apparent in those schools containing children of lower intelligence, from poor home backgrounds, in which teachers were eager to help children to read and where, prior to the use of i.t.a., they had not been as successful as they wished.

Teachers' remarks on children's confidence included the following: 'i.t.a. gives all children, even the slowest, confidence'. 'i.t.a. gives children confidence because there is no confusion; it puts children on a path which stays the same all the way.' One teacher expressed it rather differently. She said, 'i.t.a. doesn't destroy children's confidence'. She believed that children generally had a natural confidence in themselves which had tended to be undermined when they tried to read with t.o.

Very many teachers pointed out that children's confidence in their own ability to read made them eager to try anything in the way of reading materials. Even some of the youngest children picked up new books, comics, newspapers, birthday cards and cereal packets and tried to read them. One reception class teacher had noticed particularly that since she had used i.t.a., as soon as she displayed anything on the classroom walls, the children all went and tried to read it. In the days of t.o. many children would have looked at the picture but not bothered with the caption, and in the case of a notice, only a small handful of children would have attempted to read it. An infant headmistress gave a different example of children's keenness to try to read print. She had always adopted the practice, fairly common in many schools, of having groups of slower children come to her room for extra practice in reading aloud. When the school had used t.o. she had noticed that whenever a child had finished reading to her a previously prepared page in his reading book, he had begun to edge away from her desk, in case she should ask him to turn over the page and try to read something entirely new. Now, when children came to read i.t.a. books to her, she found them eager to turn over to the next page.

Closely related to children's enjoyment and confidence was the obverse advantage noted by so many teachers who commented that i.t.a. cuts out frustrations for children. The following quotations represent a variety of ways of expressing this point:

'There are fewer children who don't like reading or who are worried about reading than formerly–although there may still be the odd one. The shutters don't go down when a child meets a word he doesn't know. He'll try it.'

44

'One doesn't now find children in the middle of infant school who have, as it were, given up. Even if a child is going slowly, he feels he is making progress.'

'Backward children don't get that defeatist attitude.'

'Children feel on top of it instead of struggling.'

'Children don't get blockages as they did with t.o. Even the youngest, dullest child can have a go.'

An infant headmistress of an informal, 'progressive' school in a rather poor district spoke along these lines:

'i.t.a. prevents frustration from building up in slower children. It is true that if the beginning of reading was left until later for slower children it would be easier for them, but there are two difficulties about this. At first, in the reception class, the teacher doesn't know which are the slowest children. Even if she did, the slow child in a class of mixed abilities sees other children reading and he wants to do the same. If he finds it too difficult this makes for frustrations in him.'

Many teachers remarked that children's confidence in their own ability to read, and the fact that they could soon do so, had given children a great sense of achievement. As soon as children found they could read, they were eager to demonstrate their skill by reading aloud to teachers, parents and visitors to the school. Brighter children who learned to read with t.o. always used to be keen to read aloud to teachers, in order to demonstrate their prowess and obtain commendations. Infant teachers using i.t.a., however, have noticed that this now applied to even the slowest children. On entering most i.t.a. classrooms, visitors are almost pestered by young children anxious to read to them. This eagerness is not teacher-fostered; it is rather a result of young children's satisfaction at being able to master what they consider to be an adult accomplishment, and their very natural desire to demonstrate it.

The independence of children who began to read with i.t.a., in contrast to the dependence of many children on the teacher when t.o. was the medium employed, was noted by most teachers. They remarked that this increase in independence was particularly noticeable in the slowest children who had formerly displayed the greatest degree of dependence. One teacher commented that, 'Children's manner with teachers is now more that of equals'. As an illustration of this point she instanced a five-year-old tapping her on the shoulder to say, 'You have forgotten to write the date on the blackboard but I've done it for you'.

The different attitudes of boys and girls to reading were mentioned by some teachers. They spoke of how, when they had used t.o., they had usually found girls keener to learn to read than boys. Boys in the main had tended to be more interested in rushing about pretending to be aeroplanes or in engaging in building activities than in reading; since using i.t.a. these teachers had observed that boys were just as interested in reading as girls.

The interviewer's observations in schools, which included talking to many children and listening to them read, confirmed what teachers had to say. Adverse attitudes to reading were not noticeable. Children's enjoyment, confidence, sense of achievement and eagerness to try to read were patently obvious.

1 *Records of reading progress*

It has already been noted that it is rare for infant schools to make regular assessments of children's reading ability by means of administering objective reading tests. Accordingly, very few of the infant schools visited had based their assessments of children's reading on such results. In any case, if one had merely been interested in test results there were plenty of published records of reading test scores available. The few infant schools in which reading tests had been carried out regularly, both before and after the use of i.t.a., showed the i.t.a. children, after transfer to t.o., to be in advance of previous groups of t.o. children. One headmistress of such a school commented as follows:

> 'We are very pleased with the results of i.t.a.; it really knocks Reading Ages into cocked hats. At the end of the first year, 50% of the children can make a good attempt at Burt's Graded Word Reading Test and Southgate Word Selection Test in t.o., although some of them have only been in the school since March. Some children have Reading Ages of ten at this stage.'

Test results, however, were only rarely quoted. Infant teachers' conclusions about children's reading progress generally represented subjective impressions based on years of experience of teaching reading, by means of t.o., to children of the same age. These impressions were frequently reinforced by the type of records of children's reading progress which many teachers keep; for example, the 'sight words' recognised by individual children in the early stages of reading and notes of the dates when each child had completed a basic reading book and been given the next one in the reading scheme. Discussions regarding these records showed that when children reading i.t.a. books were compared with preceding classes of children reading t.o. books, for example in the *Janet and John* scheme, the i.t.a. children were ahead. The same was true when the number of children who had transferred from i.t.a., and were currently reading one of the later books in a t.o. reading scheme, was compared with the number of children who were reading that same book in the days of t.o. In short, whether or not teachers' assessments were backed up by records of children's progress over a number of years preceding, and during, the use of i.t.a., the majority of teachers gave examples which served to support their conviction that most children had made better reading progress with i.t.a. than could have been expected with t.o.

2 *Decrease in non-readers*

The decrease in the number of non-readers among the children was remarked on by many teachers in comments such as, 'There is less backlog of slower children'; and 'Fewer children are left behind in reading'. One example came from a teacher who had previously taught in one of the schools visited as an untrained teacher, at a time when the school was using t.o. After her college training she returned to teach in the same school and found them using i.t.a. She immediately noticed the reduction in the number of non-readers in the school.

One type of example, most frequently quoted, referred to those particular families, familiar to most teachers, in which all the children appear to be of low intelligence. In the past, notwithstanding teachers' efforts to help, the children had nevertheless passed through the infant school, and in some cases also through the junior school, without learning to read. In a large number of schools visited, teachers spoke of such families and related how one of the younger children had learned to read using i.t.a., although the teachers did not believe the child to be any more intelligent than his older siblings. In one instance, a child who during his first year at school had never spoken a word, did learn to read with i.t.a., although the teacher was certain he would not have done so with t.o. This teacher realised that the child's reading was still at what she described as 'a mechanical stage', but even so it gave the child satisfaction, and there was hope that he would later read with more understanding.

3 Progress at different ages

Examples of reading progress cited by teachers were not confined to any one age group of children. Many teachers in reception classes, particularly in schools in low socio-economic areas, commented on the number of books in i.t.a. read by children during their first year, whereas formerly only a few children in the class would have read the first book or two in a reading scheme in t.o. At the other extreme, one teacher of the reception class, in a school situated in a high socio-economic area, in which as she indicated, 'children would read anyway', remarked that most children were 'through the i.t.a. programme in four months'. Reception class teachers who now, for the first time, had many pupils able to read simple books, found not only that this gave the teachers themselves satisfaction and pleasure, but also that it lightened some of the burden of large classes by freeing the teacher for other activities.

Teachers of six-year-olds probably noticed the greatest differences in children's reading ability. Many of them talked of the proportion of children who used to come into their classes not having made a start at reading, or barely started, in contrast to the avid readers of i.t.a. books who now come up from reception classes. One teacher of this age group remarked that the children who entered her class were now about a year ahead. Consequently, she no longer had to teach 'the tools of reading', as the children were already using their reading skill. Another teacher of a class of 39 children, in a school in a slum area, stated that when the children entered her class, at $6\frac{1}{2}$ years, the entire 39 had made the transfer to t.o. For the first time she 'didn't have to teach them to read!' Now she found that reading books from a reading scheme were hardly required. The children not only read story books and used information books but they read poetry and plays for pleasure. Even the dullest child in the class could find a book which interested him and read it.

Teachers of the oldest infant classes also had many similar examples of children's reading progress to quote. One such teacher, who had been a little doubtful about the use of i.t.a. at first, spoke as follows:

'It may be a coincidence, but in three years of having this class, these children are the best readers who have come into the class – and this is the first i.t.a. class to come through the school.'

Another teacher remarked that, 'Many top infants can now read second-year junior history textbooks on their own.'

The headteacher of a school in a slum clearance area, which had used i.t.a. for three years, indicated that, of the 80 children who would be promoted to the Junior School at the end of the summer term, every child was reading in t.o. by May.

A number of schools gave specific examples of how younger children, beginning to read in i.t.a., soon surpassed older children in the school who were using t.o. In one such school the teachers were working under particularly difficult conditions in which the population of their classes was partially altered every term, a proportion of the children in the class being promoted to the next class, while an equal number of younger children came in from the preceding class. One teacher soon found that the younger i.t.a. children entering the class were well ahead of the older t.o. children in it. She felt so strongly that the older t.o. children should not be deprived of the opportunity of using i.t.a. that she re-started all the older children in the class on i.t.a., with good results.

In another school, which began to use i.t.a. with five-year-olds, the headmistress was soon so pleased with the children's reading progress that she wondered if i.t.a. would be of some help to those children in the six-year-old class who had made very little progress with reading in t.o. Accordingly, the group of six-year-olds who had made least progress in reading were allowed to start with i.t.a. She was delighted with the results. Before this class moved up to the Junior School, the weakest group of children had transferred to t.o. and had surpassed the other children in the class who had been taught solely with t.o.

4 Absentees

Some teachers commented on the reading progress of absentees. Most children in infant schools have a number of absences owing to illness. Teachers talked of how, when they used t.o., these absences nearly always resulted in children 'falling behind in reading'. An absence of two or three weeks quite often resulted in a child having to be demoted to a lower reading group. Now with i.t.a., as one teacher expressed it:

> 'Absent children don't fall behind in reading nearly as much as they used to. They come back again and pick up reading more easily.'

5 Changing standards

There was one other aspect of reading progress which cropped up quite frequently in schools. It was mentioned spontaneously by a number of teachers and it often appeared in group discussions when teachers were invited to look back over their experiences, with a view to comparing children's former reading progress with t.o. and their current progress since i.t.a. was introduced. The effort to make such comparisons had made some teachers realise that their own standards and expectations regarding children's reading progress had altered since they had used i.t.a. They were now expecting more of children. Hence it was quite difficult for them to look back to their t.o. days and make valid comparisons of children's reading progress.

One teacher of a second year infant class, typical of many, told the interviewer how, at the beginning of the year, she had felt rather disappointed with the reading standards of the children who had come up to her from the reception class. She felt they were not as good as the preceding year or two, only about half the children having reached the end of an infant reading scheme. She then went on to say that when this thought had occurred to her, she had had to jolt her memory to remind herself that three or four years ago none of the children entering her class would have reached the end of the reading scheme; some would have been reading the early books in the scheme and many would not have begun to read books at all. This rise in teachers' own standards and expectations of infants' reading can be summed up in the following comment from one headmistress:

> 'Now that the school has almost completed its third year with i.t.a., the staff and myself are all beginning to accept these delightful results as commonplace. We are more than ever convinced that we were right to use i.t.a.'

1 *Materials, Methods and Procedures*

There are countless strands in the background and forefront of the situations in which children learn to read. Probably the most important factors in the forefront, disregarding for the moment those personal factors relating to both the teacher and the child, are the medium,* the materials* and the methods* used. That these three 'm's' are closely interwoven with classroom procedure* represents one of the major difficulties of both designing an experiment to test a new medium and assessing the results. Moreover, it is pertinent to remember that the methods employed in infant classes, and equally the reading materials used, have been developed over the years as the means of teaching children to read in the medium of the traditional alphabet. Much, but not all, of what is now accepted as commonplace in both methods and materials has arisen in response to the irregularities of t.o. The use of a simpler alphabet or code may well result in the development of different materials, methods and procedures.

(*a*) *Early materials, methods and procedures.* A survey of infant classes using t.o. would reveal a use of reading materials ranging from a fairly rigid adherence to one basic reading scheme, through the use of two basic schemes to complement each other, to the class which did not use a reading scheme at all, but relied solely on a wide variety of published books alongside hand-made apparatus and books. There would be additional books available in the book corners in nearly all these classes, with the last one likely to have the largest number and variety.

In the classes which first used i.t.a., the use of such a range of reading materials was impossible. Teachers had practically no choice of published materials. Only one reading scheme, namely *Janet and John*, was available, together with a limited choice of book-corner books. Accordingly, the reading materials in the early i.t.a. classes varied mainly only in respect of home-made apparatus, charts and books.

Teachers who began to use i.t.a. (originally known as the Augmented Roman Alphabet–A.R.A.) in 1961 and 1962, as part of the Reading Research Unit's First Experiment, were asked to continue with the same methods as they had formerly used with t.o. For instance, Downing, in *To Be or Not To Be* (1962), posed the question, 'Does the teacher have to modify her methods of teaching reading if she uses A.R.A?' He replied: ' "No" is the brief answer to this question, although some adaptions may be forced on the teacher by the nature of A.R.A. However, in general it is true to say that teaching methods can remain as usual.' It seems fairly clear that in using the word 'method', Downing is referring not only to the interpretation of the word 'method' employed in this report which applies particularly to look-and-say and phonic methods, but also to what is termed 'classroom procedure' in this report.

With regard to method in the narrower sense, the observer found that the majority of the early schools visited began with a look-and-say method. Indeed, the choice of *Janet and John* reading scheme made this practice almost inevitable. The timing of the introduction of phonic work varied considerably from school to school.

Discussions with teachers and observations in schools suggested that classroom procedure in the first year or two varied more widely than method, although the limitation of published reading materials precluded certain divergences in procedure which were to be observed in schools using i.t.a. after 1963. For example, the earliest

* Please refer to 'Terminology' in Appendix A.

schools relied fairly heavily on one basic reading scheme in the early stages of reading. Other features of procedure, however, such as class organisation and grouping, formality or informality of the regime, the time devoted to reading and its extension to other aspects of literacy and to other subjects did vary from school to school. The variety of procedures adopted probably differed from those to be found in a representative sample of infant schools only in so far as the early i.t.a. schools contained a relatively small proportion of the total number of so-called 'progressive' infant schools.

(*b*) *Later changes in materials, methods and procedures.* The choice of published materials in i.t.a. increased year by year. By the end of 1966 five reading schemes, comprising 130 books, were being published in Great Britain in i.t.a., together with some 490 titles of books not connected with reading schemes. Teachers could supplement this total of approximately 620 books by additional books printed in the U.S.A. and by i.t.a. reading materials, other than books, which were published by ten different firms in Great Britain.

Accordingly, the i.t.a. classes visited in the course of this enquiry used a much greater selection of published books than had been possible even a few years earlier. A few schools still relied mainly on the *Janet and John* scheme. The majority of classes visited used *The Downing Readers* as the basic scheme and *Janet and John* as a supporting scheme. Only a very few schools dispensed entirely with a reading scheme and relied on surrounding children with a variety of books printed in i.t.a. In one such school, which had started to use i.t.a. in 1963, the teachers had avoided purchasing a reading scheme by using i.t.a. flash cards and apparatus, and sticking hand-printed i.t.a. labels into many of their existing books. As the reception class teacher said:

> 'I find i.t.a. absolutely marvellous. It does not even need a reading scheme. Even if children do start on a scheme, after the first two or three books they can easily transfer to other schemes or books.'

In a few other schools, certain teachers who believed that children's early reading should spring from the use of many different books and other forms of printed words, and who went a long way towards putting these beliefs into practice, nevertheless felt that they were still slightly handicapped by the limitations of books printed in i.t.a. They agreed that the much larger number of books now available made feasible such an approach to reading, yet they still considered the number of books published in i.t.a. to be insufficient. The main need they expressed was for more 'large, beautifully-produced and beautifully-illustrated books'.

In fact, despite the increase in books published in i.t.a., certain teachers, even when they approved of i.t.a., nevertheless rated it as a disadvantage that the supply of books was not yet adequate. In various schools mention was made of the lack of information books, reference books, picture dictionaries, comics and ancillary materials of all kinds in i.t.a. Some headteachers also pointed out that i.t.a. books were frequently dearer than t.o. books and that, moreover, schools were faced with a dual expense in that large numbers of both i.t.a. and t.o. books were required.

Regarding reading methods, nearly all schools began with a look-and-say word or sentence method, and at varying stages gave some phonic training. The timing of the introduction of phonics varied from 'after a sight vocabulary of 20 or so words' to 'towards the end of the infant school'. These schools also differed in respect of whether they gave specific graded instruction in phonic rules or whether they talked about phonic rules arising incidentally. Only one class, in one of the schools visited, began the teaching of reading with basic phonic training, that is by teaching the children the sounds of the symbols and then combining these sounds into words. No school claimed to use look-and-say methods entirely unsupported by any form of phonic work.

The wider range of the use of reading materials and methods to be seen in i.t.a. classes in 1966 was complemented by the greater variety of teaching procedures regarding reading which were to be observed. Both these features of the reading environment are reflections of the fact that by that date all types of schools were found to be experimenting with i.t.a. Schools with different attitudes towards the timing of the introduction of formal reading, with different aims, organisations and so on were almost bound to display the complete gamut of materials, methods and procedures.

In most of the schools visited, almost regardless of the materials, methods and procedures in use, teachers commented on the way in which the use of i.t.a. had resulted in changes in methods and procedures.

One noticeable trend in i.t.a. classes was towards less dependence on a basic reading scheme. Usually, when a teacher first started to use i.t.a., she adhered rather closely to a particular reading scheme. Then, quite soon, she found that the regularity of the alphabet enabled children to attempt unknown words outside the controlled vocabulary of their particular scheme and so their reading, even at a very early stage, could extend beyond the reading scheme. Certain infant headteachers, like the one quoted below, rated this as one of the main advantages of i.t.a.:

> 'With t.o., although I had always encouraged teachers to let children use reading books other than those in the basic scheme–because I think both teachers and children get bored with one scheme–yet they had to stick fairly closely to a reading scheme because of the controlled vocabulary. One of the main advantages of i.t.a. is that children very soon begin to word-build, and once they have done so, they can soon use all sorts of other books outside the reading scheme.'

The use of i.t.a. had also brought about in many schools a change in procedure, represented by an increase in children's free writing, which inevitably reinforced the process of learning to read. This change was not one which had been initiated by the teacher; rather was it an activity which had sprung from the children themselves. A full report of teacher's comments on children's writing, however, forms part of the following chapter.

Almost all teachers who had used i.t.a. for a few years reported changes, not so much in their own teaching procedure as in ways of learning, arising spontaneously from the children. These changes were all in one direction, and related to 'sounding' and phonics arising naturally much earlier than with t.o.

One example, given in detail, will serve to illustrate this point. The school was one which would be termed 'progressive'. The atmosphere was informal, children followed individual interests and no basic reading scheme had ever been used when children learned to read with t.o. The headmistress had put off experimenting with i.t.a. at first because she feared that it might be phonically orientated. In the reception class children did not have specific seats at tables because they all moved about so much. Each child had a drawer in which to keep his possessions. On the children's first day in school, these drawers were labelled with the children's names, printed in i.t.a. Each child was also given a name card, with his name printed in i.t.a., to hang round his neck. These cards were distributed each morning. In the cloakroom each child's peg was labelled with a picture, for example a pig, a rose or a ship, as is usual in an infant school. In the cloakroom the teacher, for her own information, had hung a reference list of these pictures, with the children's names in i.t.a.

It is important to note, that in this school there was no idea of beginning to teach children to read at an early stage in their school careers; in fact the situation was the opposite, with a complete absence of such pressure. Accordingly, the reception class teacher was amazed when, within their first few days at school, the children began to look at the list in the cloakroom and remark on the similar letters which appeared in each other's names. They soon began to recognise their own and each other's names on their drawers and name cards. Noting identical letters arose as a spontaneous and exciting game. It was usually the middle letters of names which were remarked on, with   being the first and the favourite. There was so much interest in it that the teacher made a big '   ' wall book for the children. All the names with   in them were written in it. Very soon there was a whole set of these large 'sound' books. The head remarked that, 'The enthusiasm of the children never palled; it went on right through their reading and writing'.

Very many other schools also gave details of children's very early interest in letters and sounds, when i.t.a. was used. One reception class teacher, in a school with an informal approach to reading, remarked that children do learn to recognise the 44 symbols of i.t.a. more quickly than they used to recognise the 26 lower-case letters of t.o. She had been surprised by this and was not quite sure how it happened as she had not set out to get children to recognise the letters. She had concluded that it probably arose because the same symbol is repeated so often. For example '   ' appears in so many of the first words the child learns – my, like, night, etc. Formerly, with t.o., the children would have met all the different spellings of these words, instead of seeing the same ones written over and over again.

Children's early recognition of the visual symbols is very closely linked with the sounds these symbols represent. The following are typical comments made by teachers on this score:

'i.t.a. makes children more sound-conscious.'

'With i.t.a. children can learn the letter sounds much more easily than with t.o., and with no heart-burning. They really need to learn the sounds of the letters in order to get the best out of i.t.a. This applies to both reading and writing.' (N.B.–This may sound like the remark of a teacher in a very formal school; in fact it was from a teacher of a vertically grouped class with children working on individual and quite informal lines.)

' "Sounding" the letters comes much earlier. It begins with incidental sounding as the children help the teacher to write news on the blackboard. With t.o., the teacher wouldn't have dared to let sounding happen because of all the irregularities.'

According to the majority of teachers, the recognition of letters and sounds led fairly rapidly to the blending of sounds to form words and to an appreciation of phonic rules. A selection of teachers' remarks on these points is given below:

'Phonic work automatically starts earlier. Bright children seem to pick up the ability to do word-building on their own.'

'The good children acquire skill in word blending before it has ever been taught. With average and dull children it is worth teaching them to do this formally.'

'Positive word building is now possible because all the words follow the same rules. It could not be positive with t.o.'

'Children soon pick out the regularities between the words themselves and so the long business of plugging flashcards is greatly reduced.'

'i.t.a. cuts down the slog and grind of word-building, for example with such rules as 'lazy e'. Children soon romp away through the rules.'

The earlier reaction of children to the greater regularity of the sound-symbol relationship in i.t.a. was frequently stressed by teachers when they noted that i.t.a. is logical in the early stages. They expressed this point in the following words:

'There is security for the child in that i.t.a. is logical, thus the child never has to unlearn things.'

'Children can have a logical method of learning which does away with contradictions. The sign-posts are true.'

'From the teacher's point of view you are not betraying the children by telling them one sound one day and a different sound on another day for the same letter.'

'i.t.a.'s biggest advantage is the regularising of the irregular words. The anomalies are ironed out and consequently children get the feeling that they aren't going to be let down.'

It could perhaps be imagined that all these comments on early sounding, blending and learning of rules reflected situations in which i.t.a. had turned infant classes into formal teaching factories, reminiscent of schools fifty or so years ago. One reception class teacher with 50 children in her class who declared that she was a convert who loved i.t.a., went on to say, 'It is to be hoped that teachers won't go back to older formal methods but will have fun with the sounds'. Judging from what the investigator saw in i.t.a. schools, this teacher need have no fear on this score. In fact, it would be a grave error to assume that the use of i.t.a. had brought about an increase in formal phonic training. What it has done, as a result of its regularity, is to spark off an enormous increase in incidental phonic work, springing mainly from the children's own observations and interest. The alert and intuitive teacher has utilised these moments of insight and strong motivation on the children's part, to reinforce their learning by brief moments of incidental teaching.

Many teachers emphasised that, not only had i.t.a. eased the teacher's task but that, for children, the drudgery had been taken out of learning to read. Referring to dull children, one teacher remarked that one advantage of i.t.a. was that its regularity had made it worthwhile for the teacher to do some simple phonic work, such as games involving recognition and sounding of letters, even with those children who might not be really ready to start formal reading for another year. Such reading readiness training gave these children something to do which would form a basis for formal reading at a later stage, while at the same time satisfying them that they were making progress. The irregularities of t.o. formerly made such work impracticable with dull children.

The changes teachers reported in children's attitudes – for instance independence, fearlessness and confidence – had resulted in certain changes in teaching procedures. The majority of teachers commented that the greater regularity and simplicity of i.t.a. enabled children to help themselves far more than was possible with t.o. Children did not now find it necessary to ask the teacher to tell them every new word they met. They soon discovered that they could 'puzzle it out for themselves'. The resultant change in procedure represented a swing away from instruction towards individual, independent learning. A small minority of teachers, however, supported the view of one who sounded a note of caution, saying, 'i.t.a. doesn't teach itself. It must be taught, but one gets more out of it for the work one puts into it.'

In the course of visits to schools, one final point about changing teaching procedures was noted. Originally some teachers had been hesitant about using i.t.a. in case it should necessitate their having to alter methods and procedures with which they were familiar. The observer found that even the originally hesitant teachers were pleased by the changes in the patterns of learning resulting from the use of i.t.a. This was particularly true of those teachers who believed in a broadly-based approach to reading and who had originally suspected that the advent of i.t.a. would herald a return to formal phonic methods. Not one teacher deplored the changes in methods and procedures which had arisen when i.t.a. was used and nearly all expressed approval of these changes.

2 What children read

If teachers had been asked what infants now read, their replies would undoubtedly have been given in one word – 'everything'. One teacher, speaking of children who were still using i.t.a., said:

> 'Children can read anything almost right from the start. They don't need to have an artificially controlled vocabulary. The teacher can use any of the words in the children's own vocabulary when she writes news items and notices for them.'

There was general agreement that children learning to read by i.t.a. took a much greater interest in notices, titles on pictures and displays, news books hanging on the walls and lists of various sorts, and that they enjoyed trying to read them more than had children taught by t.o. One teacher pointed out that even the reception class children could read the notice on the aquarium which said, 'There are sticklebacks in our aquarium'.

Many remarks were made by teachers to the effect that, with i.t.a., children of all ages read far more books than they had done when t.o. was used. As one teacher said, 'Even children in the reception class read a fantastic number of books'. These books included basic reading books, small supplementary books, book corner books, large story books and library books from both the school library and the public library. Some public libraries had co-operated with local authorities in providing children's books in i.t.a. Even young infants were borrowing such books from the public libraries and reading them. One teacher, referring to some of the very large, lavishly-illustrated story books which were available in the classroom, drew attention to the fact that infants now *read* these books, whereas formerly most of them had merely looked at the illustrations.

Teachers also pointed out that the children's own interest in reading was not confined only to books but extended to any printed matter. As one teacher said, 'These children read everything they can get their hands on'. It was noticed that many children, even before they had officially made the transfer to t.o., were trying to puzzle out the t.o. words on Christmas cards, birthday cards, grocery packets and chocolate boxes.

As soon as children had made the transition to t.o. the range of what they read increased enormously, partly because there is so much more reading matter printed in t.o. Many teachers remarked on infants reading the headlines and sometimes articles from daily papers and from publications relating to pop-singers, cars, football or other interests. Many children, who would formerly have gleaned the stories in comics and annuals by following the pictures, were now reading the stories. There was a greater traffic of books between home and school. Children themselves were reading the books which relatives had given them as presents, instead of expecting their parents to read the books to them. One teacher told of how her own personal books, from which she read stories to the children, were continually missing because children were reading them; and how, if inspection copies of reading books from publishers were left on her table, children would soon be found to be reading them. A number of headteachers, relating how they now regularly borrowed large boxes of books from the public libraries in order to cater for these infant children who had become 'thirsty for books', pointed out that this was a practice which had formerly only been necessary for juniors.

Other teachers emphasised how the increase in reading ability was changing the needs of infant schools for books. For instance, more reference books and information books were required. One teacher of upper infants found that now many more poetry books were needed. Some infant teachers now felt the need for class sets of both hymn-books and song-books. These represented quite new requirements in their schools where the former practice had been for most children to memorise the words of hymns and songs. One school had prepared duplicated hymn-sheets in i.t.a. and the younger classes could read these.

Thus the general trend of teachers' remarks, in nearly all the schools visited, was that children who had learned to read by i.t.a. read many more books and more printed materials of all kinds than had similar children who had been taught by t.o. Naturally the slower children did not read as many or such difficult books as the brighter children; yet even dull children, who with t.o. would probably not have begun to read by the end of the infant school, had now read many simple books. The content of the books read by infants had also increased: longer story books, reference books and information books, which would formerly have been read mainly by juniors, were now enjoyed by large numbers of infants. The interviewer's observations in infant schools using both t.o. and i.t.a., supported the conclusions of the teachers on this point.

3 When children read

Although teachers were not asked the actual question, 'When do children read?' very many of their unsolicited comments could well have been replies to this question. Their broad summing up of this aspect of reading progress was that children read, 'nearly all the time' or 'as often as possible'. Of course, this represents an over-simplification, as the i.t.a. schools varied in the amount of time which children chose to spend in reading, just as do schools using t.o. In those schools in which the teachers' own love of books and reading were made evident by an abundance of attractive books spread out all over the school, easily accessible to the children, the children themselves were more inclined to value reading highly, and accordingly utilised every opportunity to spend time handling, consulting and reading books. In schools in which reading appeared to be considered as a skill to be taught, rather than an area of enjoyment into which children might be initiated, there was often a smaller range of books available to the children and not quite as much evidence of children's eagerness to spend so much time reading.

Nevertheless, even allowing for this range of differences in schools, most teachers indicated that children who had learned to read with i.t.a. chose to spend much more time reading than did children who had learned with t.o. A great number of infant teachers made remarks such as, 'The children just love reading. They will read all the time – whenever they get the chance.' They were referring to time spent at home, as well as at school. For instance, in what might be narrowly described as 'lesson time', in schools in which reading was taught quite formally, even reception class teachers remarked that children spend more time actually reading. One teacher described it this way:

'Children can get on and help themselves. Formerly, when a teacher had heard a child read, she sent him to his seat and hoped that he would then read on his own. Now the teacher knows that the child will go on reading because he can read.'

A number of other teachers of young infants remarked that formerly when they used t.o., on those occasions when they had been busy with registration, savings and dinner-money and had said to children, 'Take out your reading books', most of the children had just wasted time. Now, nearly all the children could actually go on reading on their own. Among the schools just mentioned was one in which the children were given a free choice of activities on Friday afternoons. The teacher had noticed that since using i.t.a., when children were allowed to choose what to do, most of them would rather read or write than do anything else.

Indeed, the same trend was noted by teachers in less formal schools, as well as in schools with unscheduled days, when they made the following remarks:

'The book corner is now a favourite occupation, an activity, which it used not to be.'

'Poorer children are using the library corner more.'

'The long uphill grind has been cut out. Reading is more an ordinary part of childhood instead of a chore and so the children take it in their stride. They pick up a book in their free time as they would a paint-brush or a jig-saw.'

'Now, when the teacher is talking to the headteacher, or to a visitor, children take out a book and really read – even children in the reception class. It was not like this with t.o.'

The majority of teachers also spoke about the amount of time, other than 'lesson-times', which children chose to spend on reading and writing. They mentioned children who arrived at school early in the morning or who spent break-times and lunch-times burying themselves in books.

A visitor could not fail to note how this absorbing interest of children in reading was constantly demonstrated at all times of the day. The children's behaviour in i.t.a. classes must, of course, be compared with the behaviour of children in similar t.o.

classes. The investigator, as a frequent visitor to all sorts of infant schools, had usually found that when she went into t.o. classrooms to talk to teachers, the children's ability to continue with what they were doing on their own was closely related to the formal-informal rating within the classroom. In the informal situations in which children were engaged in individual, purposeful occupations, a visitor talking to the teacher caused very little dislocation. Children in such schools were, in the main, able to carry on with whatever they were doing, whether this was reading or other activities. The more formal the classroom regime, the more quickly did the work become disrupted by a visitor. Yet, in t.o. schools having both these types of organisation, the time which children had been able to spend on reading and writing on their own, unless they were very good readers, had always been seriously limited by their need to consult the teacher about words they were unable to read or write.

The differences to be observed in the time the children spent on private reading in t.o. schools and i.t.a. schools were as follows. In t.o. schools, some of the more advanced children went on reading in the classrooms for a certain amount of time when a visitor was talking to the teacher. In a formal school, the reading soon came to a halt when the teacher was unable to help the children, who were then quite likely to turn to nuisance-making or destructive pursuits than to purposeful activities. In an informal t.o. school, when children who were reading ran into difficulties they were more inclined to turn to other activities than to become restless and noisy.

A contrast could be seen in both these types of classes when i.t.a. was used. In formal i.t.a. classes, most children who were reading basic reading books continued to do so, almost without help. When they had completed the task in hand, they generally selected books from the book corner and continued to read. In informal i.t.a. classrooms, a greater proportion of children seemed to be engaged in reading and writing than in similar t.o. classrooms. Furthermore, when children had finished what they were doing, whether it was number work or creative work, there was a greater tendency for them to turn to reading and writing as alternative activities.

Children reading for their own pleasure in book corners, corridors and entrance halls, at break-times and lunch-times as well as in lesson times, were more apparent in 'progressive' t.o. infant schools than in formal t.o. infant schools, where sometimes there was very little evidence of this. When one tried to assess i.t.a. schools on this criterion it was very clear to an observer that, generally speaking, in i.t.a. schools, almost regardless of their types of organisation, children wanted to read more than t.o. children, and spent a greater proportion of all the odd minutes in a day doing so.

Teachers in i.t.a. schools were also certain that infants spent much more time reading at home than did t.o. children. They said that intelligent children from good home backgrounds had always enjoyed doing a certain amount of reading at home, but that when t.o. was used this only applied to a small proportion of infants. Teachers' comments suggest that now the majority of infants, even duller children from homes in which little reading took place, wanted to read at home and did read to their parents and themselves. One teacher said, 'Children are so keen they want to take all their books home to read, even their basic reading books.'

Teachers' comments thus represented a general conclusion, which was confirmed by the investigator's observations in schools, that usually children who learned to read by i.t.a. both want to, and do, spend more time on reading than children taught by t.o. This conclusion refers to all ages and all intelligence levels of children, and covers lesson times, free times, break-times and time at home.

Consideration of what children read and when they read leads on to the question of how they read. Some teachers indicated that originally they had wondered if the use of i.t.a. would result in 'mere mechanical reading', but they had not found this to be the case. One experienced teacher, described by the headteacher as 'an excellent teacher of reading', phrased it thus:

> 'I have always loved reading, and at first I didn't want to do i.t.a. This was because I thought it might turn out to be an approach through which children would sound out every word – but it's not so.'

Other remarks concerning how children read included the following:

> 'Young children can read and understand even long words in "news" and "topics".'

> 'i.t.a. gives greater fluency and greater comprehension. The children really do understand what they are reading.'

> 'The brighter children turn to silent reading, as opposed to reading aloud, earlier than they would have done with t.o.'

> 'There is far more reading for pleasure.'

One basic question which teachers are always asking themselves is whether children are reading mechanically or whether they are reading with understanding. In considering this point, one thoughtful headmistress made the following distinction between two kinds of reading. Many children want to read and enjoy learning to read, partly because they obtain satisfaction in getting through a page and on to the next book. Furthermore, they know that to carry out this performance pleases adults, both parents and teachers, whom they are anxious to please. This is one level of reading. In the second kind of reading, it is the task itself which is more important. Here the child becomes so absorbed in the meaning he is obtaining from the printed word that he wants to go on reading for his own personal, intellectual satisfaction. Such reading is more or less dissociated from the obvious satisfaction of completing the page or book, or of pleasing adults. Having made this distinction, the headmistress went on to say that her current observations of both t.o. and i.t.a. children led her to suspect that the i.t.a. children have the advantage here – that more of them are engaged in this second kind of reading than the t.o. children. Somehow or other this cautious, yet penetrating, appraisal of how children read carried equally as much conviction as many of the more sweeping comments on children's reading comprehension made by teachers who were extremely enthusiastic about i.t.a.

The question of the kind of reading that children are doing can also be partially answered by referring to the comments on what children read and when they read. It is highly unlikely that young children would choose to read all sorts of books silently, on their own, for long periods of time, if they were not understanding and enjoying what they were reading. The child who is merely reading mechanically usually reads aloud, tends to want to read to an adult and has a much shorter attention span than the child who is truly reading with comprehension. A large number of the children whom the observer saw reading in odd corners, as well as in classrooms, in i.t.a. schools were patently 'lost' in the books in which their noses were buried. One example will serve to represent many. The interviewer was waiting in a spare class-room which had been converted into a library. At the time of mid-morning break, the door burst open and in rushed a small boy of five. He was so intent on his own purpose that he failed entirely to notice that an adult was in the room. He went straight to a book display unit, without a second's hesitation selected a huge illustrated book about Ali-Baba and the Forty Thieves, sat down at a small table, turned immediately to a page about half-way through the book, put his elbows on the table, supported his face on his hands and became utterly absorbed in the story which he had quite evidently begun on a previous occasion. One did not need to question him to be convinced of his comprehension of what he was reading, yet this the interviewer did, although it was a shame to drag his attention away from the story which had so gripped him. He talked politely and knowledgeably about the book but was clearly anxious to be left alone so that he could go on with it

The sort of incident just described could also have taken place in a t.o. school, but the interviewer's impressions support those of teachers that much more of this type of reading goes on, and at an earlier age, when i.t.a. rather than t.o. is the medium of instruction. Teachers themselves were very willing to point out that the dullest children did not understand as much of what they read as did average or bright children. Consequently greater care had to be taken in the selection of appropriate reading materials for slower children.

In this context, a number of teachers mentioned one particular danger which sprang from the use of i.t.a. and which could equally well constitute a problem for bright children as for slower children. Once children had learned to decipher unknown words for themselves, by blending sounds together, they soon found it possible to go on and on, supposedly reading i.t.a. books that were becoming progressively more difficult. If the teacher was not alert to this situation, it was possible for children to be deciphering the words in a story, the content of which was beyond his comprehension. The following quotations from teachers relate to this problem:

> 'The content of the later books in *Janet and John* in i.t.a. can still be too difficult for the bright child of five and six who reaches this stage and can read the words but doesn't really understand them; e.g. "great feasting and rejoicing followed".'

> 'The children go ahead with reading so rapidly that they may get beyond their stage of comprehension. More books are needed at their level. For instance, our six-year-olds were able to read a book about fishermen and trawlers but the subject matter was really beyond them.'

> 'There is always a danger, with t.o. as well as with i.t.a., that the child will go on without really understanding it. The danger is greater with i.t.a. because children go ahead faster; e.g. the children met the phrase "casualty department" in a book about hospitals and afterwards were convinced that the word "depart-ment" had to do with an accident. They were unable to generalise – department store, etc. Comprehension eventually comes from talk between teacher and child, and child and child. Yet, even with plenty of discussion, more books are required at each level.'

The teachers realised that if they allowed children to race ahead to more and more difficult books, as the children themselves were so often eager to do, this would be tantamount to teachers encouraging children to 'bark at print'. They concluded that the duller the child, the more important it was for the teacher to broaden his reading programme rather than permit him to advance rapidly. The provision of many very simple books at the same level, before proceeding to a slightly more difficult level of book, was a plan which appeared to encourage reading with understanding.

The conclusions arrived at by the majority of teachers with experience of both i.t.a. and t.o. were that most children who learned to read by i.t.a. did so with comprehension. They did not claim that all children read in this way but that more did so than formerly with t.o. There was no suggestion from any teacher who had used i.t.a. that it was instrumental in making children concentrate on the mere sounding of words, regardless of the meaning of the sentences, paragraphs and stories. On the other hand, a number of teachers stressed that it was necessary to be alert lest young children's rapidly increasing skill in reading should lead them to books beyond their comprehension.

The observer's own conclusions, resulting from listening to hundreds of children reading aloud, and talking to them about what they had read, lend support to the teachers' views. The majority of children were reading with understanding. Few of even the slowest children were merely sounding words which were devoid of meaning for them, as long as they were attempting to read books suited to their capabilities.

III The transition in reading

A. GENERAL IMPRESSIONS OF THE TRANSITION

One of the main causes of anxiety to teachers when they first begin to use i.t.a. has always been the question of the difficulties children might experience when they transfer from i.t.a. to t.o. Teachers who began to use i.t.a. in the first year or two were particularly anxious on this score. Within a short space of time, however, many published accounts appeared in which teachers described the ease with which children did make the transfer. Nevertheless, even after four or five years of such reports, teachers who had begun to use i.t.a. for the first time quite recently continued to express fears concerning the transfer.

Teachers who had actually seen children making the transition, however, regardless of how long they had been using i.t.a., were almost unanimous in their conclusions that the transfer from i.t.a. to t.o. did not pose a problem to the children concerned. In every school visited, teachers expressed the wonder and delight they had experienced when children first made the transition. One teacher of six-year-olds expressed it as follows:

> 'I was absolutely amazed at the transfer. When the first child began to read his first book in t.o., I was so amazed that I had to call in the rest of the staff to marvel at it. Children can read their first book in t.o. without stumbling, even over irregular words such as "bough".'

Most teachers with a number of years' experience of watching children make the transition in reading had come to two main conclusions: namely, that it was probable that, at first, children were allowed to make the transfer at too early a stage and that their conviction now was that children should be absolutely fluent in i.t.a. before they transfer to t.o.

Many of the teachers who were among the early users of i.t.a. volunteered the information that, on looking back to the first year or two, they were now inclined to think that they had probably allowed children to make too early a transition to t.o. These teachers had since asked themselves how this had come about. They had concluded that a teacher's own anxiety concerning the transfer may have caused her to allow children to transfer too soon, in a subconscious effort to reassure herself. One head-teacher pointed out that in the early days the teacher needed to have much more confidence than the children regarding transition, because she could see many of the pitfalls of which the children were unaware.

Teachers themselves saw another related reason why some of them may have originally encouraged a somewhat premature transition. They felt that certain teachers had made the transition to t.o. a goal towards which they could aim. To have a short-term aim of this nature was quite often a help to an infant teacher who is frequently unable to assess what she is achieving owing to the fact that so much of the work she is doing will have long-term results which she will not see. In other words, it requires faith on the part of an infant teacher to continue with many activities in which tangible results may not become obvious until the children are in an older class or a different school. The stage at which a child exchanges an i.t.a. reading book for one printed in t.o. is a demonstrable achievement for the teacher, as well as for the child. One headteacher described this as a particular danger for less confident teachers. She said:

> 'One danger is that the teacher may measure her own success by the number of children who have transferred, and hence there may be a tendency for the teacher to let the children transfer too early.'

Both headteachers and class teachers were aware that this particular danger regarding transition was not necessarily confined to the early users of i.t.a., but could become operative at any time.

Nevertheless, teachers who had seen the transition from i.t.a. to t.o. over a number of years felt that the situation had changed in three ways: firstly, teachers themselves were now more relaxed in their attitude to the transition; secondly, and as a consequence of the first fact, the transition was generally taking place later; and thirdly, teachers were now convinced that children should be really fluent readers in i.t.a. before transferring to t.o. One example of later transition was given by the head-master of a primary school in a good residential area, which had always had good reading standards with t.o. After five years of using i.t.a., the position in his school was as follows. The brightest two or three children transferred after about ten to twelve months; average children usually transferred after about one and a half years. Ten per cent of the children had not made the transfer before they go into the first junior class. Another headteacher expressed the view of many when she said, 'Dull children should not be expected to transfer in less than two years and it may well take three years'. In fact, in certain schools in poorer areas, with less able children, it was suggested that 25% or 30% of children would not have transferred to t.o. before entering junior schools, although most of these children would be reading fairly fluently in i.t.a.

One difficult problem regarding the timing of the transition is still being faced by some infant schools before children are promoted to separate junior schools. This problem arises if there is little co-operation between infant and junior schools, if it is known that the headteacher of a junior school is unsympathetic towards i.t.a. or if it is suspected that the teacher in charge of the first junior class may be unable or unwilling to continue to use i.t.a. with a group of children who have not transferred. Two comments on this point made by infant headteachers are given:

'It is a bad thing if the infant school knows, or suspects, that a junior school will not carry on with i.t.a. with those children who are not yet ready to transfer, for then infant teachers may be inclined to hurry the transfer.'

'My biggest problem is the small group of children who are still reading in i.t.a. when they go into the junior school. There they will be in classes of 47 with teachers who are younger and less experienced than our teachers. This small group of children are learning to read–we can see their progress–but they need individual help. The teachers and I keep asking ourselves what will happen to these children when they leave us.'

Infant teachers are always concerned lest slower children, whom they feel have just begun to grasp the idea of reading, or those who are getting on nicely with i.t.a., should be placed in classes in which the circumstances are not likely to help them. They fear that some teachers of junior classes might not really understand these children's difficulties and that the children may be changed over abruptly to t.o. by a teacher inexperienced in the use of i.t.a. When infant teachers suspect that the reading progress of children still using i.t.a. might be jeopardised when they enter a junior school, some of them are taking the decision to hasten the transfer. The infant teachers' reasons for doing so spring solely from their concern for the children. Such teachers indicated that they did not consider it to be an ideal practice. Nonetheless, in certain circumstances, they thought it preferable for these slower children to be guided through the transition, albeit a little early, by teachers who knew them intimately and who were knowledgeable and experienced about the stage of transfer.

One further problem regarding the transition often mentioned by teachers was the question of i.t.a. children moving to t.o. schools and t.o. children coming into i.t.a. schools. In each case, it was pointed out, the child's feeling of strangeness and isolation was emphasised by the fact that he was reading and writing with a different alphabet from all the other members of the class. Many teachers spoke of wondering how certain i.t.a. children, who had not been ready to transfer when they moved to another district, got on in their new t.o. schools. The problem of the t.o. child entering an i.t.a. class was not so acute if he was a poor reader, for then the teacher usually started him at the beginning on i.t.a. It was less likely that a newcomer, reading t.o. fluently, would arrive in a class where all the children were reading i.t.a.

With regard to the question of fluency, almost every teacher who was interviewed insisted that a child should be absolutely fluent in reading i.t.a. before he changed to t.o. As one teacher said, 'Children should be able to "gabble it off" before they transfer'. Joined with the idea of fluency was a belief that children should be reading i.t.a. with enjoyment and understanding before they changed to t.o. There was general agreement that the child who was stumbling and hesitating over i.t.a. should not be offered t.o.

One headmistress who stressed that children should be fluent in i.t.a. before transferring pointed out that it is difficult to hold many children back long enough. She did not think that the child himself necessarily had an urge to make the transfer; it was rather that he had such an urge to read that he picked up everything in sight and did not always realise the difference. She gave a delightful example of two five-year-olds, who were still reading i.t.a. books in school, walking along the corridor together. One was looking at one of the popular daily newspapers as she walked along and was making comments to her friend about what she was reading; for instance, 'Fancy—Shirley Bassey going into films!'

Comments from many other schools reinforced the opinion that most children do not notice the difference between the two alphabets. It was suggested that children are much more adaptable than we think and are not necessarily troubled by two 'a's or two 'g's, by capital letters being different from small letters or by meeting t.o. outside school and i.t.a. in school. Other teachers pointed out that, when they had first used i.t.a., they had assumed that, while children were learning to read by i.t.a., all their books should be in i.t.a. Now they leave both t.o. and i.t.a. books spread out all over the school. Even the youngest children pick them up, look at them and try to read them, regardless of the alphabet. In fact, in vertically grouped classes, books printed in both alphabets must necessarily be available.'

In contrast to the headteacher who thought that children did not necessarily have an urge to make the transfer, certain teachers believed the transition itself to be a goal for some children. The following are examples of two such comments:

'Children who are beginning to read well in i.t.a. look forward to changing over to t.o. It is something for them to aim at.'

'The transition itself may be a goal for the child—which is a good thing. He feels grown up when he can read t.o. It is a definite stage for him to aim at. Children who have just transferred are so pleased that they stop me in the corridor to tell me about it.'

In one school, the teachers believed that such an aim might have been fostered in children by parents asking their children if they had yet made the transfer. Whether teachers considered it beneficial for children to have such a goal, or not, seemed to the investigator to depend on the attitude of the whole school, and the particular teacher, to reading. A school with an emphasis on early reading might not mind children having this aim, especially if the transition was the teacher's own goal. A school with a more relaxed attitude towards reading and transition seemed less likely to foster, or accept without misgivings, such an aim in children.

With regard to the actual transition from a basic reading book in i.t.a. to a basic reading book in t.o., teachers in different schools had developed various procedures relating to when and how this should be done. In the early days, when *Janet and John* was the only basic reading scheme available, a child was often considered ready for transfer to t.o. when he had read *Janet and John* Book IV in i.t.a. At that stage, many teachers gave the child the same book in t.o. In certain cases, the child was allowed to retain the i.t.a. version of the book so that if he was not sure of a t.o. word he could refer to the i.t.a. text. Later, teachers grew to consider fluency in reading to be more important than the actual reading book a child had completed. As more basic reading schemes and supplementary books in i.t.a. became available, teachers tended to give children what one of them described as more i.t.a. experience in breadth rather than height. Thus children were encouraged to read books from two or three reading schemes, in addition to the book corner books. In this way fluency at each level was maximised and it was not considered so important that a child should have reached a certain book in a particular reading scheme before transferring to t.o. books.

Indeed, in one school, teachers had begun to suspect that children could go too far in a particular reading scheme. One teacher told of children who had been very fluent readers in i.t.a. in *Janet and John* Book IV but when they reached *Once Upon A Time* the content of the stories and some of the phrasing was too difficult for them and consequently they were struggling and stumbling. When such a child was later given a t.o. book, he continued to hesitate and stumble because he had lost the habit of skimming lines of print with rapidity. Perceiving this, these teachers were now experimenting with transferring children to t.o. at a lower level, while they were fluent in i.t.a. and before they reached i.t.a. books which they might find too difficult.

As well as watching for fluency in i.t.a. children, some teachers had developed rule-of-thumb assessments of when children were ready for t.o. In many cases children were tried out on a t.o. book from another scheme with which the teacher was familiar. Books mentioned as such criteria were 'The Orange Book' in the *Gay Way Reading Scheme*, the first four books in *Key Words Reading Scheme* and various books in the *Beacon Reading Scheme*. Ability to read these particular t.o. books with ease was taken to indicate that the child was ready for transfer. A few teachers used the scores on a graded word reading test in t.o. as assessments of readiness for transfer; different numbers of correct words being considered appropriate by different teachers.

E. TEACHERS' DIFFICULTIES

One point regarding the transition in reading on which there was almost complete agreement was that to be in charge of a class in which the transition was taking place was hard work for the teacher concerned. Writing every word twice, in two separate alphabets, on blackboards, notices and pictures was extremely time-consuming and rather a strain on the teacher, as was the fact that she had always, as it were, to 'think' in two alphabets. A few teachers, who basically approved of i.t.a., nevertheless wondered if time spent in this way might have been better employed in helping slower children to read. Of course, teachers who were working in 'vertically-grouped' classes faced this problem of writing and 'thinking' in two alphabets all the time. Teachers of vertically-grouped classes mentioned the difficulties of the teacher, regarding the transition, less than did teachers of more homogeneous classes. Perhaps teachers of vertically-grouped classes took it in their stride, as they were accustomed to dealing with differences in every subject at every level. One teacher in such a school suggested that it would be of great help if children ready for transfer, in writing as well as reading, could be in a separate class.

F. ONE PUZZLING ASPECT

Teachers' comments on the transition in reading from i.t.a. to t.o. presented one rather puzzling aspect. Practically every teacher who had dealt with the transition said that it did not present a problem to the children. This fact was repeated over and over again, illustrated by telling examples of individual children. The interviewer's own observations of many children at this same stage, including children making their very first attempts to read t.o. books, endorsed teachers' comments on this point. Despite these reiterations, however, it was clear that a great deal of discussion still goes on between teachers about the transfer. 'We still need to know much more about the transfer,' was a common remark.

The investigator gained the impression that there still remained a certain uneasiness among teachers regarding the transfer, and that it was probably related to the average and below average children rather than the brighter ones. It must be stated that teachers did not explicitly express this, although they did indicate that slower children should not be expected to transfer at an early stage. However, as there was general agreement that the first group of children to transfer in every class appeared to do so spontaneously and effortlessly, the observer could visualise only two possible reasons for the uneasiness which many teachers still clearly felt on this score. It could have been that teachers had noted that those children who made the earliest transfer experienced belated difficulties in their reading. Alternatively, teachers of older infants might have noticed those children who transferred at a later stage to be having difficulties. Yet, in none of the schools visited did a teacher mention having encountered either of these problems, although one infant headmistress had clearly considered one of these possibilities. She said:

'Although I think that even the very dull child will learn to read eventually with i.t.a. because of its regularity, I have my doubts about how he will make the transfer. I wonder what will happen to him if he is still reading i.t.a. in the middle of the Junior School, when everyone else is doing t.o., and when all the subject books, for example Geography, are in t.o.'

IV   Summing up on reading

Among infant teachers who had used i.t.a. there was almost total agreement concerning its favourable effect on children's reading progress, with a slight tendency for teachers of older infants to be a little less enthusiastic than teachers of younger infants. The comments most frequently made by teachers were that i.t.a. enables children to make a good beginning with reading; the task is simpler and consequently children can begin earlier, learn more quickly and achieve greater pleasure and satisfaction in so doing. Teachers expressed approval of the independence, confidence and lack of frustration exhibited by children who had used i.t.a. They noted that children were soon able and eager to attempt to read a wide variety of books and other materials outside basic reading schemes, that they read many more books than formerly and more frequently chose to read in preference to other activities.

The use of i.t.a. was often found to bring about a change in methods and procedure in the process of learning to read. An interest in earlier 'sounding' and 'blending', followed by insight into phonic rules, appeared to arise spontaneously in the children. This growing perception of phonic regularities by children did not represent a swing towards earlier formal methods of phonic teaching which certain teachers had feared might result from the use of i.t.a. Indeed, children's early ability to make independent progress in reading had led rather towards an increase in informal classroom procedures. Another of the original fears of teachers, namely that the use of i.t.a. would lead to an increase in 'mechanical reading', was found to be baseless. The general opinion was that more children read with comprehension than when t.o. was used, although teachers had to be alert lest the rapidly expanding powers of young children in reading should lead them to books in which the concepts were too advanced for them to grasp.

The general pattern of noting a great improvement in children's reading progress was tempered by the opinion of a few teachers, mostly from schools which believed in a delayed start to reading or schools which had always had very good reading standards, who stated that they could see little difference in the reading progress of children when they used i.t.a. No teacher thought that children made less progress with i.t.a. than they would have done with t.o.

Even among the vast majority of teachers who were enthusiastic about the advantages of i.t.a. for beginning reading, there was yet a realisation that the use of a simplified alphabet is not the sole factor within the total situation affecting children's reading progress. Consequently, although the use of i.t.a. considerably eased the initial task, its use did not predetermine that all children would learn to read immediately and automatically. Thus, although fewer non-readers and slow readers were leaving infant classes, there yet remained a small proportion of children who had barely begun to read when they were promoted to junior classes.

The original anxieties of teachers regarding the difficulties children might experience at the time of transfer from i.t.a. to t.o. in reading had proved, in practice, to be groundless. From a functional point of view, teachers noted no recession in children's reading ability when they transferred. The normal practice of providing children with t.o. books at the same, or a slightly lower, level of difficulty as the i.t.a. books they had recently used, only being necessary for a very short period before they continued to advance further. Current practice was to delay the transfer until children were extremely fluent in reading i.t.a. Teachers' main worries about the transition concerned children who were still reading in i.t.a. when they had to move to, or were transferred to, other schools which would not be able or willing to support them in the use of this alphabet. From a teacher's personal viewpoint, to be in charge of an infant class in which both i.t.a. and t.o. were in use, represented a great deal of additional work for her.

CHAPTER 7

Infant Teachers' Comments on Writing and Spelling

I   Free writing

A. GENERAL IMPRESSIONS OF FREE WRITING

ALTHOUGH accounts of earlier experiments to teach children to read with simplified alphabets had noted accompanying improvements in children's written work, many teachers who had begun to use i.t.a. in 1961 and 1962 spoke of their initial amazement at its effect on the free writing of young children. It had represented to these teachers an unexpected and delightful bonus. Teachers who had started to use i.t.a. more recently were not so surprised when they found improvements, because they had heard and read a good deal about this. In listing the advantages of i.t.a., the majority of infant teachers gave priority of place to the earlier and easier reading or writing. If anything, children's free writing was rated as the main advantage more often than reading. Many teachers made this sort of remark:

> 'Of course it does help the reading, but its main advantage is the free writing. It helps expression. Thoughts come into children's minds and they can express them so easily in writing, without becoming bogged down.'

Some teachers, who had obviously always been good teachers of reading, were converted to i.t.a. almost solely on account of the writing. One said:

> 'I was against i.t.a. for the first two years because I felt that I could teach reading with t.o. Now I am all for i.t.a. The reading is better with i.t.a. but it's for the written work that I approve of it even more than for the reading.'

It was a rare occurrence, among all the i.t.a. schools visited, if headteachers and classteachers failed to comment favourably on improvements in children's free writing. The few teachers who remarked that they had perceived no difference or who did not mention free writing appeared to the observer to fall into three distinct categories. The first group of teachers worked in schools in which children's writing had clearly been exceptionally good when they used t.o., probably because the beliefs of the staff and the whole atmosphere of the schools were such as to encourage children's free writing. However, even in these schools, teachers tended to say that the children probably used a wider vocabulary now. Secondly, there were a few teachers who worked in quite formal schools where it was obvious that, irrespective of whether t.o. or i.t.a. was used, children were neither encouraged to write freely nor given much opportunity to do so. In such schools there was no evidence of children being allowed access to a supply of paper on which to do individual writing. Thirdly, one or two teachers, who were worried about children doing too much writing in a script they would later have to discard, had deliberately refrained from actively encouraging children to write, while not denying them the opportunity to do so. In only one of the classes visited did a teacher with similar doubts indicate that the children in her class had done no writing whatsoever in i.t.a. This teacher was concentrating on teaching reading and then, when children had made the transition in reading, formal written work in t.o. was introduced.

There was a further small group of teachers who expressed disappointment that the children in their classes were not producing the quantity or quality of written work which they had been led to expect. The interviewer's impression was that usually the teachers who were disappointed in this respect had assumed that the good examples of children's written work which they had observed, heard of or read about in other i.t.a. schools, could be attributed solely to i.t.a., whereas in fact, a proportion of such success was directly attributable to the whole atmosphere and aims of the schools concerned. Teachers quite often find themselves at a disadvantage, when they try to compare standards between different schools, in that they so seldom have opportunities of visiting other schools. Accordingly they do not always realise how much schools do differ, even within the same socio-economic areas, in the standards attained in various aspects of the curriculum.

B. DETAILS OF FREE WRITING

The common features which most teachers noted in children's free writing when i.t.a. was used were as follows: it begins at a much earlier age; it is greater in quantity; and the quality has improved in content, in the flow of ideas and in the breadth of vocabulary used. Teachers attributed these improvements mainly to the regularity of the spelling of words. They often commented that even young children soon found that they could make good attempts at writing any word they wished. This made children fearless, self-confident and independent in their writing, as already noted in their reading. Remarks such as the following were constantly being made:

'Everybody has been astounded at the enjoyment children find in free writing. Right from the start the child can say exactly what he has been thinking.'

'Children write down everything just as it comes into their heads.'

'There is no barrier to stop the child using the words he wants.'

'i.t.a. really improves the fluency of children's writing. I am absolutely certain of this.'

Many examples were given of the differences that i.t.a. had made to specific age-groups of children. For instance, the following remarks were made by reception class teachers:

'Formerly, with young infants, the teacher was often writing words and sentences on the blackboard for them to copy. There is very little of that now. Children write freely.'

'The children are now producing little stories which they have made up and written themselves. I've never had this before, in reception class, from these children coming from a poor area, whose parents are not concerned about reading and writing.'

'Children start writing on their own, very early, not just copying words at first, as formerly.'

'Once children know the sounds they can make any word.'

Teachers of six-year-olds made similar remarks, most of them pointing out that the children not only write at great length but that the quality is better. For example, one teacher said, 'The writing is much better; it has a conversational flow instead of being stereotyped sentences'.

The following two quotations, expressing a more cautious view, came from schools in which the teachers were very conscious of the poor home backgrounds and low intelligence of the children. The first refers to five-year-olds and the second to six-year-olds:

> 'Children from better homes still do better writing and more writing than children from poor homes and/or dull children. These poorer children are still short of ideas but ideas and experience can be given to them. Yet even slow children do write more with i.t.a.–say a couple of sentences–where formerly they wouldn't have written at all.'

> 'The change is not miraculous but in their second infant year children are doing some writing–which wasn't usual in this area with t.o.' (This was a school in a very poor, slum-clearance area.)

The fact that the regularity of the sound-symbol relationship in i.t.a. permitted children to use a much more varied vocabulary than with t.o. was remarked on by teachers in most schools. The following two comments are representative:

> 'In the reception class, at the level of the earliest reading and writing, when I am writing on the blackboard, the words or sentences the children ask me to write, say in "News", I find this difference. With t.o. I did not always write down the words the children really wanted, for example "Germolene", I automatically simplified some of what they said by substituting easier words which I thought they could read. Now the sentences can consist of the exact words that the child says and wants. Hence, i.t.a. helps children to use their normal, out-of-school vocabulary in writing, instead of the former stilted written vocabulary which was a result of the children and the teacher writing only those words which the child could read.'

> 'Children have a more varied written vocabulary–for example, six-year-olds using "causing", "ordinary" and "injection"–and they make good attempts at spelling them. With t.o. children's written vocabulary was more stilted and usually limited to those words they thought they could spell.'

Many teachers expressed their pleasure that infants had now found an additional means of self-expression in the creative writing which appeared to arise so naturally when i.t.a. was used. They pointed out that, although formerly many children had expressed themselves in paint, clay, dance or the spoken word, some had not found these modes of expression easy. With i.t.a. nearly all children discovered the ability to express themselves in written words. The results were not only descriptive of their doings and thoughts but also showed an increase in imagination and inventiveness which resulted in original stories and poems. One infant headmistress spoke in the following terms:

> 'Early writing gives the child another mode of expression. It helps him to express

his own feelings. It helps him to think. The child is able to put his own stamp on his own experience.'

A headmaster who had noted an additional advantage in children's ability to express themselves in writing said:

> 'There is a therapeutic effect in the creative writing which wasn't apparent with t.o. There is no barrier now to prevent that which is in the forefront of the child's mind getting on to the paper. Some children play out their conflicts in their diaries.'

This headmaster perceived a new problem here regarding children from broken homes. They may want to put their thoughts on paper as a form of emotional release, yet, having done so, they may not wish to show what they have written to others. He felt that it was important that a child who did not want to allow his teacher to see what he had written should not be pressed to do so.

The close connection between reading and writing was emphasised by many teachers who said, 'The children themselves can now read what they have written,' and 'The teacher can read what the children have written'. These teachers recalled that, when t.o. had been used, many of the children's early attempts at free writing had been undecipherable by the teacher. When the teacher had resorted to asking the child to read back to her what he had written, the child had been unable to do so. Such episodes had been embarrassing for both child and teacher and were unlikely to have encouraged the child to make further efforts to express himself in writing. That this situation had now changed was a source of great satisfaction to the teachers. One teacher exclaimed, 'The joy on a child's face when he first sees the adult read what he has written!'

C. SUMMING UP

Teachers in the majority of infant schools which had used i.t.a. reported enthusiastically on the improvement in children's free writing. The interviewer was shown vast quantities of this written work, most of which was good and some of which was excellent. It included vivid descriptions, deeply-felt experiences, aesthetic appreciation, humour and creativity. Probably the most telling pieces of written work were a few simple sentences, describing everyday events, which had been produced with comparative ease by slower children who would have been quite unable to engage in written expression in t.o. The standard of written work varied considerably from school to school, a fact which was not necessarily related to the socio-economic levels nor the intelligence of the children in the schools; some of the most commendable work was produced in those schools in very poor areas which were working on progressive lines. Schools in which teachers saw less improvement in written work were usually those in which the climate, organisation and procedure of school did not lend themselves to freedom of expression in any form.

In short, teachers' comments, reinforced by the investigator's observations, led to the conclusion that the introduction of i.t.a. as a medium of introducing reading and writing to young children has usually resulted in a flowering of children's free writing, which has arisen spontaneously and happily at an earlier age than formerly. This writing has become more prolific and of higher quality than before, with a tendency to be truly expressive for most children and truly creative for some.

II Spelling

The increase in the quantity and quality of children's early written work was attributed by infant teachers largely to the regularity of spelling in i.t.a. They reiterated that once the child had realised the relationship between sounds and written symbols he felt confident about translating any word from the spoken to the written form. Teachers were all agreed that children's early attempts at spelling were much more often correct in i.t.a. than when t.o. was used and that, moreover, errors were nearer to the correct spelling. As one infant headmistress pointed out:

> 'In the days of t.o. I used to collect many examples of children's spelling errors and, when I considered using i.t.a., I thought that it couldn't produce anything worse. Children always did write "sed" and "muther" or "muvver". Teachers have forgotten this. Children's i.t.a. spelling is a great improvement on t.o.'

Two further comments regarding spelling are also fairly typical:

> 'Spelling is much improved. It will always be a difficulty and must be taught separately from reading. Spelling is a problem on its own.'

> 'We haven't worried about spelling. We never did want copy work. Content comes first.'

Teachers' unanimous conclusion regarding children's spelling ability in i.t.a. was that it came more easily and was of a higher standard.

However, it was a more practical aspect of classroom procedure, regarding spelling, which brought the greatest number of comments from infant teachers. One comment can well represent a multitude here:

> 'Children can get on with writing without coming out to ask the teacher how to spell words. i.t.a. has brought about the end of long queues.'

Anyone who has taught infants or been a frequent visitor to primary schools can appreciate the heart-felt fervour of such remarks. With t.o. there were so many irregularly-spelled words that children often needed to consult their teachers. This was true even when the teacher had tried to train children to be independent and when picture dictionaries, wall charts and reference charts were available. In fact, because it was not always possible for a child to know which words were regular and which irregular, many children had so little confidence in their own ability to spell that they often came to the teacher to confirm the spelling of simple words which they were capable of spelling. Consequently, with t.o., whenever written work was going on in infant classes, long queues of children almost invariably stood by the teacher's desk or followed her around the room to ask her how to spell a word or to check their own attempts to spell it. These permanent queues of children used to prevent the teacher from giving more constructive help, in different ways, to other children. The advent of i.t.a. had brought about a welcome change. As one teacher remarked:

> 'Because so many children can carry on writing on their own, without the teacher's help, the teacher can have more time to help slower children.'

When the use of i.t.a. was first mooted, and indeed when it was first used, the problem of children changing over from spelling with one alphabet to spelling with another less-regular alphabet was probably the one which caused teachers and parents the greatest disquiet. Many teachers related how this anxiety had originally loomed larger in their minds than the problem of the transition in reading. Discussions with teachers whose experience with i.t.a. extended for three years and more revealed that many of them now had much less anxiety on this score. Teachers in schools which had begun to use i.t.a. more recently, however, were still expressing their fears on this point.

Teachers of upper infants tended to express the most concern about children's transfer to t.o. spelling, particularly if this transfer was going to occur in junior classes. In all schools it was accepted that the transfer in spelling would come later than the transfer in reading. Infant teachers saw most children make the transfer in reading before they moved into junior schools or classes. In contrast, with spelling, a greater proportion of children left their guidance still using, in their written work, either i.t.a. or a mixture of i.t.a. and t.o. Infant teachers would have felt happier if children could have remained under their tuition until the transition in both reading and writing had been accomplished.

The opposite view was expressed by some infant teachers who were confident that children taught by i.t.a. would not experience difficulty about the transition in spelling. The following are examples of their comments:

'You don't really have to teach t.o. spelling after the transfer because children who have used i.t.a. are in a state to appreciate the rules. Good spelling seems to result after the transition. Hybrid spelling exists at first; then the most common words begin to be spelt correctly and so on.'

'At the transition stage, or just after, children will be able to cope with our t.o. spelling rules, with all their exceptions, because they have been conditioned to look carefully at words.'

'The seven-year-olds seem to have much more interest in words and their different spellings and rules than formerly. They are interested to discover that one sound in i.t.a. now has many spellings in t.o. At the transition stage children look at both blackboards and notice the different spellings.'

This optimism about spelling transfer is closely related to the opinions expressed earlier regarding children becoming more 'sound-conscious' when learning to read by i.t.a., and making good attempts to spell, in i.t.a., any word which is familiar to them in its spoken form. Most teachers appreciated that the use of i.t.a. had drawn children's attention to the facts that symbols represent sounds, that spoken sounds can be expressed in written symbols and that in each case the order of sequence of sounds and symbols is important. They considered that such an appreciation would have been unlikely to arise in the early stages of reading and writing when t.o. was used.

Many teachers believed that, at a certain stage, definite teaching of t.o. spelling rules was helpful or even necessary. The following descriptions are examples of ways in which this help was given:

'With regard to the transition in spelling, we teach it. We begin by getting children to change those things which always change the same way, for example "ch" and "sh". We give some instruction in t.o. spelling rules and let children have practice by playing spelling games, rather than just leave children to pick up the new spelling.'

'Children need help with the transfer in spelling. We do this formally. We teach the children in small groups as they are ready. We begin by separating the vowel combinations–" " etc. Consequently, most of the children who began i.t.a. in September 1963 now (April 1966) show no trace of i.t.a. spelling–it has been eliminated.' (N.B. This was a school in a culturally deprived area which was run on 'informal' lines.)

On the other hand, certain teachers stated that they thought it best to leave i.t.a. spelling alone, as children would gradually change over to t.o. spelling of their own accord. A minority of teachers hesitated about correcting i.t.a. spellings and teaching the t.o. forms of the words, in case children's free writing should thereby be inhibited.

Both the teachers who taught t.o. spelling rules and those who refrained from doing so were in agreement on one point. They nearly all concluded that, even when children had almost completed the transfer to t.o. spelling, if they continued to spell certain words in their correct i.t.a. versions, these should be accepted by the teacher for quite a long time.

There was not total agreement among infant teachers about the timing of the changeover from i.t.a. to t.o. spelling. The majority opinion was that children's i.t.a. spelling should not be interfered with until it was really fluent, even if this was some considerable time after the transfer in reading had occurred. A few teachers, however, did perceive dangers in allowing children to spell in i.t.a. for too long, without encouraging the transfer to t.o. spelling. For instance, a group discussion with five teachers in one primary school resulted in the following conclusion:

'There is a danger in leaving children writing in i.t.a. for too long, instead of helping them towards t.o. spelling. Because the good children who can soon read and write fluently in i.t.a. are quiet in the class and no trouble to the teacher, it is very easy for her to leave them alone instead of pushing them on to t.o. spelling.'

This represented a minority viewpoint which was expressed by teachers of older infants and lower juniors in a rather formal school which laid emphasis on neatness, punctuation and spelling.

C. SUMMING UP

To sum up teachers' views and the interviewer's observations regarding spelling in infant schools is rather difficult, as most infant schools had some children who had not made the transfer in spelling, in addition to many children who had partially done so. Regarding spelling in i.t.a., there is no doubt whatsoever that children found this much simpler than spelling in t.o. and that the favourable effect of this on children's written work was enormous.

As far as the transfer to t.o. spelling was concerned, there was a growing belief, which was finding its way into practice, that specific, carefully-graded and quite formal teaching of t.o. spelling rules was found helpful, and indeed interesting, by the children. The interviewer's impressions were that, the longer the teachers' experience with i.t.a., the more likely they were to consider such spelling teaching to be necessary and the stronger were their beliefs that children's experiences with i.t.a. had conditioned them towards an appreciation of t.o. spelling rules.

The long-term effects of i.t.a. on children's spelling of t.o. is a question for junior rather than infant schools, and junior teachers' impressions will be given in the appropriate section of this report. It is perhaps sufficient to indicate at this point that not one infant teacher with experience of children transferring to t.o. spelling expressed the view that i.t.a. had had a deleterious effect on children's spelling in t.o. Hence, the verbal evidence given by infant teachers, as well as observations in schools, led to the conclusion that teachers' original fears that the use of i.t.a. would be likely to have a harmful effect on children's spelling have not been justified. No evidence of a decline in spelling ability was noted in infant classes and there were certain indications of improvements.

III   Handwriting

On the whole, infant teachers made very few comments about the effect of i.t.a. on children's handwriting. A small number of teachers had noticed that some children experienced difficulty in writing certain of the characters. In contrast, a few teachers thought that children enjoyed writing the characters and gained pleasure from the rhythmical movements required to form certain characters. One teacher remarked:

> 'The script itself is more attractive to children than t.o., especially the vowels. They like the shapes, and this helps them to enjoy learning to write them.'

One or two teachers expressed the view that, because children now wrote so much, there was a tendency for their handwriting to become rather slipshod. These teachers realised that the poorer handwriting was a result of children's ideas flowing freely and their eagerness to relate their experiences in writing; accordingly the teachers placed little importance on any observed deterioration in handwriting. The majority of teachers were so pleased by the quality and quantity of children's free writing in i.t.a. that they gave little consideration to the quality of handwriting.

CHAPTER 8

Infant Teachers' Comments on other Aspects of i.t.a.

I Effect on other subjects

THE effect of the introduction of i.t.a. on subjects other than the language arts or on the life of the school in general was not investigated by means of direct questions to teachers, although a certain amount of information was volunteered by them. Many teachers spoke of how the confidence and independence which children soon acquired in reading and writing spread into other subjects and other aspects of the school day. Typical comments on this score were as follows:

> 'Because children are confident about attempting to read anything, in some ways this makes them quite fearless about other things.'

> 'i.t.a. gives children an impetus for everything.'

A. SPECIFIC SUBJECTS

Teachers spoke of the children who had used i.t.a. showing more confidence in their approaches to such widely different activities as science, creative activities and the use of gymnastic apparatus. One headmaster, who spoke as follows, counted this effect of i.t.a. on other subjects as one of its main advantages:

> 'Interesting and more advanced books can be used by children, for example science books. Because children can read instructions in books and on cards, simple science experiments are going on in infant classes.'

Apart from reading and writing, the two subjects mentioned most frequently by teachers as having gained the greatest benefit from the introduction of i.t.a. were spoken English and mathematics.

I *Children's spoken language*

Many teachers picked out various aspects of children's spoken language in which they considered i.t.a. to have effected improvements. The following comments cover most of the points made in this context:

> 'i.t.a. has helped children's pronunciation.'

> 'The child with a speech defect can be picked out much earlier because his speech defect becomes apparent as soon as he begins to express himself in writing–"brudder" for "brother", etc. The talkative child could always have his slovenly or defective speech noticed and corrected–but with the quiet child in a large class this was not so. Now the early writing soon highlights it.'

(A headteacher in a school in a very poor area)

'One of the main advantages of i.t.a. is the effect it has had on spoken English. The spoken English of t.o. children in this area is not in the same class as that of i.t.a. children. The t.o. children had no ideas and one got very little response from them. But with i.t.a. children it's quite different–all their reading helps their ideas. Children talk more to the teacher and are more responsive altogether.'

'Children's spoken vocabulary has increased enormously because they read so much. They use difficult words correctly without thinking about it. For example, I went up to a seven-year-old who was using Stern's apparatus and asked him why he was doing so-and-so. Without pausing the child replied, "Well, it's really very *ingenious*, you see . . ." I am continually being amazed by this enrichment of children's spoken vocabulary.'

2 *Mathematics*

A very large number of teachers talked of how the development of children's earlier reading skills with i.t.a. had helped mathematics. One infant teacher said:

'One advantage of i.t.a. is that the earlier reading and writing spread into other lessons. For instance, our six-year-olds have all been measuring each other. They then go and write freely about what they've done.'

Other teachers noted with pleasure how even young infants could now read problems in mathematics, as well as make up their own problems and write stories about 'number'. Large quantities of 'number' booklets, devised by children and amusingly illustrated, were shown to the interviewer.

In a few schools, teachers mentioned specifically that i.t.a. had helped 'modern mathematics'. These were schools taking part in the Nuffield Mathematics Project. The teachers pointed out that they had written all the cards in i.t.a. and that the children could read them, whereas with t.o. few infants would have been able to do this. In the same manner, the preparation of work cards or instruction cards in subjects other than mathematics was now a feasible proposition, enabling many more children to work on individual lines.

B. ALLOCATION OF TIME TO DIFFERENT SUBJECTS

One further way in which i.t.a. had benefited other subjects was noted by certain teachers. It was suggested that, because children learn to read and write more easily with i.t.a. than with t.o., infant teachers now have the opportunity to devote more time and thought to other subjects. In effect, it is no longer necessary for teachers to spend such a large proportion of the day in teaching reading and writing.

In contrast, a few teachers indicated that, when they first began to use i.t.a., they may have devoted rather more time to reading and writing than formerly, owing to their own interest in the new medium and the observed satisfaction of children in the acquisition of the skill. However, they felt that after a year or two the position had righted itself. As infant teachers are usually responsible for nearly all subjects in their own classes, it is easy for them to lay emphasis on certain aspects of the curriculum without intending, or even realising, that they are doing so. This is particularly true in those classes in which 'unscheduled days' have replaced time-tabled periods. One teacher of such a class elaborated on this point in detail:

'Children like i.t.a. and find it easy and can soon begin to learn. I myself like teaching reading. It would be the easiest thing in the world for me to carry on with games and play situations related to reading, even although children did not think of them as reading. Children would enjoy this all day. If I did this, the children would all be reading in a very, very short space of time, so I can understand why some schools claim exceptionally good results. However, I believe in the all-round development of children and I want them to have opportunities for all sorts of other creative activities, so we don't spend a great deal of time on reading and writing.'

The interviewer's observations confirm teachers' own suggestions that, if more time is spent on reading and writing at first, it is fairly soon levelled out as teachers become used to i.t.a. On the other hand, it did appear to the observer that in i.t.a. schools infants spend more time in doing individual reading and writing than in most t.o. schools – not at the instigation of the teacher but from the children's own desires. Moreover, this extra time was not instead of, but in addition to, other things. All the odd minutes which might formerly have been wasted were now being enriched by children's strong interest in reading and in the expression of their own ideas in writing.

C. DEVELOPING CHILDREN'S INDIVIDUAL INTERESTS

Numerous teachers spoke of how infants' rapid progress in reading with i.t.a. resulted in their becoming interested in, and gaining information on, many more subjects than was usual in t.o. classes. The following quotations are representative:

'Children are acquiring more information of all sorts because of their fluency in reading.'

'i.t.a. opens the door to all sorts of things which were formerly closed to the children – particularly to children from culturally deprived homes.'

'Children soon meet a wide range of interests and topics in a variety of books. For instance, one six-year-old has recently been fascinated to read about muscles in the leg.'

Many examples, like the preceding one, were given of young children using their reading skill to pursue the study of new subjects independently. There was a growing awareness in teachers that the easier acquisition of reading skill merges with and focuses children's interest on additional activities, while at the same time further reading grows from these activities. It was being realised that discovery methods of learning in infant schools were greatly enriched when children were able to read. One headmistress counted this as among the main advantages of i.t.a. She expressed it in this manner:

'Education today is trying more than ever before to get children to do things for themselves and find out things for themselves. i.t.a. is in line with this.'

The interviewer did not set out to make any assessment regarding subjects other than reading, writing and spelling. Nevertheless, in most infant schools the amount of emphasis which was being laid on creative work and first-hand experience of all sorts for children, as opposed to formal work in the basic subjects, may be judged to quite a large extent by the appearance of the school and the various activities in which children are seen to be engaged. The i.t.a. schools visited ranged from, at one end, those which provided children with a rich and stimulating environment in which vast arrays of different materials were attractively displayed and children had abundant opportunities to experiment with them, to, at the other end, schools in which a few books and children's paintings were all that adorned the classrooms. In the more progressive schools the introduction of i.t.a. appeared to have further stimulated the drive towards heuristic methods. In the few very formal schools visited there was no indication that i.t.a. had prevented the development of other sides of the curriculum; rather did it appear that these were schools which had always laid strong emphasis on teaching reading and less emphasis on children's all-round development. On the other hand, between these two extremes were a number of schools in which teachers stated that i.t.a. had encouraged both them and the children to branch out into new subjects and also to develop work on more individual lines.

II   General attitudes of children

The majority of teachers expressed the view that children's general attitudes and behaviour in school had improved since the introduction of i.t.a. and a number of them said that there were now fewer children exhibiting behaviour problems. Others spoke of how even the youngest and shyest children soon gained the confidence to take messages to other teachers and to carry out simple tasks in different parts of the school. Further groups of teachers instanced improvements in behaviour in the dining room, in corridors and in the playground. The trend of these remarks was that the majority of infants who had used i.t.a. somehow or other adopted more responsible attitudes to everything in the school than did the majority of children when t.o. was used. One head spoke of 'this marvellous attitude which the children now have to everything'. Another said, 'I cannot quite put my finger on what it is, but there is a different atmosphere in the school'. Such remarks were made in widely-separated schools and, even when teachers found difficulty in expressing exactly what they meant, it was clear that they felt it strongly and considered it as one of the notable advantages of using i.t.a. The following remarks exemplify the changes noted by teachers in children's attitudes and behaviour:

'The whole atmosphere of the school is different. Everybody is interested in everything.'

'Children can be left alone when the teacher is out of the room and they get on by themselves.'

'Children are more relaxed.'

'The children are not inhibited now.'

'The children show far more initiative.'

'The children are more confident in talking to people; because of their wider reading they have more to talk about.'

'I'm not sure exactly what it is, but somehow i.t.a. children are more forthcoming, more willing to tackle anything. There is a different attitude in the school. This may not necessarily come from i.t.a. but from a difference in teachers' attitudes.'

78

With regard to the behaviour of children, their attitudes to work, to each other and to visitors, the interviewer's impressions were that in this respect children in the i.t.a. schools were noticeably better than average children in t.o. schools. Some t.o. schools have certainly developed attitudes in children as good as in any of the i.t.a. schools, but, in very many t.o. schools, a visitor could observe adverse attitudes in children to school, to adults and to other children, such as one would rarely come across in i.t.a. classes. These, of course, represent value-judgements on the part of the interviewer, yet it must be stated that her observations support teachers' conclusions on this matter.

III Staffing

A. ADVANTAGES REGARDING TEACHERS

When talking of the difference she had noted in children's attitudes, since the introduction of i.t.a., one infant headmistress already quoted linked this with a change of attitudes on the part of the staff. Other headteachers followed the same course in instancing, among the advantages of i.t.a., the beneficial effects which they had noted on members of their staffs. Some of their comments were as follows:

> 'Neither the staff nor myself would like to go back to t.o. The main reason is that we could not bear to lose this lively attitude which we now have in the school. It's entirely different for both children and staff.'

> 'One advantage of i.t.a. is the different attitude in the school of response and joining-in which is difficult to define. It affects both teachers and children.'

> 'There's a friendlier attitude between the staff, with i.t.a. Teachers consult and help each other. Those who are lacking in confidence gain it.'

> 'With i.t.a. teachers have to listen to themselves and they find that their own speech is not always correct. They have to learn again. It shakes them out of the routine they've got into and promotes discussion. Teachers too make mistakes and this makes for a friendlier attitude between staff and children. Previously, because teachers read fluently, it was easy for teachers to forget how difficult it was for children to learn. So somehow, although it's difficult to put one's finger on it, there's a different attitude.'

One headmistress thought that the use of i.t.a. had a particular advantage for less able teachers. She stated:

> ✳ 'Poor teachers obviously don't get such good results as good teachers. The rather lazy teacher finds i.t.a. a help because children aren't always coming out asking things. With a poorer teacher, the children would get on better with i.t.a. than with t.o. because they could get on more easily on their own. The weaker teacher might be reluctant to try i.t.a. and might be a bit erratic about spelling at first, but this would soon right itself.'

Most headteachers, however, considered i.t.a. to have certain advantages for all members of the staff, in addition to the improved attitudes already mentioned. The two main points made are exemplified in the following comments:

'Teachers get great satisfaction from using i.t.a.'

'i.t.a. has stirred up a great interest in reading among teachers. Since we used it there have been so many staff-room discussions about reading.'

B. DISADVANTAGES FOR TEACHERS

From the point of view of teachers, only one main disadvantage was remarked on. It referred to the difficulties experienced by teachers in classes in which children were reading both t.o. and i.t.a., but this point has already been noted earlier.

Two additional minor difficulties experienced by teachers were mentioned by headteachers:

'It is difficult for a teacher who is first starting with i.t.a. because she doesn't know what standards she is aiming at. Formerly, when she was using a t.o. reading scheme with which she was familiar, she knew where she expected to be with different groups, say at the end of each term.'

'When teachers of the second and third classes take over children who have transferred to t.o., because they are not steeped in i.t.a. like the teachers of the preceding classes, they may find it difficult to understand and have sympathy with the children's mistakes in reading and spelling.'

C. FREQUENT STAFF CHANGES

In the course of discussions, headteachers sometimes related the use of i.t.a. to the current position of frequently changing staffs in primary schools. If headteachers did not bring up this point, the interviewer asked how new teachers, who were inexperienced with i.t.a., managed when they were placed in charge of i.t.a. classes. A number of headteachers confessed that this was one of the problems which had concerned them when they first introduced i.t.a. into their schools. Their original i.t.a. teachers had attended i.t.a. workshops. Headteachers were fearful lest temporary teachers and others, joining the staff of the school later and having neither training nor experience in the use of i.t.a., would not be able to cope with the situation and that, in consequence, the children might suffer.

In the event, the majority of headteachers did not find the problem to be nearly as acute as they had suspected. Their consensus of opinion was that new teachers soon began to feel at home with i.t.a. The following two quotations from headteachers relate to this point:

'I now only have one out of the five original i.t.a. teachers left, but the four new teachers have picked it up quickly and are very happy about it.'

'It doesn't take new staff long to get used to i.t.a., as far as reading is concerned. It takes them a little longer to learn to write it. For example, when they are writing children's "news" on the blackboard, the teachers are not certain at first of the correct i.t.a. spellings of all the words the children are asking them to write.'

It was quite clear that most of these headteachers now considered it unnecessary for teachers to have special training in the use of i.t.a.

On the other hand, one headmistress expressed the views of a number of others when she said, 'It certainly makes a difference if the teachers have had some training in using i.t.a.'

The interviewer also discussed this question with teachers who had only recently begun to teach in i.t.a. schools. Few of them had attended i.t.a. workshops or courses but one or two had followed the correspondence course provided by The i.t.a. Foundation. The majority of teachers new to i.t.a. said that it had not posed much of a problem to them. The following are examples of their comments:

'i.t.a. looked strange to me at first but in two or three weeks I felt quite at home with it. The children helped me when I went wrong with the spelling.'

'It did not take me long to feel familiar with i.t.a. I did a couple of hours work on two evenings at home. Then, after about a week, I felt fairly confident – as soon as I knew the sounds.'

Married women who had returned to teaching after absences of some years, often described how apprehensive they had felt when they knew they were to be in charge of classes using i.t.a. Yet nearly all of them said they had soon got used to i.t.a. and most spoke of how happy they were to be using it. One infant headmistress summed up the position regarding married women returning to teaching, in these words:

'I have been absolutely amazed by the way older women have taken to i.t.a. This was originally one of my worries about i.t.a. – how would older married women returners and part-time teachers get on with it? Our original teachers went to workshops to learn about i.t.a. but what about the others who had to pick it up later? Yet all the part-time teachers who have joined the staff and the older women who have returned full-time have soon picked it up and they have all been delighted with the results they have obtained.'

Another headmistress made the following points regarding the relationship between the use of i.t.a. and the pattern of changing staffs in infant schools:

'(i) Many married women are now teaching in infant schools. They have not the time to spend their evenings making reading apparatus and home-made reading books, as they used to do. Even lunch-times are not usually spent in schools because they are doing household shopping. In these circumstances, i.t.a. is a great advantage, because neither apparatus nor home-made books are necessary. Once children have started to word-build, which they soon do, all they need is books and books and books!'

'(ii) Children learn to read so quickly with i.t.a. that even the less able teacher can hardly prevent children learning to read. There are more and more untrained teachers coming into the schools, so if children can learn to read in six months they are not so dependent on untrained or changing staff.'

'(iii) i.t.a. enables children to learn to read and write much earlier, thus providing an additional means of communication. This is especially important with large classes and with changing staffs. Once children have learned to read and write, this can have an important effect on all the work in the school. For example, I have prepared large quantities of written number cards. Even young infants can read these cards and so progress steadily from one stage to another, even when the staff are absent or there are changes of staff. It can be as if I am running a correspondence course directly with the children.'

The views expressed by both headteachers and teachers led to the conclusion that the problem of teachers with no experience of i.t.a. joining the staff of schools which used i.t.a. was not nearly so great as had been feared. Most teachers soon familiarised themselves with the new alphabet and enjoyed using it. On the other hand, a few headteachers indicated that it was preferable for teachers to receive some training. Certain headteachers perceived various advantages to be gained from using i.t.a. rather than t.o. in situations where staff changes were frequent and where there were untrained teachers, part-time teachers and married women returners.

IV Children's intelligence

If teachers did not speak of the effects of using i.t.a. with children of different levels of intelligence, the following question was put to them: 'What impressions have you formed about how i.t.a. works with bright, with average and with dull children?' This was a question which everyone seemed interested to answer and it was clear that many staffroom discussions had centred on this very point.

A. EFFECT OF i.t.a. ON DULL CHILDREN

It soon became apparent that the reaction of most teachers to any new approach to reading is to consider how it may help the dullest children in their classes. Quite a large body of such teachers, although not the majority of those with whom discussions took place, replied to the above question as follows, 'The bright children would learn anyway. i.t.a. helps the average and the slow children most'.

So many replies along these lines were couched in similar terms that there would be no value in duplicating them. Only one further quotation, which goes into greater detail, need be given:

> 'The intelligent children would manage anyway, although with i.t.a. they do acquire a wider vocabulary earlier. Regarding the dull children – formerly with t.o. the teacher was trying all the time, with those who were sticking, to make it easier and simpler. But one soon reached a point when one couldn't go back any further to make it any simpler, yet nothing was easy enough for them. Now, with i.t.a., reading is easy enough for dull children.'

Other teachers, without stating that bright children would learn by any means, did lay emphasis on how i.t.a. was helping the slowest children. Many of these teachers taught in schools in slum areas. The headmistress of one such school said this about the dullest children:

> 'Our dullest children are learning to read by i.t.a. and they would not have done so with t.o. After one and a half years with i.t.a. only one child out of 40 is not reading and she is going to an E.S.N. (Educationally Sub-Normal) school when she is seven.'

In a very similar school, an excellent staff of teachers, working in a delightful atmosphere, with children of low intelligence who came from poor home backgrounds, reported that only five children out of 110 had not transferred to t.o. before they left the infant school, and even these five were making progress in i.t.a. One headmistress described the home backgrounds of the children in the school as follows:

'All the children live in council houses except four families. No child ever comes to school having started to read. Most children are inarticulate. Many have to be taught to speak.'

She then stated unequivocally:

'Children are able to begin to learn to read at five with i.t.a.-even these poor children in this school.'

One amusing incident, described by the headteacher of a school in a deprived area, and relating to a family of children of very low intelligence might well be included here. There were three children in the family. The eldest two children, having passed through the infant school without the least indication of even being ready to begin to learn to read, had then gone to an E.S.N. school. The third child was due to go to this same school when she left the infant school. The parents had made no protest about their first two children going to this special school, but they objected strongly to the youngest child being sent there. They thought that this child was much brighter than her elder brother and sister, basing their assumption on the fact that she could read, which neither of the others had been able to do. The child had been taking home i.t.a. books and happily reading them aloud to her parents, whose knowledge of reading was so meagre that they were quite unaware that her books were printed in an alphabet other than the traditional one!

Not all teachers who described the way in which i.t.a. helped slower children, however, taught in schools in slum areas. One teacher of the 'transition' class, in a school in which the intelligence of the children was above average, had this to say:

'The three dullest children in my class are reading "Once Upon a Time", from the *Janet and John* Reading Scheme, in i.t.a. If the school had still been using t.o. these children would not have started to read at all or they'd have been struggling on the very early book of *Janet and John*. All the children in the class will have made the transfer before they enter the Junior School. With i.t.a., even if the slowest children are struggling they don't want to give up, and they don't have to give up because they do make progress.'

The number of teachers who expressed the view that i.t.a. did not help children of low intelligence to read was very small indeed. A further few advised caution about allowing dull children to begin to read too early, even with i.t.a. For example:

'The very, very dull child may not learn at first because he is not ready to begin, but because of the regularity of i.t.a., he will learn eventually.'

In the following section, one or two additional cautionary comments about dull children are combined with remarks concerning bright children.

B. EFFECT OF i.t.a. ON BRIGHT CHILDREN

The view that i.t.a. is valuable for intelligent children appeared to be growing among infant teachers: some considered that it helped bright children more than average and dull children, while others thought it helped bright children as well as average and dull children. The following remarks were among those stressing that most benefits accrued to bright children:

'i.t.a. helps the bright ones most. It does not really help the backward ones.'

'i.t.a. is most effective with the children who would have done well anyway. A and B children definitely benefit. C children should not start before they are ready. Both i.t.a. and t.o. are equally pernicious for the dull child if he is started too early. When he is ready to begin – yes, i.t.a. is good then.'

'Intelligent children quickly learn the rules of i.t.a. and apply them. Then nothing stops them. Average and slower children – the fixed rules help them. The teacher can plan the work, e.g. when teaching sounds. A firm pattern can be set. One couldn't do this before. Children can consolidate by practising the rules, e.g. "e*" is always the same.

As for the very dull children, I have not yet been able to make up my mind whether i.t.a. really helps the dullest children of all or not.'

'When we were considering using i.t.a. we thought that its main function might be to help slower children, but we were amazed at the phenomenal progress of average and above average children.'

C. i.t.a. BENEFITS CHILDREN OF ALL LEVELS OF INTELLIGENCE

In more than half the schools visited teachers were of the opinion that the use of i.t.a. effected improvements in the reading standards of children of all levels of ability. The following three quotations are representative: the first comes from a school in a good residential area; the latter two were made in infant schools on council house estates, the first of which represented a rather better area than the second:

'It helps children of all levels of intelligence in different ways. With bright children it's highly successful. With average and below average children it avoids the building up of an antipathy towards reading, which, because of the difficulty of succeeding, used to affect many children.'

'i.t.a. is better all along the range of intelligence. The bright child writes long stories at the end of the second term. The average child is writing good stories by the end of the first year. The slow child has had the experience of reading three or four books in a reading scheme by the end of the first year.'

'i.t.a. works with all children. With bright children there is fantastically quick learning. The average child also learns more quickly than he would with t.o. As for the dull child, it depends why he is backward at reading. i.t.a. won't cure all ills – for example, if a child is deaf. But all children want to read and they are happy when they learn with i.t.a., so all make progress.'

D. SUMMING UP

More than half the teachers with whom discussions took place were convinced that the use of i.t.a. was beneficial to children of all levels of intelligence. This conviction related to earlier, easier beginnings, as well as to increased standards in both reading and written expression. Of the teachers who did not hold this view, a proportion thought that it was most effective with children of low intelligence and least effective with children of high intelligence; the remainder reversed this conclusion.

It will be recalled that, when visiting classes, the investigator had asked teachers to present a group of the best children, a group of the slowest children and a group of average children. These children were asked to read individually, and examples of their written work were examined. In addition, the records of many teachers referring to books read by i.t.a. children and preceding t.o. children were examined. In the light of this evidence, the conclusions of the observer support those of the majority of teachers: in general, the reading and writing of children of all levels of ability was in advance of what would be found in equivalent schools using t.o. Perhaps the most impressive feature of all was to watch the slowest group of children in a class, happily reading and writing at a simple level, while being certain that most of them would not have been doing so with t.o.

To state that children of all levels of intelligence benefited from the use of i.t.a. is not meant to indicate that every child was ready to begin to read and write as soon as he entered school. In many infant schools the investigator saw occasional children of very low intelligence who had not started to read. The wise teacher had realised that the child was not ready to begin and she did not intend to try to rush him. Nevertheless, the number of children who were not ready to begin reading and writing was extremely small compared with the number to be found in t.o. schools. At the other end of the intelligence scale, the large number of children reading vast quantities of books fluently and with understanding on their own, and producing pages of flowing written work, contrasted with the small number of children in the better t.o. schools who might have reached this standard.

The remarks from some teachers that i.t.a. did not help the most able children and from others that it did not help the slowest children when viewed against the school background, led the observer to draw the following conclusions. Teachers who believed that bright children would learn anyway, and that consequently i.t.a. would not help them, had not always fully realised the importance of 'stretching' intelligent children at an early age. As for the remarks concerning slower children not benefiting from i.t.a., such teachers were sometimes referring to the small percentage of E.S.N. children who at the age of five were not ready to utilise any alphabet for formal reading and writing. When the remarks concerned large groups of duller children, the observer mentally compared these classes with similar classes in schools in poor areas where nearly every child was benefiting from the use of i.t.a. The only conclusion to be drawn from these comparisons was that, in the latter schools, there were present some positive features in the whole atmosphere of the schools and the beliefs of the teachers or in the methods and procedures used, which were lacking in the former schools.

V   Children's views on i.t.a.

Teacher's opinions of children's reactions to i.t.a., as well as the interviewer's observations, have formed an almost continuous thread running throughout this record of evidence from infant schools. Comments on children's enjoyment of learning to read with i.t.a., their keenness to continue, their pleasure in using and in demonstrating their skill have all been mentioned. Useful as these observations were thought to be, it was considered that the verbal evidence collected in this section of the report would have been enriched if one could have discovered what young children themselves thought about i.t.a. Yet, as those children who had learned to read by means of this alphabet lacked the experience of learning to read by t.o., and were therefore not in a position to contrast the two media, there was little point in asking their opinions. Fortunately, however, details of the reactions and comments of some infants who had initially started to learn to read with t.o., and later switched to i.t.a., were reported by teachers. Two examples will serve to represent the common reactions of children in these situations.

The first example concerns a child who moved from a t.o. infant school into one which was using i.t.a. In such a situation it was the school's practice, when a child had made only a meagre beginning with reading in t.o., to start him again on i.t.a. This particular child had read *Janet and John* Book 1 in t.o. and was struggling with Book 2. The teacher started the child on i.t.a., using the *Downing Readers*. The child read the first seven books in two months and was delighted, saying to her teacher, 'This is much easier!'

The second example refers to an infant school which was so organised that twice a year a proportion of children from every class was promoted to the next class. The teacher relating this particular experience was in charge of the second class. The first group of children using i.t.a. were promoted to her class from the reception class, at Easter, after having been in school two terms. The teacher of the second class found that the new group of children, using i.t.a., were much better at reading and writing than her t.o. children who were two terms older and had been in the school for four terms. By the end of the summer term, the i.t.a. children, who had then been in school three terms, were so far ahead of the older t.o. children in the class that the teacher considered the t.o. children to be at a serious disadvantage. Accordingly, she started all the t.o. children on i.t.a. She reported that when these former t.o. children were given i.t.a. books they were extremely pleased. They said, 'This is better – we can read this!'

VI Advantages and disadvantages of i.t.a.

Towards the conclusion of every discussion, the interviewer asked each headteacher and class teacher who had used i.t.a. to summarise his or her conclusions concerning the main advantages and disadvantages of i.t.a. As the majority of teachers who had used i.t.a. approved of it, it was not surprising to find that the number of advantages put forward far outweighed the disadvantages. About half the teachers interviewed had found no disadvantages. One headmaster of a primary school gave the following reply to this question, 'I can honestly say that we haven't found any disadvantages. We were afraid of some but they didn't materialise.'

Most of the remaining teachers, having listed what they considered to be the advantages of i.t.a., were prepared to put forward one or two disadvantages or, as they often phrased them, 'dangers', which they perceived and which caused them some anxiety.

Many of the advantages and disadvantages listed by teachers in response to this particular question have already been included earlier in the appropriate sections of this report. In certain places teachers' remarks on this point have been given explicitly, while elsewhere they were implicit in what has been written. To attempt to gather together all such comments at this stage is unnecessary. Nevertheless, it may serve to draw together the overall impressions of infant teachers regarding i.t.a. if an attempt is now made to summarise the most important advantages and disadvantages noted by them.

The main advantages of using i.t.a. with infants, as listed by their teachers, related to children's earlier and easier reading and writing. Teachers' emphases were always on the comparative simplicity of learning these two skills, when the medium used was i.t.a. as opposed to t.o., and the corresponding pleasure and satisfaction gained by children in so doing. That children experienced less frustration and that there was a reduction in the number of non-readers and struggling readers were also rated as advantages.

Children's early ability and eagerness to attempt to read unknown words was given a high place among advantages. Associated with this facet of i.t.a. was the fact that children could read a variety of books outside basic reading schemes. This ability resulted in a widening of children's interests and an expansion of individual study which led to exploration and experimentation, in a manner thought likely to result in an increase in modern heuristic methods in infant schools. Infant teachers were also impressed by the advantageous effect which i.t.a. had on particular subjects in the curriculum, mathematics, spoken English and science being most frequently mentioned in this context.

The third group of advantages noted by infant teachers referred mainly to attitudes, behaviour and social relationships of children and staff. Among the advantages mentioned were the confidence and independence which children displayed in many aspects of school life, other than reading and writing, and improvements in their general behaviour, reflecting more responsible attitudes and easier social relationships with each other, with teachers and with visitors. The effect of using i.t.a. on members of the staff, as reported by headteachers, included friendlier attitudes towards each other, an increased interest in reading and greater satisfaction in the work they were doing.

Of the three disadvantages of i.t.a. brought forward most frequently in infant schools, two were more often termed 'dangers' than 'disadvantages'. These three main disadvantages concerned the difficulties encountered by teachers of transition classes, the dangers of allowing children to transfer to t.o. reading at too early a stage and the danger of children being permitted to read beyond the level of their comprehension. Two additional disadvantages were mentioned much less frequently than the preceding three. Certain teachers considered the quantity and variety of reading materials available in i.t.a. still insufficient for their needs. A small proportion of teachers also spoke of some children finding difficulty in writing i.t.a. symbols.

In addition to the preceding disadvantages one further point cropped up fairly frequently in group discussions with teachers. One infant headmistress spoke in the following terms of this dilemma, with which she confessed she had not yet come to terms:

't.o. has a much greater wealth of books than i.t.a. and everything the children see around them outside school is in t.o. Current learning practice tends to use the whole of the child's environment, but we cannot do this if we use i.t.a. in schools when the child is seeing t.o. all the time outside school. Yet I should not like to give up i.t.a., especially for the lovely attitude it has brought into the school.'

In a number of the t.o. schools visited, and especially in those schools which had seriously considered using i.t.a. before deciding not to do so, this particular dilemma had frequently proved the deciding factor. It was also a point mentioned by many advisers, inspectors and other visitors to the schools, as reported in Chapter 10.

A number of teachers had also noted that the use of i.t.a. with infants resulted in certain advantages and disadvantages, as far as children's parents were concerned. These points, however, are reported in Chapter 12.

CHAPTER 9

Evidence from Schools involved in Experiments

I Preliminary points

THE first schools in England and Wales to use i.t.a. were those which took part in the Reading Research Unit's original experiment in 1961 and 1962. Consequently, it was within these schools that teachers with the longest experience of i.t.a. were to be found, some of them, by July 1966, having had five years of such experience. These teachers' conclusions, based on practical experience and reinforced by discussions among themselves and with other people, proved an invaluable source of information to the interviewer. Certain of these teachers combined two sorts of experience; for example, being in charge of the original control classes and later using i.t.a. Thus, although certain schools visited were using i.t.a. experimentally on their own, while others worked completely outside any experiment, it was inevitable that the majority of the schools visited in the course of this evaluation should have taken part in Downing's first experiment.

The total numbers of schools visited and teachers with whom discussions were held are categorised in Tables D/3 and D/4 in Appendix D. The schools concerned with experiments were divided as follows: 39 connected with the Reading Research Unit's first experiment, 2 with the Reading Research Unit's second experiment and 7 carrying out their own experiments. The numbers of teachers involved were 146, 7 and 21 respectively.

Of the 39 schools connected with the Reading Research Unit's first experiment, 9 were control schools and 5 were separate junior schools fed by children from the original experimental infant schools. The information collected from teachers in these 14 schools has not been presented earlier in this report. The remaining 25 schools were infant or all-age primary schools and much of what these teachers had to say has been embodied in earlier chapters of this report. In this particular chapter, all teachers' comments relating to experimental conditions and the effects of taking part in experiments have been gathered together.

The majority of these remarks occurred when headteachers and teachers were asked to give their general impressions of i.t.a. If teachers who had taken part in experiments failed to say anything on this score, the interviewer usually asked the following question: 'Have you any comment to make on the experiment itself?' Apart from factual questions on such points as testing and numbers of visitors, direct questions requesting teachers' views on particular aspects of experiments were not asked. Accordingly, the information which follows is based on unsolicited comments arising during interviews and on teachers' replies to the preceding question.

II The Reading Research Unit's first experiment

1 *Reasons for becoming an experimental school*

When the headteachers of the 25 schools which had taken part in the Reading Research Unit's first experiment were asked their reasons for joining the experiment, two indicated that they had been asked or persuaded to join, while the remainder had volunteered. The reasons they gave for doing so fell into three categories. The majority of headteachers gave interest in new ideas and in the teaching of reading as their main reason: it was frequently associated with a second reason, namely, dissatisfaction with t.o. and its irregularities which made learning to read 'a grind' for children. Many headteachers had decided to experiment with i.t.a. after listening to talks, reading about it and concluding that, in the words of one, 'it was a good hypothesis'. A minority of headteachers volunteered to experiment with i.t.a. because they were dissatisfied with the standards of reading in their schools. Very many of the headteachers of the original experimental schools stated that it had been their intention, if they found i.t.a. unsatisfactory, to abandon it after a year or so.

2 *Early enthusiasm*

The comments which were volunteered most frequently in the first experimental schools referred to the enthusiasm which the teachers had felt in the first year or two and the stimulus which came from knowing that they were part of an important experiment. The following were among the remarks made:

'It was so stimulating to be in an experiment.'

'In a new experiment teachers have enthusiasm which makes them want to do well.'

'Because it is easier, children are most interested in reading and they read more. Some of the children's interest and keenness enthuses the teacher. I felt very keen at first – not because I wanted the experiment to succeed but because the children were so keen.'

'i.t.a. went off with a bang, right from the beginning. I'm not sure whether this was because of the alphabet or because of the enthusiasm.'

In one joint discussion with an infant headmistress and four teachers, the following comment was made: 'The enthusiasm of the teacher bounces back on to the children'. They all agreed about this and one continued, 'A new scheme or idea stimulates the teacher who may have got bored with the old books'. The interviewer pursued this point by asking: 'Would a new scheme in t.o. have had the same effect?' The group were all in agreement with the answer of one who replied, 'It would have had some effect, but not as much as i.t.a.'

A particularly interesting conversation took place with a headmaster who had been in charge of one school where i.t.a. was originally used and who later became head of a second school which, at that time, had been using i.t.a. for three years. The following are some of his observations:

'At first my staff and I went to lectures by enthusiastic teachers. We became enthusiastic. Once the teachers were familiar with i.t.a., they all began to make a lot of apparatus and this created even more enthusiasm and discussion. In the second school, when i.t.a. had been in use for three years, there wasn't the same enthusiasm, although the staff approved of it. There was more an attitude of everyday occurrence.'

'The real fear is that a completely new thing, i.e. i.t.a., makes the mediocre teacher think more about it than about other subjects, and so good results are produced. This enthusiasm then tails off. It becomes mundane. The stimulus of further thought given to the subject loses its impetus.'

3 Earlier and later results

Closely connected with the remarks about the original stimulation and enthusiasm were comments comparing later results with earlier results. The trend of these remarks was that the first year's results were nearly always better than succeeding years. The following are examples of teachers' comments on this score:

'Our first-year results seemed better than later results. Maybe it was a better year of children or maybe the teachers were more enthusiastic.'

'The results in the second and third year of using i.t.a. were not as spectacular as in the first year.'

'The results were never as good as the first year. Now perhaps i.t.a. teachers are taking it a little slower. They are more relaxed. The transfer is made a little later than in the first year.'

These remarks did not imply that the teachers concerned did not approve of i.t.a. Nearly all of them did so. They were merely noting what they had observed and attributing the particularly good results in the first year to a combination of exceptional circumstances such as the stimulation of a new idea, initial keenness and the knowledge that they were part of an important experiment.

4 Publicity and visitors

Many teachers made adverse comments about the publicity which had accompanied the original i.t.a. experiment, as the following quotations illustrate:

'My staff and I thought that all the publicity was a mistake. We disagreed with the reports of test results coming out too early – after i.t.a. had only been in use one year.'

'The claims for i.t.a. were published too early. I had expected that the results would not be published for three years. Early publication made some people cynical.'

'It has been a mistake to make too many claims. i.t.a. is good, but people have been put off by extravagant claims.'

Some of the early experimental schools also complained about the large number of visitors in the first year or two, while other schools said that they had not suffered from a surfeit of visitors. The two comments given below relate visitors to the time which children spent on reading:

'Perhaps more time was spent on reading because of all the visitors. This was not intentional on the part of the teachers but the children liked reading to visitors and many of them were very good readers.'

'Extra reading lessons were taken for the visitors, but not necessarily the reading lesson the teacher had intended to take, so the time probably evened itself out.'

5 Books and methods

Most teachers of experimental classes remarked on the shortage of i.t.a. books during the first year or two and particularly in the first two terms, that is autumn 1961 and spring 1962. The majority also mentioned that they had consciously tried to continue with their former methods of teaching reading but that i.t.a. itself had, because of its regularity, led to an almost involuntary evolution of a change in method. One example of such a comment is given:

'We really did try to use the same methods and approaches as formerly, but children began to abstract the sounds for themselves earlier with i.t.a.'

6 Testing

In some of the experimental schools visited, the headteacher had carried out the testing, helped occasionally by one or more members of staff. In other schools, outsiders who had received a little training in testing carried out all or part of the testing. In some cases, headteachers were not altogether happy about the ability or qualifications of these outside testers. However, regardless of who had carried out the testing, most of the headteachers and teachers who took part in the first experiment expressed dissatisfaction at the large amount of testing and recording which took place. They felt it to be a strain on teachers and more particularly on children who were so young, and they often wondered if so much of it was absolutely necessary. A few typical comments are given:

'The testing took far too long.'

'The testing was so time-consuming.'

'There was too much testing for infants, although we understood and appreciated the reasons for it. But infants had to be asked to do all sorts of things they'd never done before, e.g. dictated spellings. The teachers enjoy using i.t.a. much more now that we are out of the experiment and have no testing to do.'

A few headteachers who had carried out all the testing themselves because they were interested in it, spoke as follows:

'I was very impressed with the Neale Analysis Tests – children do understand what they read.'

'I did all the testing myself. I didn't ask for help because I was fascinated by what I was finding out. Otherwise the testing would have been very frustrating.'

One headmistress, who had been in charge of an original control school before moving to another school in which an experimental class was commencing, made this thoughtful comparison of the test results of control and experimental classes:

'As a control school we retained our former methods of teaching. Our own policy had always been not to introduce word-building until the second year. This showed up in the test results of reception-class children who, because they had not been trained to decipher new words, could only recognise words they had met in their reading scheme. On the other hand, i.t.a. children, because of the alphabet they were using, knew how to tackle new words. If things are taught later, they should be assessed later. Early tests would assess good results in i.t.a. Children were tested at the same chronological age but not at the same stage in their reading programmes.'

The general feeling was that, although it was interesting and stimulating to be involved in an experiment of this nature, the amount of testing which took place constituted a serious disadvantage. Some headteachers even went so far as to say that if they had known in advance how much testing and recording would need to be undertaken, they would not have agreed to take part in the experiment.

7 Results related to teachers

A number of headteachers brought up the question of the calibre of teachers who were in charge of the original experimental classes. Quite independently, they stated that, on reflection, they had concluded that their first experimental classes had been given to experienced and exceptionally able teachers. Two reasons for this were given. Firstly, it was often the lively, able teacher with a keen interest in new ideas and in the teaching of reading who was the one eager, or at any rate willing, to experiment with i.t.a. Secondly, a headteacher who wanted to try i.t.a., and having the interests of the children at heart, knew that if the new alphabet should prove unacceptable in use, the children would be less likely to suffer serious harm if they were in the charge of a good, experienced teacher. Such a teacher would, in all probability, be able to counterbalance the possible disadvantages which might become apparent as i.t.a. was tried out. One headmistress discussed the problem in this way:

'Our original i.t.a. class had the same teacher for three years and she was a very good teacher. Hence the children had continuity of approach. Also they were a good year of children. These facts, plus the original enthusiasm, may account in part for our exceptionally good results. I would not say that the good results were entirely due to i.t.a. It would not be fair to say so. Later results are not likely to be as spectacular as earlier results.'

Other headteachers noted that some less able teachers, as well as others who were 'anti-i.t.a.' did not obtain such good results as the more able teachers. One headmaster described how one of the older members of his staff, who did not like change of any sort, was definitely against i.t.a. As a consequence, the reading results in her class were rather poor. The headmaster had noticed that in the reception class the children did well; in the second class, in the charge of the 'anti-i.t.a.' person, there was little progress; then in the third class the reading progress soared ahead again. In a different school, the headmistress had this to say:

'We had two teachers who originally would not try i.t.a. They were prejudiced without trying it. Later they did begin to use it but they did not get such good results as other teachers in the school because, although they were good teachers, they were not so keen.'

93

Teachers who took part in the Reading Research Unit's first experiment were those with the longest experience of i.t.a. and consequently those most competent to express opinions. The schools and the teachers who first used i.t.a. were nearly all volunteers who had a lively approach to new educational ideas and who were particularly interested in reading. Most of the original teachers were both experienced and able. Headteachers had noted that the best results were obtained by those teachers who were both able and keen to experiment with i.t.a.

Teachers referred to the difficulties encountered because of the initial shortage of books. They had tried to continue with their former methods of teaching reading, as requested, but changes in methods had occurred almost unconsciously on account of the regularity of the alphabet. Many teachers made adverse comments about the publicity which i.t.a. had received and felt that rather extravagant claims had been made in the early days. There was general agreement that the testing had been too time-consuming, although a few headteachers had been interested in carrying it out for themselves.

Practically every one of the original teachers had found it stimulating to be part of the experiment and to try out i.t.a. They talked of their early enthusiasm and the enjoyment and satisfaction of the children. Many of the teachers were amazed and delighted by their early successes and, although results in the following years were not as spectacular as in the first year, nearly all were still in favour of i.t.a. and hoped to continue to use it.

B. CONTROL SCHOOLS

I   *Reasons for becoming a control school*

Nine of the control schools in the Reading Research Unit's first experiment were visited in six different education authorities. In one local authority certain schools had been informed that they would be control schools, without having any choice in the matter. In the remaining authorities the control schools had been volunteers.

The reasons given by different headteachers for volunteering to be control schools revealed considerable identity of aims. These headteachers were usually people interested in new ideas, interested in reading and anxious to be associated with an experiment of this nature. Most of them would have liked to take part as experimental schools but were prevented from doing so either by administrative problems or by lack of interest on the part of their staffs. They had decided that the next best thing was to be control schools, as in this way they would be kept in touch with the experiment and the results. The following are typical comments from headteachers about their reasons for becoming control schools:

'This school had wanted to be an experimental school but due to administrative reasons we couldn't. We thought that to become a control school was the next best thing. Later we became an experimental i.t.a. school.'

'I was interested in i.t.a. My urge was to do it, but we are involved in the new mathematics, vertical grouping, etc., and so I didn't think it wise to do too many new things together. We became a control school to keep in touch and so that we would get information.'

One headmaster of a school in a poor socio-economic area explained in detail his reasons for volunteering to act as a control school:

'Formerly, when children passed from the infant department to the first junior class, I always used to take the slower readers in groups. I then noticed all the anomalies in word-building. Consequently I was interested in i.t.a., which I thought might be a solution to this problem. Yet the teachers were rather doubtful about trying what seemed, at that time (1961), to be a rather revolutionary idea. I still wanted to be in touch with the i.t.a. experiment, so we became a control school–partly to help the experiment and partly so that we would know what was going on.

I was rather disappointed as time went on that, as a control school, we did not get to know more about test results.'

The headmistress of an infant school in a high socio-economic area, where the reading standards had always been good, explained, in these terms, why she volunteered to be a control school:

'I went to the first meeting about i.t.a. and thought it might have something, but I feared that there would be difficulties later with writing and spelling. Yet I wanted to co-operate with any venture which might help reading. I discussed the matter with my staff and they agreed that they'd like to be part of the experiment but that they'd prefer to be a control school.'

In the discussions with 26 headteachers and class teachers of control schools in the Reading Research Unit's first experiment, there was not the faintest suggestion that anyone had been anxious to prove that his or her method of teaching reading was superior to any new idea such as i.t.a. In fact the contrary was true. Teachers in control schools were mostly interested in the new approach and eager to watch its progress, although sometimes being cautious about actually experimenting with it for themselves in the early days. Many of them made a point of stressing to the interviewer that they had not been 'anti-i.t.a.'

Quite a large proportion of the staffs of control schools had demonstrated their interest in the new alphabet by visiting schools which were using it; also, in some cases, by attending courses and lectures on i.t.a. The results of their interest were that seven of the nine original control schools visited were, by 1966, using i.t.a. The two schools which were continuing to use t.o. were doing so for different reasons. In the first school the teachers did not approve of i.t.a.: they had disliked the publicity which had surrounded it and the early publication of results. They felt that the control schools had been treated rather shabbily. Furthermore, those who had visited i.t.a. schools said that they did not consider the i.t.a. children to be any further forward than the children in their own school, and they had gained the impression that more time had been devoted to reading in the experimental schools than in their own control school.

The attitude in the second school was very different. This was the school mentioned earlier, in the good socio-economic area, which wanted to co-operate in any venture which might help reading. The teachers and the headmistress were clearly very capable and vitally interested in reading. They emphasised that they were not 'against i.t.a.' In fact, they had discussed the matter a great deal and were just not convinced that the use of i.t.a. would give any better results than they were already obtaining–

the standard of reading in the school being well above average. In their visits to i.t.a. schools, they said they had not seen either reading or free writing which was better than their own. Accordingly, they were very happy to stay with t.o. at present, although continuing to observe the results of i.t.a. and to discuss the question among themselves.

2 *Materials, methods and results*

Of the nine control schools visited, seven had previously been using the *Janet and John* reading scheme and so continued to use their old books. The remaining two schools, one of which had both a control and an experimental class, were provided with new *Janet and John* books.

In all the control schools, teachers were at pains to indicate that they had just gone on teaching reading as formerly, without changing their methods or devoting more time to reading. They said:

'We just went on as we always did.'

'We did not try any harder to teach reading.'

'Nobody worked at reading any more than we formerly did.'

'We did not feel that we should work hard in order to prove i.t.a. wrong. We did no more work in reading than formerly because we had always done a lot.'

Headteachers in most of the control schools stated that during the time that particular classes were acting as control classes, their reading standards remained about the same as they had been before they entered the experiment. For example, in one school the headmistress said:

'We had good reading standards previously. The results at the end of the first and second year were very similar to what they had been before.'

In certain schools, where records had been kept for a number of years of children's reading ability at the end of each year of the infant school, the results for children in the control class closely resembled the results for similar children in preceding years. Thus the indications were that the mere fact of being a control school had not resulted in an alteration of methods and procedure in the direction of a greater emphasis on reading.

3 *Visitors, meetings and lectures*

All the control schools stated that they had had very few visitors, apart from an occasional one from the Reading Research Unit. As the headteacher of one school said:

'Why should visitors want to come and see us, when they can go and see something new being tried out in an i.t.a. school?'

Regarding the meetings arranged for headteachers of control schools, the usual remarks made were to the effect that the meetings were few and were mostly concerned with telling the headteachers about testing and warning them to keep to their former methods of teaching. One headteacher commented:

'We only had three meetings in three and a half years and most of them were a waste of time.'

In four of the nine control schools, no mention was made of lectures on reading which may have been arranged for teachers of control schools. In five of the schools, however, the headteacher or members of the staff specifically stated that the lectures had been 'not helpful', 'useless', or 'a waste of time'. One headmistress summed up the situation regarding visitors, meetings and lectures in this way:

'The Reading Research Unit may have meant well, but any idea of stimulating control schools just did not work. We had few visitors and the odd meeting about filling in forms. We also had odd lectures, but the odd lecture by someone about t.o. is not the same as lectures by enthusiasts about new ideas like i.t.a.'

4 Testing

In nearly all the control schools visited, the headteacher, occasionally assisted by class teachers, had done the whole, or the major part, of the testing. Many of them complained, as had the staff in experimental schools, about the amount of testing which was required. On the other hand, despite considering that too much testing was demanded, a minority of teachers had enjoyed this aspect of being a control school, as evidenced by the following comments:

'I didn't mind being a control school because I found the testing so interesting.'

'I did all the testing myself. I found it fascinating. I learned a lot about individual children from doing the Neale Tests and Raven's Matrices. As a result of what I learned about individual children from this testing, the "tail" in reading in this school has completely disappeared during the last few years.' (i.e. while continuing to use t.o.)

One headteacher had doubts about the value of one of the tests, as the following remark indicates:

'Regarding the Accuracy Measurement in the Neale Tests, which Downing uses in some of his tables–better readers, i.e. children with the highest Reading Ages, do not always achieve the highest scores for accuracy, because, if they attempt more words, their percentage of success is likely to be lower.'

5 Summing-up

The majority of the control schools in the Reading Research Unit's first experiment which were visited had volunteered to join the experiment. Many of the headteachers would have liked to experiment with i.t.a. but were not in positions to do so, for instance because their staffs were not eager to try the new alphabet.

Of the nine control schools visited, two had received new *Janet and John* books for the experiment. All the schools tried to continue with their former methods of teaching reading and, in fact, their results during the experiment were similar to their previous results. Most teachers complained that too much testing was done but a few headteachers enjoyed doing the testing. They said they had few visitors and only rare meetings. None found the few lectures on reading which were arranged to be helpful.

The control schools were interested in the use of i.t.a. and many of their teachers visited i.t.a. schools. By 1966, seven of the nine original control schools visited were using i.t.a.

In noting the above summary of the comments made by teachers in control schools, it is important to remember that it is not known how closely the nine schools visited

97

approximated to a representative sample of all control schools. (Reference should be made to Chapters 3 and 4 for details of how the schools were selected.) Thus, generalisations concerning all control schools cannot be drawn from the group of control schools visited. For example, it might well have been that the seven control schools which had turned to i.t.a. were proposed by local education authority officials as likely to provide fruitful visits for the interviewer, in that the teachers in them would be able to offer information and comments from two different angles, control classes and i.t.a. classes. Consequently, it would be impossible to draw the conclusion that because seven of the nine control schools visited were using i.t.a. by 1966, 77% of all the original control schools had likewise taken up i.t.a. This may be the case, but evidence regarding this point was not available in this investigation.

C. JUNIOR SCHOOLS FED BY EXPERIMENTAL SCHOOLS

1 The differences between schools

By the spring and summer terms of 1966, some pupils aged eight and nine years who had begun to learn to read with i.t.a. when they were four and five years old, as part of the Reading Research Unit's first experiment, had entered junior schools or the junior classes of all-age primary schools. Five such junior schools were visited in addition to five all-age primary schools which had experimental children in the junior classes. These ten schools varied in so many important background features, as well as in the aims and opinions of their headteachers and staff, that it has proved impossible to formulate a general description of teachers' reactions and comments, as has been done in the case of experimental and control schools. Any attempt to combine the views of teachers of junior children in generalities would fail to do justice to varying conclusions arrived at in different sets of circumstances. Accordingly, it has been deemed more appropriate to describe, in Appendix F, the points which emerged in each school, separately, against a few relevant background details of the school.

The procedure adopted on these visits to junior schools was the same as already described for infant schools, combining visits to classes with discussions with headteachers and teachers. Comments of class teachers, however, are only recorded in the summaries in Appendix F where they supplement or diverge from the headteacher's comments and conclusions.

2 Summing-up the reactions of junior teachers

The reports given, in Appendix F, of visits to junior schools and junior classes in all-age primary schools, illustrate the impossibility of drawing general conclusions from comments made in schools in which the socio-economic backgrounds, the sizes, the working conditions, the organisations, the aims and the expectations show such diversity. The following points are therefore presented merely as a very tentative summary.

(a) General reactions

(i) In those all-age primary schools in which i.t.a. children had reached junior classes, teachers had much less to say about the effect of i.t.a. on eight- and nine-year-old children than had teachers in separate junior schools. It seemed that once an all-age school had accepted i.t.a. for its infant classes, the thoughts of the staff were centred on the advantages to the infants rather than on its effects on juniors.

(ii) In all five of the junior schools, teachers had clearly been interested in the i.t.a. children who had entered the school and had consciously endeavoured to assess the differences between them and t.o. children. The overall pattern revealed was usually one of only small perceivable differences.

(iii) In these ten schools, although some teachers saw minor advantages and disadvantages in i.t.a. regarding its observable effect on young junior children, there was not one instance of a junior teacher or headteacher condemning the use of i.t.a. with infants.

(b) Comments on specific subjects

(i) *Reading.* Definite comments were made about reading progress in all ten schools, in contrast to writing and spelling which in certain schools were not mentioned. In six of the schools favourable comments about children's reading were made; these included a decrease in the number of non-readers entering junior classes, improvements in reading standards and better attitudes to reading. One school spoke of a slight improvement. Three schools saw no difference in reading standards, and in two of these junior schools the teachers' views were supported by the results of standardised reading tests given to both t.o. and i.t.a. children when they entered the school.

(ii) *Writing.* In two of the ten schools no comment was made about children's free writing. One school perceived no difference in the free writing and another said that it was no different, except that i.t.a. children tended to use a wider vocabulary. In five schools, the free writing of junior children was considered to have improved. In one primary school, teachers in junior classes spoke of the difficulty of teaching children, who had been used to writing freely and fluently, to punctuate and formalise their written work.

(iii) *Spelling.* In five of the ten schools no comments were made regarding children's spelling, and in one school there was considered to be no difference. Teachers in one school were of the opinion that children experienced difficulty in changing from i.t.a. to t.o. spelling, while in another school teachers had doubts on this score. In two schools an improvement in children's spelling had been noted.

III The Reading Research Unit's second experiment

.A. INTRODUCTION

Two schools which took part in the Reading Research Unit's second experiment were visited, both of which were organised on progressive lines. Discussions took place with the two headteachers concerned and with five teachers who had taught experimental classes, all of whom appeared to be good, experienced teachers.

B. COMMENTS COMMON TO BOTH SCHOOLS

The following comments were common to the headteachers and class teachers in the schools visited:

1 Although the teachers who took part in the experiment had been willing and interested to do so, they found the practice of being responsible for either Reading

or Number in two different classes neither easy nor personally satisfying. The practice was more exhausting for the teachers and afforded them less variety of subject matter and interests in the course of a day than did the usual procedure of being totally responsible for one class. The situation proved to be rather a strain on the teachers because it was so different from the procedure prevalent in normal infant classrooms in which subjects and activities overlap, mingle with and reinforce each other. The teachers felt themselves to be in artificial situations and would not have liked to continue in this way for long.

2 Headteachers, as well as teachers who had been in charge of the first- and second-year classes for reading, agreed that the i.t.a. children 'got off to a better start' in reading, but that by the end of the second year the t.o. children were about level.

3 Writing started earlier with the i.t.a. children and there was much more of it than ever before. In contrast, in the t.o. classes, the teachers always had queues of children waiting to ask them about spellings.

C. ADDITIONAL COMMENTS

Two additional points were made in one of the schools. It was a large school in an area in which there had been recent large-scale population changes, resulting in influxes of new children into the school, half-taught to read on t.o. As a consequence it had been necessary to continue to run one or two t.o. classes for these children. The headteacher of this school commented that whenever she asked a teacher to be responsible for a t.o. class, the usual response was for the teacher to groan and reply in these terms, 'If I take a t.o. class this year, will you give me an i.t.a. class again next year?'

The teacher who had been responsible for Number in both the t.o. and i.t.a. classes in the Reading Research Unit's second experiment in this school commented on the strikingly different attitudes of the two classes. She said:

'The children who were using i.t.a. showed more confidence in everything, even to their paintings: they were more adventurous altogether.'

D SUMMING-UP

1 Both headteachers are now in favour of i.t.a. and are using it in preference to t.o. One headmistress summed it up in this way:

'My satisfaction with i.t.a. is expressed in the fact that I have adopted it for the whole school. It is a happy way for the children to learn to read and write. Even if i.t.a. children are only level with t.o. children at eight years, they have learned easily and happily.'

The other said:

'I should never go back to t.o. I'd be very unhappy if I had to move to a school which was committed to t.o. and where I couldn't use i.t.a., for instance because the staff didn't want to.'

2 When the five class teachers concerned were asked the 'key question', regarding whether they would choose to use i.t.a. or t.o. if they became heads of infant schools, they all replied that they would use i.t.a.

IV Schools with their own experiments

Seven of the schools visited were carrying out their own small experiments in which an i.t.a. class was matched with a t.o. class. In contrast to experiments set up by research workers, these were essentially experiments in which individual headteachers wanted to observe in their own ways the effect of using i.t.a. and t.o. on parallel groups of children, over a period of two or three years, before making decisions about using i.t.a. throughout their schools. Consequently, the control of experimental conditions varied from school to school, but in no case were the variables tightly controlled. For instance, in none of these schools was a testing programme being carried out at regular intervals with a view to ascertaining and comparing reading, or other attainments and progress, between the parallel classes.

In all seven schools the experiments had commenced with reception children, the two groups being matched for age. In some cases children were matched for intelligence on the results of intelligence tests, and in other cases they had been allocated randomly to the two classes. In every school the headteacher had aimed at equating the two teachers for ability and experience. In two of the seven schools both the t.o. and i.t.a. classes used *Janet and John* books; in one case both classes had new *Janet and John* books and in the other only the i.t.a. class had new books. In the remaining classes a variety of books was used in the two experimental classes: for instance, in one school the i.t.a. class used *The Downing Readers*, supplemented by *Janet and John*, while the t.o. class used *Key Words Reading Scheme* supplemented by *Janet and John* and *Happy Venture*. In five of the schools, the two experimental classes had each been allocated £100 to be spent on new books – either basic readers, book-corner books or a selection of both. In all seven schools the teachers used whatever method and procedures they felt to be appropriate to the alphabet, the books or the apparatus being used.

These schools were all infant schools, but they varied in size from a one-form intake to a three-form intake and the school buildings ranged from new to very old. In socio-economic levels they covered the entire range extending from one school in an area consisting almost entirely of owner-occupied houses to an extremely poor school in a redevelopment area. The average levels of intelligence in the schools were equally varied. In three of the schools the classes were vertically grouped, while in the remaining four schools children were in age-groups. Six of the schools had not used i.t.a. prior to beginning their own experiments, but of these one had been a control school in the Reading Research Unit's experiment in 1961. The seventh school had been an experimental school in the original experiment. The school which had commenced as a control school had started its own experiment in September 1963; the remaining six schools began their experiments in September 1964. At the time when the interviewer visited these schools, one was in the second year of its own experiment, five were just beginning their third year and the last had almost completed its third year.

Despite all the differences just enumerated between these seven schools, they had nevertheless a certain number of common features. The similarities noted, although they quite clearly represent subjective assessments on the part of the interviewer, were so striking that they should be stated.

1 The schools were all very good infant schools.

2 The headmistresses were first-class.

3 The schools were staffed by above-average teachers.

4 In every school the 'atmosphere' was excellent, demonstrating very good relationships between staff, between children and between adults and children.

5 In all the schools the children had great freedom and yet there was a noticeable purposefulness and orderliness about all that the children were doing. Behaviour problems were almost non-existent, even in those schools in the poorest areas.

6 The headteachers and the staff were interested in the all-round development of children. Accordingly, all observable aspects of children's work, for example, mathematics and creative work, appeared to be of a high standard.

7 There was no strong emphasis on reading in these schools, nor anxiety to see the children reading early or quickly. Indeed in some schools headteachers stressed that there was no pressure upon children to read, while others stated that they believed in a delayed start to reading.

8 The headteachers were really prepared to take a careful look at i.t.a. with a view to reaching an unbiased conclusion as to its value. Their attitudes and those of their staffs were of general interest and considered appraisal, which contrasted with the total forthright enthusiasm evinced in many i.t.a. schools.

C. DETAILS OF SCHOOL VISITS

In the seven schools carrying out their own experiments, discussions were held with seven headteachers and fourteen members of staff. Reports on these talks are given in Appendix F. In two cases, it was considered necessary to present teachers' views within the context of certain background details referring to the individual schools. It was then possible to group the comments from the remaining schools.

D. SUMMING-UP

Of the seven headmistresses of infant schools who were conducting their own experiments, none expressed disapproval of i.t.a., although a few minor disadvantages were pointed out. Their views may be summarised simply by noting that five approved of i.t.a. and intended to continue to use it, either for part or the whole of the school; two had not yet made up their minds; none said she disapproved of i.t.a.

The reactions of the 14 members of staff who had used i.t.a. to the 'key question' of which alphabet they would use if they were appointed as heads of infant schools, were as follows: 11 said they would use i.t.a.; 2 were not sure or they would use both i.t.a. and t.o.; and one would use t.o.

This brief summary and the more detailed reports in Appendix F indicate that, in these good schools which were taking a cautious look at i.t.a. by means of their own small experiments, there was a marked tendency for headteachers and class teachers to approve of i.t.a. The majority of headteachers intended to continue to use it and the majority of class teachers were eager to do so.

CHAPTER 10

Evidence from Visitors to Schools

I The importance of visitors' evidence

THE verbal evidence supplied by teachers who had used i.t.a. forms an important part of this evaluation, yet this evidence, viewed in isolation, would not suffice to present the total picture of the use of i.t.a. in schools. Evidence from teachers in individual schools needs to be viewed against a broader background of the variety of schools within an area and the total pattern of primary schools in the country as a whole. Both the close-up and the long-range views are necessary and, in fact, complementary.

Headteachers and teachers used and observed i.t.a. in the practical situation, at that vital point of contact when children were meeting, using and reacting to the new alphabet. The strength of their evidence lies in the fact that their observations were close-ups of the actual learning situations in which they themselves were deeply involved. They discussed their observations and conclusions freely and fairly with the interviewer. Great weight must therefore be given to the views they expressed.

These close-up views of i.t.a. being used in particular schools, however, needed to be complemented by the broad observations in wider contexts which could often be supplied by knowledgeable visitors to schools. The views of local education authority advisers and inspectors were considered to be of particular importance in this respect. Many such visitors were in a position to view each school in its relation to the enormous variety of conditions to be found within their areas, and were able to relate their observations to this diverse pattern of primary schools. H.M. Inspectors, education lecturers and other knowledgeable visitors to schools were frequently able to broaden the picture even further, as their experiences usually covered schools in more than one local education authority.

Accordingly, during this enquiry, the views of as many as possible of these experienced visitors were collected. Discussions took place with a total of 63 such people, of whom 35 were local authority officials. Further details regarding these visitors are set out in Tables D/1, D/2, D/5, and D/7 in Appendix D. In addition, written evidence in the form of letters was received from other local authorities and reports drawn up by H.M. Inspectors were made available to the investigators. In these ways, a great deal of information was amassed to form a long-range view which would complement the close-up view provided by teachers.

II Local education authority officials

A. THE DIVERGENT VIEWS OF L.E.A. OFFICIALS

It can rarely be an easy task to present a large body of collected evidence in a simple, clear and fair manner. In recording the views of teachers in this report, the task was facilitated in that the majority of them reported similar findings. In contrast, it proved extremely difficult to present, in any sort of concise framework, the views of the 37 local education authority officials with whom discussions took place.

For instance, there were certain questions regarding the use of i.t.a. in infant schools to which it seemed likely that local advisers and inspectors might be able to give fairly conclusive answers. However, when the written reports on individual discussions with 20 local officials were reviewed, so many divergent opinions emerged that there was a clear need for further evidence. Accordingly, at a group discussion attended by an additional 15 local advisers and inspectors, certain predetermined topics were introduced, as talking points, by the interviewer. (See Table E/4 in Appendix E.) They consisted of those aspects of the use of i.t.a. with infants on which conflicting reports had previously been made, and additional questions to which the members of the group, because of their experience, were likely to be able to formulate answers. Yet, although interesting points were brought forward and discussed at the group meeting, few clear answers emerged. In effect, this corroborated the previous tentative conclusion derived from individual interviews that, in their appraisals of i.t.a., local education authority advisers and inspectors were far from unanimous.

One problem was that the very breadth of some local advisers' experience, providing as it did the opportunities for viewing a variety of schools using both t.o. and i.t.a. in different ways and with differing results, led them into difficulties about formulating conclusions. Some advisers had found it impossible to form definite conclusions and were frank enough to state this; others had arrived at tentative or qualified conclusions. A second problem encountered in summarising this evidence was that a proportion of the officials who had reached definite conclusions presented conflicting assessments, and, moreover, these divergences could not always be seen to follow a distinct pattern. The consequences were that the long-range view, as seen by local advisers and inspectors, was not nearly as clear or definite as the close-up view presented by teachers who had used i.t.a.

It may help to give some form to the reports which follow, if the interviewer's observations regarding the diverging views of local officials are related to the facts about the incidence of the use of i.t.a. in the various local authorities, as set out in Chapter 3. The interviewer formed the impression that local inspectors and advisers who gave evidence could be roughly divided into the following four broad divisions of opinion. It would, however, be impossible to generalise regarding the proportion of evidence in each category, as in the first place there was some overlap, and secondly there were considerable variations in the range of experiences from which the views of different people were derived. The four broad groups are as follows:

1 Those definitely in favour of i.t.a.

2 Those who expressed certain doubts or misgivings.

3 Those who could see no necessity for i.t.a. or who were not very interested in it.

4 Those who stated that they were still reserving judgement.

It can be seen that the first three categories represent varying positions on a continuum of approval-disapproval of i.t.a. It should also be noted that not one inspector or adviser declared outright disapproval of i.t.a. and, consequently, there is no category for 'those who definitely disapproved'.

It was noticed by the observer that a certain amount of correspondence existed between the number, or percentage, of schools using i.t.a. in a local authority and the position of the local official on the approval-disapproval continuum. For instance, those officials who expressed little interest in i.t.a. or who stated that they could see no need for it almost invariably came from local authorities where a negligible number of schools was using it. At the other end of the scale, advisers who were very enthusiastic about i.t.a. had usually had the widest experience, both in terms of number of schools and length of time of observing it in use. Even so, not all advisers with this breadth of experience fell into the definitely favourable category; some still had certain misgivings or had not yet made up their minds.

This observed relationship between the spread of i.t.a. and the opinions of local officials may be regarded from two angles. It might be suspected that interested officials had advised schools in their areas to use i.t.a. or, alternatively, that when advisers were not keen on i t a , they had discouraged schools from using it. The observer came across practically no evidence to support such assumptions. Most advisers reiterated that no pressures of any sort had been brought on headteachers to persuade them to use, or refrain from using, i.t.a., and as mentioned earlier, teachers themselves corroborated these statements.

The interviewer's impressions were that the manner in which the views of local officials appeared to reflect, or be reflected in, the number of schools using i.t.a. in the authority, was an expression of much more subtle relationships than direct pressures or suggestions. Headteachers, while valuing their freedom of choice in so many aspects of the life of their schools, are still sensitive to and, in most cases, respect the ideas and opinions of their local advisers. Furthermore, in county boroughs particularly, there can be very close liaison between local officials and teachers. For instance, one adviser in a county borough explained, in the following terms, why some of their schools joined the first experiment:

'The experimental schools did volunteer. However, it was not so much because they were keen to experiment with i.t.a., it was rather that they were loyal to the local education authority, and if the local authority wanted to be in on the experiment, the headteachers were willing to go along.'

Thus, the fact that local officials were known to be, or considered to be, either enthusiastic or indifferent towards i.t.a. could, in different areas, have resulted in greater or lesser amounts of experimentation with it. These variations were much more likely to have sprung from rather tenuous and often unconscious circumstances than from direct suggestions.

It is not possible to judge which of these two factors, local officials' views on i.t.a. or the number of schools in the authority using i.t.a., is cause and which is effect. It is, however, worth noting that, in general, those local officials with the greatest opportunities of observing infants using i.t.a. tended to be the most enthusiastic and those who had seen little of its use were disinterested or doubtful.

Regarding the opinions of the third category of advisers noted earlier – those who were not interested or saw no use for i.t.a. – the interviewer noted that they had two features in common. Firstly, they considered the reading standards in their authorities to be good and believed that reading was not a great problem to their teachers. Secondly, these advisers and inspectors had certain beliefs about infant education in common, and they tended to think that the introduction of i.t.a. into infant schools would result in changes in attitude and alterations of methods and organisations which they considered important. They had what is usually termed 'progressive' ideas on infant education and they laid emphasis on the importance of children having first-hand experience before beginning to read. They believed in a wide curriculum, a delayed start to reading and an informal approach to learning. They feared that the introduction of i.t.a. into infant schools would lead to early instruction, formal methods and a disregard or curtailment of other aspects of the curriculum. This description of the common beliefs of advisers in this third category should not be taken to imply that all advisers and inspectors with these progressive ideas fell into the same category of opinions regarding i.t.a. There were also many such progressive infant organisers in the remaining three suggested categories.

Most of the fourth group of people, who stated that they had not come to any clear decision, worked in local authorities in which i.t.a. had been in use in a small proportion of schools for one or two years. They, although genuinely interested, felt the need to observe the effects of i.t.a. for a longer period before making up their minds. A few of the advisers in this category had been in contact with schools using i.t.a. for three or four years, and yet, because they could perceive both advantages and disadvantages in its use, were genuinely unable to formulate definite conclusions.

The points noted above are expanded in the report which follows, in which the evidence from individual interviews has been amalgamated with the views expressed at the group meeting of local advisers and inspectors. However, owing to the diversity of views represented, it was considered necessary to formulate the interviewer's general impressions of the opinions of local officials, at this point, as without this skeleton framework, the evidence might well have appeared as a meaningless kaleidoscope of varied comments.

B. LOCAL ADVISERS' OBSERVATIONS

1   *The schools which have used i.t.a.*

(a) *The varied schools using i.t.a.*

It was pertinent to enquire whether i.t.a. had been taken up mainly by schools possessing particular characteristics: for instance, with regard to the socio-economic level of the areas in which they were situated, the intelligence of the children, the organisation of the schools, the ability of the staff, and so on. It has already been stated that the schools visited demonstrated among them combinations of all the background factors one might care to list. Yet, because of the method of selection of schools, it might be suggested that they did not constitute a representative sample of all schools using i.t.a. On the other hand, local advisers covering areas containing 41% of all schools in the country using i.t.a. with infants, might have been expected to discern common features in these schools, if such patterns existed. The fact that no clear pattern emerged is an indication that i.t.a. is being used in many different types of schools containing infant pupils.

Local advisers spoke of observing i.t.a. in use in schools in good residential areas with pupils of above-average intelligence, and in schools in poor areas with children of below-average intelligence. There was no strong evidence to suggest that these factors had affected headteachers' decisions to adopt i.t.a. A few advisers, however, did suggest that schools in deprived areas, which frequently had reading problems, had shown more initial eagerness to experiment with i.t.a. than schools in good residential areas with high reading standards, but that they had recently observed some of the latter groups of schools beginning to use i.t.a.

All-age primary schools and schools containing only infant pupils had been equally interested in, and had gained similar results with i.t.a., according to many reports. On the other hand, one adviser had noted that, at first, men headteachers of all-age primary schools in which reading standards were not very good had been those most inclined to experiment with i.t.a.

Schools with very different internal organisations, grouping of children and formality or informality of procedures had all been observed using i.t.a. Some advisers thought that initially the more formal schools had tended to be most interested in i.t.a., but others did not agree with this generalisation. The early fears of certain educationists that the introduction of i.t.a. would lead to an increase in formal teaching did not appear to have been justified. Indeed, certain inspectors reported that in some of the more formal schools the use of i.t.a. had led to greater informality in the grouping of children and in classroom procedures, as a result of children quickly becoming independent of the teacher when they found they could make good attempts at reading and spelling on their own.

There was a measure of agreement about the attitude to reading of the schools which had adopted i.t.a. The general opinion was that most of the early schools to experiment with i.t.a. believed in an early start to learning to read. More recently, however, schools which believe in a delayed beginning to reading were also using i.t.a.

Advisers reported that schools currently using i.t.a. included a wide range of methods of teaching reading. The same was true of the reading books used. Most of the early schools had had little choice but to rely fairly heavily on a basic reading scheme, supplemented by book–corner books. A number of advisers reported that in some schools which had previously followed a reading scheme rather rigidly, i.t.a. had had a liberalising effect. Children who had used i.t.a. wanted more books earlier and were interested in dipping into a variety of books, including some in t.o. Among schools which have begun to use i.t.a. more recently were some in which the teachers did not believe in using basic reading schemes, but preferred to let children use a variety of books. Some inspectors indicated that a number of such schools would not yet consider using i.t.a. because, in their view, there were still not sufficient good books available in i.t.a.

(b) Headteachers of schools using i.t.a.

A fairly close measure of agreement was evinced between local advisers concerning the quality of the headteachers who had adopted i.t.a. and, consequently, the quality and vitality of the schools. Words such as 'quality', 'progressive', 'good' and 'poorer', in this context, refer to the whole atmosphere and work of the schools and not to the level of interest or the home backgrounds of the children. These terms represent value-judgements on the part of the advisers and they would prove difficult to define precisely. Nevertheless, these words were meaningful to the people using them and were understood exactly by other advisers and by the observer. Consequently, it is impossible to avoid mentioning and quoting such terms of description.

There was a noticeable trend among local inspectors to believe that many of the more progressive headteachers had begun to use i.t.a. and that, conversely, some of the more conservative headteachers had not yet contemplated using it. The following comments stress this viewpoint:

'The schools which have taken up i.t.a. are often schools in which a rich variety of things is going on. A few are schools with reading problems but certainly not the majority.'

'The schools using i.t.a. tend to be the larger and more progressive schools.'

'The original experimental i.t.a. schools and control schools, as well as schools which have taken up i.t.a. since then, seem to be the "best" schools in the way of good headteachers and lively, interested teachers.'

'There was no pressure on headteachers to use i.t.a. It was completely voluntary, so the lively heads and enthusiastic teachers tended to take it up. Some were schools in poor areas and some were in good areas.'

Yet even on this point there was not unanimity among local advisers, some of whom were of the opinion that certain progressive headteachers were unlikely to use i.t.a. as they were satisfied with the standards of reading and free writing in their schools and thus saw no necessity for changing from t.o. to i.t.a. As one adviser commented:

'In our authority we have one or two very good schools in poor residential areas who have marvellous reading and free writing with t.o. They say, 'Why should we change to i.t.a?'

Another inspector put forward a different reason for some progressive infant head-teachers not being interested in i.t.a.:

'The high-pressure salesmanship of i.t.a. at first put off the headteachers of many good infant schools. Consequently, some of our best infant headteachers still tend to distrust i.t.a. in this area.'

An additional point of view was expressed by a few inspectors regarding the schools using i.t.a. They mentioned that there was always a certain percentage of headteachers who were 'in the habit of jumping on every new bandwagon', and that some of them had undoubtedly begun to use i.t.a.

(c) Schools which had discontinued the use of i.t.a.

One further aspect on which local officials might have been able to offer evidence, related to schools which had discarded i.t.a. after experimenting with it. The figures relating to such schools, set out in Table 2(g) in Chapter 2, record only 2% of schools which had used i.t.a. with infant pupils in England and Wales discontinuing its use. Consequently, it was not unexpected to find the majority of local advisers comment-ing that nearly all teachers who had tried i.t.a. wished to continue using it. As one adviser said, 'I have not come across any dissatisfied customer'. Where schools had reverted to t.o., the reasons were often administrative – for instance a change of head-teacher or of staff.

In certain cases, however, advisers offered explanations for schools discontinuing the use of i.t.a. which did relate to the alphabet itself. For instance, it was occasionally suggested that the decision to revert to t.o. sprang from anxiety about the timing of the transition and about spelling. In a few instances it was considered that schools with too high expectations of the effectiveness of i.t.a. had reverted to t.o. when their expectations were not realised. Following this line of thought, one or two inspectors spoke of sensing a reluctance to admit reservations about i.t.a., on the part of some teachers who were still using it and who had embarked on its use with high enthusiasm. This represented a minority viewpoint. One adviser who was acquainted with three schools which had discarded i.t.a. had noted that they were all formal schools, staffed by headteachers and class teachers of above-average age.

2 Comments regarding experiments

A number of local advisers volunteered comments relating to the experiments with i.t.a. As some of the remarks refer to the reasons for certain results being obtained and others refer to test results, it would seem appropriate to give the verbal evidence on this score prior to the straightforward observations on results. Some of these remarks refer to the Reading Research Unit's experiments, some to schools' own experiments and some to the mere fact that teachers using i.t.a. for the first time, even outside any experimental framework, were in effect experimenting with something new.

Remarks on teachers' initial enthusiasm included the following:

'There has never been, in my experience, such a wave of educational enthusiasm for anything as the wave of enthusiasm for i.t.a. Modern Mathematics is now taking away some of this enthusiasm.'

'There is always a great deal of zip in the first stages of trying something new.'

'There is always so much enthusiasm about a new approach at first, and this is unavoidable.'

In some cases it was pointed out that this initial enthusiasm, whether or not schools were part of experiments, made it difficult to know whether good results were wholly a result of using the new alphabet or partially the effect of the enthusiasm. On the other hand, one adviser from a local authority which had taken part in the Reading Research Unit's first experiment had this to say:

'Teachers who took part in the first experiment felt more committed than teachers who used i.t.a. later. The later ones seemed to regard it more soberly and yet they approve. They still think it's a quicker and more effective way of teaching children to read.'

One adviser from an authority which joined the Reading Research Unit's experiment in 1961 was convinced that teachers in the experimental classes had worked harder at reading than ever before, as the following quotation shows:

'Once the experimental classes started, the teachers were keen and worked hard. They put their best foot forward. One man headteacher who had never bothered much about reading before was always taking i.t.a. reading groups in his room. I am sure that this went on in most or all of the i.t.a. schools. I am certain that they all spent more time on reading than formerly.'

A few other inspectors suggested that originally teachers' enthusiasm had led to more than the normal amount of time being spent on reading and writing but the majority did not offer comments on this point.

The large amount of testing which took place in both experimental and control schools in the Reading Research Unit's first experiment came under fire from a certain number of local officials. For instance, one adviser said:

'There was far too much testing and mainly it was the teachers who were expected to do it. The headteacher of one control school would have withdrawn from the experiment because of the weight of testing, if the Reading Research Unit had not finally agreed to send out testers to do it for him.'

Even more seriously, the quality of the testing and the reliability of the results were questioned by a few advisers. Examples of such comments, from three different local education authorities which took part in the Reading Research Unit's first experiment, are given in detail:

'I was very unhappy about the results which were being published because of my doubts about the testing. The Reading Research Unit did send out a few testers but it was mainly the teachers who did it. I doubt if test results obtained by teachers and by outside testers are ever comparable, because teachers find it almost impossible to test without helping the children. To give you one example, I was running a small experiment on i.t.a. myself. In one i.t.a. school, the reading test results as obtained by the teachers were so high that knowing the school I couldn't believe them. So, I got the educational psychologist to test both the i.t.a. and the t.o. schools. The results as obtained by the educational psychologist were lower in both sets of schools. The t.o. schools' results dropped a little; the i.t.a. schools' results dropped tremendously. Therefore I think that exactly the same thing may have happened in the Reading Research Unit's first experiment.'

'At the end of the third and fourth years of the experiment, Schonell's Graded Word Reading Test in t.o. was given to every child at the stage of transfer to the Junior School. The control schools had considerably better results than the i.t.a. experimental classes—but a small proportion of children in the latter classes had not transferred at that time.'

'When the first experimental groups were tested at seven plus, I was extremely surprised by the good results. (The testing had been undertaken by one person sent by the Reading Research Unit and one person from the school.) The remedial staff therefore retested the same children on the same test—Schonell's Graded Word Reading Test. The results were a lot lower than the research results. In fact, in the group of children with the reputedly highest scores, i.e. Reading Age of 7+, there was an average drop of 1·3 years.'

'Our educational psychologist did some reading testing on new entrants to one junior school. The children came from two different infant schools. They were both in the same sort of areas and the quality of the teaching was the same in both schools. One infant school had used i.t.a. and one had used t.o. The test results showed no significant differences between the two groups of children.'

One comment was also made regarding the validity of one specific assessment of reading progress used by the Reading Research Unit, that is the basic reading book which the children were using. This adviser pointed out the difficulty of knowing exactly what is implied when a report says, 'Children can read such and such a book'. He had retested some of the same children in the experiment by 'hearing them read' the books they could reputedly read. He found that the children were making as much as 20% errors.

Finally, regarding the question of testing reading ability, there were a few proposals that some objective testing should be undertaken when the novelty of i.t.a. had worn off. One adviser expressed the view that it would be extremely interesting, 'now that the hubbub has died down and after teachers have had five years' experience with i.t.a.,' if testing could be carried out in the original experimental and control schools. This would prove of particular interest, in that 'some of these original schools are now involved in Nuffield Mathematics and Science Projects, and so reading would only be getting its fair proportion of time and attention.'

3   *Observations of results in infant classes*

(a) *Progress in reading and writing*

Teachers' beliefs concerning the results of using i.t.a. with infants were sometimes confirmed by local advisers and sometimes contradicted or tempered.

Certain local officials, and more particularly those who had observed i.t.a. in use for the longest time in the greatest number of schools, were very favourably impressed, and convinced that the introduction of i.t.a. had resulted in an increase in the standards of reading and free writing in those infant classes which had used it. The following are typical remarks made by this group of advisers:

'I was not very enthusiastic at first but after seeing i.t.a. in use I firmly believe that it is more effective than t.o.'

'This simplified alphabet does definitely make it easier for children to learn to read and it makes an enormous improvement in creative writing.'

'Reading certainly seems easier and happier in the early stages.'

'I believe that it is natural for children when they begin to learn to read to expect that sounds and written symbols will have a one-to-one correspondence. One could say that children want to find a regular and ordered pattern when they learn to read; i.t.a. provides this.'

As it happened, the remarks of most local advisers with wide experiences of observing infants using i.t.a. were similar to those of teachers in respect of children's earlier, easier and happier progress in reading and writing. No purpose would be achieved by quoting additional comments on this score.

A few officials noted that children's rapid progress in reading had led to a change in the expectations of those teachers who had used i.t.a. for a number of years, without their always realising it: some of them had begun to forget the standards of reading which had been considered normal when t.o. was used.

In contrast to these favourable reports by local officials, were a few which indicated that little or no improvement in reading and writing had been noted. In some cases these remarks came from local authorities in which tests of children's reading ability were carried out annually at the age of 7+. In one such authority the adviser spoke in these terms:

'Whatever the headteachers say, I am certain that i.t.a. has not made a scrap of difference to their reading standards. However, in one school which started to use i.t.a. it has added life and vitality to the school. It brought enthusiasm to the teachers and the attitude of the school was revitalised.'

Occasionally a rider was added to an otherwise favourable report on results in connection with the slowest group of children, as in the following comment:

> 'It has relieved children of spelling problems so that we now get uninhibited writing. The bright and average children learn to read more quickly but I'm not sure about slower children. These children certainly have more confidence with i.t.a.; they believe they can read more easily but there still seem to be some slow readers who take as long to read on i.t.a. as on t.o.'

A number of other officials expressed doubts or disappointments regarding the discernible results of using i.t.a. with the slowest children in infant schools as follows:

> 'Even many schools which approve of i.t.a., and many do, are disappointed that it has not really helped the slowest children. For example, an infant school which usually sent up about twelve non-readers to the junior school sent up the same number last year after using i.t.a.'

> 'I had hoped that i.t.a. would help the slower children. My impression now is that it has not improved the standards of the very slowest children. Schools on some council house estates which always had poor readers, now with i.t.a. still have many children going up to the junior school not reading. Probably no reading approach will help these children as the fault lies in their lack of language development.'

> 'A few of the original (1961) experimental children had not made the transfer to t.o. by the beginning of the school year in September 1965–i.e. after four years.'

On the other hand, in one authority, remedial teachers who worked with the non-readers entering junior schools seemed to think that there was an untestable bonus in the non-readers who had been exposed to i.t.a. They found them a little easier to teach than the non-readers from t.o. schools.

Additional views representing doubts about children's reading progress with i.t.a. more often came from those advisers who had seen least of it in use. For instance, it was said that the best use of t.o. had not yet been fully explored and that if the same enthusiasm was applied to exploiting the potentialities of t.o. as had been applied to experimenting with i.t.a., the results might be very satisfactory. Certain officials also pointed out that reading standards in general were improving, in schools which used t.o. as well as schools using i.t.a., while others suggested that increased reading standards in i.t.a. classes might be the result of teachers spending more time on reading because of their own interest in a new approach.

(b) The transition in reading

Certain observations regarding the transfer in reading from i.t.a. to t.o. were made. A number of officials, like the one below, reported that children did not find the transition troublesome:

> 'We have not hurried the transition, but those who have transferred have not experienced difficulty.'

There was also a tendency to emphasise that children should have read plenty of books in i.t.a. and be fluent readers before the transition to t.o. was effected. Certain other advisers saw a danger when heads of infant schools were doubtful about junior schools giving adequate help to those children who were still reading in i.t.a. at seven plus. There was concern lest this worry should result in infant teachers forcing the transition before children were ready for it.

One local official made an interesting observation about the transition from the teacher's point of view. This adviser had sent out a questionnaire to all class teachers in the authority who were using i.t.a. By chance, some of the completed questionnaires were forwarded directly to the adviser while others arrived via headteachers. A difference was perceived in these two batches of returns. In those sent directly to the adviser, most teachers stated that, although they felt that i.t.a. had something to offer in the early stage, the weight of teaching at the transition stage when two blackboards had to be kept going and everything written twice, was too heavy for the teacher, especially with classes of 40. Such a viewpoint was not expressed so strongly in the replies which teachers had handed in to their headteachers.

(c) *Additional observations*

It will be recalled that certain topics on which local advisers were expected to have drawn conclusions were listed and brought up in discussions. As it happened, on some of these topics, for example the effect of i.t.a. on children's spelling ability and on other aspects of the curriculum or life of infant schools, few comments were made. On the other hand, with individuals as well as in group discussion, many aspects of i.t.a. other than those listed were talked about. Two examples of ideas which sprang from local advisers are given.

One adviser put forward an interesting question regarding children making an early start to reading, expressed in the following terms:

'If headteachers really believe, as they say they do, that i.t.a. helps children to learn to read more easily in the early stages and if so many children entering schools have poor spoken language, as they do seem to have, why do these schools begin to teach reading to children on entry? Why don't they spend a few terms in enriching children's spoken vocabulary before beginning to teach reading with i.t.a. – a task which shouldn't take long?'

In the same vein, another adviser also expressed concern lest the introduction of i.t.a. should lead to an undue emphasis on reading skills to the neglect of the development of speech.

An additional point of view was raised by certain local advisers, who were so conscious of the advantages of using i.t.a. for remedial work with older children who had failed to learn to read with t.o., that they would have preferred infant schools to continue to use t.o. while at the same time exploring ways in which this medium might be used to the best advantage. Good teaching with t.o., they felt, would result in few children failing to learn to read. These few failures could then be given a new start with i.t.a.

Certain other points raised by advisers and inspectors, without being expanded here, are included in the list of advantages and disadvantages which concludes this section of the report on the verbal evidence of local officials. These represent views which have already been developed fully in the report on teachers' evidence, and consequently require no elaboration of points which are self-explanatory.

113

4 Observations of results in junior classes

Verbal evidence regarding results in junior classes, for those children who had used i.t.a. as infants, could only be obtained from officials in those authorities which had begun to use i.t.a. in 1961 or 1962. Reports on this score varied. A written report from one local authority, summarising junior headteachers' opinions, indicated that reading standards of children coming from i.t.a. infant classes had risen. A further few advisers were of the opinion that, as a result of i.t.a., fewer non-readers were entering junior classes.

One adviser noted a difference in the observations of headteachers of junior schools which were fed by i.t.a. children and heads of all-age primary schools, as follows:

'I perceive a difference in the attitudes of heads of junior schools to heads of all-age primary schools. The former do not seem to think that i.t.a. has made as much difference to children by the time they are eight or nine as do the heads of all-age schools.'

As has already been reported, a few authorities who carried out regular reading tests on children at the age of 7+ saw very little or no difference in reading standards as a result of i.t.a. being used in infant classes. One adviser remarked on the difficulty that heads of junior schools experienced in pin-pointing differences in standards between i.t.a. and t.o. children.

'By the time children reach the first or second junior class there doesn't seem to be much difference between t.o. and i.t.a. children. When I ask the headteachers about standards of reading and writing they find it difficult to answer. They tend to say that it is difficult to judge because years of children are always different.'

Further observations on junior classes came from certain other advisers who commented that teachers in junior classes had not yet learned to exploit, or build upon, the fluency of reading and writing which had been fostered in children who had used i.t.a. in infant classes.

5 Results as related to staff

There was some diversity of opinion among local advisers regarding the effects of teachers of varying degrees of experience and ability using i.t.a. However, no adviser who had observed teachers using i.t.a. expressed the opinion that teachers of any level of ability obtained lower standards than they would have done if they had used t.o., and there was a pronounced tendency to believe that most teachers obtained better results.

Certain advisers who supported these views noted that not all schools in their authorities obtained identical results with i.t.a. The variety of standards attained was attributed by them mainly to the quality of the staff. For instance, one said:

'In our authority, the schools have had varying results. Some schools still have non-readers after two years. But one very good school, with a stable staff, has done much better with i.t.a. than the other schools. They have no non-readers after two years and have had to rewrite the syllabus for their top infants because they can all read.'

Advisers in this group usually emphasised that the ablest teachers obtained the best results and the less able teachers, although doing better with i.t.a. than with t.o., nevertheless did less well than their more able colleagues–a position which the advisers pointed out was true in any teaching situation.

In fact, there was a strong measure of support for the idea that the introduction of i.t.a. had led to the greatest increase in the efficiency of reading teaching among less able teachers. Local inspectors who had reached this conclusion instanced ways in which they felt i.t.a. was raising the level of competence of such teachers. Factors mentioned in this context centred round the regularity of the alphabet, the enthusiasm engendered by using a new approach, and rethinking about reading and specific training, as can be seen in the following remarks:

'Because the alphabet is regular and clearly structured it is easier for young teachers and less able teachers to do better with it.'

'A general improvement in the approach of the less able teacher may arise, in that i.t.a. encourages them to think more analytically than does t.o.'

'The use of i.t.a. has engendered a great deal of enthusiasm and resulted in much discussion among teachers which has given new impetus to some average and below-average teachers who had got into a rut with t.o.'

'It has made teachers listen carefully to their own pronunciation of words.'

'Teachers who have never attended courses in their lives have gone to courses on i.t.a.'

'I found that many infant teachers really knew very little about teaching reading and so the course on i.t.a. which the local education authority arranged for those teachers who volunteered to use i.t.a. did give them some training in reading teaching.'

'Not only young teachers are interested in i.t.a. and eager to learn more about it. Even teachers near retiring age are going to courses and conferences.'

In contrast to those local advisers who had noted the greatest improvement in the efficiency of less able teachers, certain officials had been extremely impressed with the results obtained in classes taught by teachers of the highest calibre. One such adviser described how in the classes of the ablest of the teachers in the authority, the results obtained with i.t.a. were 'fantastically higher' than with t.o.

An opposing point of view emerged when certain inspectors who reported that the use of i.t.a. had helped to raise the standards of teaching of the less able and the less experienced teachers, sometimes went on to remark that good teachers had always obtained good results. The following comments illustrate this point:

'In the hands of the right teachers i.t.a. does very well, but these are the teachers who would have done well even with slates and slate-pencils.'

'Miss —— has adopted i.t.a., which she uses with good results. She is a keen and enthusiastic teacher and would, I think, have succeeded by any method that she herself believes in.'

In one local education authority, an adviser had wanted to observe i.t.a. in use in one of the 'best' infant schools in the authority. This was a school which had never used a basic reading scheme in t.o. but had relied on the children reading widely from different books which interested them. The standard of reading had always been high and the children's free writing prolific. The headmistress had agreed to use i.t.a., with one of three parallel classes, to see if it did improve children's reading performance. After two years she was contemplating discarding i.t.a. because the children's reading and free writing were no better than they would have been with t.o.

One local adviser, with very wide opportunities for observing schools using both i.t.a. and t.o., had definitely concluded that good teachers did no better with i.t.a. than with t.o., but that less able teachers, as well as the children in their classes, had benefited. The opinions which follow were reiterated by a number of local inspectors:

'Good schools have done no better with i.t.a. than with t.o. as regards reading; they have maintained their standards but not improved them. The poorer schools have improved their standards because there has been more attention focused on reading and more enthusiasm. More teachers have gone to courses and learned something about reading.'

'The free writing in the poorer schools has improved. Many teachers who never used free writing before alongside reading are now finding that it occurs automatically. This is particularly true of all-age primary schools in the charge of headmasters. In some of these schools there was no free writing previously, so there has been a definite improvement. However, in good schools where children always did write, i.t.a. has probably enabled the children to use a wider vocabulary.'

Many local inspectors who had observed both i.t.a. and t.o. in use in numerous infant classes were obviously facing a dilemma here. They constitute the two categories mentioned earlier: those who were doubtful or who had certain misgivings, and those who had not yet reached firm decisions. Their dilemma was partially related to the calibre of the staff in different schools and their observations of excellent reading and free writing in both t.o. and i.t.a. classes. A number of advisers emphasised that the quality of the headteacher and the staff was more important than the medium used. Two examples of some comments are quoted:

'Results with both t.o. and i.t.a. depend so much on the quality of the staff.'

'The schools in our area have had varying results with i.t.a. One very good school (meaning good teachers) did much better with i.t.a. than all the others. Yet, on the other hand, we have one or two very good schools in poor residential areas which have marvellous reading and writing with t.o.'

One or two officials who were not particularly interested in i.t.a. clearly had in mind that the ablest teachers in their areas did very good work with t.o. and that, if all teachers could be trained or encouraged to do the same, there would not be any need for i.t.a.

On the question of teachers receiving special training in the use of i.t.a., a few advisers thought it should be compulsory. One suggested that Colleges of Education might do some of this training with their students. Another adviser drew attention to an additional problem concerning training: in an area of changing staff, the teachers who attended courses on i.t.a. would not necessarily be those who were teaching the children with i.t.a. in the course of a year or so.

C. LOCAL ADVISERS' CONCLUSIONS

1 General conclusions

The conclusions drawn by local officials who have observed infants using i.t.a. and noted the results when these infants reached junior classes, were extremely diverse and also extraordinarily difficult to summarise. In some areas, notably those in which the use of i.t.a. was most widespread, the advisers concerned were very favourably disposed towards it. Yet in a number of similar areas, the officials were still uncertain of the conclusions to be drawn or they had certain misgivings.

No local education authority official expressed outright disapproval. Those who were least favourably disposed to i.t.a. or who showed little interest in it were usually satisfied with the reading standards in their schools and so thought it unnecessary to consider the use of a simplified alphabet.

Many local inspectors who had observed i.t.a. in use and compared it with their experience of observing large numbers of schools using t.o. still felt unable to formulate definite conclusions. Sometimes the very breadth of their experience or their realisation of, as one adviser phrased it, 'the difficulty of separating all the strands which lead to better reading,' was the cause of their reluctance to form hasty judgements.

The difficulty experienced by many officials in reaching definite decisions is highlighted by the following two telling illustrations from advisers in different authorities. In one authority the adviser, who was quite favourably disposed towards i.t.a., had observed a few infant schools using *Words in Colour*, and was of the opinion that in these schools the reading standards were higher than in the schools using i.t.a. The second example gives a very clear picture of why an adviser who has observed i.t.a. in use for four years is still reluctant to formulate definite conclusions. It should first be noted that this was an authority in which the adviser had stated that the majority of schools which had taken up i.t.a. were progressive schools; that no school which had started to use it was thinking of giving it up; and that 'reading with i.t.a. seems easier and happier in the earlier stages'. Nevertheless, this inspector's uncertainty about the rival merits of i.t.a. and t.o. is well demonstrated in the following remark to the interviewer:

'If you were to visit all the infant schools in this authority, you might be more impressed by the reading in the t.o. schools than in the i.t.a. schools.'

2 Advantages and disadvantages

The foregoing brief summary of the general conclusions regarding i.t.a. arrived at by local inspectors can probably best be amplified by reference to the advantages and disadvantages noted by them. Accordingly, the points for and against i.t.a. which were put forward by local officials in individual interviews, as well as in the group discussion, have been amalgamated and summarised in the following points. It should be noted that certain of the points included in these lists have not been expanded earlier in this section of the report but are included here in order to complete the report of the verbal evidence of local advisers and inspectors. Those advantages and disadvantages –

or dangers, as they were often termed – which are starred, were mentioned by a number of officials; the remainder were made by individuals.

(a) *Advantages*

* (i) Children read earlier.

* (ii) Children learn to read more easily and are happier.

* (iii) Children's morale is high.

* (iv) Children soon gain confidence in their own ability and so read books other than their reading books. The use of the library corner has increased.

* (v) There is an increase in children's free writing.

* (vi) i.t.a. has stirred up a new interest in reading among teachers. There has been more discussion, more reading and an increased attendance at lectures and conferences by teachers.

* (vii) The standard of teaching reading by less able and less experienced teachers has improved.

(viii) The early good reading has helped other subjects, e.g. mathematics.

(ix) Children listen to how words are sounded.

(x) It increases parents' morale when their children read earlier.

(xi) The very slowest children, for whom, when they first come to school, reading is too hard anyway, may gain a secondary advantage from i.t.a. in that their teacher will have more time to spend with them.

(xii) It has made teachers listen carefully to their own pronunciation of words.

(xiii) It helps children to get a 'learning set'; then early success is likely to lead to further success.

(b) *Disadvantages*

* (i) There is a problem when children change schools.

* (ii) There is a problem relating to children who have not transferred to t.o. going to junior schools in which they may not receive adequate help with i.t.a. In these circumstances, there is a danger that infant teachers may be tempted to introduce a too-early transfer.

* (iii) The young beginning reader is exposed to one alphabet in the classroom and another one outside it, whereas what he most needs is regularity.

* (iv) Some parents are still anxious when they know that their children are going to use i.t.a. This applies particularly in good homes with plentiful supplies of t.o. books.

* (v) Even now (December 1966), the choice of books printed in i.t.a. is not sufficiently large.

* (vi) The quality of i.t.a. books is not yet good enough; transliterated copies of t.o. books do not adequately cater for children's requirements.

* (vii) Schools are faced with the dual expense of both t.o. and i.t.a. books.

(viii) The feeling of failure of children who do not learn to read in the infant school may be increased because of an emphasis on reading and the fact that more children do learn to read.

III Her Majesty's Inspectors

Two confidential reports on i.t.a. prepared by H.M. Inspectors, relating to information collected in May 1963 and September 1964, were made available to the researchers. The second report was more comprehensive than the first: for instance, it recorded that H.M. Inspectors had observed i.t.a. in use in 171 of the 174 schools which began to use it in 1961, 1962 and 1963. Furthermore, the second report reversed or amended the views expressed on certain points in the earlier report, which had been based on more limited observations. Accordingly, this evaluation has leaned more heavily on the second than the first report.

Conclusions from the written reports are here amalgamated with the impressions gained in a few personal conversations with members of H.M. Inspectorate. Altogether they represent a considerable body of evidence from people with wide experiences of observing and assessing the staff and children, the media and methods employed, and the results obtained in a large variety of schools in different parts of the country. The importance of this evidence requires no stressing.

A. GENERAL IMPRESSIONS

The views of H.M. Inspectors presented a much more consolidated body of opinion than those of local advisers. The general impression is that, despite certain misgivings on a number of aspects of the use of i.t.a. in the first year or two, by September 1964 the majority of H.M. Inspectors tended to be favourably impressed by i.t.a.; it being noticeable that those who had seen most of it were the most enthusiastic, while those who were doubtful were those with least experience of i.t.a.

B. SCHOOLS WHICH HAVE USED i.t.a.

Although early impressions had led to the suggestion that the schools which first used i.t.a. were the less good schools, namely those which found difficulty in teaching reading or which were in areas with special reading problems, further observations had contradicted this suggestion. H.M. Inspectors' observations led them to conclude that both the schools using i.t.a. in the Reading Research Unit's first experiment and schools using i.t.a. outside the experiment were on the whole rather above average. It was also noted that, almost without exception, those 'good' headteachers who had experimented with i.t.a. were completely convinced of its efficacy.

The schools which had begun to use i.t.a. were usually those in which a belief in the importance of reading was reflected in an early start to teaching it. Few of them, however, were schools with a marked emphasis on phonic methods, the majority beginning reading with a 'look-and-say' method. Most of the schools using i.t.a. had not changed their previous methods of teaching reading, although some had slightly modified their previous practices in the direction of phonics or by beginning reading a little earlier.

By September 1964, H.M. Inspectors throughout the country had only noted four schools which had actually dropped i.t.a., and four additional schools which were considering discarding it. The reasons given were mainly due to extraneous circumstances such as staffing problems or shortage of books. In no case had a good school been observed to abandon i.t.a. after a considered appraisal in properly controlled circumstances.

Commenting on the publicity which had accompanied the introduction of i.t.a., H.M. Inspectors concluded that although a few of the original experimental schools seemed to have suffered from the publicity which led to them having large numbers of visitors, the general effect of publicity had been stimulating. Many teachers had felt themselves caught up in a successful and important experiment and they had thought afresh about their methods. In contrast, a lack of stimulus in the majority of the control schools was commented on, in the first report. However, in the latter report, the opinions of H.M. Inspectors on this point were divided: half felt that the control schools they had observed had been well served in the way of lectures and visits; the other half thought that they had been badly served. It was considered probable that these different views represented variations in experimental conditions in different areas.

D. OBSERVED RESULTS OF USING i.t.a.

1 *Reading*

The majority of H.M. Inspectors who had seen i.t.a. in use with infants had concluded that children learned to read more quickly and more easily than with t.o., the few who had reservations on this score being inspectors with little experience of i.t.a. A marked decline in the number of non-starters in reading had been observed to result from the easier and speedier learning which i.t.a. had made possible. With regard to the question of transfer, every inspector who had observed children transferring from i.t.a. to t.o. supported the view that the children experienced little or no difficulty at this point.

The opinions of the vast majority of H.M. Inspectors were that the use of i.t.a. had resulted in an improvement in children's attitudes to reading. The same was true with reference to children's comprehension of what they read, most of H.M. Inspectors believing that i.t.a. had brought about an improvement in this respect. Some doubts were expressed as to whether all schools were catering adequately, in their provision of books, for children whose reading ability, comprehension and interests had increased. It was felt that both the requisite quantity and quality of books was lacking in certain schools.

Of the total number of H.M. Inspectors who had observed i.t.a. in infant classes, only a small proportion had had the opportunity of noting the reading progress, at 7+ and 8+, of those children whose beginning reading experience had been with i.t.a. Some of this small group of inspectors felt that the children who had learned to read quickly and easily with i.t.a. had retained their advantage at 7+ and 8+; some thought otherwise.

2 *Written English and spelling*

In respect of written English, the majority view was that the use of i.t.a. had effected an improvement. One inspector with a large experience of observing i.t.a. was particularly impressed with the very significant improvement in the quantity and quality of the written work of the less able children which he had noted. Comments on the effect of i.t.a. on spelling were not so conclusive: certain inspectors mentioned improvements, some deterioration, and others no noticeable effect.

3 Effect on the general life of the school

Opinions on the effect of the use of i.t.a. on other aspects of the life of the school were varied. More than half of the members of H.M. Inspectorate had observed good effects, such as children being more confident and better behaved, and less able children having healthier attitudes. Some had observed no differences in the life of the schools, but several of these remarks referred to schools which were considered very good before the introduction of i.t.a. In a few schools it was thought that the introduction of i.t.a. had led to a neglect of creative work. Conversely, in a few schools the creative work and other subjects were considered to have benefited, because the introduction of i.t.a. had released the teacher from spending so much time on teaching reading.

E. SUMMARY OF THE VIEWS OF H.M. INSPECTORS

The observations of H.M. Inspectors on the use of i.t.a. in the early stages of reading and writing represented a cohesion of opinions which was in contrast to the diversity of views expressed by local authority advisers and inspectors. In fact, the conclusions of the majority of H.M. Inspectors were very closely in line with those of local officials who had a breadth of experience of observing i.t.a. Most of H.M. Inspectors were favourably impressed with i.t.a., the same tendency being noticeable as among local inspectors for those who expressed doubts to be those who had seen least of it. Many of H.M. Inspectors who had harboured certain misgivings in the early years of its use had, by September 1964, found most of their fears unjustified and their doubts resolved.

H.M. Inspectors had concluded that over the country as a whole both the schools which took part in the Reading Research Unit's experiments and schools using i.t.a. outside experiments were mostly rather above average, that 'good' headteachers were convinced of the advantages of using i.t.a. and that in no case had a good school been observed to discard i.t.a. after giving it a fair trial.

The majority of H.M. Inspectors were in agreement regarding children's reading progress with i.t.a., their improved attitude to reading, their comprehension of what they read, and the fact that they experienced no difficulty in transferring to t.o. Doubts were felt about the quantity and quality of books available to cater for children's expanding reading ability. Of those members of H.M. Inspectorate who had observed the results of using i.t.a. by the time children reached the ages of seven and eight, opinions were divided as to whether infants who had learned to read early and quickly had retained this advantage in junior classes. The majority opinion was that the use of i.t.a. had brought about an improvement in written English: conclusions concerning spelling, however, varied. More than half of H.M. Inspectors had noted improvements in children's confidence, behaviour and attitudes; the remainder saw no change.

IV Education lecturers

Among those knowledgeable visitors to schools who had observed i.t.a. in use, local inspectors and members of H.M. Inspectorate represented the two groups of people with the widest and most continuous opportunities for comparative assessments. A third group of people, having rather more limited opportunities for visiting schools using both i.t.a. and t.o. than the preceding two groups, consisted of University and College of Education lecturers. Individual discussions were arranged with eight such lecturers; they were supplemented by two group discussions with five and three additional lecturers respectively. Further evidence from lecturers in Universities and Colleges of Education came from listening to lectures which they gave and from receiving written evidence from an additional few.

A minority of the lecturers concerned had only observed i.t.a. being used in one or two schools; others had visited more schools. Most of them had read and thought a good deal about i.t.a. Nevertheless it should be noted that their total experience of observing i.t.a. in use was considerably less than that of the advisers and inspectors in the first two groups.

A. GENERAL IMPRESSIONS

In general, the appraisal of i.t.a. made by lecturers in Colleges of Education and University Departments of Education was not very enthusiastic. It was certainly much less favourable than the reports of H.M. Inspectors and of those local advisers who had had most experience of i.t.a. In many respects, the opinions of lecturers were in line with the views expressed by certain local inspectors with limited experience of seeing i.t.a. in use.

The majority of lecturers interviewed tended to query the value of, or the need for, i.t.a., rather than to applaud or decry its use. The main points made by lecturers are summarised quite briefly, since many of them have already been developed in detail earlier in the report.

B. DOUBTS ABOUT i.t.a.

One of the main doubts about the use of i.t.a. related to infants being surrounded by t.o. outside school and at home, while using i.t.a. in the classroom. A second doubt concerned 'the problem of unlearning' in both reading and spelling. Fears were also expressed that, in the teaching of reading, the use of i.t.a. might lead to an emphasis on phonics and on technical competence without due regard for comprehension. A further danger mentioned was that those schools which took up i.t.a. merely in order to have children reading earlier might tend to neglect other activities. Concern was expressed for children who had to change schools, in that the use of i.t.a. might lead to a floating population of children who could read neither i.t.a. nor t.o. A certain mis-use of i.t.a. was remarked on by a few lecturers who gave instances of children, able to read in t.o. before they began school, being started again on i.t.a.

Doubts about the value of i.t.a. were often related to a belief that, if teachers put the same energy into the use of t.o. as they did into i.t.a., they would obtain similar results. One further point relating to t.o. was expressed in the view that, with many children who cannot read, it is not the orthography that is the chief stumbling block. Such children might be able to learn to read with t.o. if they were taught differently.

C. OBSERVED ADVANTAGES OF i.t.a.

The advantages of i.t.a., as observed by some lecturers, included earlier free writing and earlier acquisition of the skill of decoding words which, in turn, caused children to exhibit more independence about endeavouring to read books outside a basic reading scheme. Fewer non-readers passing from infant to junior classes, with a consequent reduction in the amount of remedial work required, was also mentioned.

Of the reasons put forward by lecturers in education for the observed success of i.t.a. only the following one related specifically to the alphabet itself.

'The real problem in the teaching of reading for the practising teacher is that our system of spelling so often departs from principles of alphabet writing. i.t.a., although not entirely phonetic, has fewer inconsistencies, is more logical and therefore easier to teach. Hence its popularity with teachers of large classes.'

Other reasons suggested for some of the success were that, in the first experiments, the best teachers in the school were given the i.t.a. classes, and that the later as well as the earlier schools to use i.t.a. were in the charge of headteachers who were 'keen types who would make a good shot at anything'. Another reason advanced to explain some of the success of i.t.a. was that once schools had spent a lot of money on i.t.a. books, teachers felt they ought to work hard at it. An additional suggestion was that i.t.a. had a 'halo effect' with some teachers.

One particularly interesting suggestion came from a College of Education lecturer in Infant Education. Her observations had led her to conclude that some of the teacher's enthusiasm stems from the fact that she herself is coping with i.t.a. It represents a challenge to the teacher. Part of her pleasure in using it is in mastering i.t.a. herself and knowing that she is then capable of using two alphabets. Her pleasure in meeting and overcoming this challenge increases her enthusiasm for 'getting it over' to the children. In infant schools, with their constantly changing staffs of new, young teachers and married women returners, i.t.a. may continue to represent this sort of challenge to fresh teachers.

D. CONCLUSIONS

The fact that most of the lecturers in University Departments of Education and Colleges of Education who expressed their views on i.t.a. had grave reservations about its value is exemplified in the replies to the 'key question' put to eight College of Education lecturers at the conclusions of the two group discussions. They were asked if they would use i.t.a. or t.o. if they were now in charge of infant schools. One lecturer indicated that she would use i.t.a., but not for all children; five said they would use t.o., and two had not seen sufficient of i.t.a. in use to enable them to make decisions.

Two observations made by the interviewer regarding the views of lecturers ought to be included at this point. It became quite clear in the course of discussions that many of the lecturers, particularly the older and more experienced ones, had taken exception to the original publicity regarding i.t.a. and to what they considered the premature and continuing publication of results. They were inclined to think that the original claims of the early users were exaggerated, and that the whole project was not in line with the professional procedures usually adopted for either carrying out long-term research projects in comparative obscurity or for the introduction and development of new ideas into schools. This original reaction against i.t.a. had in some cases coloured later observations. In certain instances, the lecturers had visited i.t.a. schools in the early days, been rather doubtful about the effects of visitors on the children and various other aspects of some of the first experimental classes, and had visited few schools using i.t.a. in the succeeding years.

Secondly, it was noted that most of the lecturers who subscribed to the view that results with t.o. were equally as good as results with i.t.a. were fairly new recruits to the staffs of Colleges of Education. They had usually come from infant schools where they had proved themselves exceptionally good headmistresses. They had sometimes visited only a few i.t.a. schools and were not yet acquainted with a large variety of t.o. schools. Consequently, they did not always realise that they might have been comparing the results achieved in average or below average i.t.a. schools with the high standards obtained by themselves in their former t.o. schools.

V Summary of evidence from visitors to schools

A. INTRODUCTION

In trying to form a global impression of the long-range view of the use of i.t.a. with infants, as represented by the views of knowledgeable visitors to schools, certain factors regarding the different experiences of three specific groups of visitors should be borne in mind.

Lecturers from Colleges of Education and University Departments of Education formed the group with the least experience of observing i.t.a., owing to the fact that only a small proportion of their time was spent in schools.

The group comprising local education authority advisers and inspectors consisted of people of whom the majority had a breadth of experience of observing t.o. in use in infant schools but whose experiences of observing i.t.a. varied greatly. Some had observed only a few schools using i.t.a., while others must be regarded as ranking among those who had made the most continuous observations of the largest number of children using i.t.a., over the longest periods of time.

The third group, comprising H.M. Inspectors, had certain features in common with local inspectors, while differing in other respects from this group of observers. The main similarity between the two groups lay in the fact that visits to schools formed part of their daily routines and, consequently, their powers of assessment, based on their observations, were generally highly developed. The second similarity lay in the range of schools using i.t.a. seen by members of both groups. As with local advisers, some of H.M. Inspectors had visited many i.t.a. schools while others had visited few.

Despite these similarities between the two groups of inspectors, they differed in certain respects. For instance, it was likely that those local advisers in whose authorities many schools were using i.t.a. had studied the effects of i.t.a. more intensively and more continuously than H.M. Inspectors, whose visits to any one school are usually less frequent. On the other hand, many of H.M. Inspectors have wider experiences of infant schools, throughout the country, than have most local officials. Furthermore, H.M. Inspectors tend to communicate more with each other, at meetings as well as by written reports, than do local officials between one authority and another. The result is that, while in some instances local officials may have a deeper knowledge of the day-to-day working and the results of i.t.a., many of H.M. Inspectors have broader backgrounds of experience of infant schools teaching reading by means of the traditional alphabet, against which they may judge i.t.a.

The general impressions of the use of i.t.a. formed from all the opinions expressed by knowledgeable visitors to schools may be summarised broadly under three main conclusions.

1   Those people with the widest experience of assessing various aspects of infant education, namely H.M. Inspectors, and those with the greatest experience of observing numerous children using i.t.a. for the longest periods, namely local education authority officials in authorities containing large numbers of schools using i.t.a., were mainly favourably impressed by the results obtained when i.t.a. was used with infants.

2   Those who were least favourably disposed towards i.t.a. tended to be those who had seen least of it. Their attitude generally took the form of expressing doubts or raising queries regarding the use of i.t.a. This questioning attitude was some-times reinforced by a belief that children could learn to read satisfactorily with t.o.

3   Not one knowledgeable visitor to schools who had made more than a superficial observation of i.t.a. being used expressed outright disapproval of it.

The first two points should only be taken to represent broad generalisations, there being exceptions to the majority views expressed in each statement. For instance, although there was no doubt that the most enthusiastic supporters of i.t.a. were those who had closely observed its use in many schools, nevertheless, certain local inspectors with this same sort of experience still had misgivings on certain scores and felt unable to come to definite conclusions regarding the relative merits of t.o. and i.t.a. The same was true of a minority of H.M. Inspectors. Moreover, even among those visitors to schools who had perceived much to commend i.t.a., there were comments regarding certain disadvantages, queries on a few points and cautionary notes about it being too early for final assessments of various aspects of the use of i.t.a. to be made.

C. MORE DETAILED OBSERVATIONS

The foregoing short summary of the impressions of all these visitors to schools can probably best be rounded out by setting out two brief lists of the doubts and queries put forward by the minority, and the advantages or good results noted by the majority.

Doubts and queries

(*a*) The children who use i.t.a. in school will be surrounded by t.o. out of school.

(*b*) t.o., properly used, can be an efficient medium for teaching children to read and write.

(*c*) The use of i.t.a. may lead to an increase in formal teaching and an undue emphasis on phonic training.

(*d*) The use of i.t.a. may lead teachers to stress the importance of reading and so it may contribute to a neglect of other aspects of the curriculum.

(*e*) There may be a problem of 'unlearning' when children have to make the transfer in both reading and spelling.

(*f*) The transfer may be rushed prior to the promotion of children to those junior schools which are thought to have little interest in i.t.a.

(*g*) Children who move from i.t.a. schools to t.o. schools, while still in the early stages of learning to read, are likely to experience setbacks.

(*h*) 'Progressive' schools still consider the quantity and quality of books in i.t.a. to be inadequate.

(*i*) i.t.a. does not help the very slowest children.

(*j*) The use of i.t.a. produces little or no noticeable improvement in children's ability in reading and writing at 7+ or 8+.

Observed advantages

(*a*) Children learn to read earlier, more easily and more happily.

(*b*) Children soon become confident, independent and self-reliant. This leads to an increase in the number of books which infants read on their own.

(*c*) The transition in reading is not a problem for children.

(*d*) The use of i.t.a. results in a reduction of the number of non-readers in infant classes.

(*e*) There is an increase in the quantity and quality of children's free written work.

(*f*) The use of i.t.a. has led to an improvement in the standard of reading instruction, particularly among less able teachers.

D. COMMENTS ON EXPERIMENTS

There were differences of opinion regarding the schools which had first begun to use i.t.a., some visitors thinking that schools with reading problems were the first to use i.t.a., and others believing that many lively headteachers had been among the early volunteers. There was general agreement that the teachers in charge of the original i.t.a. classes were exceptionally able. The majority of visitors to schools also commented on the unprecedented amount of interest in, and enthusiasm for, reading, which soon manifested itself in the experimental schools. There were certain complaints about the amount of testing which was undertaken with infants.

E. SCHOOLS USING AND DISCARDING i.t.a.

Although there was a divergence of opinion in respect of the kind of schools which had first begun to use i.t.a., there was general agreement among knowledgeable visitors to schools that i.t.a. was currently being used with infants in all types of school.

Regarding the small number of schools which had used i.t.a. and later discarded it, opinions were that most of these schools had done so for administrative reasons, such as staff changes. In the few instances in which an abandonment of i.t.a. was more directly related to the alphabet itself, it was suggested that worries regarding the transition in reading and spelling were the main reasons. Two reasons relating to staffing were also put forward. Firstly, a few headteachers who were conservative and had older members of staff had returned to t.o. Secondly, a few headteachers of very good schools, in which the reading and writing had always been above average, were returning to t.o. on the grounds that they had noted no improvement when i.t.a. had been used.

CHAPTER 11

Additional Evidence from Interested People

I Introduction

IN addition to the 63 people who are classified as 'local education authority officials' and 'other visitors to schools' in Table D/7 in Appendix D, and whose evidence is reported in Chapter 10, it will be noted that discussions also took place with a further 46 people who were knowledgeable about, or interested in, certain aspects of i.t.a. They included members of the staffs of both the British and the American i.t.a. Foundations, members of the Reading Research Unit of the Institute of Education of London University, educational psychologists other than those employed by local education authorities, linguists, publishers, writers, lecturers and other educationists from at home and abroad. It was originally intended to report the views expressed by all these people in full. However, when this section of the report came to be written, the original plan was amended for the following reasons.

Firstly, as certain of the points raised by people in this group had also been expressed by teachers and visitors to schools, they were recorded earlier in this report. Secondly, a considerable number of those interviewed who were most closely involved with i.t.a. in the roles of inventor, administrator, supporter, researcher or author of i.t.a. reading schemes and books (as for example, Block, Downing, Harrison, Mazurkiewicz, Pitman and Tanyzer) had already published their views and findings in numerous articles, books and research reports. Many of these publications are listed in the bibliography at the end of this report and will no doubt be read by the interested reader. The views of teachers,* advisers, inspectors and parents, on the other hand, had received comparatively little publicity: hence the emphasis in Part Two of the report is on this new, independent and close-up aspect of verbal evidence.

Furthermore, the publication of views on i.t.a. by people other than those with direct or practical experience of its use has increased in 1966 and 1967 so that an abundance of research reports and comments by experts is now available. Two symposia, arranged by the National Foundation for Educational Research, provide valuable views from many different angles. The first, *The i.t.a. Symposium: Research Report on the British Experiment with i.t.a.*, was published by the N.F.E.R. in January 1967. It was followed by a conference entitled, *i.t.a. Research Evaluated*, which the N.F.E.R. arranged in April 1967, the proceedings of which are to be published. Among the speakers and writers in these two symposia were some whose conclusions the interviewer had already obtained in private discussions. To summarise views which are already published would merely lengthen this report without placing new evidence before the reader.

Accordingly, this chapter has been considerably curtailed to include only those

---

* SCEATS, John: *i.t.a. and The Teaching of Literacy* (Bodley Head) was published in the spring of 1967 after the above was written.

comments from educationists and other interested and knowledgeable people which have either not been noted, or have been mentioned but not expanded earlier in this report. It may appear to the reader that in this chapter are reported only those comments which represent doubts or unfavourable views of i.t.a., and he may draw the conclusion that the majority of the 46 people in this group were not in favour of the use of i.t.a. Such was not the case. For example, the views of people from abroad tended to follow the pattern of British opinions, with a majority of those who had used i.t.a., closely observed it in use or been involved in research employing it, being mainly favourably impressed, while a minority were hesitant or against it. Such views have already been expanded, unlike the more critical observations which follow, but which nevertheless need to be reported in order to present a fair picture of the total verbal evidence.

The decision to reduce this chapter does not in any way indicate that the discussions with many of the people concerned were not helpful. Indeed, the reverse is true, for these particular talks, supplemented by reading the publications of the people concerned, have provided the interviewer with a background of most useful information which must inevitably have influenced the whole tenor of this part of the report relating to verbal evidence.

II Comments on simplified spelling systems

A. IS A NEW SPELLING SYSTEM NECESSARY?

A number of people in this group stated quite firmly that, in the words of one, 'i.t.a. is an entirely unnecessary invention'. A proportion but not by any means all of those holding this view were authors of reading schemes and other reading materials in t.o., and some could be considered as reading experts. They tended to believe that the anomalies in our traditional spelling system did not represent a major cause of children's difficulties in learning to read. It was suggested that i.t.a. had clearly been devised by someone who had not taught infants to read and who took an adult and often erroneous view of children's difficulties. The general conclusion of this group of people was that if, in the early stages of teaching reading, the emphasis was on the regularities of the language, equally good results would be obtained with t.o., without any necessity for going to the length of inventing a new spelling system. Reading materials and approaches which were mentioned as concentrating on regular elements in the early stages included linguistic approaches such as that of Freis, *The Royal Road Readers* by Daniels and Diack, *Words in Colour* by Gattegno and Stott's *Programmed Reading Kit*.

In contrast, there were others who firmly supported Pitman's and Downing's hypothesis that the irregularities of the English spelling system represent a major cause of children's reading difficulties. As one reading expert commented:

> 'Any fairly consistent spelling would be likely to be easier to read and write than the present one.'

An educational psychologist expanded this point of view more fully. He suggested that there was one important advantage which i.t.a., or any regular, simplified spelling system was likely to have over t.o. He had come to believe that the irregularities of t.o. almost certainly prevented children from making generalisations in their concepts. He gave the following example of a child who may just be beginning to form a concept of the sound of the letter 'a', after having met it in, for instance, 'man', 'cat' and 'ham', when he encounters the word 'ball' and his newly crystallised concept is revealed as inapplicable. As this psychologist said, we do not really know how this sort of experience, which must occur very frequently when t.o. is used, inhibits the child's concept formation and prevents him making generalisations; but such experiences must undoubtedly constitute a continuing series of setbacks to the child.

B. QUESTIONS CONCERNING PROPOSED NEW SPELLING SYSTEMS

1   *The importance of trying different systems*

Certain linguists, educational psychologists and others deeply regretted that, when a large-scale experiment with an orthography other than the traditional one was being considered, it had not been preceded by a small experiment designed to discover, from among the various possible simplified spelling systems and coding systems, the one most appropriate for the purpose of helping young children to learn to read. Suggestions of alterations to the normal form of the written language, which might have been assessed alongside i.t.a. in a preliminary experiment, included amendments to t.o. by the use of colour or the addition of diacritical marks, simplified spelling systems employing solely the traditional alphabet and alternative spelling systems which either supplemented, or were substitutes for, the traditional alphabet.

Those who held the view that large-scale experiments with i.t.a., before it had been carefully appraised in experimental situations in conjunction with various likely alternatives, had been premature, were often not surprised that i.t.a. had been shown to simplify the task of reading for children. On the other hand, they were gravely concerned lest the success of i.t.a. should lead people to draw hasty and often unwarranted conclusions. For instance, it was considered that it would be disastrous if it was assumed, from the results of the current experiments and the extensive published literature referring to them, that i.t.a. was not only a 'better' medium than t.o. but also that it was the 'best possible' medium. Such an assumption could well lead to a closing of the door on careful and continued appraisals of all possible means of simplifying, for children, the initial stages of learning to read and write.

2   *Possible alternatives to i.t.a.*

(a) *Criticisms of i.t.a.*

A number of those who denied the necessity for a new spelling system also went on to level certain criticisms at the actual alphabet which constituted i.t.a. They were supported by others who, although they approved of the idea of producing a simpler spelling system or coding system likely to help children with the early stages of reading and writing, nevertheless considered i.t.a. to be unnecessarily complex.

Certain reading experts and others gave examples from i.t.a. demonstrating how someone who was neither a teacher nor a reading expert could assume that certain aspects of our written language caused children difficulties in learning to read, whereas classroom practice showed these assumptions to be unfounded. For instance, one person said, 'Pitman has assumed that children find digraphs difficult to read and write: this is not so'. Others gave concrete examples, pointing out that in t.o. most children experienced little difficulty in either recognising or writing such common digraphs as 'sh', 'ch', 'th', 'oo' and 'ee'. Educationists expressing these views believed that i.t.a. could have been simplified, while at the same time made to present an appearance more similar to t.o., if many of the new characters devised to replace such digraphs had been omitted. The assumption that the use of capital letters in t.o. constituted a major stumbling block to children was also denied by some of the people in this group, but this was not considered to be such a serious criticism as that concerning digraphs.

One or two linguists and others instanced additional ways in which i.t.a. might have been simplified. They were of the opinion that certain fine distinctions had been introduced which were superfluous, particularly for English-speaking children. The most frequent example to be given was the two forms of the 's' sound forming the plurals of words. It was pointed out that when English-speaking children are reading the words 'cows' and 'cats', they automatically make the distinction between the two final sounds and never substitute one for the other. Thus, the use of these two different characters in situations which children do not find confusing, merely complicates the deciphering and writing of the words. The use of two forms of 'th' and the retention of both 'c' and 'k' to represent the same sound were also given as examples of unnecessary complications.

This report is clearly not the place for detailed comments, either for or against the actual form which i.t.a. has taken. It is sufficient to report that certain experts who were interviewed had concluded that, even if a new spelling system consisting of a new alphabet was deemed necessary, the present form of i.t.a. could with advantage be simplified.

(b) Alternatives to Pitman's alphabet

While realising that Pitman had studied alternative alphabets before devising his own, a few people still continued to wonder if the 'New Spelling' devised by the Simplified Spelling Society in 1940, and revised in 1948, might have been preferable. Another suggestion from a linguist was that, if we must employ a different alphabet for teaching children to read and write initially, it might be worth considering the use of the International Phonetic Alphabet. (See example B/6 in Appendix B.) This alphabet would not need to be completely discarded and forgotten when children transferred to t.o.: it would continue to prove useful to them throughout their lives, for example to check the pronunciation of English words and in learning foreign languages.

(c) Alternative uses of the traditional alphabet

Certain critics of i.t.a. denied entirely the necessity for inventing a new alphabet, as they believed that a variety of amended uses of the traditional alphabet would be equally effective in overcoming the anomalies of written English. They drew attention to the disadvantages arising from the introduction of new characters. These disadvantages included the increased difficulties for the child both at the time when he was using a different alphabet in school from that in use elsewhere and also at the stage of transfer, and the problems raised for teachers, parents and publishers when new characters were introduced.

Opponents of the introduction of new characters followed two main lines of thought regarding an improved use of our traditional 26-letter alphabet. One trend of development consisted of retaining the whole of the traditional alphabet and spelling system, while superimposing upon it a variety of temporary clues which would act as signals to the child regarding the sounds which certain letters represented. Such systems are termed 'signalling systems' in this report and those suggested as possible alternatives to i.t.a. included the addition of diacritical marks to all or some of the letters, the use of capital letters within words to represent different sounds and the use of colour. Certain samples of such 'signalling systems' were sent to the investigators by people who had heard of the current evaluation of i.t.a., while others were collected by the investigators. Three samples of signalling systems are included in Appendix B; Fry's Diacritical Marking System (Example B/2), Gattegno's *Words in Colour* (Example B/3) and Jones's *Colour Story Reading* (Example B/4).

The second line of thought centred around the production of a simplified spelling system using only the 26 lower-case letters of the alphabet. In this context, undoubtedly the most scholarly example, based on meticulous research by an expert, is Wijk's 'Regularized Inglish' (Example B/5 in Appendix B). It was mentioned most frequently as a feasible alternative to i.t.a. by those knowledgeable people who had misgivings about i.t.a. One linguist's comment was:

'Wijk's "Regularized Inglish" is the least deviant system and it uses only the letters of the normal alphabet.'

Accordingly, as experts spoke so highly of 'Regularized Inglish', the interviewer arranged to have discussions with Professor Wijk. As the bibliography contains a number of references to Wijk's work, in which his ideas are fully expanded, it will suffice here to give only the barest details of his comments regarding his simplified spelling system.

Wijk agreed with Pitman that, in order to teach reading more rapidly and more successfully than is now the case, it is essential to employ a transitional spelling system which is phonetic in character, but he disagreed with the necessity for a new alphabet. His investigations into English spelling revealed that about 90–95% of English words actually follow certain regular patterns in regard to their spelling and pronunciation. He found that English spelling could be regularised by means of changes in only 10% of the total vocabulary. A large proportion of the changes required would only be slight, and certain of them would be unnecessary if English-speaking children were using the alphabet.

Wijk's intensive research led him to develop his 'Regularized Inglish', in which the necessary changes to traditional spelling have been made in order to produce a regular spelling system, using the 26 letters of the traditional alphabet. These alterations to about 10% of the spellings of the total vocabulary have resulted in approximately 70% of the running words on any page remaining the same. (In contrast, the use of i.t.a. leaves approximately 30% of the running words on a page the same as in t.o.) The results are that a page printed in 'Regularized Inglish' does not look very different from a page printed in t.o., and the final transfer to t.o. should be easier for children than from i.t.a. to t.o.

Professor Wijk stressed that not only does 'Regularized Inglish' employ the regular alphabet, but it uses the various letters and combinations of letters in the same way as they are normally used in the present orthography. Thus children are introduced to all the regular patterns of English spelling as they go along and before they meet the exceptions. He was not surprised at the results which had been achieved with i.t.a., as he thought that any comparatively regular and phonetic alphabet would be likely to be easier for children to read than t.o. Yet he was certain that the same results could be gained, without the disadvantages attached to the introduction of a new alphabet, if 'Regularized Inglish', employing the traditional alphabet and replacing all the irregular spellings with regular ones, were used as a transitional spelling system during the first year or two of a child's school life.

Other people in this group supported Wijk's views and were anxious to see 'Regularized Inglish' being tried out with infants in at least a few British schools. Pitman himself has made certain objections to Wijk's system, and both he and certain other educationists were of the opinion that none of the spelling systems or 'signalling systems' which retained the 26-letter alphabet was likely to result in the improvement in children's writing observed when i.t.a. was the medium for initial reading instruction.

3 Is a new system necessary for all children?

A number of educationists queried the necessity for using a new spelling system with all children. They pointed out that a large proportion of children did learn to read and write with t.o., and consequently they doubted the wisdom of having such children using a transitional system of spelling for their first year or two in school. Two alternatives were suggested to the policy of every child in a class beginning with a new spelling system. A few people, while recognising the difficulty of diagnosing the probable slow reader at an early stage in the infant school, nevertheless wondered if only the slowest children should be taught by a new spelling system or 'signalling system', while the majority used t.o. The alternative suggestion was that all children should begin by using t.o.; the majority would soon begin to read and write in this medium; then those who were clearly failing or struggling could be introduced to the chosen alternative to t.o.

C. SUMMING UP

The evidence regarding different spelling systems is complex and highly technical and, consequently, full justice can only be done to the arguments put forward by the proponents of various schemes for revising English spelling by reading the appropriate literature. The evidence on simplified spelling systems and other means of simplifying initial reading materials accumulated during this enquiry in no way approximates to even a small representative sample of all the possibilities. The points which have been reported can merely be taken to indicate that there was considerable support for the belief that, before a wholesale turnover to i.t.a. took place in infant schools, other spelling systems and 'signalling systems', as well as different approaches to the use of t.o., should be closely investigated. Of all the alternatives to i.t.a. put forward by those knowledgeable and competent to judge, Wijk's 'Regularized Inglish' was mentioned most frequently.

Among those who supported the need for a simplified spelling system to help slower children were a number who queried the necessity for its use with all children.

III Publishers' problems

The introduction of i.t.a. experimentally, and its adoption in an increasing proportion of schools, has caused those publishers who are concerned with publishing reading materials for infants to be faced with unprecedented problems. In interviews with members of publishing firms these problems came in for a good deal of discussion;

they were also commented on by certain educationists who were sensitive to the publishers' dilemma.

The requirement of a new typeface, which to the layman might appear to be one of the chief difficulties, does not basically concern the publisher: rather is it a problem for the printer and a comparatively minor one at that.

A. A MINORITY MARKET

The major problem for the publisher is one with which he is already familiar: how to produce appropriate reading materials for a minority market without incurring a financial loss. This is a problem which he has already faced in respect of, for example, books for older backward readers or for deaf children. Even when such books are priced at a higher level than similar books intended for a normal market, their production may still result in a loss rather than a profit. In these circumstances, it is understandable that publishers should be hesitant regarding the publication of a large variety of books in i.t.a. The problem is accentuated in that, whereas with other minority markets reasonably accurate forecasts of the probable demand can be made, with i.t.a. no one is in a position to estimate the future potential market.

B. COMPLETE READING SCHEMES

One of the most difficult problems for publishers has concerned complete reading schemes. When Nisbet originally agreed to publish *Janet and John* in i.t.a., this was undoubtedly a courageous decision taken in the general interests of educational experiment and advancement, at a time when no one was really in a position to forecast the eventual outcome. The dilemma regarding reading schemes confronted other publishers after the restrictions of the sale of i.t.a. books were withdrawn in the summer of 1963. To publish a complete reading scheme, consisting as it usually does of a teacher's manual, pre-reading books, basic reading books, supplementary books, pictures and supporting apparatus, involves a publisher in great capital expenditure. It is an undertaking which many publishers are understandably reluctant even to contemplate until more accurate assessments of probable sales can be made. Consequently, some publishers have deliberately postponed any consideration of the publication of an i.t.a. reading scheme at the present time.

Among the publishers willing to publish reading schemes in i.t.a., the tendency has been to settle for transliterations of an already established t.o. scheme, in preference to having new reading schemes devised. Although this solution might possibly be the safest one from the publisher's viewpoint, it is certainly not the ideal one from an educational standpoint.

Although many publishers are hesitant about publishing an entirely new reading scheme in i.t.a. yet the writer sensed in some of them a reluctance to stand back entirely from what might eventually prove to be an expanding and lucrative market. They cannot fail to have considered the possibility that, if the use of i.t.a. should increase, a publisher who was first in the field with a new reading scheme, based not on former needs and principles but on fresh needs which practical experience with i.t.a. had thrown up, would find himself in an extremely enviable position in relation to his competitors. Such a view is understandable, but it would be unfortunate if keenness to be first in the field with publications designed to fulfil needs of a market

133

estimated to be expanding should result in the adoption of reading materials ill-fitted to the new situations.

Neither should it be overlooked that the uncertainty of both educationists and publishers regarding the eventual increase or decline of the use of i.t.a. must in some measure have had an inhibiting effect on the publication of complete new reading schemes in t.o. No publisher can afford to regard with equanimity the possibility of finding himself in the position of publishing a new reading scheme in t.o. at a time when the majority of schools might be changing to i.t.a.

C. SUPPLEMENTARY BOOKS

The hesitancy of publishers regarding complete reading schemes in i.t.a. is demonstrated in a tendency to print mostly supplementary books, and more particularly those transliterated from t.o. into i.t.a. Even so, the number of suitable supplementary books, including books of stories and verse, information books, reference books, picture dictionaries, and so on, published in i.t.a. at each level falls far short of the number available in t.o. Moreover, because of doubts regarding sales, the majority of the supplementary books published in i.t.a. have tended to be of the cheaper variety: relatively few children's books of high quality having so far been printed in i.t.a.

D. ARE i.t.a. READING MATERIALS APPROPRIATE?

One further important point, of great concern to certain far-seeing educators and publishers, is the appropriateness of i.t.a. books and materials. All reading schemes, and to some extent other reading materials previously published in t.o., had been devised to facilitate the task of learning to read with a more complex and irregular spelling system than i.t.a. It appears unlikely that any of these reading schemes, including those founded on different basic principles, will prove of maximum efficiency when the spelling system to be used is more regular. Furthermore, practical experience with i.t.a. has not yet been sufficiently extensive for clear indications of the most appropriate reading materials to emerge.

Thus publishers are not only faced with decisions regarding whether or not to publish i.t.a. reading schemes and books, but they must continually be asking themselves how the use of i.t.a. is likely to affect the type and quantity of new books required in both i.t.a. and t.o. The following are some of the possible changes in requirements which the writer considers might occur:

(i) The currently accepted type of reading scheme with its supporting supplementary books, designed originally to give additional practice in the recognition of irregular words, may be considered unnecessarily cumbersome if a regular system of spelling is employed, and thus basic reading schemes may become much shorter and simpler.

(ii) Basic reading schemes, at least in the form we have recently come to accept as normal, may be entirely discarded.

(iii) If reading schemes are retained, a great deal of fresh thinking about the principles of learning involved when the task to be mastered is simpler and more systematic than formerly needs to be undertaken and could well result in great changes in basic reading materials.

(iv) More individual titles of easy reading books might be bought in both i.t.a. and t.o. in preference to groups of books of the same title.

(v) In both i.t.a. and t.o., books which utilise a more advanced vocabulary, while retaining the simple ideas and sentence structure appropriate for young infants, are likely to be needed. For instance, if the five and six year old can read and understand words formerly thought of as belonging to the vocabulary of average seven and eight year olds, these words will need to be used within a language structure suited to his chronological and mental age.

One overriding question which haunts most publishers is likely to inhibit the flow of new i.t.a. books. It is unavoidable that they should wonder if this first simplified alphabet to be given an extensive trial in Great Britain is the forerunner of further experiments with alternative simplified spelling systems or, conversely, if continued experience with i.t.a. will reveal that it might benefit from certain modifications.

F. SUMMING UP

The introduction of i.t.a. has presented publishers with many problems, regarding the publication of both i.t.a. and t.o. books for young children, which lack of information and experience prevents them from solving at the present time. The result is that although the number of available books in i.t.a. is increasing, the books are frequently more expensive than equivalent t.o. books, and the supply is still not entirely satisfactory in certain ways. i.t.a. books are considerably less in number and variety than comparable t.o. books and few of them reach the level of the highest quality of t.o. books. Moreover, quite a large proportion of the reading materials published in i.t.a., being merely transliterations from t.o. materials, cannot be considered as absolutely appropriate either for the medium they utilise or for the children concerned. New problems springing from the introduction of i.t.a. also extended into the realm of the publication of t.o. books for infants and juniors. The question for publishers which overrides all others refers to whether i.t.a. in its present form has come to stay, whether it will be superseded by other simplified spelling systems or whether the majority of schools will disregard such innovations and will continue to use t.o.

IV   Miscellaneous points

The few points which follow, although they cannot be regarded entirely as fresh evidence, are mentioned in that they represent a greater emphasis on certain aspects of the use of i.t.a. than has so far been reported.

A. THE EARLY STAGES OF READING

Certain people in this group stressed that children's early writing helps the teacher to obtain a clearer idea of what children actually hear when they listen to spoken words. As the child tries to express himself in writing, the teacher can actually see what the child hears, as well as how he attempts to speak the words. Such insight should enable the teacher to co-ordinate listening, speaking, reading and writing in a total learning pattern more easily than previously. The fact that teachers themselves are learning more about the spoken word and the structure of the language, and thinking more about how children learn, should also prove beneficial in this respect.

Certain Americans who gave evidence were of the opinion that an important contribution which i.t.a. had made to beginning reading in the U.S.A. was that it had given both teachers and children freedom to break away from basic reading schemes. (It will be noted that this echoes a view already expressed by British teachers.) Americans who gave evidence frequently mentioned with approval, in this context, the increasing use of the 'language experience approach' with i.t.a.

Other educators stressed that this trend away from formal reading schemes and formal instruction had led teachers to re-examine certain practices of reading teaching which they had formerly accepted, for example that children at different grade levels were only capable of mastering particular features of reading skills. One person interviewed suggested that when a teacher who had used t.o. had built up expectations of what children would be able to do at certain stages, there was inevitably the danger that he or she would teach towards these standards. Thus one of the advantages of i.t.a. had been that at first teachers did not have a set of standards, and so there was more opportunity for children to forge ahead.

The preceding views were also closely linked with theories regarding children's growth and development. One American stated that close observation of i.t.a. in use had enabled him to draw together psychology, learning theories, methodology, the philosophy of education and so on into a composite whole. He felt that the child was continually struggling towards independence and i.t.a. released him and enabled him to approach this goal in a way that t.o. could never do.

B. READING AFTER THE FIRST TWO YEARS

A number of reading experts in both Great Britain and America were concerned by their observations of what was happening to children who had made good reading progress with i.t.a. in the early stages and who had transferred easily to t.o., after two or three years of schooling. Appearances suggested that in many cases the rate of progress of these children lost its early acceleration and was generally reduced to an extremely modest speed. American comment on this point referred rather despairingly to teachers, once children had transferred from i.t.a. to t.o., going back to the old basal reading schemes. From Britain emerged the conclusion that junior schools are not capitalising on children's increased reading ability by raising either the level of their expectations for the children or the level of their own teaching. Experts from both sides of the Atlantic concluded that much of the impetus of children's early reading progress with i.t.a. could be wasted if attention was not directed towards later developmental skills.

CHAPTER 12

Parents' Evidence

1 Comments from teachers and others on parents' reactions to i.t.a.

A. PARENTS' ORIGINAL DOUBTS

IN the first few years of experimenting with i.t.a., the majority of headteachers invited parents to meetings at which the Reading Research Unit's experiment was explained and their co-operation invited. Copies of a pamphlet written by Downing entitled *How your children are being taught to read by i.t.a.*, were also handed out to parents. This procedure is still followed by most infant schools before they begin to use i.t.a. for the first time. The parents whose children took part in the early experiments were naturally more suspicious of the use of a new alphabet than those parents whose children have begun to use i.t.a. more recently as the latter have heard about i.t.a. for a number of years and may also know children who have been taught to read with this alphabet.

A few local advisers and inspectors, as well as teachers, remarked on the early doubts of certain parents. The importance of parents being taken into the confidence of headteachers, in order that their fears might be allayed before a school began to use i.t.a. was stressed. One adviser exemplified parents' doubts by relating how they had asked him if they should still buy books for their children and whether they should continue to read them stories. Another recounted how, when i.t.a. was first introduced into the schools in his authority, a few parents had come to the Education Office to complain about their children being asked to learn something that they would later have to unlearn. This adviser had noted that these parents were not professional people as might have been expected; rather were they intelligent working-class parents who prized education highly.

The differences between the reactions of early and later parents, however, were not nearly so great as those demonstrated, at every stage, between parents in contrasting socio-economic areas. The comments of nearly all headteachers and members of staff in poor socio-economic areas indicated that most parents originally showed, and still show, little concern about the use of i.t.a. In one such school, although the parents were circularised regarding the proposal to use i.t.a., and invited to school to talk about it, only one parent came along for a discussion. In another similar area, in which a few mothers did respond to the invitation to come to school to discuss the proposal, they said that they were quite content for the headteacher to use whatever means of teaching reading she thought best, for as one mother expressed it: 'Yu learns them proper luvly!' On the other hand, in one poor socio-economic area in which there was no reaction from parents when i.t.a. was first used, a number of parents of large families later told the headmistress that they had noticed that their younger children who were using i.t.a. were learning to read better, and wanting to read at home much more than their elder children had done. In contrast, in higher socio-economic areas, parents were not always so approving or so acquiescent when schools proposed the introduction of i.t.a. Headteachers of schools in such areas commented as follows:

'The parents were alarmed at first but I talked to them and explained things and gave them the booklets.'

'There was quite a bit of difficulty at first with parents who were dubious about children using i.t.a. Their main fears were about the spelling.'

'The parents were rather dubious at first. This soon became apparent at parent-teacher meetings. Also, once children had started to learn with i.t.a. the parents were perturbed because they found they couldn't help their children with reading.'

Most headteachers of schools containing children of professional parents mentioned at least a few parents having doubts in the early stages. In contrast, one or two spoke in this way:

'The parents in this area accept my judgement. Their only reaction was to enquire how they might help. These parents are always interested and helpful.'

B. PARENTS' INCREASING INTEREST IN READING

A certain number of teachers, local education authority advisers, and other educationists counted it as one of the advantages of i.t.a. that it was causing parents to take an increasing interest in their children's reading progress. Instances were given of parent-teacher associations borrowing film about i.t.a., and of a certain local authority arranging an evening class for those parents who wished to familiarise themselves with i.t.a.

One infant headmistress linked parents' interest in the earlier reading, resulting from the use of i.t.a., in the following manner. She believed that it was important for children to read as early as their ability would permit because reading is the one measure that parents have of their children's reading progress. The one question that all parents seem to ask teachers on parents' days at school is 'How is my child getting on with reading?' Parents whose children are not reading by the age of seven feel this badly. If parents are worried or despondent about their children's inability to read this can be reflected in home life and does not help children's attitude to reading. Consequently, this headteacher believes that anything that will help children learn to read earlier and more easily is worthwhile and, in this respect, she considered that i.t.a. possessed advantages over t.o.

C. CO-OPERATION BETWEEN PARENTS AND TEACHERS

Parents' growing interest in their children's reading and writing with i.t.a. had engendered a closer relationship between parents and teachers; a result which was considered advantageous by many teachers. Examples, including the following, of closer co-operation between parents and teachers were cited in schools in all types of areas:

'Parents are more helpful now that the school uses i.t.a. than they were when t.o.

was used. Parents are intrigued by the idea of i.t.a. and delighted by the children learning so quickly.'

'At first, when duplicated sheets of i.t.a. printing had to be pasted into t.o. books, parents came to school one afternoon a week to do this. In this way, the parents also learned to read i.t.a.'

'Our classes are very large and we believe in someone hearing the children read every day. So we are now trying the experiment of a group of mothers coming in every day to help with this.'

'Some parents found that when their children were trying to write at home, and asked their help with certain words, they were not able to give this help because they did not understand the alphabet, so at their request I am holding a class for parents, once a week, to teach them to write in i.t.a.'

Although certain parents felt handicapped originally because they could not help their children with reading, some of the above examples show how, when the relationship between teachers and parents was good, the stimulus of the new alphabet could result in even closer links between school and home. A few headteachers also mentioned that the use of i.t.a. resulted in closer relationships between parents and children regarding reading, as the following examples illustrate:

'Mothers who never bothered to buy their children books formerly, now do so because the children are so keen on reading.'

'Children can now read a book to mother. Formerly, either mother read a book to the child or, when the child tried to read to her, she had to tell him so many words that it was not satisfactory. Now the child can really read to her and this gives them both pleasure.'

D. PARENTS' REACTIONS TO THE TRANSITION

A number of infant teachers made remarks such as the following, relating to parents' reactions to the transition in reading:

'Parents get a bit anxious when their children are reaching the stage of transfer.'

Some teachers wondered if this anxiety on the part of parents might have resulted in their frequently questioning children as to whether they had yet progressed to 'grown-up printing', and if such insidious pressure could have set up a certain amount of anxiety in children regarding the transfer. (Parents present at the group discussion, however, denied this.)

One headmaster of a junior school, in which a proportion of children from an i.t.a. infant school were still reading in i.t.a. in the first year junior class, supported the views of infant teachers in respect of parents' anxieties about a delayed transition. He said:

'There was a bit of trouble with some parents on open-days. They complained to the teachers about children who were still doing i.t.a., "They" (meaning teachers in the infant school) "told us that children would have finished with i.t.a. by the end of the infant school," said the parents. This disgruntled attitude of parents may well have affected the children.'

139

Many teachers in infant schools are now married women with children of their own, and in the course of visits to schools the interviewer talked to a number of such teacher-parents who were experienced i.t.a. teachers. As it happened, not one of these teacher-parents had a child who had learned to read using i.t.a., but all had comments to make referring to their own older or younger children. Without exception, these teachers either wished that their own older children had had the opportunity of using i.t.a. or hoped that their younger children would have this opportunity.

II Discussions with parents

A. INDIVIDUAL DISCUSSIONS

On a number of occasions when the interviewer was in i.t.a. infant schools, parents came to the schools either to see the headmistress or to collect their children. It was sometimes possible to have discussions with these parents regarding their reactions to their children using i.t.a. As it happened, most of these parents came from low socio-economic areas and their comments were invariably favourable. Whenever the child concerned had older brothers and sisters, the mother almost invariably commented that this child was a far better reader than her older children who had learned to read with t.o.

One local inspector, whose five-year-old child had recently begun to read using i.t.a., put forward the viewpoint of a professional parent. He said that most of the time he was indifferent about whether she was learning by t.o. or i.t.a., but that on certain occasions he felt slightly irritated. For instance, when he was reading a story to the child and she wanted to see the words: because the book was printed in t.o. he was placed in the position of not knowing whether he should let her see the words or not. He added that when the child was shown the print she often wanted to try to sound out the words and did not seem to notice the difference between i.t.a. and t.o. The reaction of this professional parent was in line with the remarks of certain parents to headteachers and of other parents present at the group discussion.

Written evidence from one father, on another problem, was brought to the attention of the investigators by Sir James Pitman who kindly made the relevant correspondence available to them. This father had found himself in the position of having to move his family to another area, at the time when his child, who had started to learn to read by i.t.a., had not reached fluency in this medium. There was no school in the area using i.t.a. and the father wrote of the difficulties his child had encountered in an infant school which used t.o. Although there were certain exceptional circumstances in this case, it nevertheless tends to confirm the suspicions of a number of educationists that the situation described can present a very real problem to such children and to their parents.

B. A GROUP DISCUSSION

1 *Arranging the group discussion*

Towards the end of this enquiry, it was felt that the individual discussions with parents had not been sufficient to provide adequate information, and that it was desirable that the views of parents should be further explored. It was hoped that two group discussions could be arranged with parents: one in a high socio-economic area and the other in a poor socio-economic area. In the event, it only proved possible to arrange the first of these proposed meetings.

In one school in a good area, the headmistress was interested in the idea and thought the children's parents would like to participate in such a discussion. This was a school which had been running its own experiment of one t.o. class matched with one i.t.a. class. The parents of the class of children who had started to use i.t.a. two and a half years previously, were invited to an evening meeting. Letters were sent to all the parents, explaining the project, emphasising the independent nature of the enquiry and inviting their views.

There was a good response to this invitation: 34 parents, of whom 12 were fathers, attended the meeting. One parent who was unable to attend went to the trouble of sending the interviewer a letter stating her views. This action was in line with the general attitude of the parents who evinced, not only a particular interest in their own children's progress, but also a general interest in i.t.a. and in this independent evaluation.

2 Procedure at the discussion

The procedure adopted at the meeting was to ask the parents certain specific questions regarding their views and then invite them to make any other comments they wished. The parents proved to be eager to express their views: in the course of the meeting, nearly every parent present made some contribution to the discussion. The four direct questions asked were as follows:

(*a*) How did you feel when it was first suggested that your child should use i.t.a.?

(*b*) What advantages have you seen in i.t.a.?

(*c*) What disadvantages have you noticed?

(*d*) How do you feel about i.t.a. now after two and a half years?

3 Parents' comments

(*a*) Parents' first reactions. Regarding their reactions to the headmistress's original proposal to use i.t.a. with their children, about one third of the parents had felt apprehensive at first. Their fears were mainly centred on the problem of the transfer to t.o. The remaining two thirds of the parents had not felt anxious about the proposal because they had faith in whatever the headmistress suggested.

(*b*) Advantages. Although these particular parents were articulate, they did not find it easy to list advantages and disadvantages of i.t.a. As one father pointed out, if the child concerned was their first child, they had no means of comparing his progress with others. Furthermore, as they remarked, children in the same family differ. However, the following comments in favour of i.t.a. were put forward by certain parents:

(i) The children soon acquire a wide vocabulary in reading, writing, and speech.

(ii) The regular alphabet seems easier for children to read than t.o., and consequently they thought that children learnt to read earlier and quicker.

(iii) Reading makes sense more quickly.

(iv) One father rated it as an advantage of i.t.a. that his son was aware of being part of an experiment and this made him more interested in reading than he might have been with t.o. When asked to elaborate on the child's awareness of being part of an experiment, the father stressed that it was not the school which made him feel so. It was rather that the child knew that his books were in a different alphabet from the books at home and those being used in other classes in the school. As a consequence, adults and other children coming into the house were interested in this fact and quite often looked at his i.t.a. books. In fact, the family and friends tended to talk about 'Robert's alphabet'. This made the child feel rather special and had perhaps increased his desire to read.

(*c*) *Disadvantages.* Parents at this meeting appeared to experience more difficulty in commenting on the disadvantages than the advantages of i.t.a., which suggested that the majority had failed to note disadvantages. Nevertheless, after a short discussion, the following disadvantages which certain parents had perceived were voiced:

(i) At first the school did not have many library books in i.t.a. which the children could take home, nor did the parents find it easy to locate bookshops selling i.t.a. books which they could purchase for their children.

(ii) When the children wanted to read at home, parents found it difficult to help them.

(iii) The children were not able to read comics or the words printed on household articles. When children did attempt to pick out words from comics or newspapers, as they often did, they found it rather disheartening.

(*d*) *The transition.* One point made by parents in this discussion was in contrast to the comments of certain teachers, who had noticed that the transition from an i.t.a. to a t.o. reading book was a goal towards which some children strove and a landmark which gave them pleasure when it was attained. These parents were almost unanimous in their conclusion that their children had not been concerned about making the transition. Only one child had actually gone home and told his parents that he had changed from an i.t.a. to a t.o. book. Quite clearly the children in this class had taken the transition in their stride, a situation which may well be attributable to a relaxed attitude in the school, brought about by teachers consciously refraining from putting children under pressure.

(*e*) *Children's reactions.* In this discussion, one of the main conclusions could be drawn from what was not said, rather than from the actual comments. Although the parents had been encouraged to talk freely, and indeed had done so, no mention was made of a child being unhappy or worried about learning to read at school with i.t.a. Towards the end of the meeting, when the interviewer realised this, she questioned the parents on this score. The consensus of parents' opinions was that their children seemed very happy with i.t.a.

(*f*) *Parents' later reactions.* At the conclusion of the meeting, the parents were invited to give their reactions now that two and a half years had elapsed since their children had begun to use i.t.a. They were asked if they felt able to decide whether they were pleased their children had been taught by i.t.a. or if, on looking back, they would have preferred t.o. to have been the medium of instruction. About one-third of the parents indicated that they considered it too early yet to reach such a decision: they preferred to wait until their children concluded their time in the infant school. The remaining

142

two-thirds were in favour of i.t.a. Not one parent said that he would have preferred his child to be taught with t.o.

III Summary of parents' reactions

The evidence collected from parents of children taught by i.t.a., and from the reports of teachers and local officials regarding parents' reactions, led to the following conclusions:

1 The majority of parents whose children were taught by i.t.a. had not considered this innovation a cause for concern.

2 Of those parents who were apprehensive, most came from good or average socio-economic areas, although even in such areas parents with doubts were in the minority.

3 Parents' original doubts centred on the problems of transition in reading and writing.

4 In schools in above average socio-economic areas which had started to use i.t.a. recently, there were still parents who showed apprehension, although the proportion appeared to have decreased slightly from the time when i.t.a. was first used.

5 Only very rarely were examples cited of parents either refusing to have children taught by i.t.a. or objecting very strongly to it.

6 In poor socio-economic areas, a number of parents of large families of low ability remarked on the fact that younger children taught by i.t.a. liked reading, in contrast to older siblings who had failed to learn to read.

7 The main disadvantages of i.t.a. noted by some parents, mainly from above average homes, were as follows:

(*a*) They had difficulty in helping their children with reading and writing.
(*b*) Newspapers, comics and books in the home, in t.o., tended to confuse or dishearten the child when he first tried to read the words.

8 Some headteachers felt that i.t.a. had established close links between parents and teachers, as well as between parents and children. Instances were given of parents coming to school to help with the preparation of i.t.a. books for the children as well as to learn to read and write i.t.a. for themselves.

9 There were suggestions by certain teachers that some parents tended to become anxious if they thought their children were late in making the transfer. On the other hand, 34 parents in one school in a good socio-economic area firmly denied this suggestion.

10 No instance was reported of a parent, whose child had learned to read by i.t.a., expressing disapproval of it, saying that he would have preferred the child to have been taught by t.o. or requesting that a younger child should be taught by t.o.

11 The main impression to be gained regarding the reactions of parents whose children had learned to read and write by means of i.t.a., was that these parents were pleased by the results, having observed that their children learned happily, easily and quickly.

CHAPTER 13

Summary of Verbal Evidence

I Introduction

THE report on the verbal evidence obtained from nearly 400 people who were interviewed, on the use of i.t.a. with infants as a means of beginning reading and writing, has necessarily run to great length. Even a summary of the views expressed on the many aspects of the use of this alphabet must prove rather extensive. Accordingly, it may give clarity and make for easier appreciation of the points raised if the overall pattern of the verbal evidence, as noted by the interviewer, is reported first.

The majority of the verbal evidence represented favourable reports on the use of i.t.a. with infants. Only a small minority of the people interviewed expressed unfavourable opinions or doubts. The most noticeable trend in this mass of evidence was that the people nearest to, or most knowledgeable about, actual teaching and learning in infant classes, were mostly favourably impressed, while those who saw dangers and had misgivings were generally those who had neither used i.t.a. themselves nor closely observed it in use.

The majority group, with favourable impressions of i.t.a., consisted of most teachers who had used it, a large percentage of H.M. Inspectors, many but not all local education authority advisers and inspectors with wide experiences of observing it and the majority of the parents concerned.

The minority group, of those least favourably impressed, included a few teachers in schools which had always attained good reading standards with t.o., certain of H.M. Inspectors, local education authority inspectors, College of Education lecturers and University staff with little experience of observing i.t.a. being used, and a few parents. In this group could also be found linguists, people who strongly supported other simplified writing systems and approaches to beginning reading and a number of other educationists and writers, of whom a few had not visited any school using i.t.a. In contrast to most of the people in this minority group who had little experience of observing i.t.a., the group also included a certain number of officials from local authorities in which i.t.a. was being used quite extensively, but who were not convinced that it was preferable to t.o. as a medium of beginning reading instruction.

Against this broad background of the general trend of verbal evidence noted by the interviewer, an attempt will be made in this chapter to summarise briefly, under various headings, the main views expressed by the many people with whom discussions took place. Such a summary cannot hope to include all the shades of belief which were put forward. Indeed, any attempt to extract the broad pattern of findings from a large body of evidence must clearly fail to do justice to minority views; these, however, have been expanded quite fully throughout the preceding chapters of Part Two of this report.

II Schools using and discarding i.t.a.

1 The schools which first began to use i.t.a., according to both local advisers and H.M. Inspectors, were usually those with a marked tendency towards early reading. Later, however, it was noted that certain 'progressive' schools with a belief in a delayed start to reading were also beginning to use i.t.a. By 1966 local officials had observed i.t.a. being used with infants in schools which exhibited every possible variety and combination of such factors as socio-economic level, range of intelligence, size, organisation, attitudes to reading and formality and informality of working procedures.

2 There was fairly general agreement between the majority of local inspectors and H.M. Inspectors that, in both the early days and at present, it was usually 'good' headteachers who had begun to experiment with i.t.a.

3 By the summer of 1966, only a tiny percentage of schools which had begun to use i.t.a. were reported by local inspectors and H.M. Inspectors to have abandoned its use. Their reasons for so doing were stated to be administrative, rather than representing dissatisfaction with the alphabet itself.

III Observed results of using i.t.a.

A. READING

1 The majority of teachers who had used i.t.a. as a medium of beginning reading with infants, found that children made better progress than could have been expected with t.o. The children learned to read earlier, more easily and more happily. They understood what they read and developed habits of independent reading which led to an extension of their interests in many subjects.

2 The observations of H.M. Inspectors supported those of teachers regarding children's reading progress, their improved attitude to reading and their comprehension of what they read.

3 The majority of those local advisers with wide experience of observing i.t.a. in infant classes were in agreement with teachers and H.M. Inspectors regarding children's reading progress.

4 A minority of local advisers thought that the introduction of i.t.a. had made little difference to infant reading standards. While certain of these advisers had only slight experience of i.t.a., others had observed its use quite closely.

5 The parents of infants who had been taught to read by i.t.a. were generally pleased with their progress.

6 The effect on children's reading standards of having learned to read initially with i.t.a. was not nearly as pronounced by the age of about eight as in the early infant classes. Opinions were fairly equally divided as to whether or not those infants who had learned to read early and quickly with i.t.a. retained this advantage in junior classes.

7 Certain teachers of junior classes, containing children taught to read originally both by i.t.a. and by t.o., found their reading performances at eight and nine to be indistinguishable. Other teachers, although stating that the level of reading ability was similar for the groups of children taught by both media, had nevertheless noted that children who had originally learned to read with i.t.a. read independently, more

often, for longer periods and with greater interest and understanding than children taught to read entirely with t.o.

8 Some headteachers and class teachers of junior schools, H.M. Inspectors and local education authority advisers commented that the use of i.t.a. had resulted in fewer non-readers and slow readers entering junior classes. Others had noted no reduction in the numbers of such children.

9 Not one teacher who had used i.t.a. with infants, or who had been in charge of such children when they entered junior schools or classes, remarked on any injurious effect on children's reading progress which he or she had observed. The same was true of H.M. Inspectors, local inspectors and other frequent and knowledgeable visitors to i.t.a. schools.

10 Without exception, every teacher who had seen children transfer from i.t.a. to t.o. in reading was of the opinion that this transition caused no difficulty. H.M. Inspectors, local inspectors and other visitors to schools who had closely observed this stage were in full agreement with the teachers.

11 Teachers themselves, as well as knowledgeable visitors to schools, commented that the use of i.t.a. had resulted in less dependence on basic reading schemes in infant classes.

12 Doubts were expressed by all concerned as to whether the quantity and quality of books available was yet* adequate to cater for children's expanding reading ability and interests.

13 Teachers who were in charge of classes in which children were transferring from i.t.a. to t.o. found themselves faced with difficult tasks.

B. WRITING

1 An overwhelming majority of infant teachers who had used i.t.a. expressed their pleasure in the increase in the quantity and quality of children's free writing; many of them rating this as the chief advantage of i.t.a.

2 It was particularly emphasised that this free writing arose spontaneously, at an earlier stage than when t.o. was used, and that children were able to pursue this form of expression almost independently of the teacher.

3 The majority of H.M. Inspectors and local inspectors supported the views of teachers regarding the free writing of infants.

4 The minority of infant schools in which no improvement in children's free writing was observed, consisted mainly of very good schools which had always excelled in this respect with t.o.

5 The opinions of teachers of junior classes were divided concerning the free writing of children who had learned to read initially with i.t.a.; about half of them noted an improvement, while the remainder saw no difference or made no comments.

C. SPELLING

1 The overwhelming opinion of infant teachers and all knowledgeable visitors to schools was that the use of i.t.a. as a writing system had enormously simplified the task of spelling for children. It was this factor which was mainly responsible for the increase in children's free writing.

* This refers to the summer of 1966. Many more books printed in i.t.a. were available by 1968.

2 It was generally concluded that children's attempts at spelling in i.t.a. were much more often correct than they would have been in t.o.; even young children soon gained confidence in their own ability to spell any word and so became relatively independent of the teacher.

3 Certain parents rated it as a disadvantage that, when their children were writing at home, they were unable to help them with i.t.a. spelling.

4 Infant teachers did not consider that the transfer from i.t.a. to t.o. spelling caused children any difficulty, but a few teachers in junior schools took the opposite view.

5 There was general agreement among infant teachers, as well as among advisers and inspectors, that the transfer in spelling should take place later than the transfer in reading and that mixed t.o. and i.t.a. spellings should be accepted for a considerable time. Many infant teachers found some direct instruction in t.o. spelling rules to be helpful to children at the transition stage.

6 No infant teacher expressed the view that children who had been taught by i.t.a., once they had made the transfer to t.o. spelling, were less able spellers than children who had used i.t.a. from the beginning.

7 Most teachers of junior classes had little to say concerning children's spelling ability. Of those who did comment, some spoke of an improvement in children's spelling ability while others had doubts about the transfer. The views of H.M. Inspectors and local advisers also varied regarding the effects of i.t.a. on the spelling ability of junior children.

8 The one main fact which did emerge from the small amount of available evidence on the spelling ability of junior children was that there had been no clearly observed deterioration in the spelling of children who had learned to read and write with i.t.a. and later transferred to t.o., although such a result had originally been rather widely feared.

D. EFFECT ON OTHER ASPECTS OF SCHOOL LIFE

1 Infant teachers who had used i.t.a. were generally impressed by its beneficial effects on subjects other than the language arts. It was noted that the shorter time required to master the skills of reading and writing enabled more time to be spent on other aspects of the curriculum. Children's early skill in reading and writing helped them with other subjects, for example mathematics, and facilitated an increase in the use of individual heuristic methods of learning. Most H.M. Inspectors and local advisers also counted this as one of the advantages of i.t.a.

2 On the whole, junior teachers had much less to say about the effect of i.t.a. on other subjects than had infant teachers, although certain headteachers mentioned this point.

3 The majority of infant teachers who had used i.t.a. commented on improvements in children's attitudes and personal behaviour; interest, liveliness, confidence, independence and responsibility being mentioned in this context.

4 Many junior teachers, although not such a large majority as among infant teachers, commented favourably on the general attitudes of children taught by i.t.a.

5 More than half of H.M. Inspectors had noted an improvement in children's attitudes and behaviour; most of the remainder saw little change. The views of local inspectors on this point were similarly divided.

E. RESULTS RELATED TO CHILDREN'S INTELLIGENCE

1 Most of the comments regarding the results of using i.t.a. with children of different levels of intelligence came from infant teachers rather than from visitors to schools. More than half of the teachers who had used i.t.a. were convinced that children of all levels of interest made better progress in reading and writing than they would have done with t.o.

2 A small minority of infant teachers thought that as the brightest children were likely to learn to read quite easily with t.o., there was probably no need for them to use i.t.a. In contrast, certain teachers considered i.t.a. to be particularly valuable for the brightest children by 'stretching' them, in that its use permitted them to forge ahead on their own in so many subjects.

3 A minority of infant teachers spoke of their disappointment that i.t.a. had not helped the dullest children as much as they had hoped. A few local advisers also expressed their doubts on this point, in contrast to other local inspectors and H.M. Inspectors who remarked on significant improvements in the reading and writing progress of less able children.

F. RESULTS IN JUNIOR CLASSES

1 Although opinions were divided regarding the long-term effect of using i.t.a. to be observed in the reading, writing and spelling of eight and nine year olds, two clear trends of belief emerged from the evidence:

(a) Junior children had not suffered by learning to read and write initially with i.t.a.
(b) The exceptional rate of progress noted by most infant teachers was decreasing rapidly and had often reached a normal rate by the time children were in first and second year junior classes.

2 Certain reading experts, teachers and other skilled observers had formed the opinion that teachers of upper infant and junior classes had not yet learned to capitalise on the early reading skill gained by children who had used i.t.a. It was considered that teachers of junior children needed not only to increase their expectations of what children could do but also to realise the need for giving children guidance and instruction in the more advanced reading skills, as part of a continuous developmental programme.

IV Observations regarding staff

1 Headteachers and local advisers were in complete agreement that all teachers did not achieve the same results with i.t.a., even when the children in their classes were considered equivalent. In other words, exactly as in any other teaching situation, the results obtained by the most able and experienced teachers were always better than the results of less able and inexperienced teachers.

2 There was also an extensive measure of agreement between headteachers and local officials that, with teachers of all levels of ability and experience, children's progress was better with i.t.a. than with t.o. The exception to this statement was represented by the views of certain local inspectors who concluded that children's progress in reading and writing was equally as good with the 'best' teachers using t.o. as with the 'best' teachers using i.t.a.

3   Support for the idea that the introduction of i.t.a. had led to a general improvement in the level of reading tuition came from teachers themselves, headteachers, inspectors and most other visitors to schools. It was concluded that the publicity about i.t.a., and the fact that many teachers had read reports on the subject and attended lectures and workshops, had contributed to a renewed interest in both i.t.a. and t.o. schools, resulting in many staffroom discussions on varied aspects of reading. Greater thought has thus been given to the actual learning and teaching process, leading to a noticeable improvement in the standard of reading tuition.

4   Many local inspectors and certain headteachers were particularly favourably impressed by their observations of less able and inexperienced teachers using i.t.a. with infants. They noted that, as the comparative regularity of the alphabet simplified the initial process of learning to read and write, inexperienced and below average teachers were able to teach these skills more competently, with beneficial effects on the children in their classes.

5   One of the problems originally feared by headteachers concerned frequent staff changes, resulting in an influx of teachers who were neither trained to use i.t.a. nor experienced in its use. In practice, however, the majority of headteachers and local inspectors had been pleasantly surprised by the ease and speed with which new members of staff, including young teachers straight from college and married women returning to teaching, had familiarised themselves with the alphabet–a view corroborated by the teachers concerned.

6   A proportion of headteachers and advisers, as well as members of The i.t.a. Foundation, believed that teachers' competence in the use of i.t.a. could be increased by tuition in the form of lectures, correspondence courses and workshops.

7   Certain headteachers were of the opinion that the use of i.t.a. had contributed towards a friendlier attitude between members of staff.

V   Observations regarding experiments

A. THE READING RESEARCH UNIT'S FIRST EXPERIMENT

1   Knowledgeable visitors to schools were mostly of the opinion that, in the Reading Research Unit's first experiment, the schools which had volunteered to use i.t.a. were usually in the charge of good headteachers who took a lively interest in new ideas in education. In most of these schools there was a belief in an early rather than a delayed beginning to reading.

2   The main reasons given by the headteachers themselves for becoming experimental schools were, in this order: an interest in new developments in reading, dissatisfaction with the difficulties caused to children by the irregularities of the traditional alphabet and concern about the reading standards in the school.

3   There was general agreement among headteachers of experimental schools that the most experienced or most able teachers in the school had been placed in charge of the original i.t.a. class, a view which was endorsed by local inspectors and other visitors to schools.

4   The majority of the teachers in the first experimental classes spoke of the original stimulus of knowing they were part of an important experiment, and their increasing enthusiasm as they observed children making good progress with i.t.a.

Local advisers, H.M. Inspectors and other visitors to schools also remarked on this exceptional wave of enthusiasm in the classes which first used i.t.a.

5   Teachers, advisers and inspectors all mentioned the shortage of books printed in i.t.a. during the first few years of the experiment.

6   Many teachers of experimental classes commented that, in spite of the lack of books, the results in their first year were better than the results in succeeding years. Headteachers, advisers and inspectors had noticed the same trend. These exceptionally good results in the first year were attributed to the quality of the teachers in charge of experimental classes, the pioneering spirit which resulted from being the first to experiment with this new alphabet and the stimulation arising from early success. (Despite the less striking results in succeeding years, the majority of the first experimental class teachers were still favourably impressed by i.t.a. and hoped to continue to use it in preference to t.o.)

7   Teachers in the experimental classes stressed that they had tried to continue to use their former methods of teaching, as requested. Yet, in many cases, they had found that the sounding of words and grasping of phonic rules had arisen quite naturally in children at an earlier stage than with t.o. Nevertheless, neither the teachers themselves, nor local and national inspectors, saw this trend as a movement towards more formalised phonic work–a trend which would have been disapproved of by many of them.

8   Many educationists, including lecturers, writers, inspectors and advisers, had taken strong exception to the publicity surrounding the Reading Research Unit's first experiment, to the frequent visitors to certain of the experimental schools and to what they considered to be the premature publication of results. Numerous teachers of experimental classes also made adverse comments on the excessive numbers of visitors and continual publicity.

9   The large amount of testing and recording which took place in both experimental and control classes was deplored by the majority of teachers concerned. It was considered by them to be a strain on young children and far too time-consuming both from the point of view of the children and the teachers who had to undertake it. On the other hand, a minority of headteachers reported that they found the task of carrying out the testing to be interesting.

10   A proportion of advisers in those local authorities which took part in the first experiment also criticised the amount of testing which had to be carried out. Even more seriously, the quality of the testing and the reliability of the results were questioned by a few of these officials; their views, in certain instances, being supported by independent test results.

11   As the nine control schools visited in the Reading Research Unit's first experiment form only a small proportion of the total number of control schools, and as no special rules of guidance for the selection of these schools was employed, it should be noted that general conclusions regarding control schools cannot be drawn from the following observations.

12   The main reason given by the headteachers of the nine control schools for taking part in the first experiment was interest in new developments in reading. They were eager to be involved in such an experiment and many would have preferred to be experimental rather than control schools, but they had been prevented from doing so by the doubts of their staff. In fact, by 1966, seven of these nine control schools had begun to use i.t.a.

13   Of the nine control schools visited, two had been provided with new *Janet and John* reading books, while the remaining seven had continued to use *Janet and John* books already in the school.

14   The majority of the control schools had had few visitors and only occasional meetings and lectures had been arranged for them. No teacher or headteacher indicated that any of the lectures had been helpful and many voiced the reverse opinion.

15   Local authority advisers, as well as H.M. Inspectors, were divided in their views as to whether control schools had been well or badly served in the way of meetings and lectures.

16   Not one of the control schools visited appeared to have regarded the experiment as a contest between different schools using different media for beginning reading. The staffs stated that they had consciously tried to give no more emphasis to reading than formerly and to continue to use their normal methods. The majority of local inspectors concerned endorsed these statements. Further corroboration came from the results of standardised reading tests which were given annually at 7+, in some instances, and which showed little variation after the schools became control schools.

B. THE READING RESEARCH UNIT'S SECOND EXPERIMENT

1   As only two of the schools taking part in the Reading Research Unit's second experiment were visited, it cannot be assumed that the views expressed were representative of all the experimental schools.

2   Although the teachers concerned had been interested to take part in the experiment, they had found the experimental conditions neither easy to work under nor personally satisfying. The separation of the day's timetable into two parts, in the charge of two separate teachers, represented an artificial division, at variance with normal infant-class routine in which all the subjects of the curriculum overflow into, merge with, and reinforce each other.

VI   Miscellaneous points

A. SIMPLIFIED SPELLING SYSTEMS

1   Certain educationists questioned the need to introduce any new simplified spelling system, in the belief that 'good' teaching using t.o. would produce the same results as employing i.t.a. However, there were considerable variations in what different people meant by making 'the best' use of t.o.

2   A few people considered that, even if a new spelling system was required to help slower children to learn to read, it was unnecessary for the majority of children, who learned to read quite successfully with t.o.

3   Certain linguists and other educationists were of the opinion that, even if a new spelling system was required, i.t.a. was not the only one which should have been considered, as there were a number of criticisms which could be levelled against it.

4   The alternatives to i.t.a. which were suggested included different simplified spelling systems, utilising both the traditional alphabet and other new alphabets, and various schemes for retaining the traditional alphabet and spelling system while superimposing upon it certain signals to pronunciation, such as colour codes or

additional differentiating marks, in order to make it easier for children in the early stages.

1 The introduction of i.t.a. has presented publishers with those problems always inherent in the provision of books for a minority market, accentuated by the fact that the ultimate size of this particular market is a matter of pure conjecture.

2 The question of overriding importance for publishers concerns whether i.t.a. in its present form has come to stay, whether it will be superseded by other simplified spelling systems or whether the majority of schools will disregard such innovations and continue to use t.o.

3 Until there are quite clear indications of the likely outcome to the foregoing questions, publishers are naturally hesitant about committing themselves to the expense of publishing both i.t.a. and t.o. books. The result is that the reading books available in i.t.a. are less in number, variety and sometimes quality than equivalent t.o. books, as well as tending to be more expensive. Furthermore, books and reading materials in i.t.a., many having merely been transliterated from t.o., are not always entirely appropriate for the medium in which they are printed or for the children who use them.

VII The advantages and disadvantages of i.t.a.

It should be emphasised that the majority of the verbal evidence collected in this evaluation weighted the advantages of using i.t.a. for beginning reading and writing with infants much more heavily than the disadvantages; the latter being frequently expressed as doubts or dangers rather than disadvantages.

When asked about the advantages and disadvantages of i.t.a., more than half the infant teachers who had used it approved of it so thoroughly that they could see no disadvantages and, accordingly, were only able to list advantages. Other teachers who basically approved of i.t.a. were nevertheless aware of certain dangers. The same was true of H.M. Inspectors, local officials, other educationists and parents, who noted a few disadvantages, even when their conclusions were in favour of i.t.a.

Many of the misgivings originally felt by certain people, when the use of i.t.a. was first proposed, had proved in practice to be unfounded. Nevertheless, some of these doubts continue to be expressed by people who are lacking in personal experience of working with, or observing, children using i.t.a.

The main advantages and disadvantages put forward by all the different categories of people interviewed are summarised in the following lists. Those doubts or dangers which were mentioned by people who had seen little of i.t.a. in practice, and which experience had disproved, have not been included.

A. THE MAIN ADVANTAGES OF i.t.a.

1 The use of i.t.a. has made the early stages of learning to read easier and more enjoyable for children. As a consequence they learn to read earlier and in a shorter space of time.

2   This early reading is not merely sounding words but is usually reading with understanding.

3   Children soon find they can make successful attempts to read unknown words themselves, without help from teachers. As a result, young children choose to read individually more often than when t.o. was used, read for longer periods of time and read many more books.

4   The materials read by infants soon extended beyond those of a basic reading scheme into a wide variety of story books, information books and reference books, as well as comics, newspapers, magazines, pamphlets and so on.

5   i.t.a. has brought about a reduction in the number of non-readers and struggling readers in infant classes and has consequently reduced the frustration and lack of confidence formerly experienced by children who found difficulty in reading with t.o.

6   The beneficial effect of the introduction of i.t.a. on children's free writing was listed as one of its main advantages quite as frequently as its effect on reading.

7   The comparative regularity of the sound-symbol relationship has resulted in children's early discovery that they can make good attempts at spelling any word for themselves. The result has been a marked increase in the quantity and quality of children's free written work.

8   Children who have learned to read and write easily and happily with i.t.a. tend to develop confidence and independence and to show initiative and responsibility in other aspects of school life at a quite early age.

9   The early mastery of the skills of reading and writing, together with the independent and confident attitudes developed by children, has led naturally to an increase in individual study and exploration which is in line with current heuristic methods of learning.

10   The use of i.t.a. has benefited work other than reading and writing in infant classes in two different ways. Firstly, children's earlier skill in reading and writing has been instrumental in extending their understanding of other subjects, for example mathematics and science. Secondly, the fact that children master the basic skills of reading and writing with greater ease and speed has enabled the teacher to devote more time to the needs of individual children and to aspects of the curriculum other than the language arts.

11   Teachers themselves obtain greater pleasure and satisfaction in children's progress in reading and writing. They spoke with feeling of the end of the 'long uphill grind' of children learning to read with t.o., and the abolition of long queues of children waiting to ask for help in spelling words.

12   Teachers also rated it as an advantage that the introduction of i.t.a. has stirred up a great interest in reading among themselves; attendances at lectures and conferences, as well as staffroom discussions have contributed to an increase in teachers' own understanding of children's learning, with a consequent increase in their teaching proficiency. This view was supported by headteachers, local advisers and other visitors to schools, who also noted particularly an improvement in the proficiency of less able and less experienced teachers when they use i.t.a. rather than t.o.

13   Teachers and others counted it an advantage of i.t.a. that its introduction has resulted in an increasing interest by parents in their children's reading, often exemplified by closer co-operation between parents and teachers.

153

1   Certain people, including teachers, parents, local inspectors and educationists, who were not only familiar with i.t.a. being used with infants but also favourably disposed towards it, continued to have misgivings about the effect on the children of using i.t.a. in the classroom while encountering t.o. in every other situation in their total environment.

2   There were instances of parents reporting the frustrations experienced by children, who were not yet ready to transfer from i.t.a. to t.o., when they attempt to read t.o. print at home in books, comics, newspapers and other printed materials.

3   Certain parents find it a disadvantage to be unable to give the help requested by their children who are reading or writing in i.t.a. at home.

4   Many parents, teachers and other educators are very conscious of the problem which arises when a family moves and a child who is not a fluent reader in i.t.a. has to attend a school using only t.o.

5   Local inspectors, as well as teachers themselves, are aware of the danger of infant teachers endeavouring to hasten children's transition in reading from i.t.a. to t.o. This problem is most likely to arise when slower infants are about to be promoted to those junior schools known, or thought, to be not very favourably disposed towards i.t.a.

6   Owing to publishers' doubts regarding the possible extension of the use of i.t.a. the number and variety of books and other reading materials available in i.t.a. for beginning readers is still small compared with early reading materials printed in t.o. Furthermore, experience with i.t.a. has not yet been sufficiently extensive as to result in the most appropriate reading materials for the early stages being devised.

7   Once children have mastered the initial stages of reading, H.M. Inspectors, local advisers, teachers and others do not consider that the quantity and quality of books available for infants cater adequately for their expanding reading ability. This lack is felt not only in i.t.a. books but also in suitable t.o. books for young readers who have made the transition from i.t.a.

CHAPTER 14

Conclusions drawn from the Verbal Evidence

I Implications for teachers of infants

A. THE MAIN CONCLUSION

THE overriding impression of the interviewer, after visiting 46 primary schools and having discussions with some 250 teachers, arose not so much from what the teachers said about i.t.a., t.o. or reading in general, but rather from their whole attitude to teaching and to the children in their care. Their genuine concern for the children, their desire to do their best for them, and their interest in the progress and well-being of every individual child, were patently obvious and totally admirable.

This concern of infant teachers to do their best for children is demonstrated in their desire to make the early stages of learning to read as pleasant, simple and successful as possible. With this aim in mind, teachers tend to look hopefully at all new approaches to reading, whether these incorporate changes in media, methods, materials or procedures. Thus their interest in this evaluation will be centred on the search for an answer to a simple question. The basic question in the mind of a head-teacher who has never used i.t.a. with infants runs somewhat along the following lines: 'If we were to change the medium of reading instruction in this school from t.o. to i.t.a., would the children be given a better start to reading, would they be happier and would certain children be prevented from failing? On the other hand, if we continue to use t.o. in preference to i.t.a., should we be depriving the children of certain benefits which they might otherwise gain?' These represent direct and practical questions to which an evaluation of this nature ought to attempt to give definite and honest answers, unless the evidence proves to be either so inconclusive or so conflicting as to preclude straightforward answers. This, as we have seen, is not the case with the present evidence.

Accordingly, before adding several riders, the straightforward answer to the headteacher's straightforward question is, 'Yes–as far as the verbal evidence is concerned, if the headteacher of a school now using t.o. decides to use i.t.a. with infants as the medium for the initial stages of learning to read, there is a strong likelihood that, in a large majority of cases, such a change will be to the advantage of most of the children'. There are certain circumstances in which this might not be true; there are a few drawbacks to the use of i.t.a.; and there are alternative ways of simplifying the task of learning to read and improving teaching procedures so that children's reading progress is eased and accelerated. Such factors constitute a proportion of the conclusions to be drawn from the verbal evidence. Headteachers of primary schools will want to consider these factors alongside the preceding broad conclusion, before reaching a decision regarding the adoption of i.t.a.

If a headteacher, after reading the preceding detailed report of the discussions which took place and considering the points which follow, decides to introduce i.t.a. into infant classes, he can feel almost certain that, at the very least, the children will be unlikely to suffer, while there is a substantial body of evidence which indicates that most children will benefit in a variety of ways.

B. CONVINCING EVIDENCE

The verbal evidence offered on certain points by those with the greatest experience of either using i.t.a. with infants or observing its use is almost unanimous. The following are the main points of most importance to the questioning headteacher, as they led to the preceding general conclusion:

1 Examples of every conceivable type of school are now using i.t.a. with infants and, with only rare exceptions, the teachers concerned have no desire to revert to the use of t.o.

2 The majority of teachers who have used i.t.a., as well as knowledgeable visitors to schools, have concluded that, when i.t.a. is used with infants, better progress is made than when t.o. is used. The observed results include easier and earlier reading skill acquired without frustrations for the child; an increase in the time children choose to spend on reading, in the number of books they read and on their understanding of the contents of the books; an increase in the quantity and quality of children's free writing; an improvement in children's attitudes and behaviour; and beneficial effects on other school subjects and the general life of the school.

3 The teachers who reached the foregoing conclusions were teachers with many years of experience of using t.o. They were comparing the results of using i.t.a. with their own previous experiences with t.o. when using different methods, every possible kind of material including all the well-known t.o. reading schemes and a variety of classroom procedures. Furthermore, many of these teachers were among those who had first begun to use i.t.a. in 1961 and 1962, and whom it is now generally accepted were exceptionally able teachers. Such a group of good teachers must necessarily have comprised the very ones who had previously obtained the optimum results with t.o. That the majority of such teachers find i.t.a. preferable to t.o. must be counted as strong evidence in favour of i.t.a. A similar argument applies to the views of H.M. Inspectors and local inspectors: their breadth of opportunities for closely observing the levels of work in all types of schools, using both t.o. and i.t.a., demands that their views should be taken very seriously.

C. ORIGINAL DOUBTS WHICH PROVED UNFOUNDED

The first users of i.t.a., as well as many who deplored its use, had several grave misgivings concerning the dangers of allowing infants to begin to learn to read with this medium. Certain headteachers and teachers contemplating the adoption of i.t.a. still express the same misgivings. According to the verbal evidence, however, experience with i.t.a. has shown some of these fears, of which the following three are the most important, to be unfounded.

1 *The transition in reading*

Doubts regarding the difficulties which children would be likely to experience when they change from books printed in i.t.a. to books printed in t.o. have proved to be unfounded. In the whole of the verbal evidence collected in the course of this enquiry, no teacher or anyone else who had closely observed children at the stage of transfer, reported children experiencing difficulties. On the contrary, those who had been close to children were almost unanimous in expressing their amazement and delight when they first observed the ease with which children moved from one medium to the other, often without even appearing to notice the difference.

2 *The transition in spelling*

Originally there were serious misgivings about the effect which the employment of a temporary spelling system was likely to have on children's later ability to spell using the traditional alphabet and spelling system of written English. The evidence collected in this evaluation indicated that the early use of i t a had not adversely affected later spelling in t.o.

3 *Changing staff*

One of the main fears of headteachers regarding the introduction of i.t.a. related to the current position in infant schools of frequently changing staffs. Headteachers were anxious about how those probationary teachers and married women returning to the teaching profession, who were entirely inexperienced in using i.t.a., would manage. In the event, it has proved little of a problem, the teachers concerned soon feeling quite at home with i.t.a.

D. REMAINING DISADVANTAGES

Although experience showed some of the early forebodings about i.t.a. to have been unduly pessimistic, a proportion of them were confirmed as constituting dangers. About half of all those teachers experienced in working with i.t.a., and basically approving of it, nevertheless noted certain disadvantages, although these were considered to be less important than the advantages. Headteachers considering the introduction of i.t.a. into their schools need to be aware of these dangers so that they may measure them against the disadvantages of other approaches to reading (for every approach has both advantages and disadvantages) and, equally, in order that they may plan how best to circumvent these dangers. The four main disadvantages which follow are arranged in the order of their importance, as judged by the writer from the verbal evidence.

1 *Continuity of i.t.a. instruction*

The greatest danger to a child who begins to learn to read with i.t.a. lies in the possibility that the learning process may be interrupted at a stage before he is ready to transfer to t.o. There are two situations in which this is most likely to occur. First, the child's family may move to an area in which the child has to attend an infant school which uses t.o. only. There is little that headteachers can do to prevent such a situation arising. This danger may cause the headteacher of a school with a somewhat itinerant population to hesitate about introducing i.t.a. into the school. In schools which are using i.t.a., parents of new entrants to reception classes might be questioned about possible moves, and t.o. instruction offered to children expecting to move, but this would do nothing to alleviate the situations arising from unexpected moves. The t.o. school to which the i.t.a. child is going should certainly be supplied with information regarding the child's level of attainments, if not the actual books on which he is working, as co-operation between schools in such a case could, to some extent, help to diminish the child's difficulties.

The second situation is that in which a child still using i.t.a. is being promoted to a junior school which is not anxious to continue i.t.a. instruction. Infant teachers, knowing of, or suspecting, such a situation may tend to rush the transition. Alternatively the junior teachers concerned may cause children to transfer too early. The clear answer to this danger is that an infant headteacher would be unwise to even contemplate the introduction of i.t.a. into the school until she is absolutely satisfied that the junior school to which the child will be promoted is willing and able to continue to use i.t.a. with those children requiring to do so. Continuity for the child would, of course, be more easily assured by co-operation between the infant and junior school: visits of junior teachers to the i.t.a. infant school, joint discussions on a case-study basis and the passing on of detailed records from infant to junior schools represent some of the more obvious ways of providing such continuity.

2   The transition and the teacher

One of the disadvantages of i.t.a. mentioned most frequently by both infant headteachers and class teachers was the heavy demand made on any teacher in charge of a class in which both i.t.a. and t.o. were being used by different children. It should be noted that in a vertically-grouped school all teachers find themselves in this situation, while in schools in which children are grouped according to chronological age, most teachers face this dual task because children transfer from i.t.a. to t.o. at such widely different ages. Writing and 'thinking' in two spelling systems all day, preparing duplicate charts and notices and organising two sets of reading materials is extremely hard work for these teachers. Nevertheless, the majority of infant teachers, even while stating that the transition was hard for them, considered that the benefits to be gained by the children and also by themselves in various other ways, when i.t.a. was used, more than compensated for this additional work.

3   t.o. outside school

The modern trend in infant schools is to utilise the child's total environment as the learning situation. Certain local advisers, infant teachers and other educationists who disapprove of the whole idea of utilising simplified spelling systems as media for beginning reading are committed to this belief. Consequently, their aversion to i.t.a. springs mainly from their concern about the child being faced with one form of printed words in school and a different form elsewhere. It should also be noted that those teachers who avoid i.t.a. because they consider this to be one of its main disadvantages are usually those who, if they did use it, would be likely to extend the critical period of children's exposure to two spelling systems. They are frequently teachers who believe in a delayed start to reading and are opposed to direct instruction as such, preferring children to learn with a minimum of guidance. In such circumstances, that period which precedes the stage at which children become independent of adult help is considerably lengthened: yet this is the very time when any danger occasioned by dual spelling systems would be most likely to exist.

However, it was not only opponents of i.t.a. who were concerned about this particular danger. This same fear that children might be confused by the two alphabets was also expressed by a few of the teachers who used i.t.a. and approved of it.

Parents' verbal evidence gave a certain amount of confirmation to the existence of this particular danger. A minority of parents, mainly those who were most interested in their children's progress, reported that children using i.t.a. in school sometimes experienced frustrations when trying to read t.o. at home. The parents themselves experienced difficulties when trying to help their children to read and write in i.t.a. at home. Reports of how parents' difficulties on this score could be eased came from headteachers who had helped such parents to master i.t.a. themselves, and from local authorities where evening classes on these lines had been arranged for interested parents.

Most of the verbal evidence given by teachers who had used i.t.a., however, as well as the interviewer's observations in schools lead to the conclusion that this represents less of a danger than the preceding two disadvantages. For instance, in vertically-grouped schools, where both i.t.a. and t.o. books are available in every class-room, teachers reported that children picked up examples of both types of books without appearing to notice the difference.

Another aspect of children being exposed simultaneously to two different spelling systems arises from a phrase sometimes used in educational psychology, namely that 'perception is functionally selective'. This simply means that, although the human eye is capable, at any one moment, of seeing a wide field before it, in practice a person only perceives or pays attention to such phenomena as are of interest to him at that time. Thus it would be a mistake to imagine that all infants are constantly noticing the words printed in t.o. in their environment and mentally comparing them with the i.t.a. words seen in class. Many children may show little interest in printed words on shops, buses, cartons and so on until the time when they begin to try to decode words for themselves at school. A comparatively short time generally elapses between this moment and the time when they are reading fluently in i.t.a. and beginning to pick up t.o. books without realising they are different. It is only during this brief period that confusion between the two spelling systems might be likely to occur.

The interviewer's conclusions on this agree with the common view that children are much more adaptable than adults usually suppose. The child starting school meets anomalies all the time. He often finds dual standards of behaviour or speech at home and at school: to these he generally adapts himself. Children who learn to read with t.o. demonstrate great adaptability, for example when they learn to accept that a letter represents one sound in one word and a different sound in another word. It could well be that it is simpler for many children to reconcile themselves, for a short period, to i.t.a. in school and t.o. outside school, than to adapt themselves in the initial stages to all the various rules governing the pronunciation and spelling of words in t.o. It might also be that the hardest step in learning to read is one of the early ones, namely that of realising that a spoken word is an assembly of discrete sounds blended together and that these sounds are represented by specific letters printed on the page in a particular order. i.t.a. would seem to ease this first step and it could be that the child is then in a more receptive state for accepting the rules and anomalies of t.o.

The real truth about this suspected danger of children encountering dual spelling systems simultaneously is that we have very little evidence available. Research into this question is certainly needed. What does seem fairly certain is that it cannot constitute a very serious problem; if it did so the reading progress of those children whose early medium of reading instruction was i.t.a. would not be so great as the verbal evidence so clearly shows it to be.

159

4 Reading materials

Although the supply of reading books and other materials published in i.t.a. has continued to increase since 1961, by the academic year 1966–67 certain teachers, local advisers and H.M. Inspectors still considered the supply of reading materials to be inadequate in quality and in variety and, consequently, counted this as one of the disadvantages of i.t.a. The contention that there are fewer i.t.a. books than t.o. books available in many categories is undoubtedly true: for example, basic reading schemes, information books, picture dictionaries and story books of high quality. The same is true of the supply of supplementary reading materials of all kinds. Nevertheless, there are two reasons why the writer considers this to be the least important of the four disadvantages mentioned.

Firstly, it should be noted that those children who learned to read so easily with i.t.a., in the first few years, did so with a much smaller selection of reading materials than is now available. Indeed, the most spectacular results of all were obtained in the first year, when the supply of i.t.a. materials could well have been described as totally inadequate. A variety of interesting conclusions might possibly be drawn from this fact. For instance, it could be assumed that the fewer printed books available and the more the teacher and the children have to produce their own form of written words, the better children's early reading progress is likely to be. Alternatively, the conclusion might be drawn that reading materials are of little importance compared with other factors in the total reading situation, of which, in this instance, the medium employed or the teacher's enthusiasm and drive may be the most potent. Whatever the reasons may be, it can be said that many children have already learned to read easily and speedily with i.t.a. despite a shortage of books. Secondly, if i.t.a. continues to be used, the supply of reading materials in this medium is bound to increase. Concurrently, practical experience with i.t.a. should lead to the production of materials appropriate to the medium itself, in contrast to the mere transliteration of books designed originally to help children to master an irregular spelling system.

E. SUMMARY OF MAIN IMPLICATIONS FOR TEACHERS

The headteacher of a school containing infant pupils, who is considering the possibility of changing from t.o. to i.t.a., is likely to find the following points which emerged from the verbal evidence of most relevance to his decision:

1 Reading progress does not depend solely on the medium used. For instance, certain of the best schools using t.o. had approximately the same standards of reading and writing as similar schools using i.t.a. Likewise, in those schools with similar background features in which i.t.a. was being used, widely different standards were noted.

2 It follows that alterations in the other factors relating to reading can effect improvements without changing from t.o. to i.t.a.; for instance, changes in the attitudes of the staff, an increase in reading drive or alterations in the methods, materials and procedures adopted with t.o. might well produce better results than many schools are currently obtaining with t.o.

3 Nevertheless, even while bearing in mind the foregoing two points, there is a wealth of evidence from able and experienced teachers which indicates that this particular form of simplified spelling system is easier for children to learn than t.o., and that its use is usually accompanied by a variety of benefits. There is very little

evidence available of children suffering, or being placed at a disadvantage, as a result of beginning to read and write with i.t.a.

4 Many of the original doubts and dangers envisaged when the use of i.t.a. was first proposed have proved unfounded. A few disadvantages still remain and will need to be weighed against the difficulties and drawbacks of t.o.; some of which adults are well aware of and others they have grown to accept, although they are nonetheless present for children. None of the disadvantages is insurmountable, except perhaps the case of the child who has to move to a t.o. school before he is fluent in i.t.a., and they certainly do not appear so formidable as to outweigh the many advantages noted by those with the greatest experience of using i.t.a.

5 The following notes of caution regarding the introduction of i.t.a. can be drawn from the verbal evidence:

(a) If the school has an itinerant population of children, the use of i.t.a. might be inadvisable.

(b) An infant school would be unwise to consider using i.t.a. before ascertaining that the junior school to which the children will be promoted at 7 years of age is both willing and able to continue to use i.t.a. with those children who need to do so.

(c) Before beginning to use i.t.a. the headteacher needs to be certain that the staff are eager to experiment with it or at least willing to co-operate fully.

6 The bulk of the verbal evidence given by teachers having the longest experience of using i.t.a., and by experienced observers, emphasises the advantages to be gained when i.t.a. is the medium for beginning reading and writing, rather than t.o. as it is currently employed in many infant classes.

II Additional conclusions

Those conclusions drawn by the writer from the verbal evidence, and considered to be of most relevance to the headteacher thinking of adopting i.t.a., have been included in Section I of this chapter. Additional conclusions are presented in this section.

A. VIEWS VARY WITH PROXIMITY

The writer was struck forcibly by the fact that the closer the experience of a person to the task of actually helping young children to master the beginnings of reading and writing in i.t.a., the greater his or her approval of i.t.a. tended to be. Teachers of reception classes and younger infants were usually more enthusiastic than teachers of older infants or juniors. Inspectors and advisers with the greatest experience of observing i.t.a. in use generally evinced most approval, while those who had seen little of it in practice were more likely to condemn it. Inspectors and advisers who were well acquainted with i.t.a., but who were doubtful about its overall value, rarely had doubts relating to children in their first year or two of schooling. Therefore the conclusion to be drawn from the verbal evidence must be that i.t.a. has proved beneficial to infants, in the early stages of learning to read and write.

B. EARLY READING

All the verbal evidence, as well as published reports, emphasises that children begin to read and write earlier with i.t.a. than with t.o. Certain educationists who regard this as a disadvantage of i.t.a., usually believe that early reading is a bad thing in itself; they sometimes suspect that i.t.a. is a tool designed to force early reading on children willy-nilly and they appear to be under the impression that, in all schools using i.t.a., early reading is the rule.

The writer's conclusions represent the opposite view. Early reading *per se* is not to be decried unless the child is being forced to attempt something beyond his capabilities. There is no evidence whatsoever of this happening with i.t.a.; in fact, the reverse is true, in that the impetus towards early reading comes from the child and not the teacher. Most children come to school eager to learn to read and write and, with this particular simplified spelling system, they soon find themselves able to do so.

Those teachers who believe in a delayed start to reading need not consider their belief to debar them from using i.t.a., as certain schools in which the same views are held are currently using it. Although teachers in such schools are finding it impossible to delay the beginning of reading and writing as long as formerly, they are learning to accept the fact that an easier task–that is, learning to read with a more regular spelling system–can be mastered with pleasure at an earlier age than the more complicated task represented by an irregular spelling system.

It is concluded that this trend towards earlier reading and writing, which springs from the child himself, carries with it considerable advantages, many of which have been detailed earlier in this report. Among them should be counted the child's pride and satisfaction when he masters the skills of reading and writing; the value to him of acquiring an additional means of communication; and the development of his confidence, initiative and independence which results in an extension of his interests. Moreover, the early reading and writing of the large majority of children leave the teacher more time to devote to slower children and those with other special needs.

C. A DIFFERENT CLIMATE IN SCHOOLS

The benefits of the earlier and easier reading and writing with i.t.a. have made a considerable difference to many other aspects of infant school life, which are reflected in the attitudes and behaviour of both children and adults and in the whole atmosphere and work of the school. Two separate yet interwoven strands which have contributed towards these changes can be discerned.

When t.o. is the medium of initial reading instruction, its irregularity makes it inevitable that children are dependent upon the teacher for perhaps the first year or two, and sometimes for considerably longer. The child needs to be taught to recognise new words and then to practise them in a variety of ways before he is ready to progress to the next page or story in a reading scheme, the timing of each stage of progress usually depending on the teacher's decision. When the child begins to make attempts at reading and writing on his own, he is handicapped by the necessity to consult the teacher frequently regarding the pronunciation or spelling of words. Within this sort of working framework, in which the teacher always initiates the next step in the learning process, and the child frequently needs to consult her, it is un-avoidable that the teacher should, to some extent, represent an authoritarian figure. On the other hand, when i.t.a. is employed, the diminution in the necessity for the teacher to teach and the child to consult, leads the child to regard the teacher as much less of an authoritarian figure and himself as more of an equal. Thus the relationship between teacher and child, and the classroom regime, nearly always becomes more democratic and more informal.

The second strand activating these changes also springs from the child's growing independence of the teacher. It very frequently results in the development of confidence, initiative and so on in the child, as already mentioned. These two forces working together, when i.t.a. is used, have increased the noticeable movement in infant schools towards heuristic methods of learning, embodying individual interests and exploration, within informal working relationships. Certain good schools using t.o. already exemplify these attitudes and this atmosphere: many do not. Since using i.t.a., many more schools are finding themselves being carried along quite naturally on these lines of development; moreover it seems likely that a large proportion of such schools would have been unlikely to move in this direction if they had continued to use t.o.

D. TEACHERS OF READING

Part of the success of i.t.a. can undoubtedly be attributed to the current position in this country regarding the training of teachers of reading. In Colleges of Education, even those students who are training specifically as infant teachers spend only a very small proportion of their time in studying or practising teaching the various aspects of reading. Thus, infant teachers leaving college can in no way be considered as reading specialists, nor, in some cases, even adequately equipped teachers of reading. Furthermore, many infant classes are in the charge of teachers whose training related to older pupils, married women who have returned to teaching after absences of many years and untrained teachers. Accordingly, in some infant schools, the teacher who is experienced and knowledgeable about teaching infants to read may well be the exception rather than the rule.

Teaching children to read in t.o., with all its irregularities and anomalies, is a difficult and often long-term operation. The able, experienced teacher has, in many instances, achieved remarkable success in this task. The remarks made by advisers and inspectors about the excellent reading results in 'good' t.o. schools spring from observations of just such teachers. The less-good results observable in many other t.o. schools can be partially attributed to changing populations of teachers who have been inadequately prepared for the difficult role of teaching reading through the medium of an irregular spelling system.

In contrast, learning to read with i.t.a. requires less skilled teaching than learning to read with t.o. In fact, it needs much less teaching altogether; the simplicity of the almost general rule that one symbol represents one sound and vice versa enables the child, once he has grasped this rule and learned the grapheme-phoneme correspondences, to make a great deal of progress on his own. Consequently, children are much less dependent for their progress on teachers who may have received little or no training in teaching the early stages of reading; equally, they are less affected by staff absences or changes. Thus, in the particular circumstances at present prevalent in infant schools in this country, the use of a simplified spelling system for beginning reading is clearly advantageous.

It would be unfortunate if the foregoing comments were taken to imply that, when i.t.a. is used, no training is required in order to teach children to read. The writer firmly believes that training in the teaching of reading results in an improvement in reading standards with both t.o. and i.t.a., and that consequently, teachers who have

163

received some training in the use of i.t.a. will generally be more competent than those lacking such training.

E. THE ADVANTAGES OF i.t.a. DO NOT LAST

Comments made by teachers in junior classes, by knowledgeable visitors to schools, as well as reports of research findings, all indicate that by the age of approximately eight, the early advantages in reading and writing gained by children who have used i.t.a. are diminishing or have almost disappeared. The observer's visits to junior classes generally confirmed this view, although certain junior teachers spoke of other advantages in the form of personal attributes which they had observed in the i.t.a. children.

In the writer's opinion the slowing down in reading progress is not unexpected, for it is closely related to the training of teachers and to current reading practice in schools in this country. As already stated, students training as infant teachers receive very little tuition in reading teaching: it can be added that those training as junior teachers receive even less and it is rare for students training for secondary schools to have even considered the teaching of reading to be a subject of concern to them. Moreover, across the whole range of teacher training, such tuition in reading as is given is almost solely concerned with the initial stages of reading, either at the infant level or in the form of remedial teaching for non-readers among older pupils.

The assumptions behind these practices in teacher training are carried over into the schools, where it tends to be assumed that by the time a child has attained a reading age of seven or eight, the skill of reading has been mastered, and that the mere presentation of progressively harder books will automatically cause this skill to be increased. The acquisition of reading skills in schools is not looked upon as representing a continuous task for all teachers, with all pupils, from infants to school leavers. The result is that in our overcrowded infant classes, teachers are not unnaturally inclined to consider that those children who have completed an infant reading scheme and begun to read a variety of books on their own, are less in need of tuition and guidance than the slower children in the class. The same pattern continues in junior and secondary schools, where it is a rare event to find a comprehensive reading programme planned for systematic improvement in word analysis skills, vocabulary extension, comprehension skills, varying rates of reading, and so on, or specific training in the utilisation of the various skills which comprise the total subject of reading.

In these circumstances, it is not surprising that the children in our schools usually reach a plateau of reading attainment round about a reading age of eight. The brightest children eventually raise themselves above this plateau in certain areas in the acquisition and application of the various reading skills, although their progress in other areas may be minimal. The majority of children rise only slowly and unevenly above this plateau, while duller children rarely progress beyond this stage and some slip back. All that is happening at present is that the i.t.a. children reach this plateau earlier than the t.o. children who, within two or three years, catch up with them. They are then all prevented, through lack of guidance and instruction, from making a continued surge of progress.

A somewhat similar picture can be noted with regard to children's free writing. It was disappointing to observe some children, who in i.t.a. infant classes had expressed themselves in original, flowing, free writing, including poetry as well as prose, writing stilted, formal 'compositions' in t.o., all on one set subject, in certain junior classes. It may be suggested that the loss of spontaneous free writing is a function of maturation or a necessary concomitant of transfer to t.o. Such a suggestion was refuted by the observation that, in certain other schools, the same originality and spontaneity of free written work seen in infant classes was encouraged and achieved in junior classes. Thus the writer concluded that the decline in the standards of free writing, often noted in first and second year junior classes, reflected an undue emphasis on punctuation, paragraphing and the formal planning of essays, in a manner likely to obliterate the spontaneity of children's free written expression.

The earlier and more enthusiastic interest and ability of young children in reading and writing presents teachers of junior classes with a new problem requiring careful thought and experimentation in order to discover how these early skills can be fully utilised and expanded

It should also be emphasised that an acceptance of the view that the reading and writing of i.t.a. and t.o. children are approximately the same at the age of eight, does not discredit the use of i.t.a. for the initial stages of reading and writing. No claim was originally made to the effect that i.t.a. would produce better readers in the long run. The aim was to simplify the initial task of learning. Thus, even if i.t.a. children are only at the same level of attainment as t.o. children after three or four years, if learning to read has been easier and more pleasant for them, if fewer children have experienced frustrations and failures and if many have known the enjoyment and value of reading a year or so earlier than they would have done, it can fairly be claimed that its use has been justified.

F. SLOW-LEARNING CHILDREN

One important factor in the assessment of i.t.a. is its effect on children of different levels of intelligence. Teachers' evidence on this point, and observations in schools, led the writer to conclude that i.t.a. has proved helpful to children of all levels of intelligence, including the slowest learners. Teachers are usually particularly interested in the effects which new approaches to reading may have on the dullest children, and in view of the fact that Downing's (1967) conclusions on this score might be interpreted by some teachers as implying that i.t.a. is of little value to the slowest 10% of children, it is important that the following observations leaning towards the contrary view should be considered.

Many teachers and advisers spoke of how the introduction of i.t.a. had resulted in a reduction in the number of non-readers and poor readers to be found in infant classes and entering junior schools. Numerous examples have been quoted of schools in poor socio-economic areas, using i.t.a. with children of below average ability, in which whole age-groups of children were being promoted to junior classes with practically no non-readers among them; even the slowest children having made a good start to reading in i.t.a. Thus, whether those children who would have been non-starters if t.o. had been used were of low intelligence or suffered from other handicaps affecting reading progress, i.t.a. had undoubtedly helped many of them to read.

These statements lead to two important questions. Why were a minority of teachers and advisers doubtful about i.t.a. helping the slowest children? And why might certain of Downing's test results be taken to support this view? With reference to the first question, the writer concluded that teachers who were disappointed in this respect were those who had expected too much of i.t.a., optimistically hoping that its use would automatically cause every child to read easily and speedily. This expectation had, in certain cases, resulted in two unhelpful practices. Firstly, the assumption that a simplified alphabet itself was all that was required for reading progress had led to the neglect of many of the other facets of learning to read. Secondly, in some instances, there had been a too early introduction to formal reading of children who might have benefited from a later beginning. In contrast, the teachers who had the greatest measure of success had accepted that, even with a simplified spelling system, slow-learning children might not be ready to begin formal reading work as soon as they entered the school, that a pre-reading programme was still required and that, even so, it might be likely to take three years or so for such children to master the initial stages of reading.

The second question might conveniently be viewed in the light of the following points, which the writer considers important, regarding the results of reading tests administered to slow-learning children in their first two or three years at school.

1   With slow-learning children, whether the medium of instruction is t.o. or i.t.a., measurable progress in reading should not be expected in the first year, as this period can probably be most profitably devoted to an enrichment of the child's total experience, with an emphasis on speaking and listening and on practising those verbal and auditory sub-skills which will lay a foundation for later more formal reading tuition.

2   Reading readiness tests are not generally used in this country and thus the progress made in this preparatory stage is judged intuitively by the teacher.

3   The reading tests currently used, even when they purport to measure the very earliest stages of reading, are extremely blunt instruments for the task. Slow-learning children remain in the earliest informal stages of learning to read much longer than average and bright children. Many slow-learning children, in their first year or so at school do achieve a sound basis for beginning to read and some take the initial steps. These early stages in learning to read, although clearly discernible to the teachers, will, nevertheless, fail to register on most reading tests currently in use in this country.

4   To test children in a different medium from the one in which they are engaged in learning to read is not a practice to be generally commended. The exposure of the slowest children to this trial is to be strongly deprecated, as it may undermine the children's confidence in their own ability to read and, furthermore, is unlikely to give meaningful results regarding their actual reading standards.

5   If one accepts that the slowest children will take much longer than bright children to learn to read, it might be agreed that for such children to be able to read easy books in i.t.a. in about three years, even if at that point they have not transferred to t.o., would be acceptable progress. It then follows that the most appropriate time to compare the effect of using different media on the reading progress of slow-learning children would be at, or later than, this stage. Thus the most meaningful comparisons between groups of slow-learning children using t.o. and i.t.a. would be the results of tests administered, in the medium being currently used, at the end of the infant school, supplemented by later tests in t.o. after the i.t.a. children had transferred to t.o.

Downing (1967) gives test results regarding High Achievers (three-tenths of the total number of experimental children), Middle Achievers (four-tenths of the children) and Low Achievers (three-tenths of the children). If we term all the children in the Low Achievers' category 'slow-learning children' and then describe those in the upper two-thirds of this group as 'rather slow children' and those in the lower third as 'very slow children', the results present the following picture.

In the earliest reading tests (presumably those administered in the first year), when both control and experimental children were tested in their own medium, no difference between the two slow-learning groups was apparent. In fact, neither group of slow-learning children had made much progress, as recorded by test scores. After one and a half years, when the children were again tested in their own medium, the rather slow children in the i.t.a. group had made better progress than the rather slow children in the t.o. group, but the very slow children in both groups showed no difference in progress.

When both groups were tested in t.o. after one and a half years, the t.o. group gained higher scores than the i.t.a. group. It is fair to assume that few, if any, of the slow-learning i.t.a. children would have made the transition to t.o. at this stage. After three years, when both groups of slow-learning children were tested in t.o., the original i.t.a. children were superior to the t.o. children, although it must be presumed that some of the very slow children in the i.t.a. group had still not made the transition.

The writer is of the opinion that results of t.o. tests administered to slow-learning i.t.a. children after one and half years, when few of them were likely to have transferred to t.o., should be ignored, as they constitute a useless comparison as far as a practical assessment of i.t.a. is concerned. If this is done, it can be seen that the pattern of the progress, as represented by test scores, is in line with the five points suggested as being important in this context. Little progress is recorded for either group in the first year and, thereafter, an increasing gain by the i.t.a. group of slow-learning children until, by the end of the third year, their scores were superior to those of their t.o. counterparts, when tested in t.o., although a proportion of i.t.a. children had not then made the transition. These test results confirm the views of the majority of teachers and inspectors, and the writer's conclusions, that, when a long-term view is taken, slow-learning children have been shown to benefit from using i.t.a.

Two further points regarding slow-learning children should be mentioned. Firstly, teachers have noted additional improvements, far removed from test scores, when slow-learning children use i.t.a.: these include more interest in reading, a greater eagerness to attempt to read and write and an increase in the pleasure and satisfaction of so doing, with a concomitant decrease in the frustrations and occasional despair which some slow-learning children experience when using t.o.

Secondly, certain visitors to i.t.a. schools criticised the fact that when they listened to some of the slower children reading easy books aloud, these children were reading mechanically and sometimes without any real understanding. The observer also met a few very slow children reading in this way, and compared them with similar children in t.o. classes who had either not started to read at all or who were stumbling horribly. Without in any way wanting to suggest that all slow-learning children should be taught to read mechanically at an early age, it is realised that it is often difficult for the teacher to refrain from allowing a slow child to start on a book. The conclusion was drawn that, for the following reasons, the situation of the slow-learning i.t.a. child who found himself able to read aloud to an adult, had, therefore, certain features to commend it:

(i) The child was taking great pride in his own reading aloud, even if it was at a

167

rather mechanical level;

(ii) The child was prevented from appearing and feeling different from other children in the class who were reading, because, in his own mind, he too was reading;

(iii) In this way a feeling of failure which might have built up in him was being avoided;

(iv) His present rather mechanical reading would be likely to form a basis on which later reading with understanding could be built.

G. THE TRANSITION

Of all the verbal evidence collected in this enquiry, the fact most frequently and most emphatically stated was that children did not experience difficulty in making the transition in reading from i.t.a. to t.o. Teachers and those experienced visitors to schools who had observed the transition taking place had no doubts whatsoever on this score. In the light of this unanimity in the views of those closely involved in the practical aspects of children's transfer, it is surprising to find that their conclusions are at direct variance with Downing's (1967) results of reading tests, which reveal what he described as a 'setback' immediately after transfer.

What the teacher means by the child experiencing no difficulty in making the transition is somewhat as follows. The child begins to read in t.o. the same book as he has just completed in i.t.a., one of a similar level of difficulty or one of a slightly lower level of difficulty. He reads it to himself with apparent ease, enjoyment and understanding. He consults the teacher only rarely about words which he finds troublesome. When the teacher asks the child to read aloud a paragraph or so from this book, he does so with almost the same ease as if the book had been in i.t.a.; he stumbles over, or requires help with, only the odd word. Within a few days, or a week or two at most, even the child who attempted a slightly easier t.o. reading book than his last i.t.a. book is reading t.o. books of an equivalent level with facility. Thus, children who were fluent readers in i.t.a., as most of them were before transfer, are, within a week or so, fluent readers in t.o. without any apparent diminution in accuracy and comprehension. This evidence from teachers represents a functional assessment of reading progress by those most competent to judge. The writer considers it to be absolutely irrefutable evidence as, had a functional setback in reading occurred in practice, the experienced teachers and observers who gave evidence would have noted it and would not have hesitated to include it with other disadvantages of i.t.a. which they reported.

On the other hand, Downing's evidence clearly indicates that the scores on t.o. tests of accuracy and comprehension, of those children who had transferred from i.t.a. to t.o. at least six weeks previously, were less than their earlier scores on i.t.a. tests. The only conclusion the writer finds it possible to draw from these two conflicting pieces of evidence is that the reading skills required in order to respond to reading tests are not identical with the skills required for functional reading as viewed by the teacher; in other words, an operational definition of reading is different from the so-called 'reading' done in test situations. It follows that differences in test scores, even when they are statistically significant, do not necessarily represent operational differences. Moreover, to employ the term 'setback' to describe a statistically significant decrease in test scores was possibly not the most appropriate phrase to have selected, as it might be considered by many people to imply that a functional setback occurred at the stage of transition.

The fact that children's scores on certain reading tests are less in t.o. than in i.t.a. for a period after transition, is of course of interest to the teacher as well as the researcher. It may well be that an examination of children's errors in t.o. could lead to a consideration of the need for a certain amount of instruction in reading, both those words which follow regular yet different rules in t.o. to i.t.a., and likewise irregular words. Instruction similar to that being given by many teachers, at the stage of transition in writing, regarding spelling rules in t.o. may be required. The two conflicting pieces of evidence from practitioners and researchers must also necessarily lead to an examination of the validity of tests of reading ability and further attempts to equate tests and test situations more closely with actual reading situations.

One further point regarding teachers' evidence on the transition should be noted. Practically every infant teacher who was speaking of children's ease of transfer, was referring to average and above average children, as slow-learning children do not usually transfer until junior classes. Certain infant teachers clearly had some anxiety about how slow-learning children would cope with the transfer. The small amount of evidence available from junior teachers about children transferring to t.o. after three or four years of using i.t.a., suggested that these anxieties were unnecessary. Junior teachers who had seen slow-learning children transferring to t.o. tended to speak as the infant teachers had done, regarding their surprise at the ease with which the change had been effected. Nevertheless, there was some indication that, while brighter younger children had tended to transfer themselves in infant classes, the question of when a child should make the transfer and how he might be helped to do so were decisions which junior teachers needed to make. Further research on the transition, with special reference to slow-learning children, obviously merits serious attention.

H. i.t.a. NOT NECESSARILY THE FINAL ANSWER

The undoubted fact that the majority of infant teachers consider children's reading progress to be of great importance could well lead to a serious danger regarding the conclusions to be drawn from the results of experiments with i.t.a. The many published reports in the last few years setting out the advantages of i.t.a., reinforced by the evidence presented in this evaluation, which mainly supports these claims, could well lead teachers to conclude that the use of i.t.a. is the total and final answer to the perennial question of the best way of initiating children into the skills of reading and writing. The writer is perturbed lest this should happen, as she considers it would be a regrettable waste of the discoveries made and the good achieved in the course of these experiments; experiments which could possibly have the most far-reaching consequences of any recent development in primary education.

What has been achieved in the six years between 1961 and 1967 is remarkable. A medium for initial reading instruction was devised by someone who was neither a teacher of young children nor an educational psychologist. It was used in large-scale experiments with infants, without even a single pilot study to discover how children would react to an alphabet different from the one prevalent in their normal environment, or how they would transfer to the traditional orthography. Wide publicity, deplored by many educationists, nevertheless persuaded educators, teachers and parents to launch into these quite revolutionary experiments in an educational field in which tradition is strong and changes normally take place only slowly. Results have been achieved which, in 1961, none but the inventor of the alphabet and a small handful of supporters would have imagined possible. It is probably a fair supposition that in 1961 few, if any, experienced infant teachers and no reading experts would have been prepared to predict the course which events have taken. That so many schools have been willing to experiment, that so many children should have learned to read and write so easily, that so many of the original fears should have proved groundless, that so much discussion about reading should have taken place among teachers and that the public at large should also have evinced such interest, has represented a phenomenon unique in the history of primary education in this country.

The experiments with i.t.a. have undoubtedly revealed that this particular medium has made the initial stages of learning to read and write considerably easier for children than do most current practices employing t.o. But to conclude from the results that the use of i.t.a. is the final answer to initial reading instruction would mean that the ultimate benefits which might spring from this adventurous undertaking could be partially or almost wholly wasted. The experiments with i.t.a. have demonstrated other points than the obvious one that a simpler code is easier to learn than a complex one, of which the following three may be the most important. Firstly, we have been brought face to face with the realisation of how little we all know about how children really do learn to read. Secondly, when someone who is not a reading expert can produce an idea which has proved so advantageous, one must consider what might be done if experts from different fields – for example, teachers, linguists, reading experts, educational psychologists, educational researchers, neurologists and so on – combined to consider reading teaching. Thirdly, it has been demonstrated that, given sufficient stimulus and support, British teachers, parents and educators, who are traditionally rather conservative, can be caught up in and become deeply involved in an interesting experiment with mutual gain for everyone.

These points lead to one major conclusion. The use of i.t.a. over six years has shown that an alteration in only one of the factors which affect reading progress can effectively simplify the task of learning to read. The time is now clearly ripe for pursuing these investigations into simplifying reading and writing for beginners by comparing all possible means of simplifying the task, including comparisons of different media, materials, methods and procedures.

Although this evaluation was not designed to collect and assess evidence as to the efficacy of other approaches to reading as compared with i.t.a., a certain amount of evidence on this score did nevertheless come to light. For instance, there are reports from certain local education authority advisers that the best schools using t.o. do as well as the best schools using i.t.a. This inevitably leads to a consideration of whether many schools now using t.o. could achieve higher reading standards with t.o. if other factors in the reading situation, for example teachers' attitudes, reading methods, materials or procedures, were altered. Comments on the use of certain published reading materials, for example, *Words in Colour, Key Words Reading Scheme* and Stott's *Programmed Reading Kit,* indicated that their use had brought about striking improvements in certain schools. In addition, claims for the value of other possible signalling systems have been put forward, as well as suggestions for improving i.t.a.

The whole tenor of the verbal evidence, while supporting the view that this particular simplified spelling system has made it easier for the majority of children to master the beginnings of reading and writing, nevertheless points forcibly to the need for further research in numerous directions, some of which are suggested in the following section of this chapter.

III   Implications for future research

A. INTRODUCTION

Although this research project has been basically concerned with collecting and evaluating evidence regarding the use of i.t.a. as a means of teaching infants to read, it was inevitable that visits to schools and discussions with so many teachers should throw up additional evidence on other facets of infant education. For instance, in this enquiry information came to light on teachers' varied aims in infant education, on their ways of trying to achieve these aims, on the whole process of learning to read, on problems relating to the conduct of experiments with infants, as well as on additional aspects of the use of i.t.a.

In particular, as so many of the schools visited had participated in the Reading Research Unit's experiments, numerous problems relating to the conduct of experiments in reading in infant classes were noted and discussed. The views of teachers who had participated in these experiments, and of inspectors and others whose experiences qualified them to compare a wide range of schools using both t.o. and i.t.a., provide a valuable commentary on the practical aspects of planning reading experiments with infants, which could prove of considerable help to future research workers in this field. Those factors considered to have most relevance for future experiments of this nature are outlined here.

B. FACTORS AFFECTING READING EXPERIMENTS

1   *Reading attitudes and drive*

Visits to schools and the collected verbal evidence reinforced an appreciation of the large differences between infant schools in respect of the attitudes of the staff to children's reading progress. The clearest demarcation lay between those schools in which the staff emphasised their belief in the importance of reading and favoured an early beginning, and those schools in which reading was considered to be only a small part of the child's environment and thus beginning reading tuition was delayed.

The attitudes of the staff to reading were reflected in expectations that children would, or would not, learn to read at an early age, resulting in reading drives of different strengths being in force in these contrasting schools. In schools in which the first attitude was prevalent a strong reading drive was permanently in force, while in the latter schools very little, if any, reading drive existed.

Attitudes to reading and reading drives were found to be partially, although not entirely, related to the organisation in force in a school. The attitude represented by a permanent reading drive was more often found in the comparatively formal schools, while the weak or non-existent reading drive was generally observed in progressive schools in which the organisation was centred on informal, individual, learning situations; but this was not an inevitable relationship. A few progressive schools were visited, in which strong reading drives were demonstrated in early starts to reading, using basic reading schemes. In other progressive schools the reading drive was manifested by the expectation that, if children were surrounded by interesting books which the teacher shared with them and encouraged them to handle, they would grow to love books and would soon learn to read. Nevertheless, to find a strong reading drive in force in a progressive school was the exception rather than the rule.

Large differences were noted in the reading progress of young infants in schools with these contrasting reading drives. In the first sort of school, in which the staff considered learning to read as the first priority, children generally learned to read early and well. This happened almost regardless of the media, materials, methods, or procedures employed. This factor was so important that it frequently overrode other important factors such as the intelligence and socio-economic background of the children. The observer visited schools in poor socio-economic areas in which reading standards were far higher than schools consisting of children of higher intelligence from good socio-economic areas, even when the same media and materials were used: the crucial factor being the attitude to reading prevalent among the staff, demonstrated in the reading drive in force in the school. In the second kind of school the teachers' beliefs in a delayed beginning to reading were clearly reflected in the children's slower mastery of the skill.

The implication for future experiments with infant reading is obvious; attitude to reading and reading drive is a variable which cannot be ignored.

2   The effect of experimenting with new techniques

When teachers in primary schools have the opportunity of experimenting with a new way of teaching reading, whether it involves a change in media, materials, methods or procedures, the result is almost invariably an increase in their interest in reading, leading to greater attention to the subject.

In the Reading Research Unit's first experiment, the teachers in the original experimental schools were not only trying out a new alphabet but using new books. They were conscious of being pioneers in a quite revolutionary experiment in educational research. Most of these teachers reported their early feelings of excitement representing almost a state of tension, which was nonetheless stimulating. It appeared to foster a pioneering spirit which enabled them to overcome the many early difficulties, including book shortages. The original, rather fearful stimulation was quickly followed by enthusiasm as good results emerged. Inspectors who visited these schools corroborated the teachers' own comments when they reported that never in their experience had they observed such a wave of interest and enthusiasm about reading.

Teachers in schools now taking up i.t.a. for the first time still experience, although to a lesser extent, a feeling of increased awareness and enthusiasm for reading teaching because they are trying out something new. These more recent experimenters also share another experience with the earlier teachers. In schools beginning to use i.t.a., teachers exhibit a community spirit which appears to draw them together, as they share their experiences, their fears and their triumphs and give each other mutual support in this common project.

The interest and enthusiasm engendered in teachers trying out something new in the field of reading, inevitably increases the reading drive in the school. This is equally true whether the school normally has a strong reading drive in force or whether it usually lays little emphasis on reading. That the results obtained in the original i.t.a. schools were almost invariably less spectacular in succeeding years than in the first year can be attributed very largely to the initial stimulation of the teachers with its concomitant increase in reading drive. (That the original i.t.a. teachers were mainly well above average in ability and experience probably accounts for the remainder of the difference.)

The stimulus of experimenting with new ways of teaching reading thus undoubtedly constitutes a second important factor in reading experiments.

3 Infant school practices

Infant schools in Britain, although they display a wide range of practices, nevertheless have certain features in common which make it especially easy for drives in any one subject to take place, often without conscious intent. This is particularly true in the case of a reading drive.

The infant teacher is generally with her own class all day, being responsible for all subjects and all sides of the children's development. The task of teaching children to read is part of a broader concept of acquiring all language skills—listening, speaking, reading and writing—which are closely interwoven. Every minute of every day in school contributes in varying, and immeasurable, degree to the acquisition of these language skills. Very few infant schools now work to rigid timetables with narrow blocks of time devoted to teaching specific subjects. Some schools have fairly fluid timetables marked in broad divisions; others have no timetables, the teachers working in what are termed 'unscheduled days'. Finally, the teachers have a large measure of freedom to work in the ways they choose.

Clearly, the situation represented by the degree of freedom enjoyed by teachers in British infant schools provides the opportunity for both conscious and unconscious emphasis on a particular subject. Experimenting with a new way of teaching reading, whether this takes place within the framework of educational research or not, almost inevitably increases the emphasis on, and time devoted to, the language arts. This was precisely what was seen to happen in most infant schools employing for the first time either i.t.a. or any new means of teaching reading in t.o.

4 Teacher ability and training

As already noted, there was general agreement among headteachers and inspectors that the original i.t.a. teachers had been of above average ability and that this, in part, accounted for the exceptionally good results of the first year. In addition, throughout this enquiry, headteachers and advisers emphasised the close relationship between the reading progress of children and the ability and experience of their teachers. With first-class teachers children made better progress than with less able teachers whatever the media, materials, methods or procedures; teacher ability in many cases overrode such factors. It was further noted that the interest fostered in teachers by the opportunity of using a new approach to reading and the resultant thought, reading and discussion which took place, even apart from those experimental situations in which teachers attended special workshops, contributed to teachers' increased proficiency for the task in hand. In other words, experimenting with reading produced better teachers of reading. Both these aspects of teacher ability and teacher training have important implications in reading experiments.

5 Control schools

Visits to control schools, discussions with teachers of control classes and with inspectors who had visited them led to an important conclusion. Some people had at first assumed that teachers of control classes in the Reading Research Unit's first experiment would look upon the exercise as a competition in which they would put forward special effort in respect of reading in t.o. No such evidence came to light in this evaluation. Teachers in control schools had usually been interested in new approaches to reading and willing to participate in experiments, but they had preferred the more cautious role of acting as control, rather than experimental, schools. In this way they felt they could help the experiment, without being committed to using a medium about which they had doubts. At the same time they expected to be in advantageous positions from which to observe and appraise the results of the innovations.

In all such schools visited the teachers spoke of how they had consciously tried, during the first experiment, to do as they had been asked, by teaching reading as they had formerly done. The results of reading tests at the end of the infant school confirmed that, in the majority of cases, they had been successful in their aims. It has thus been demonstrated that in such experiments teachers are dependable and capable of intelligent co-operation with research workers. It also suggests that fears regarding a Hawthorne effect in the control schools were unfounded.

This finding also highlights a fallacy in Downing's reasoning regarding control schools and possible Hawthorne effect. There is a contradiction in exhorting teachers of control schools to carry on using exactly the same methods and procedures as formerly, while at the same time inviting them to attend lectures designed to increase their interest or competence in reading teaching. In fact, odd lectures delivered at infrequent intervals, by different lecturers, could hardly be expected to result in such a stimulation and increase of knowledge in teachers that the effects would be noticeable in children's reading progress.

With regard to the control teachers' original hopes of the value to themselves of taking part in the experiment, many of them confessed their disappointment. They had frequently found themselves seriously inconvenienced by the unexpectedly large amount of testing and recording which took place, without the compensating interest of experimenting with a new way of teaching reading. They had been disappointed that they were not kept informed about the results of tests in both i.t.a. and t.o. classes and there was a general feeling that while they had been used, they had also been neglected.

It would seem that researchers need not only to appreciate more fully the burden of unrewarding work which is placed on teachers in control schools, but also to demonstrate this appreciation. Keeping teachers in control schools informed about what is happening and allowing them access to test results whenever practicable, would be gestures which might at least encourage them to co-operate in future research projects.

C. MATCHING GROUPS IN READING EXPERIMENTS

The assessment of reading progress in experiments in infant classes, when different media, methods, materials or approaches are being utilised, represents an extraordinarily difficult task, owing to the enormous number of variables which are known, or suspected, to affect the results. In particular, in British infant schools, the number of variables in the situation is substantially increased by the amount of freedom accorded to headteachers and class teachers.

The following main factors in the situation, each consisting of many subsidiary factors, all have bearing on the infant learning to read: the child himself; the teacher who helps the child to master the task; the situation in which the task is learned; and the techniques and tools of teaching and learning employed–that is the medium, method, materials and procedures. No experiment, however large or carefully designed, can hope to match or control all these variables. The crucial problem in setting up a research design for such an experiment is to arrange the variables in rank order, according to their effects on reading progress. Those variables considered to have the greatest effect on reading progress should be given the highest priority regarding careful matching of experimental and control groups, at the expense of discounting those variables believed to have only marginal influences. To fail to identify and match those variables most directly affecting reading progress in infant schools could completely vitiate the results of the experiment.

The verbal evidence given by teachers, advisers, inspectors and others in this evaluation, combined with the writer's own experience of teaching infants and observing them using both t.o. and i.t.a. in numerous schools, has led to certain conclusions regarding the relative weight of certain variables affecting experiments in reading in infant schools in England. This list of priorities differs, in both content and order, from the assumptions about the importance of variables which frequently appear to underlie the designs of experiments drawn up by researchers lacking first hand experience and intensive observation in infant schools. These points are clearly not intended to represent a complete list of noteworthy variables–a subject dealt with in detail in Part Three of this report: rather does it emphasise certain practical factors affecting reading progress which are not always appreciated by researchers in this field.

1   The writer is convinced that the most important variable, in the total situation of children learning to read, is the attitude towards reading which is prevalent in the school and the consequent reading drive in force. The implication of this conclusion for future reading research projects is that an attempt must be made to match all experimental and control schools according to the attitudes of the staff to reading. If this is not done, this important variable could so outweigh the matched variables as to completely distort the results, by disguising those differences which might be attributable to the experimental variable. For purposes of matching, this variable could be assessed by combining the results of an attitude scale, administered to the staff of the school, with the opinions of local inspectors and records of the reading standards of children in the school at the age of $7+$.

2   The second most important factor affecting children's reading progress which emerged in this part of the evaluation was the ability of the teacher. Like the preceding variable its effect was observed to outweigh differences in media, materials and methods, as well as partially to overcome certain intellectual and social factors. Thus, in any experiment concerned with teaching reading, an attempt must be made to match the ability and experience of the teachers of experimental and control classes. This could probably best be achieved by a combination of headteachers' and local advisers' ratings.

3   When the two preceding factors are equal, schools containing children of above average intelligence, living in high socio-economic areas, usually make better progress in reading than children of below average intelligence coming from homes of low socio-economic areas. Accordingly, in any experiment which is concerned with measuring children's reading progress in different circumstances, schools, classes or

individual children should be matched on intelligence and on the socio-economic status of their parents.

4 Experimenting with new ways of teaching reading, whether these involve changes in media, materials or procedures is usually found by teachers to be a stimulant leading to increased emphasis on the subject. Results are thus generally better than those achieved by the use of familiar ways of learning to read. Consequently, any experiment designed to assess the value of one specific new way of learning to read needs to evaluate this new way, not only against familiar ways, but also against other ways which are novel to the teachers concerned.

5 The matching of materials, methods and procedures in infant classes in Britain is likely to represent a much more difficult task than in countries in which teachers are recommended to use certain reading texts according to strictly defined procedures. The matching of these variables could perhaps best be done by carrying out experiments in two separate and contrasting types of schools: the most formal and the most progressive.

The most formal group of schools would be likely to rely rather heavily, although not entirely, on one basic reading scheme; the progressive group of schools would be more likely to employ a diversity of printed and handwritten materials. In an experiment based on more formal schools, it would be important for the basic reading schemes to be the same, and it would also be preferable for supporting materials to be equated. In experiments with progressive schools, such matching of materials would be both impossible and unnecessary; impossible in that the materials would be constantly supplemented by additional materials produced and collected by the teacher and the children, and in that individual children would be using different materials; and unnecessary in that the actual materials would be completely subordinate to the learning procedure in force. If the beliefs and aims of the teachers in these schools were in accord, it would only be necessary to ensure equality in the quantity, quality and variety of available printed materials.

If the emphasis on reading in matched schools within each category were judged to be equal, regular group meetings of teachers should lead to agreement on broad lines of action which would equate all that is implied in the matching of materials, methods and procedures, the latter including time devoted to and emphasis on reading and the other language arts. It would also be advisable for all classes to be visited frequently by a knowledgeable researcher, to verify that the agreed procedures were being adopted and were remaining equivalent.

6 Teachers using different new ways of teaching reading should have equivalent training sessions arranged, both before and during an experiment, in order to ensure that the use of the new idea is properly understood and is being used in the same manner by all teachers. Teachers in control classes should not be invited to meetings or lectures designed to interest them in particular aspects of their reading teaching or to improve in any way their current proficiency.

D. TESTS AND TESTING

An assessment of the evidence collected in Part Two of this report has led the writer to form the following conclusions regarding the testing of infants and lower juniors in reading experiments.

1 Testing programmes, even when these are undertaken by external testers, and

the keeping of records, represents a serious additional burden to primary school teachers, most of whom are already fully occupied in catering for the needs of large classes of children of mixed abilities and attainments. Consequently, testing, record keeping and so on should be reduced to a minimum.

2 All testing should be undertaken by external testers who are not only adequately trained but also used to dealing with young children. If the testing is not properly conducted by reliable, independent testers, the whole edifice of statistical calculations which often forms the bulk of research reports, and likewise the conclusions based on this evidence, can prove valueless or downright misleading. It follows that any research report based on test results should include full details of the backgrounds and training of the testers who were employed.

3 In experiments relating to the use of i.t.a., it would appear unnecessary, in future, to continue to test every child after the age of transfer to junior classes. All the evidence indicates that most children have not suffered by using i.t.a. as an initial alphabet. The continued testing of children who have long ago transferred to t.o. more nearly represents an assessment of what later teachers have taught, or failed to teach, than an appraisal of the approach used in the children's first year or so of schooling.

4 To make a regular practice of administering reading tests in t.o. to children who have not yet transferred from i.t.a. is unkind, unnecessary and misleading. It would be well worth considering the possibilities of testing children at certain functional stages in their reading progress, rather than at stated intervals of time. For example, every child might be tested in i.t.a. immediately before he made the official transfer to t.o. books, and then in t.o. at stated intervals for a specified period afterwards. Thus the only children to be tested in junior classes would be those who had transferred to t.o. immediately prior to, or after admission to, these classes.

In those circumstances, the comparison of results between t.o. and i.t.a. children would need to be arranged on some other basis than that of whole classes. One possible method would be, at specified intervals, to test the proportion of i.t.a. children in a class who had transferred and compare their results, on t.o. tests, with an identical proportion of the best children in the t.o. class. Alternatively, individual children might be matched and compared at intervals.

5 The majority of reading tests standardised and employed in this country represent inadequate assessments of the skills they attempt to measure: this is particularly true of tests for the youngest children. The evidence collected in this part of the present research project reveals the following flaws in test materials purporting to assess reading attainments in the first three years of children's schooling:

(a) No one reading test, standardised in Britain, appears to be appropriate for comparing, in the early stages, the attainments of children who have begun to learn to read by different approaches. For instance, certain tests in common use favour children who have begun to read by phonic methods. To apply such tests to children whose phonic training will not take place until a later stage is clearly a meaningless exercise, in that processes which are taught later can only be fairly assessed later. In contrast, certain other tests favour children whose early reading experience is based on a look-and-say method; yet the opportunities of such children to score on these tests are unequal in that the early sight words they have learned by using different schemes or approaches may, or may not, be included in the early items of the test. Moreover, such children, because of the way in which they have started to learn, are not usually equipped to attempt to read words other than those already constituting part of their small reading repertoire. Chall's (1967) work in the U.S.A. also has a bearing on this point. Reporting on the 1962–1965 Carnegie Study, in which numerous research results relating to beginning reading were evaluated, she concluded that 'different methods . . . tended to produce a different course of growth. They showed strengths on the different components of reading and spelling at different times. Thus, depending on what was tested and when it was tested, one approach tended to come out better than the other.'

In future reading research relating to infants it would be advisable, even before deciding on the form of test to be used, to give prior consideration to the question of the earliest stage at which children taught in different ways can fairly be compared on the results of the same test. The writer would suggest that two or three years after entering school would be more likely to represent a realistic estimate than two or three terms.

(b) The inadequacy of current tests of the earliest stages of learning to read, for instance those administered in the first year, was clearly illustrated by the number of children using both t.o. and i.t.a., who failed to score on the Reading Research Unit's early tests, and by the evidence relating to slow-learning children. Test results consistently indicated a much larger proportion of children to have failed to make a start at reading than teachers and inspectors knew to be the case. Teachers working with these children were able to recognise certain stages in their progress which standardised tests were unable to measure.

The conclusion is drawn that assessments of reading attainments in the earliest stages should probably be more in the nature of diagnostic tests, attempting to map, in exact detail, those areas in which some learning has taken place, as well as disclosing those areas of reading skills into which the child has not been initiated. Tests such as those in current use, consisting of brief samples of items standardised in respect of average children at various ages, are of very little value when applied to young children who, although they have taken the first important steps in the process of learning to read, have done so by learning quite different words in different ways.

(c) The third flaw concerns the child who has acquired fluency in reading in either i.t.a. or t.o. He has learned to concentrate on the ideas being developed in the prose and to make rapid appraisals of the probable and actual meanings of new words, in relation to the whole context of the story or passage. To present such a child with a list of unconnected words is to ask him to perform an entirely different task from the one he has learned to enjoy. The results may show statistically significant differences between children, but these certainly cannot be taken to represent operational differences. Furthermore, even when so-called 'comprehension tests' of reading ability are employed, they rarely represent adequate assessments of what is meant by 'reading with understanding' in its broadest sense.

It is concluded that, in future research projects designed to compare different ways of beginning reading, attempts should be made to devise methods of assessment which more closely reflect the functional reading of children, at every stage, than do tests in current use.

178

The evidence collected in this part of the evaluation suggests the necessity for further extensive research into the early stages of learning to read. This research may conveniently be divided into the following six broad divisions, each of which could well have many sub-divisions:

1 Extensive and fundamental research is required into how children actually do learn to read in the initial stages.

2 Research into the production of reading tests, which will give more detailed and more effective measurements of the early stages of reading and which will more nearly represent valid assessments of functional reading, is required.

3 There is a need for well-designed experiments into the optimum ways of teaching children to read using our traditional orthography. Such research projects should include variations in methods, materials and classroom procedures.

4 The effect of employing, in early reading materials, a variety of 'signalling systems' in which marks or colours are superimposed as temporary signals on t.o. merits investigation.

5 Similar investigations are needed into the effects of various simplified spelling systems, other than i.t.a., which utilise the traditional 26-letter alphabet, as well as new or augmented alphabets, as the media for beginning reading.

6 Numerous additional research projects connected with the use of i.t.a. can be seen to be desirable including, among others, the following:

(a) the question of whether i.t.a. itself might be improved

(b) investigations into the effects of using i.t.a. with different methods, materials and procedures; this is particularly important as the materials and methods so far employed were mainly devised to fulfil the needs of learning to read with an irregular spelling system and thus may be far from appropriate for a spelling system with a comparatively regular grapheme-phoneme relationship

(c) detailed research into the transition and how it works, especially with slow-learning children

(d) the effect on children of meeting one alphabet in school and another alphabet outside school, with experiments into extending and decreasing the period in which this double exposure is in force

(e) further research into the use of i.t.a. in remedial situations with those children who have failed to learn to read with t.o.

PART THREE

i.t.a IN PRACTICE:
EVIDENCE FROM RESEARCH

CHAPTER 15

The Report on Research

A. THE PLAN OF THE REPORT

THE general plan of Part Three of this report is to suggest, in Chapter 16, some principles of experimental designs for researches into classroom teaching. This entails asking some forty questions concerning the scope, design, conduct, techniques and implications of past and future investigations of i.t.a.

Chapters 17, 18 and 19 are each based on the answers to these forty questions. Chapter 17 summarises each of 17 researches carried out in Great Britain or the United States. Chapter 18 collates the information obtained in the investigations and presents the main results. Chapter 19 evaluates these results.

B. THE SCOPE OF THE REPORT

The review of experimental studies has been confined to published books, articles and research reports, and to theses deposited in the libraries of British Universities, available in the spring of 1967. The report has also been restricted to investigations that are mainly concerned with the use of i.t.a. as a means of teaching reading in the early stages. Specific researches confined to closely allied media, such as Wijk's 'Regularized Inglish', diacritical marking systems, and work with special groups of children such as remedial reading groups or non-English speaking learners, have not been included. It is not claimed that the review is comprehensive, but it is sufficiently large and representative to make the conclusions typical of research in this area.

Two important distinctions have to be drawn between different types of investigations into the efficiency of i.t.a. First, we have to distinguish between the approach to the problem through linguistic and experimental psychology, and that based on the performance of children in schools. The former type of experiment would best take place under closely controlled conditions, e.g. children would be taught individually, possibly by programmed instruction. Each individual item of behaviour would be observed, timed and recorded, and account taken of the various types of errors, guesses, irrelevancies, reversals, repetitions, sequential processings, left–right orientations, perceptual sets, etc. The pupils' auditory and visual memory, recognition, discrimination and association could also be investigated. These researches would be somewhat similar in subject matter to those carried out by Sister John (1964), Elkonin (1963) and Tensuan and Davis (1963). In contradistinction to this, we are concerned in this report with the study of reading performance, not under laboratory conditions, but in the course of classroom instruction in the schools of Britain and the United States. This is primarily an educational problem, and its solution requires the additional investigations of such matters as differences between school areas, schools, classes and pupils, teaching method, textbooks, classroom procedure and school climate.

The researches discussed in the present section are those concerned with attainment in school.

The second distinction to be borne in mind when reading this report is between the reading performance of children, (i) when the criterion tests are in the medium of instruction, the i.t.a. group being tested in i.t.a. script and the t.o. group in t.o. script, and (ii) when the criterion tests are administered in t.o. for both groups.

CHAPTER 16

Suggested Principles of Experimental Design

I Experimental treatment of variables

A. INTRODUCTION

THE first and most important stage in drawing up a research design is to determine the methods by which the main variables are to be controlled.

A striking feature of any problem in the social sciences is its extreme complexity, i.e. the large number of relevant and irrelevant influences which have to be taken into account. It would not be difficult for example, to list a hundred factors influencing a child's ability to read, and it would no doubt be possible to enumerate a thousand.

When we say that human behaviour is complex, we imply that any single act or type of behaviour is influenced by a large number of factors. We select certain variables in which we are interested, such as efficiency in reading, and attempt to relate them to certain other variables, such as i.t.a. Thus i.t.a. is an 'antecedent' variable leading to the 'consequent' variable 'reading attainment'. Alternatively, we can use the terms cause and effect or (with reservation) independent and dependent variables, and, more satisfactorily perhaps, for a different type of problem, predictor and criterion. There will, of course, be more than one antecedent variable; attainment in reading might depend not only on the medium used but also on the method of teaching adopted, the materials used, the amount of time devoted to reading, the skill and attitudes of the teacher, the size of the school and class, the incentives provided, the motivation, age and sex of the pupils, the home background and many other factors.

Psychologists sometimes adopt an 'SOR' system as a general model, i.e. the effect of a stimulus (S) on an organism (O) leading to certain responses (R), or in terms of educational research, (i) the effect of environmental conditions on (ii) certain pupils, leading to (iii) certain responses.

The factors we wish to study in researches into classroom teaching can thus be conveniently classified into:

(i) environmental influences which affect the child in the school, home and neighbourhood, such as teaching media, the size of class and home background, and

(ii) personal influences, such as age, sex.

The planning of a research may be regarded primarily, although not entirely, as a statement of the way in which a large number of antecedent variables, both personal and environmental, are to be experimentally treated, and how the 'consequent' variables are to be assessed.

We first consider, using everyday vernacular terms for our purpose, the whole range of relevant influences and their relative importance (bearing in mind that the scope of the research must be realistic, and that we must not attempt to cover every conceivable aspect of the problem). It is only after this first general stage has been completed that operational definitions are drawn up and statistical techniques decided upon. Sampling, i.e. the provision of human bodies, comes last, and if we can find enough of the right sort to satisfy our specifications we should be able to gain adequate answers to our problems. As research proceeds, modifications have to be made in the original plan, but we have at least started off on the right foot, and know which one it is.

In short, it is important to consider the broad implications of an investigation first and the details last, in contrast to much research planning in which exigencies of time and space, and the practical advantages of taking convenient samples of subjects and measuring instruments are given first place, and the gaps in the general argument and proof become apparent only when the findings are being written up.

When an experiment is finished, most research workers feel an urge to make improvements and to repeat the whole investigation on sounder lines. Often the second design could have been adopted just as easily at the outset of the experiment, simply by taking thought beforehand. It is vitally important to think the problem out to the end at the beginning.

Researches into the efficiency of different methods of teaching are basically concerned with testing an hypothesis, such as that children taught to read by i.t.a. learn more quickly than children taught by t.o. The following notes are chiefly concerned with the method of analysis of variance, which is in a sense the fundamental statistical method used in this type of investigation as it is based essentially on the comparison of mean scores. In other types of researches, however, other statistical techniques might be more appropriate.

Antecedent and consequent variables are discussed in this chapter according to the following plan:

Consequent variables
Criteria of success

Antecedent variables
1   Crucial variables underlying success
2   Disturbing variables selected by the experimenter for statistical analysis
3   Disturbing variables matched with one another by the experimenter
4   Variables held constant
5   Error
6   Excluded variables

B. CONSEQUENT VARIABLES

Criteria of success

The first main step in planning a research is to decide upon the criteria of success. Are we, for example in a research into the efficiency of i.t.a., to test comprehension, accuracy, speed, expression, or only some of these? We may decide, on educational grounds, that it is essential to test comprehension, since that is the main purpose of learning to read; that we are very interested in accuracy, and have some concern with speed (particularly with older children) so that we would also wish to include these two variables in our investigation; and another important criterion is the child's degree of interest in reading resulting perhaps from the relative comfort of reading in i.t.a. There is a great deal to be said for Hemming's (1967) suggestion of matching

185

Book Corner and other play facilities and then recording how many pupil minutes were voluntarily spent on the Book Corners during a spell of free activity periods. On the other hand, expression in reading seems too difficult to assess reliably and too slight in importance to be worth inclusion.

C. ANTECEDENT VARIABLES

Crucial variables underlying success

After the criteria have been selected, the next step is to choose the crucial variables underlying success, i.e. those selected by the researchers as forming the crux of his problem, so that the skeleton of the research may become apparent at the beginning of the planning stage. These variables are indicated by the major objectives of the research. For example in a research into the effectiveness of i.t.a. the crucial variables underlying success are i.t.a. and t.o., and the bare outline of the investigation might be as follows:

Crucial variables	Criteria of success
initial teaching alphabet (i.t.a.)	comprehension
traditional orthography (t.o.)	accuracy
	interest in reading

When we have completed these first essential steps, and are satisfied that the relation between the two reading media (the crucial antecedent variables underlying success) and the ability to read with comprehension, speed and accuracy and to take an interest in reading (the criteria of success) can be satisfactorily investigated, we should next proceed to ask what other variables, i.e. other antecedents, might influence the results, and consequently have to be taken into account if we wish to be reasonably sure that the observed differences between the efficiency of the two media are, in fact, due mainly to the media themselves and not to other factors. From the point of view of a given research, these are 'disturbing' variables or factors.

It is not to be supposed—to reduce the argument *ad absurdum*—that if one class is taught to read in i.t.a. and another in t.o. differences between the two media will be the only factors that influence the results, or that if the i.t.a. group reads more successfully than the t.o. group, a case has been made out for the introduction of i.t.a. into schools. We have, of course, also to consider what other factors might exert a strong influence on reading performance. As we have seen, these influences can be conveniently and pertinently divided into personal and environmental factors.

In respect of personal variables chronological age is not of crucial importance in the present instance, since the sample can be confined to school entrants. Similar considerations hold for initial attainment, as almost all children who enter school are unable to read, and the rare exceptions can be excluded from the experiment. On the other hand, intelligence, vocabulary, sex and socio-economic status are all highly relevant and should be investigated—any research which ignored these factors would not carry conviction—whatever the experimental results. The pupil's personality, motivation and attitudes to school are also important, even at this early stage, but they are difficult to assess reliably in very young children, and may have to be excluded for this reason. School attendance is another factor that might have to be taken into account, probably by excluding children who are frequently absent from school.

The chief environmental variables to be considered are the influence of the school and the home. Although reading opportunities and encouragement will no doubt differ from home to home, and help to determine the level of children's reading, it is impossible for the experimenter to control this factor systematically. In any case, it is covered roughly by taking the children's socio-economic status into account.

It is relatively easy to study differences between schools. In a large-scale experiment we can include schools from different geographical areas—urban, suburban, city centre, rural, market town, etc.; the size of the school and the building amenities are also highly relevant. The attitude of the school to reading and allied activities is particularly important since the classroom atmosphere, teaching procedure and methods of instruction will all vary with this factor. Teachers frequently stress the extreme importance of taking such attitudes into account.

Differences between teachers in such respects as age, experience, qualifications, competence, attitude and volunteering are also likely to influence the results. The children's performance in reading will also be crucially affected by the texts and materials used and by the classroom teaching procedures. Books and supplementary materials vary widely in their level of difficulty, and in the sequence of experiences they present to the children. No reliable conclusions concerning the effectiveness of media can be drawn by comparing classes which have used different materials. The teaching methods employed, e.g. look-and-say, phonic, or mixed, and the general classroom organisation in such matters as time schedules and group activities, might also be decisive in determining reading performance and have to be brought under control before we can venture any firm opinion on the relative merits of the two media.

D. TABULATION OF VARIABLES

The variables so far considered may be tabulated as follows:

TABLE 16(a)

Variables considered

Criteria of success	Crucial antecedent	Other antecedent variables (personal)	Other antecedent variables (environmental)
comprehension	i.t.a.	age	school characteristics (attitudes of school to reading;
accuracy	t.o.	initial reading attainment	urban-rural, size, building amenities
		intelligence	school climate)
interest in reading		verbal ability, memory	
speed		initial vocabulary	classroom characteristics (size, books and reading materials,
		sex	methods of instruction, lesson procedure,
expression		socio-economic level	amount of reading per week, incentives offered to pupils)
		personality	
		motivation to read	teacher characteristics— (experience, qualifications,
		attendance	competence, attitudes)

187

As we have seen, the categories of variables relevant to the present problem are:

    1   Criteria of success

    2   Crucial variables underlying success

We next have to consider the appropriate experimental treatment for the remaining environmental and personal conditions. It is suggested in this report that these can be best allocated to one of five types of treatment categories, as follows:

1   *Disturbing variables selected by the experimenter for statistical analysis*

There are usually some disturbing variables whose effects we wish to examine in detail, i.e. to treat statistically (usually by the method of analysis of variance) in the same way that we treat the main predictors; since we do not wish merely to keep them under experimental control. In researches into reading media, for example, we are interested in the influence of intelligence, i.e. whether a given medium is specially effective for bright or dull children, for both or neither. Similar considerations apply to vocabulary, sex and socio-economic status. We may therefore decide to include these four variables on our list of variables to be analysed.

On the environmental side, the attitude of the school to reading is clearly of vital importance. We might best assess different methods of teaching reading (possibly (i) phonic and (ii) look-and-say plus phonic) together with appropriate reading books and materials, e.g. the *Royal Road Readers* with the phonic method and *Key Words* with look-and-say plus phonic methods (the combination of 'method' and 'materials' being taken to constitute a 'system' of teaching reading). It might also be possible to include schools in both urban and rural areas and to estimate the effects of this variable. We need to make a rigorous statistical estimate of all these influences by the methods of analysis of variance in order to ascertain their separate and conjoint effect on the four criteria of comprehension, accuracy and speed of reading and interest in reading. This will require a precisely balanced sample in which, in the present instance, there are equal numbers of (i) highly intelligent boys in urban schools which emphasise reading, (ii) girls of medium intelligence in rural schools which do not emphasise reading, and so on for all possible sub-divisions of these three variables. For practical reasons it is not always possible to obtain such samples; for example, it would probably be difficult to obtain properly balanced groups in respect of socio-economic status, so that this variable would have to be included in an additional analysis of more restricted scope than the main analysis.

2   *Disturbing variables matched with one another by the experimenter*

Although it is not usually practicable to analyse (i.e. to include in an analysis of variance) all the relevant variables, it might nevertheless be important to control some of them, as their influence would otherwise vitiate the findings. These may be called 'matched' variables because their effects have to be evenly matched. In the research under discussion, for example, it would almost certainly not prove possible to form precisely balanced sub-groups in respect of teacher characteristics and school characteristics, but we can at least ensure that the i.t.a. and t.o. media are not used by groups of teachers or types of schools which differ appreciably from one another. For this purpose the most common techniques are 'matched pairs' in which each individual is matched with a 'twin' of the other group, and 'matched groups', in which the means of the variables to be matched are kept approximately the same in all experimental groups.

3   Variables held constant

A variable can be held constant, i.e. at a single level. For instance in some researches, the effect of sex is eliminated by studying girls only or boys only. This method (which is frequently applied in the physical sciences) has obvious disadvantages, since many crucial factors are not held constant in nature. We do not really know that swans are black if we confine our sample to Queensland. Alternatively, we might hold the effect of some variables constant by employing the statistical techniques of 'analysis of covariance'. This method is rather cumbersome, and sometimes gives misleading results, as the statistical assumptions on which it is based are not always fulfilled. It also has the disadvantage of burying the constant variable whose effects cannot be assessed by this method, but this does not matter if we merely wish to hold it steady.

Nevertheless, it is sometimes the safest procedure to hold a variable constant. For example, visits by the public to experimental classes are probably best kept constant, viz. at zero level, instead of matching various levels of interference by strangers.

It is highly important in any experiment to control the motivation of the subjects taking part and the incentives they are offered. For example one motivational influence, the 'Hawthorne effect' (which derives from the *novelty* of the experimental situation and the awareness of the people taking part, both pupils and teachers, that their performance is under observation) should obviously be held constant as far as possible by the provision of pre-experimental and in-service courses, and by the supervision of the experiment by the research workers.

Many variables have to be kept constant in the interests of simplicity. In the present experiment, for instance, it is probably best to restrict the population to non-readers entering school at the normal age, and on the environmental side to equalise the length of time spent on instruction in reading, and on group and individual activities in the classroom.

4   Error

Variables which necessarily influence the results because they exist either in the make-up of the child or in the environment, but which it is impracticable to analyse by the method of analysis of variance or to match or hold constant, have to be ignored; i.e. we are compelled to regard them as error. Variables with no discernible influence, such as eye-colour or cloud cover do not require to be investigated, nor do others of which the effect is presumably very slight, such as comfortable desks. More important, some variables may be regarded as error when they are not susceptible to reliable measurement, e.g. it is difficult to assess children's motivation and personality at the age of four or five. These, we trust, will be of equal influence in all experimental groups.

Other variables sometimes have to be regarded as error because of exigencies of time, finance, and labour, although we know they are important, e.g. class size, school size and attendance.

It is not to be supposed, however, that the influence of variables we choose to ignore is in any way diminished by our ostrich-like behaviour; we simply hope in the light of earlier experience that their effect will be evenly spread among the experimental groups. But, if we choose to ignore variables which may have a considerable influence on the criteria, then the whole investigation becomes of doubtful validity; e.g. the number of hours of reading activity in t.o. and i.t.a. is obviously highly important, since a medium which is used more frequently (possibly by an amount of hundreds of hours of tuition) might well prove superior for that reason alone, and the results simply demonstrate that attainment depends in part on the length of instruction. Any finding which regards this factor as error is very tentative, and certainly does not merit any radical changes being made in the reading media used in schools.

5 Excluded variables

The distinction must be drawn between variables regarded as error, and excluded variables. Some personal and environmental influences are *necessarily present* and cannot be excluded from the situation, such as pupils' personality, motives and health, or the size of class and average attendance. Such variables must be treated as either predictors, criteria, analysed, matched or error variables, as their influence cannot be entirely removed. Some variables, on the other hand, can be completely excluded, such as alphabets other than t.o. or i.t.a. Restriction in the range of measurement also leads to exclusion, e.g. the investigation may be confined to children in l.e.a. schools, excluding children attending private schools. Similarly, some types of school, teacher and class will be excluded from the experiment.

The suggested experimental treatment of variables is summarised in Table 16 (b).

II Choice of sample

The next important stage after the nature and control of the experimental variables have been fully considered is to select the most appropriate experimental samples. This will depend on practical exigencies of time, money, labour and social acceptability as well as on educational, psychological and logical relevance and completeness. The investigator has to take into account what can actually be done rather than what is highly desirable. In a thoroughgoing (but not necessarily large) experiment on classroom teaching the number and the balance of the experimental variables will probably depend in the main on the demands of the method of analysis of variance, which is the most appropriate statistical method when the fundamental consideration is the comparison of mean scores. The chief practical difficulty, however, in the use of this method is the exacting demand made for precisely balanced sub-samples.

The first step is to consider the analysed variables and to decide the lowest number of levels into which it would be reasonable to classify them. For example, in the case of the i.t.a. experiment we might draw up the following list:

> intelligence (3 levels)
> vocabulary (3 levels)
> sex (2 levels)
> socio-economic status (3 levels)
> attitudes of school to reading (2 levels)
> 'phonic' v. 'look-and-say plus phonic' system (2 levels)

TABLE 16(b)

Treatment of variables

Criteria of success	Crucial Antecedent variables	Analysed variables	Matched variables	Constant variables	Error	Excluded variables
Personal						
comprehension		intelligence		initial reading ability	personality	expression in reading
accuracy		sex			attendance	enjoyment in reading
speed		initial vocabulary		age		
interest in reading		socio-economic status				private school children
						ESN children
Environmental	i.t.a. alphabet	emphasis placed by school on reading	school characteristics (size, building amenities, pupil–teacher ratio)	incentives to read		Wijk's regularised alphabet, diacritical marking system
				volunteering		
	t.o. alphabet	teaching system, i.e. teaching methods used with appropriate reading books and materials		classroom procedure		individual tuition
			teacher characteristics (experience, qualifications, competence)	amount of reading instruction		
				pre-experimental training of teachers		amount of reading at home
				supervision of research		
				teacher relationships with public and parents		teaching machines, etc.

The next step is to determine whether it is practicable to include all those variables in a single analysis of variance or whether difficulties in securing properly balanced samples will necessitate the calculations of more than one analysis. (Other things being equal, it is preferable to include as many variables as possible in a single analysis as their conjoint as well as their separate effects can then be determined.)

It is difficult to match vocabulary and intelligence since the method demands a precisely balanced sample, i.e. a large number of children of (i) high intelligence and low vocabulary, and (ii) low intelligence and high vocabulary, which it might prove impossible to obtain. Similar troubles arise in respect of socio-economic status, so that this variable and vocabulary may have to be analysed separately. Obvious difficulties will also arise in the comparison of teachers, as each teacher cannot be asked to teach in each type of school without introducing a completely artificial teaching situation. This leaves us with the following experimental design (Tables 16 (c), (d), (e)):

TABLE 16(c)

School areas

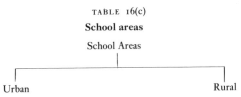

III Analyses of Variance

Analysis of Variance 1

	d.f.
Alphabets (Al)	1
Areas (Ar)	1
School types (Sch.T)	1
Reading Systems (R.A.)	1
Sexes (Se)	1
Intelligence levels (I)	1
Interactions	88 (1)
Schools (or teachers) within Ar. × Sch. T. × R.A. × Se × I	48 (2)
Schools (or teachers) × Alphabets within Ar. × Sch. T. × R.A. × Se × I	48 (3)
Residual (within cell)	192
Total	383

(1) There are 57 interactions in all, 15 first order, 20 second order, 15 third order, 6 fourth order, and 1 fifth order yielding a total of 88 degrees of freedom. All these could be tested if necessary, although in practice significance is likely to be confined to the lower order interactions.

(2) The 48 degrees of freedom could be partitioned further as follows:

Schools	d.f.
within Ar. × Sch. T. × R.A.	8

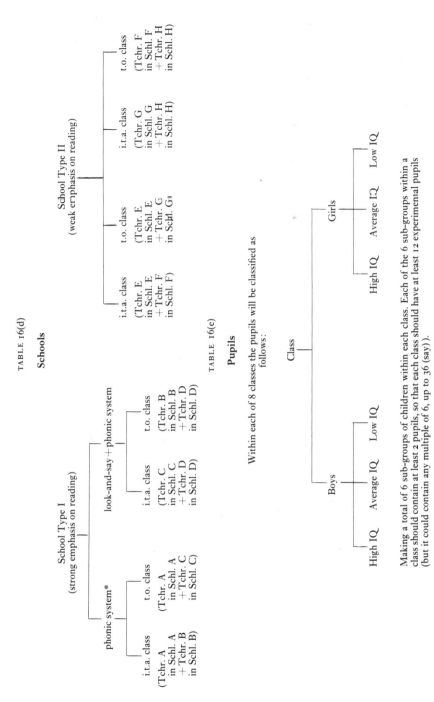

TABLE 16(d)

Schools

School Type I (strong emphasis on reading)

- phonic system*
  - i.t.a. class (Tchr. A in Schl. A + Tchr. B in Schl. B)
  - t.o. class (Tchr. A in Schl. A + Tchr. C in Schl. C)
- look-and-say + phonic system
  - i.t.a. class (Tchr. C in Schl. C + Tchr. D in Schl. D)
  - t.o. class (Tchr. B in Schl. B + Tchr. D in Schl. D)

School Type II (weak emphasis on reading)

- i.t.a. class (Tchr. E in Schl. E + Tchr. F in Schl. F)
- t.o. class (Tchr. E in Schl. E + Tchr. G in Schl. G)
- i.t.a. class (Tchr. G in Schl. G + Tchr. H in Schl. H)
- t.o. class (Tchr. F in Schl. F + Tchr. H in Schl. H)

* system = method used with appropriate materials.

TABLE 16(e)

Pupils

Within each of 8 classes the pupils will be classified as follows:

Class
- Boys: High IQ, Average IQ, Low IQ
- Girls: High IQ, Average IQ, Low IQ

Making a total of 6 sub-groups of children within each class. Each of the 6 sub-groups within a class should contain at least 2 pupils, so that each class should have at least 12 experimental pupils (but it could contain any multiple of 6, up to 36 (say)).

The author is indebted to Dr D. G. Lewis of the Department of Education, Manchester University, for the improvements he suggested in the analysis of variance design.

193

Schools × Se
with Ar. × Sch.T. × R.A.   8
Schools × I
within Ar. × Sch.T. × R.A.   16
Schools × Se × I
within Ar. × Sch.T. × R.A.   16

(3) These 48 degrees of freedom could be similarly partitioned.

Analysis of variance 2   d.f.

Between alphabets   1
Between socio-economic levels   2
Alphabet × socio-economic level   2
Residual   388
Total   393

Analysis of variance 3   d.f.

Between alphabets   1
Between initial vocabulary levels   2
Alphabet × initial vocabulary level   2
Residual   378
Total   383

Minimum population

The minimum experimental population would be as follows:

Pupils   384
Teachers   16
Classes   32
Schools   16
School Areas   4

but since this presupposes experimental classes of 12 and only 4 school areas the total population might very well be considerably larger. This would certainly be advisable in view of the low Between Groups degrees of freedom.

The above design could also be applied to other criteria, such as vocabulary, spelling and creative writing.

IV   Allocation of subjects to treatments

When the school classes that are to take part in the experiment have been identified they should be allocated to experimental treatments at random. If this precaution is not taken, it is not statistically permissible to generalise the findings to children beyond the experimental sample, i.e. to other schools of the same type.

V Notes on general procedure

The author of the present section of the report would also make the following suggestions concerning general procedure.

1 *Media*

The media investigated are best confined to i.t.a. and t.o., and should not be extended to other alphabets for purposes of comparison. It is difficult to include more than two alphabets in a single investigation if we make the important condition, from the point of view of experimental control, that the same teacher give lessons in both media in the same school. For reasons of convenience therefore any crucial experiment would have to be limited to a straightforward comparison of i.t.a. and t.o.

2 *Volunteering*

The teachers taking part in the experiment should all be volunteers, since the tradition in British education is that schools decide for themselves what teaching methods to adopt, and the future population of schools to which the findings are to be generalised will, at least in Britain, also be volunteers.

3 *Allocation of media*

The difficult problem of allocating media at random to separate schools and teachers, which is essential if the findings are to be generalised to a wider population, can be avoided if each teacher takes both the i.t.a. and the t.o. group in his own school. Within schools, media should be allocated to classes at random.

4 *Classroom procedures*

Some degree of control should be exercised over the classroom procedures adopted over the whole investigation (although not in individual lessons) if the findings are to be meaningful. In the classroom differences will arise between teachers in respect of important features of the classroom procedure such as the degree to which the structural analysis of linguistic skills and relations plays a part in the teaching programme, or the extent to which creative and controlled writing is required, the use of practice periods, group activities, individual supervision and the stress laid on word cards, supportive materials, and marking and scoring schemes. In many researches teachers are asked simply to use their own teaching methods. This is a sound procedure only if the same teacher takes both classes, and even then it provides no direct precaution against the use of atypical and bizarre procedures.

5 *Amount of instruction*

Some attempt should be made to check that neither of the experimental groups gains a great deal of additional reading practice, i.e. that the weekly amount of reading activity is similar. Otherwise it is difficult to see how the research can have any validity whatsoever, as we would not know whether we were carrying out an investigation into the effect of i.t.a. or of solar time on children's ability to read.

6 *Lesson records*

The teacher should keep a brief account of the general conduct of reading activities in terms of material covered, total amount of instruction given, etc. A two or three line summary would suffice. The purpose of this is to balance these *factors over the whole experiment*. It does not involve teaching to a set plan day by day.

7 *The Hawthorne effect*

At least two sub-control schools (similar in type to the experimental schools) should be included, in which the pupils are taught in t.o. and take the criterion tests in t.o., but the teachers are not aware that these tests are related to the enquiry. This is the only way in which the effect of the novelty of an experiment (the Hawthorne effect) can be fully controlled.

8 *Pre-experimental courses for teachers*

As an additional attempt to control the Hawthorne effect, separate pre-experimental courses should be held of approximately the same length in time for teachers of t.o. and i.t.a. A two-day course would probably be sufficient. Emphases and pressures should be kept as similar as possible. It will not be necessary to run two courses if the same teacher takes both groups within his own school.

9 *Supervision of teachers*

Little supervision of the teachers will be required, but a member of the research team might visit each teacher for a standardised discussion every four weeks (say).

10 *Relations with parents and public*

The public should be forbidden to visit the experimental classes. This is not because reading is not a matter of public interest, or because it is not the parents' business, but because extraneous influences must be kept under strict control if the results are to be meaningful. It might be an advantage, however, to discuss the project with parents both *before* and *after* (but not during) the experiment.

11 *Matching techniques*

The traditional method of matching different experimental groups is to use 't' or 'F' as a test of the significance of the difference between means. But since levels of statistical significance are basically measures of the degree of 'confidence' we can have in the observed differences—whether large or small—we also need a statement of differences in terms of standard deviations so that a check can be kept on their educational significance.

12 *Time schedule*

An attempt should be made to keep the amount of time spent on reading activities approximately equal for the two groups over the whole experiment, although not for individual lessons.

(*a*) *Length of investigation.* The investigation should proceed until all (or almost all) of the children have transferred from i.t.a. to t.o. This would entail a research lasting at least three years.

(*b*) *Time of transition.* The stage at which children make the transition to the traditional alphabet should be determined by their reading score on an objective test of reading. Otherwise the time of transition will depend on the ability and temperament of the teacher as well as the child.

VI Summary

Media

The experiment should be confined to i.t.a. and t.o.

Samples

School areas, schools, teachers, classes and pupils should be heterogeneous and balanced.

Allocation of media

The tests and media should be allocated to classes at random. The schools and teachers should be volunteers. The same teacher should teach both groups in the same school.

Classroom procedure

The materials used, the method of teaching reading, the classroom approach, and the allocation of time, should be evenly balanced over the whole course for the two media.

Supervision

The length of pre-experimental training courses for teachers, and the amount of supervision and recording of lessons should be held constant for the two media.

Relationships with public

The public should be banned. Meetings should be arranged with the parents before and after the experiment.

Results

The analysis of results and matching techniques should be mainly based on the comparison of means, using the methods of analysis of variance and covariance.

CHAPTER 17

Summary of Individual Researches

I List of researches summarised

1 BOSMA, R. L. (1965). Teaching reading with i.t.a.: a research report. *Reading Horizon*, 6, 6–19

2 DELL, G. A. (1967). The i.t.a. approach to reading. The Corporation of Glasgow Education Department

3 DOWNING, J. A. (1967). Chapter 1. Historical background and origins of i.t.a. research. *The i.t.a. Symposium*, National Foundation for Educational Research in England and Wales

4 DOWNING, J. A. and JONES, B. (1966). Some problems of evaluating i.t.a. A second experiment. *Educational Research*, 8, No. 2, 100–114

5 FRY, E. B. (1966). Comparisons of three methods of reading instruction. Results at the end of second grade. Office of Education Co-operative Research Project No. 3050. Rutgers University, New Brunswick, New Jersey

6 HAHN, H. T. (1965). Relative effectiveness of three methods of teaching reading in grade one. Lansing, Michigan: Michigan Department of Public Instruction, Office of Education, Co-operative Research Project No. 2687

7 HARRISON, M. (1964). *Instant Reading*. London: Pitman & Sons Ltd

8 HAYES, R. B. and NEMETH, J. S. (1965). Factors affecting learning to read. Harrisburg, Pennsylvania: Department of Public Instruction, Office of Education, Co-operative Research Project No. 2697

9 McCRACKEN, R. A. (1966). A two-year longitudinal study to determine the ability of first grade children to learn to read using the *Early-to-Read* i.t.a program (An Interim Report of the First Year). In A. J. Mazurkiewicz (ed.) *i.t.a. and the World of English*. Hempstead, N.Y.: i.t.a. Foundation

10 MAZURKIEWICZ, A. J. (1967). The initial teaching alphabet in reading instruction. Comprehensive Final Report, Lehigh University and the Bethlehem Area Schools

11 MILNE, A. (1966). The Scottish i.t.a. research. Paper read at the Third International Conference, Cambridge University

12 ROBINSON, H. M. (1966). Effectiveness of i.t.a. as a medium for reading instruction. In A. J. Mazurkiewicz (ed.), *i.t.a. and the World of English*. Hempstead, N.Y.: i.t.a. Foundation

13 SHAPIRO, B. J. (1966). A comparison of the reading achievement of i.t.a. and t.o.

groups in first grade. Cleveland, Ohio: Educational Research Council of Greater Cleveland.

14 STEWART, M. R. (1966). Two years with i.t.a. An interim Report of the Bethlehem-Lehigh Research Project. In A. J. Mazurkiewicz (ed.), *i.t.a. and the World of English*. Hempstead, N.Y.: i.t.a. Foundation

15 SWALES, T. D. (1966). The attainments in reading and spelling of children who learned to read through the initial teaching alphabet. M.Ed. thesis, Department of Education, University of Manchester

16 TANYZER, H. J. and ALPERT, H. (1965). Effectiveness of three different basal reading systems on first grade reading achievement, Hempstead, N.Y.: Hofstra University Office of Education, Co-operative Research Project No. 2720

17 TANYZER, H. J., ALPERT, H. and SANDEL, L. (1965). Beginning reading: effectiveness of different media. Mineola, N.Y.: Nassau School Development Council.

II List of questions asked

The research design suggested in Chapter 16 has been used as a guide to summarising research reports. This design leads to the need to find answers to the following questions:

A. BASIC PLAN

1 What media were investigated?
2 What were the criteria of success?
3 How long did the investigation take?

B. CONTROL OF SAMPLES

1 *School Areas*
(a) How many school areas took part in the investigation?
(b) What types of school area took part in the investigation?
(c) Did the school areas volunteer?
(d) Were the school areas matched?
(e) How were the media allocated to the school areas?

2 *Schools*
(a) How many schools took part in the investigation?
(b) What types of school took part in the investigation?
(c) Did the schools volunteer?
(d) Were the schools matched?
(e) How were the media allocated to the schools?

3 *Teachers*
(a) How many teachers took part in the investigation?
(b) What types of teacher took part in the investigation?

(*c*) Did the teachers volunteer?
(*d*) Were the teachers matched?
(*e*) How were the media allocated to the teachers?

4 *Classes*

(*a*) How many classes took part in the investigation?
(*b*) What types of class took part in the investigation?
(*c*) How were the media allocated to the classes?

5 *Pupils*

(*a*) How many pupils took part in the investigation?
(*b*) What types of pupil took part in the investigation?
(*c*) Were the pupils matched?

C. CLASSROOM PRACTICE

1   What materials were used?
2   What methods of teaching reading were used?
3   What general classroom procedures were adopted in teaching reading?
4   Was the number of minutes spent in reading activities controlled?
5   When did the pupils make the transition from i.t.a. to t.o.?
6   Who administered the tests?

D. SUPERVISION

1   What courses of pre-experimental training for teachers were held?
2   To what extent was the experiment supervised by research staff?

RELATIONS WITH PUBLIC

1   Were the public allowed to visit the experimental classes?
2   What contacts were made with the parents of the children taking part in the experiment?

F. ANALYSIS OF RESULTS

1   What statistical techniques were used in the analysis results?
2   What statistical matching techniques were used?
3   What variables other than the media were included in the main statistical results?
4   How were the results interpreted?
5   What were the results of the investigations?

III   Plan for summarising researches

The description of the individual researches covers these questions arranged under the following headings:

A. BASIC PLAN

Media used, criteria of success, length of investigation, time of transition from i.t.a. to t.o., time of administration of criterion test.

B. SCOPE

Number and type of school areas, schools, teachers, classes and pupils.

C. ALLOCATION OF MEDIA

Volunteering, matching and allocation of school areas, schools, teachers, classes and pupils.

D. CLASSROOM PRACTICE

Reading materials, methods of teaching reading, classroom procedure, time allowance for reading instruction.

E. SUPERVISION

Pre-experimental courses of training, supervision of lessons by researchers, teachers' records of reading activities.

F. RELATIONS WITH PUBLIC

Visits of public; contacts with parents.

G. STATISTICAL TECHNIQUES

Statistical matching techniques, statistical techniques for analysing results.

H. RESULTS

I. EVALUATION

The main interest in the individual researches is, of course, whether they show i.t.a. or t.o. (or neither) to be the superior medium for learning to read. When the main results have been established, the next major task is to evaluate them in order to determine whether any significant differences between the two groups are likely to be due to the nature of the media themselves or rather to 'disturbing' factors with which they have been associated to a different extent – e.g. teacher enthusiasm. The purpose of Chapter 16 on Experimental Design was to draw up a list of such factors and to suggest means by which they might be brought under control. It must be borne in mind however that the experimental designs actually adopted by researchers will, for reasons of convenience, time, finance and acceptability, be less rigorous than those put forward in the present report, which did not suffer from such constraints. The tendency in the actual investigations will be for the variables to be less rigorously controlled, i.e. for the 'analysed' variables of Table 16(b) to be treated as either 'matched', 'constant' or 'error' variables. Such changes do not necessarily destroy the validity of these researches. Matching gives less information than variance analysis, but it is nevertheless an effective and logical method of experimental control. Similarly, if the number of pupils and schools is large, randomisation might be effective, provided that there is no reason to believe that the variables concerned – e.g. sex, competence of teachers – are particularly associated with either t.o. or i.t.a.

It proved extremely difficult to summarise some of the reports adequately as they give incomplete accounts of a series of overlapping researches which have been modified during the course of the experiment. Omissions and apparent contradictions abound. Vital information such as the time of testing, the medium in which the children were tested and the proportion who had made the transition to t.o., is often not given, or muddled up. Most of the researches examined were either too limited in scope or too illogical in design to give much insight into the influence of disturbing factors and the evaluations are in consequence rather uninformative. (An attempt has, however, been made in Chapter 19 to gather up information from the whole range of investigations concerning the influence of various extraneous factors and to examine their relevance in interpreting the results.)

IV   Summaries of seventeen researches

1   BOSMA, R. L. (1965)

Teaching Reading with i.t.a.: a research report. *Reading Horizon*, 6, 6–19.

A. *Basic plan*

One class of children was taught to read by i.t.a., and two classes by t.o. for a period of nine months, at the end of which time the Metropolitan Achievement test was given in t.o. to both groups. No information is given about who carried out the testing.

B. *Scope*

Two groups, each of 22 children (11 boys and 11 girls) were included in the final analysis, the i.t.a. group being the entire first grade class of a University Campus school, and the t.o. group 22 pupils from the two first grade classes of a neighbouring school.

C. *Allocation of media*

The schools were invited to take part in the research by the experimenter. The t.o. classes followed their normal programme. The pupils from the experimental classes were matched for sex, chronological age, I.Q. and reading readiness and were 'judged similar in socio-economic status'. In the t.o. class neither teachers nor pupils were aware which pupils were included in the experiment (although they were presumably aware that an experiment was taking place).

D. *Classroom practice*

The *Downing Readers* were used for i.t.a. and various other readers for t.o. No writing was done in the i.t.a. class as it was felt that writing in i.t.a. would produce excessive reinforcement of the mental images of such word forms, and would thus contribute in a major way to later spelling problems.

E. *Supervision*

No supervision by the research staff is reported.

F. *Relations with public*

Not reported.

G. *Statistical techniques*

Means, S.D.'s and 't' tests were used for purposes of matching, and presumably for the analysis of the results.

H. *Results*

The i.t.a. group were significantly superior to the t.o. in reading skills even without the benefit of experience in writing. They also had a 'more enriched and extensive vocabulary'. The tests were in 't.o.', presumably after transfer as the author says that transfer did not raise a significant problem.

I. *Evaluation*

The superiority of the results shown by the i.t.a. class is not necessarily due to the use of i.t.a. since it could also have been due to differences in the type of school used, the i.t.a. classes being in a University Campus school with a strong experimental bias, and the t.o. classes in an ordinary public school, or it might have been due to differences between the teachers, the reading materials, the organisation of the lessons, the teaching methods or the time spent on reading. With so many relevant factors uncontrolled the results can at best be described as inconclusive. This is an exercise rather than a research.

2 DELL, G. A. (1967)

The i.t.a. approach to reading. The Corporation of Glasgow Education Department.

A. *Basic plan*

The media used were i.t.a. and t.o. The subjects were tested after four school terms (i.e. at about 15 months) with Schonell's Graded Word Reading test (an i.t.a. version was provided for the i.t.a. subjects), and in written expression. An analysis was made of errors in the main tests. No information is given about who carried out the testing.

B. *Scope*

Fifty-four boys and girls (26 i.t.a. and 28 t.o.) were included in the final analysis. They were members of two primary classes in a Roman Catholic school in a low socio-economic urban district in Scotland. The children had been randomly assigned to the two classes. They were just beginning to learn to read, their average age being $6\frac{1}{2}$ at the end of the experiment. The two teachers were both experienced and very competent.

C. *Allocation of media*

The i.t.a. teacher was convinced of the method; the t.o. teacher was less experienced and uncommitted. The incidence of dullness, speech defects, left-handedness and maladjustment appeared to be equally distributed between the two classes.

D. Classroom practice

The i.t.a. class used the *Downing Readers* and a predominantly phonic method, the t.o. class used *Janet and John* with a combination of phonic and look-and-say methods.

E. Supervision

Supervision of the experiment is not mentioned in the report.

F. Relations with public

The i.t.a. class had many visitors.

G. Statistical techniques

't' tests and correlation coefficients.

H. Results

The i.t.a. class (tested in i.t.a.) was about $1\frac{1}{2}$ years ahead of the t.o. (tested in t.o.) class in reading age after 4 terms. This superiority was not confined to the 'best readers', but was maintained at least two-thirds of the way down each class. Nevertheless, both groups included some very poor readers. Reading and Matrices scores were more highly correlated in the i.t.a. than in the t.o. group, suggesting a closer association between learning to read and general ability in the i.t.a. group. i.t.a. is also claimed to have a good effect on morale, particularly with the slower children. The i.t.a. group did not show any marked superiority in written expression, possibly because the vocabulary level of both classes was too low to enable writing capacity to manifest itself at this stage.

I. Evaluation

This report on a small experiment gives a valuable account of some of the major issues raised by i.t.a. in schools. In respect of experimental design it is perhaps best regarded as a case study, since it is confined to one school and the differences observed might be due to the teachers, the textbooks or the teaching methods and procedures adopted in the classroom.

3 DOWNING, J. A. (1967)

> Chapter 1, Historical background and origins of i.t.a. research. *The i.t.a. Symposium.* National Foundation for Educational Research in England and Wales.

A. Basic plan

The media used were i.t.a. and t.o. The criteria of success included the Schonell Graded Word Reading test, the Neale test of Reading Ability, and the Standish N.S. 45 test. Tests were administered at intervals from the end of the first year to mid-fourth year. From the middle of the fifth term they were given in t.o. to both groups. Teachers, but not the children's own teachers, carried out the testing.

B. Scope

One hundred and fifty-eight classes in 24 school areas were used, 89 being taught with i.t.a., and 69 with t.o. In all, 1,746 pupils and 158 teachers took part. There were 33 pairs of matched schools and 8 pairs of matched classes. The schools varied widely in type, being urban and rural; English, Scottish and Irish; North country, Southern and Midland; infants and infant/junior. The children were beginning to learn to read.

C. Allocation of media

Schools and teachers (both volunteers) were allocated to media according to their own choice. Schools were originally matched on location (urban or rural), size, pupil-teacher ratio, amenities of school building, minimum age of entry, and social class. Pupils were matched for age, sex, social class, I.Q. (Matrices) and Crichton Vocabulary Scale scores. (Certain minor modifications were made in the matched variables as the experiment proceeded.)

D. Classroom practice

Janet and John readers (transliterated for the i.t.a. classes) were used. Additional books in i.t.a. were supplied for the 'book corners' The i.t.a. class libraries were at first less well furnished with books than the t.o. but this situation improved with time. A field approach was used, teachers being asked to use their normal methods for teaching reading in both i.t.a. and t.o. classes. For the most part this involved initial look-and-say methods followed by a mixture of look-and-say and phonic.

E. Supervision

Teachers of each method attended a one-day course before the experiment began. These classes were intended to have an equal impact on each group, but it is possible that in practice this was not achieved. Evening meetings were held for each group of teachers, seven in the first year, three in the second year and two per annum thereafter. Record cards were kept for the i.t.a. classes. Visits of the research staff to the classroom were equalised for classes in both media.

F. Relations with public

Meetings were held for parents of children learning i.t.a. and booklets were distributed. The i.t.a. classes received more publicity than the t.o. classes.

G. Statistical techniques

The one-tailed Kolmogorov-Smirnov test for differences between pairs of samples was applied to the test score. Where considered suitable, the Wilcoxon matched pairs sign test was used. These procedures (like most non-parametric techniques) raise considerable doubts and could have been supplemented with advantage by 't' tests of differences between means. Standard deviations might also have been cited with advantage for purposes of interpretation. The interquartile range is usually given, but this is not an adequate substitute.

H. Results

Twice as many i.t.a. children had completed the reading scheme after $2\frac{1}{2}$ years instruction and 83% of the i.t.a. group were placed above the t.o. median in respect of progress through the basic readers, i.e. more than four-fifths of the 'superior' readers were from the i.t.a. groups. By this time the i.t.a. group was about two books ahead. After three years, the i.t.a. classes showed significantly superior achievement to t.o. classes in word recognition, accuracy and in speed reading, when the medium of testing was t.o. In comprehension the i.t.a. group was superior according to the Neale test, but not by the Standish N.S. 45 test. Except in speed, reading scores fell off immediately after the transition to t.o., by weeks according to the Neale test and by months according to the Schonell test, but the i.t.a. group remained significantly ahead. The i.t.a. group was also superior in t.o. spelling (the authors suggest that this is perhaps a generalised transfer effect of the i.t.a. pupils' early experience of the regular grapheme-phoneme relations in i.t.a.). The i.t.a. groups showed superior results in written composition and in children's written vocabulary.

I. Evaluation

This is clearly an important research. The sample was outstandingly large, many of the experimental samples are over 500 (although some became smaller) and seven over 1000, and the schools and pupils were on the whole adequately matched, although it is doubtful whether attempts to equalise the Hawthorne effect were entirely successful. The teacher variable was not fully controlled, as different teachers taught classes in the different media and were not allocated to the media at random. Lesson procedures, teaching methods and time allowances were not standardised, but since the same tests and materials were used in both media it may be that sheer weight of numbers can be taken as having randomised the influence of the remaining variables. Unfortunately orthodox tests of statistical significance were not applied to the data, which makes evaluation of the results extremely difficult. The closer controls used in the later experiments by Downing and Jones (1966) are to be preferred and their results will carry more conviction.

4 DOWNING, J. A. and JONES, B. (1966)

   Some problems of evaluating i.t.a. A second experiment. *Educational Research*, 8, No. 2, 100–114

A. *Basic plan*

The media used were i.t.a. and t.o. The criteria of success were the Schonell Graded Word Reading test given at the end of the first year and at mid-second year, and the Neale Analysis of Reading Ability given at mid-second year. Progress through the reading primer was also checked. No information is given concerning who carried out the testing.

B. *Scope*

1102 children who were beginning to read (548 i.t.a. and 554 control) from 13 schools.

C. *Allocation of media*

The schools volunteered for the experiment. They were matched for size, urban-rural location, type of organisation, pupil-teacher ratio, minimum age of entry, socio-economic status of area and building facilities. Classes were allocated at random to media. No significant differences were found between the two groups of pupils in respect of age, sex, social class, intelligence or vocabulary. The teachers were volunteers. The matching of teachers was perfect as the same teacher taught reading in both the i.t.a. and t.o. classes in a given school.

D. *Classroom practice*

The *Janet and John* readers (transliterated for the i.t.a. classes) were used on the ground that they were the most commonly used textbooks in the country. Classroom libraries were also provided with books in the appropriate script. There was some shortage of library books in i.t.a. during the first half term. Teachers were asked to use the same methods and to give identical time to teaching in each of the media.

206

The importance of observing the prescribed procedures was frequently stressed. In practice, however, there was a tendency for rather more time to be given to i.t.a.

E. *Supervision*

A record was kept of the time spent on reading. Those classes were eliminated where the ratio of time spent with either class exceeded 60/40.

F. *Relations with public*

Meetings were held for parents of both i.t.a. and t.o. classes. Outside visitors to i.t.a. classes were usually 'scheduled' elsewhere. If exclusion was not possible, the visitors were compelled to visit the t.o. classes as well.

G. *Statistical techniques*

The distributions of scores in the criterion tests were markedly skewed for many of the sub-groups and a logarithmic transformation was applied to the raw scores.

H. *Results*

The i.t.a. group was significantly superior in all the Neale criterion tests when tested in the medium of instruction after eighteen months. Within individual schools, 16 out of 17 significant differences were in favour of i.t.a. However, when all tests were given in t.o., the i.t.a. group was slightly but not significantly superior, and three out of the four significant differences within schools (all in the same school) were in favour of t.o. It must be remembered, however, that only 17% of the i.t.a. pupils had at this time made the transition to t.o. so that the findings are purely tentative. Later results, however, after three years' instruction when about three-quarters of the children had transferred to reading t.o. show no change in this position, and four of the six significant differences within schools are in favour of t.o.

I. *Evaluation*

This is the most efficiently designed research that has been carried out in this field and hence the most convincing. An attempt has been made to control all the major 'extraneous' variables that might influence the results. The pupils were all matched, and the fact that the same teachers took both groups in the same school equates a large number of influential differences between teachers, schools, methods and class-room procedures. The reading texts and materials were the same in both groups; relationships were established with the parents; the public was excluded from the experimental classrooms as far as possible and attempts were made to control the Hawthorne effect and to standardise and supervise the teaching procedure. Unfortunately, orthodox tests of statistical significance were not applied to the data, and the interpretation of the results thus becomes less conclusive.

5 FRY, E. (1966)

Comparisons of three methods of reading instruction. Results at end of second grade. Office of Education Co-operative Research Project No. 3050. Rutgers University, New Brunswick, New Jersey

A. *Basic plan*

The media used were i.t.a., t.o. and d.m.s. (diacritical marking system). The criteria of success for the main sample were the Stanford Achievement Test, the Detroit Word Recognition test, the Gilmore Oral Reading test and the Gates Word Pronunciation test. The investigation has so far extended over two years, i.e. the same classes have been followed up in Grade I and Grade II. The tests do not appear to have been administered by teachers. They were given after 140 days in Grade I and in December and May during Grade II.

B. *Scope*

21 first grade classes (7 to each medium) from 21 schools in one school area participated. The children were just beginning to read. In the second year the numbers dropped from 390 to 347.

C. *Allocation of media*

The classes were randomly allocated to the media at the beginning of the experiment. The pupils were matched by I.Q. (Pitner General Ability Test), the Metropolitan Reading Readiness test and the Murphy-Durrell Diagnostic Reading Readiness test. There were, however, large differences in I.Q. and reading readiness in favour of the t.o. classes that were not taken into account in analysing the results.

D. *Classroom practice*

The t.o. and d.m.s. groups used the Sheldon Basal Reader program, the latter with diacritical marks added. The i.t.a. groups used the *Early to Read* series. The methods used were those recommended by the Teacher's Guides accompanying the readers. Time allocations (as indicated by the teachers) showed no significant differences. Attendance was generally high. Size of class is not specified. Teachers were rated by three or four raters on the basis of class visitations. No significant differences in competence were found. Nor did they differ significantly in age, experience, second grade teaching experience, or attendance.

E. *Supervision*

Supervision is not mentioned.

F. *Relations with public*

Not mentioned.

G. *Statistical techniques*

Analysis of variance.

H. *Results*

In year I, when a large proportion of children had already made the transition to t.o., there was no difference in achievement as measured by the Stanford Achievement test. The i.t.a. children were significantly superior in the Phonetically Regular Words test of oral reading. (This test was given to 132 children randomly chosen in three groups of 44 from the the three sets of subjects.) In t.o. spelling the t.o. children were significantly superior. The range of differences between the mean scores for classes was much greater than the range of differences between media, but since there were 21 classes and only three media this is to be expected, the former being less heavily averaged.

In year II, no differences were found on the Stanford tests, the Gilmore Oral

Reading test or the Gates Word Pronunciation test. Differences were found favouring the i.t.a. on a list of phonetically regular words read orally. The i.t.a. children wrote significantly longer stories, but this might have been because they were given more practice and were told to disregard spelling.

Many interesting sidelights were thrown up. There were no significant interactions between media and intelligence or sex, and there were low positive correlations between reading achievement and total length of teaching experience, age of teacher and, very suprisingly, short amount of instruction time (possibly because the poorer teachers have to put in more time.)

I. *Evaluation*

In many respects this is a well conducted experiment; but as each medium is used with a different set of materials no convincing conclusions can possibly be drawn about the differences between the effectiveness of the two alphabets considered in isolation. The author was, of course, concerned with differences between three overall methods of reading instruction rather than between alphabets *per se*.

6 HAHN, H. T. (1965)

Relative effectiveness of three methods of teaching reading in grade one. Lansing, Michigan: Michigan Department of Public Instruction, Office of Education, Co-operative Research Project Number 2687

A. *Basic plan*

Three approaches (rather than media) were used, i.t.a., t.o. and b.r.a. (Basic Reader Approach). The investigation lasted 140 days, and the Stanford Achievement test was then administered in t.o., together with the San Diego Reading Attitudes test. Individual tests, viz. the Gilmore Oral Reading test, Fry Phonetically Regular Words, Gates Word test and Karlsen's Phonemic Words were given to a small sample. The teachers did not carry out the testing. A course of training was provided for the project director's staff and a number of local school district supervisors. Eighty per cent of the pupils had made the transition to t.o. before the close of the school.

B. *Scope*

Twelve school districts, 36 schools (3 in each district), 36 teachers and 890 children – 294 i.t.a., 283 t.o. and 313 b.r.a. – took part in the investigation. The average size of the classes was 26, comprising boys and girls. The mean age was 6.6, and the pupils were heterogeneous in social background. The schools were of three comparable socio-economic groups: the teachers, who were volunteers, had been judged competent by administrators.

C. *Allocation of media*

Certain school areas volunteered to take part in the experiments. The schools were then selected by local administrators. Within the schools the teachers were volunteers. The schools were matched for teaching approach according to the San Diego Scale. Pupils were matched by the Pitner-Cunningham I.Q. test, the Durrell-Murphy Reading Readiness test, the Metropolitan Reading Readiness test, and the Thurstone P.M.A. (identical forms and patterns copying). Eighteen i.t.a. children were not beginners, having received previous instruction in t.o.

D. Classroom practice

The method of teaching with i.t.a. and t.o. was the modified Language Arts method. Significant differences were found in the classroom approaches to i.t.a. and t.o., there being great differences in the materials used, methods and time allocations.

E. Supervision

Teachers of each of the three media attended a one-week course of instruction before the experiment began. In the course of the experiment, teachers in each media attended ten half-day meetings for discussion, advice and preparation of material. No mention is made of teachers' records.

F. Relations with public

Not mentioned.

G. Statistical techniques

The techniques used were orthodox and appropriate. Differences were tested by 't' scores, and two-way analysis of variance (for treatment and district) was included. Chi-square was used for matching, and correlation coefficients were calculated in order to determine the relationship between reading and intelligence in the two groups.

H. Results

The i.t.a. groups were poor in spelling (in t.o. but not in i.t.a.), when about 80% of the i.t.a. children had made the transition to t.o. The t.o. groups were superior in paragraph meaning (taking intelligence into account). The i.t.a. group scored higher on word lists, but not on contextual material. According to the authors 'The i.t.a. children have learned to sound through a word one element at a time, and they employed a broader range of word attack skills which served them particularly well on word lists'. No significant differences were found between the children's attitudes to reading. Significant differences were found not only between the mean reading attainment in different districts (which is not surprising) but also in the interaction between district and approach, i.e. certain approaches were relatively more efficient in different districts, possibly due to socio-economic influences.

I. Evaluation

This investigation, despite the thoroughness and soundness of the analytic methods used, and the size of the sample, provides very little information on the relative merits of the two media, as they were experimentally confounded with different materials, methods and time allocations. Moreover, significant differences were found between the teachers' approach to reading. The observed differences might be due to the alphabets used, and, equally well, they might not. The authors were, of course, primarily interested in three broad approaches to reading rather than differences between the i.t.a. and t.o. alphabets.

7 HARRISON, M. (1964)

   Instant Reading. London: Pitman & Sons Ltd.
   This book reports part of Downing's (1967) experiment carried out in Oldham. This local education authority led the field in Britain in pioneering i.t.a. in schools, and the findings may fairly be regarded as a separate research contribution.

A. *Basic plan*

The media used were i.t.a. and t.o.; the criteria of success were the books reached by the children in their reading series and scores on the Southgate Group Reading tests, and the Neale Analysis of Reading Ability tests. These were given in t.o. at the end of the third, fourth, fifth and sixth terms. The tests were administered by an expert in reading tests.

B. *Scope*

In the early stages of the experiment at Oldham, the sample comprised 5 entry classes from 5 schools of varying type, with predominantly working-class background. 135–163 children were in i.t.a. and 241–273 in t.o. classes. They were children just beginning to read aged 4.1 to 5.0 years.

C. *Allocation of media*

Schools and teachers were volunteers; pupils were not specially allocated to classes, but taken as they were found (subject to parental consent). No formal matching techniques are reported.

D. *Classroom practice*

Janet and John readers were used in both media. Teaching methods, classroom approaches and time allocations appear to have varied considerably.

E. *Supervision*

i.t.a. teachers were given instruction in the use of the new alphabet and in the maintenance of the children's record cards. t.o. teachers also were given instruction regarding record cards.

F. *Relations with public*

Pamphlets on the initial teaching alphabet were distributed to teachers and parents; children were not put into i.t.a. classes without their parents' consent. There was an absurdly large number of visitors (over 4,000), chiefly to one newly-built school.

G. *Statistical techniques*

Not mentioned.

H. *Results*

The i.t.a. classes were one year ahead in reading age of the t.o. class after 18 months' teaching (the test being in t.o. script), despite the fact that less than half of the children had made progress through the basic readers beyond the t.o. median. They also showed very considerable superiority in creative writing, and (in the view of their teachers) in reading standards, reduced failure rates, vocabulary, speech, comprehension, speed, general knowledge, confidence, enthusiasm, independence, steadfastness of application and maturity. Later results confirmed a marked superiority for the i.t.a. group after three years, when more than twice as many children taught by i.t.a. had completed the reading series (over 80% compared with 40%) even when allowance had been made for the Hawthorne effect.

I. *Evaluation*

An extremely useful pioneering experiment, without full controls. The results are highly suggestive rather than conclusive.

8   HAYES, R. B. and NEMETH, J. S. (1965)
Factors affecting learning to read. Harrisburg, Pennsylvania Department of
Public Instruction, Office of Education Co-operative Research Project No. 2687

A. *Basic plan*

Four approaches to reading instruction were investigated.
(i) eclectic 'whole word' (Scott, Foresman)
(ii) phonic (Lippincott)
(iii) combined eclectic 'whole word-phonic' (Scott, Foresman)
(iv) i.t.a. (Language Arts Approach)

The investigation lasted 140 days and the criteria of success were scores on the
Stanford Achievement test (given in i.t.a. and t.o. scripts on the 82nd day, and in t.o.
only on the 141st day), and the San Diego Inventory of Reading Attitudes. Three
separate random samples of 30 pupils also took part in the Gilmore Oral Reading test,
the Gates Word Pronunciation test and the Phonetically Regular Words Oral
Reading test. The field director undertook the individual testing, but the group
tests were carried out by teachers, with neutral observers.

B. *Scope*

The subjects were 365 first-grade pupils beginning to read from 19 classes, representing 10 of 12 schools comprising one school area.

C. *Allocation of media*

Teachers volunteered for both the experiment and the method used. The pupils
were matched according to father's occupation, the Detroit Word Recognition test,
the Murphy-Durrell Diagnostic Reading test, the Metropolitan Reading Readiness
test, the Thurstone P.M.A. (Pattern Copying Identical Forms), the Stanford
Achievement and Lee-Clark Reading Readiness test.

D. *Classroom practice*

Materials used were the Lippincott Readers (phonic), Scott, Foresman Readers
(whole word eclectic) together with 'Phonics and Word Power' and i.t.a. publications, i.e. the *Downing Readers*. Teaching methods for t.o. were thus phonic,
look-and-say and eclectic; for i.t.a. they were those recommended by the publishers.
650 minutes weekly were given to reading activities in each approach.

E. *Supervision*

For each approach there was a three-day pre-school course for teachers, run by the
book companies' consultants and authors. Each class was visited about 20 times in the
year by a consultant, the research director or the project director. Teacher logs were
kept, including a record of instructional time.

F. *Relations with public*

Enquiries were made of parents concerning the number of books in the home and
the amount of pre-school reading.

G. *Statistical techniques*

The statistical techniques used were extremely interesting, matching being achieved by covariance techniques. At first, correlation coefficients were computed to see which of the pre-experimental variables correlated best with the dependent variables, and those which had the highest statistically significant correlations with silent reading achievement on the Stanford test were then chosen as covariates. These covariates proved to be the Murphy-Durrell Phonemes, Murphy-Durrell Letter Names, the Metropolitan Reading Readiness and intelligence tests. In addition, ratings of teachers' effectiveness and the educational level of the parents were treated as covariates. Subsequent analysis was chiefly by 't' tests of the differences between achievement scores, educational level of parents and the number of books in the home.

H. Results

There was some evidence that the more analytic approaches, i.e. phonic and i.t.a., were superior as aids to word recognition. There was no interaction with intelligence, groups differing in intelligence obtaining similar results.

I. Evaluation

The findings were of little value as regards the relative merits of i.t.a. and t.o., as the media were very much confounded with methods, materials, and procedure in four different approaches. Thus this is a research into general approaches to reading rather than into reading *per se*. The supervision of the experiment was thorough and the criteria included attitudes to reading, but the experimental design is too muddled to be regarded as an investigation into the relative merits of i.t.a. and t.o. The investigation was not primarily intended to throw light on differences between media, as one of its stated objectives is 'to refine, extend and strengthen knowledge of beginning reading by comparing methods and materials of four separate educational publishers, Scott, Foresman, Lippincott, American Educational Publishers and i.t.a.'

9   McCRACKEN, R. A. (1966)

A two-year longitudinal study to determine the ability of first grade children to learn to read using the *Early-to-Read* i.t.a. program. (An Interim Report of the First Year). In A. J. Mazurkiewicz (ed.), *i.t.a. and the World of English*, Hempstead, N.Y.: i.t.a. Foundation

A. Basic plan

This is an interim report on the first year of a two-year study. The media used were i.t.a. and t.o.; the criteria of success were the Standard Reading Inventory (S.R.I.), Gray's Oral Reading test (at 70 and 140 days), and the Stanford Achievement test (at 140 days). The first two tests were transliterated for the i.t.a. classes. Eleven examiners were appointed who were presumably not participating teachers.

B. Scope

Sixty children (34 taught by i.t.a. and 26 by t.o.) forming two classes in one school, were the main group of subjects. Three randomly chosen classes from neighbouring schools served as sub-control groups. It was thought that these three classes, which received no attention other than initial and final testing, would be completely free of Hawthorne effect. The two teachers were randomly assigned to the main experimental classes. The pupils were in the first grade, and just beginning to read.

C. *Allocation of media*

The teachers were those already at the school, randomly assigned to the two experimental classes. Pupils were randomly assigned to these classes.

D. *Classroom practice*

The i.t.a. class worked with the *Early-to-Read* series and the t.o. class with the Ginn Basal series. Each class had a comparable library in the appropriate script. The time spent on reading and writing together appeared to be the same in both classes. The i.t.a. groups spent significantly more time than the t.o. group on writing and the t.o. group significantly more than the i.t.a. group on reading.

E. *Supervision*

There were no pre-experimental classes for teachers, but a time-study was made in both experimental and control groups, with systematic whole-day observation made by observers once a fortnight throughout the first year. There is no mention of teachers' records.

F. *Relations with public*

No intrusion by the public is mentioned, and no contacts appear to have been made with parents.

G. *Statistical techniques*

Various methods were used including analysis of variance, 't' tests, the Wilcoxon two sample test, chi-square and a sign test.

H. *Results*

The i.t.a. pupils did not show any clear-cut superiority when reading in t.o. in overall achievement at the end of the first grade, although they were superior in word recognition. (No information is given about how many children had made the transition.) Their spelling achievement was then equal to that of pupils taught by t.o. When reading from i.t.a. script the i.t.a. pupils were markedly superior to the t.o. pupils; although this tended to be limited to above average and average achievers, with the least able third of the class continuing to be in difficulties. The Hawthorne effect is clearly very considerable, but as no S.D.'s are given it is impossible to make an accurate estimate of its extent. However, the median grade level of the Stanford Achievement test when both groups were tested in t.o. is 1·95 for the i.t.a. group 2·00 for the t.o. groups, but much lower (1·70) for the sub-controls, who were not aware that they were taking part in the experiment. Inspection of mean sub-test scores suggests that the Hawthorne effect might account for some two-thirds of the observed differences. The experimental t.o. group scored about 20% higher than the sub-control group in which no Hawthorne effect was present.

I. *Evaluation*

This research is chiefly valuable in indicating methods of investigating the Hawthorne effect. As the two groups used different readers, and the t.o. group spent significantly more time in reading instruction whilst the i.t.a. group spent significantly more time in independent writing, the results bear no definite relationship to the media used. The author was concerned of course with the differences between reading programmes rather than between the media themselves.

The initial teaching alphabet in reading instruction. Comprehensive Final Report, Lehigh University and Bethlehem Area Schools.

A. *Basic plan*

The media used were i.t.a. and t.o. The investigations were carried out during 1963–7 and involved two first grade entries, 1963–4 and 1964–5. The 1963–4 first-grade experiment was primarily intended to give the teachers experience of i.t.a., but a number of results were given in connection with this group, and the progress of the pupils concerned is followed up to the third grade.

Criteria of success were the Botel Reading Inventory and the Stanford Achievement test. A sub-sample was tested with the Phonetically Regular Words, the Gilmore Oral Reading test, Gates Word Pronunciation test and Karlsen's Phonemic Words. Randomly selected sub-samples of 30–40 children were tested in informal word recognition inventories and the Stanford Achievement test (transliterated for the i.t.a. groups) after 70 days' instruction. All the group tests were administered by specially trained teachers under the supervision of school district administrators and research personnel, but the sub-sample tests were given by the research staff.

B. *Scope*

Initially, 30 first grade classes from 26 schools (i.t.a. group 455, t.o. group about 460) in one school district took part in the experiment. The final population in the main experiment (1964–5 entry) consisted of 118 matched pairs who had completed all the tests.

C. *Allocation of media*

The total first-grade intake in the school district was about 1,400. These were assigned randomly to classes within their schools, except that heterogeneity within each class in regard to reading readiness test marks was ensured. The experimenter selected 15 classes for i.t.a. in schools such that rural, suburban, urban and low, medium and high socio-economic areas were proportionately represented; there was, however, a rather larger proportion of low-economic status pupils in the i.t.a. than in the t.o. classes (40% against 25%). Teachers of i.t.a. and t.o. were volunteers, but the volunteers were also selected for teacher competence as judged by supervisors, principals and curriculum consultants. They were all about 40 years old, and equally experienced. Their training was varied, some being certified only, others were graduates, and some had higher degrees. Pupils included whites, Negroes and Puerto Ricans.

D. *Classroom practice*

In the main experiment, the materials used for i.t.a. classes were the *Early-to-Read* series for the more able pupils and the *Downing Readers* for the less able. The t.o. classes used *Alice and Jerry* for the more able and the American Book Company Language Arts book for the less able pupils. In both groups there was a language arts emphasis. In both media the time allocation was 655 minutes for all language activities, including 510 minutes for direct reading instruction. The time allocation seems to have been adhered to fairly well.

E. *Supervision*

There were separate two-day pre-experimental workshops for teachers in both groups.

Mimeographed materials with specific teaching suggestions were distributed to all teachers. Instructional supervisors visited each classroom at least once a week and very frequently more often. They gave advice and constructive criticism and generally conferred with the teachers. All teachers met monthly for discussion and mutual help. Teachers' logs were kept, including time records.

F. *Relations with public*

Visitors were 'scheduled' into the i.t.a. classes; 'authorities' had complete freedom to question the teachers. There was some indication that these visits had a disorganising and disheartening effect, which it was hoped might counteract rather than reinforce any Hawthorne effect. (It is not clear if there were visitors to t.o. classes.)

No mention is made in the report of contact with parents.

G. *Statistical techniques*

The statistical techniques were orthodox, chiefly comprising the calculation of means, S.D.'s and 't' tests of significance.

H. *Results*

(i) 1963-4 *First Grade*
In the follow-up of the 1963-4 first-grade children it was found that at the end of the second grade when most (60%) of the children had made the transition to t.o., the i.t.a. children were significantly superior in vocabulary and spelling to t.o. children (testing 196 pairs matched for I.Q., sex, socio-economic status and age). At the end of Grade III with the same sample i.t.a. pupils were still found significantly superior in spelling. They also retained their significant superiority in writing (number of running words, polysyllabic words, capitalisation, spelling).

(ii) 1964-5 *First Grade*
The i.t.a. sample was two books ahead, after five months, being significantly superior in the Botel Reading Inventory (72·6% having progressed beyond the t.o. median) and in word reading on the Stanford Achievement test when each group was tested in its own medium of instruction. By this time 5·7% of the i.t.a. children and 2·9% of the t.o. group had completed the reading scheme. When tested in t.o., about two-thirds of the children having made the transition, the t.o. children showed significant superiority in spelling and word study and the i.t.a. children in word reading (for matched pairs of 118).

According to a later report at the end of the second year, when nearly all (97%) of the children had made the transition, the i.t.a. children in a matched sample of 68 pairs showed significant superiority in language skills on the Stanford Achievement test, and in spelling and writing (polysyllabic words, running words). A random sample of 33 pairs showed the i.t.a. children to be significantly superior in word recognition according to the Fry Phonetically Regular Words test.

I. *Evaluation*

Although some control was exercised over classroom procedures, no less than four sets of readers were used according to the medium of instruction and the level of ability of the children. This makes it impossible to draw logical conclusions about the relative effectiveness of the media employed considered in isolation from other factors. Nevertheless, this large scale and important research admirably achieves the author's purpose in giving valuable information about general approaches to reading (in which the medium might or might not play some part).

11   MILNE, A. (1966)

The Scottish i.t.a. research. Paper read at the Third International i.t.a. Conference, Cambridge University

A. *Basic plan*

The approaches investigated were i.t.a., t.o. and the Stott *Programmed Reading Kit* (p.r.k.). The criteria of success were the Burt-Vernon Word Recognition test, the N.F. E.R. N.S. 45 test (both given in t.o. at the end of the second year) and fluency in writing. The tests were administered by the local principal psychologist and trained teachers from Colleges of Education.

B. *Scope*

Initially 720 children from 21 admission classes in seven schools from three school areas were involved. Two of the areas were urban and one rural. Twenty-one teachers took part. The number completing the experiment is not stated.

C. *Allocation of media*

The teachers (who had agreed to take part in the experiment) and the children were both allocated to the media at random. Matching criteria for the experimental group were the Crichton Vocabulary test and the occupational status of the father. Information was also obtained in I.Q. (Moray House Picture Intelligence Test) and on the cultural background as indicated by the number of books in the home, the amount of T.V. watched and comics read. The experimental groups were also matched with groups using the same media throughout Scotland (the sub-controls) by the Crichton Vocabulary Test score. Teachers and children in the sub-control groups did not know that they were being used for this purpose.

D. *Classroom practice*

Janet and John were used in all three groups. Teaching methods were look-and-say initially, probably mixed with phonics later. The p.r.k. group did some additional phonic work.

E. *Supervision*

The media and the methods were discussed with the teachers before the experiment began. One meeting was held each term for discussion and information. Teachers who would be taking the children during the third year at school also attended some of these meetings in order to preserve the continuity of the experiment.

F. *Relations with public*

Visits by the public were discouraged; if it was not possible to funnel visitors into non-participating i.t.a. classes, care was taken that classes from both groups were visited an equal number of times. Two questionnaires were issued to parents, and for each one there was a 90% response.

G. *Statistical techniques*

Presumably analysis of variance.

H. Results

This is an interim report, covering the first two years of the experiment. The i.t.a. children are shown to have done better than t.o. children (by about one-quarter S.D.) in the N.F. E.R. N.S. 45 Group Reading test and (by about one-fifth S.D.) in the Burt-Vernon Word Recognition test. At the time of testing (in t.o.), however, the i.t.a. children had only very recently transferred to t.o. script, and as many as 40% had not transferred at all. The i.t.a. script appeared to have helped the lowest I.Q. group most, a result contrary to that found in most investigations, although the tables showing reading attainment plotted against I.Q. levels show little evidence of interaction either for reading or word recognition scores.

The i.t.a. group were markedly more fluent in writing (by about 25%), both as regards the number of words used and the number of different words used.

Later results, after three years, show no significant differences between t.o. and i.t.a. groups in respect of reading in t.o. (Burt-Vernon and Southgate tests), spelling (according to the Mann-Whitney test of statistical significance) and composition. By this time, almost all the children had made the transition to t.o., suggesting that the t.o. children eventually catch up.

I. Evaluation

This is a closely controlled research. There are some excellent attempts to allow for the effect of sub-control groups; of shunting visitors to non-experimental classes, and of questioning parents. The same material was used for all of the experimental groups, but it is not clear to what extent teaching methods and classroom procedure were standardised. Variations between schools were controlled by ensuring that both media were used in all schools (except in rural areas, where this was impossible). Differences between teachers may influence the results as each teacher within a school used a different reading medium.

12 ROBINSON, H. M. (1966)

Effectiveness of i.t.a. as a medium for reading instruction. In A. J. Mazurkiewicz (ed.), *i.t.a. and the World of English*. Hempstead, N.Y.: i.t.a. Foundation

A. Basic Plan

This report is confined to a plan of a research. The media are i.t.a. and t.o.; the criteria of success are the Basal Reader tests, the Huelsman Word Discrimination test and the Metropolitan Achievement test. Gray's Oral Reading test is to be given to about 50 children from each group. Reading attitude tests of Strong's open-ended type, 'I'd rather read than . . . ' are also to be administered, and creative writing and the amount of personal reading will be evaluated. The tests will be given near the end of the first grade.

B. Scope

The research involves 450 pupils and 42 classes from 10 schools in two school areas. Nine of the schools are suburban, one is situated in a city slum; two of them serve upper-middle, two middle and two lower-class populations. Classes vary from all-Negro to all-Caucasian. Pupils were just beginning to read.

C. *Allocation of media*

Schools and teachers volunteered; pupils were allocated randomly to the media. The teachers will switch from i.t.a. to t.o. or vice-versa after one year, so that each teacher will teach both groups in the same school, although not the same year. The children are matched according to their scores in the Metropolitan Reading Readiness test, the California Mental Maturity Reading Readiness test, the California Mental Maturity test and the Kuhlman-Anderson intelligence test.

D. *Classroom practice*

The Scott, Foresman Multi-Ethnic Readers with supportive material (transliterated from the i.t.a. group) will be used for both media. Teaching methods are those advised in the Scott, Foresman guide. The general approach will be free, with stress on creative writing. Equal time is to be allocated to each medium.

E. *Supervision*

Pre-experimental workshops of equal duration were held for teachers in each medium. Research assistants will keep a regular check on time allowances and skill sequences in the classroom. Records are being kept of the books read and time spent on reading instruction.

F. *Relations with public*

Parents were informed about the experiment, and those who wished to do so were able to withdraw their children. A record of books read at home by the children is being obtained. Books used in the i.t.a. classes for other lessons such as arithmetic, social studies and science, are printed in i.t.a.

G. *Statistical techniques*

Statistical techniques are not mentioned. This report contains no results.

H. *Results*

The findings are not yet known, but the hypothesis is made that higher reading achievement will be attained by the i.t.a. groups of average and high, but not of low socio-economic levels.

I. *Evaluation*

This experiment is very well designed, with adequate control of media, materials, procedures and time allowances. The yearly change of teachers from one media to the other has disadvantages, since different children are taught by different sequences of teachers. Nevertheless, this investigation ranks with Downing and Jones's (1966) research as having the most thorough experimental design in the literature.

13   SHAPIRO, B. J. (1966)

A comparison of the reading achievement of i.t.a. and t.o. groups in first grade. Cleveland, Ohio: Educational Research Council of Greater Cleveland

A. *Basic plan*

The media used were i.t.a. and t.o. The criteria of success were the ERC Reading Mastery test administered after seven months in the medium of instruction and the

Stanford Achievement test, administered after eight months (in t.o. for both groups). No information is given about who carried out the testing. The length of the experiment was one school year.

B. *Scope*

1018 first grade pupils (430 i.t.a. and 588 t.o.) were observed, these forming 47 classes (21 i.t.a. and 26 t.o.) from schools in 10 school areas. There were 47 teachers.

C. *Allocation of media*

The methods of allocating the media to school areas, schools, teachers and classes is not stated, and we are not told whether schools and teachers were volunteers. Nor is any description given of the teachers. Pupils were matched by sex, I.Q. (Lorge-Thorndike) and reading readiness (ERC).

D., E., F. *Classroom practice, Supervision, Relations with public*

These are not mentioned in the report.

G. *Statistical techniques*

The statistical techniques used were the 't' test of differences between (i) unadjusted mean scores and (ii) mean scores adjusted by covariance techniques, holding I.Q. and reading readiness constant.

H. *Results*

In the Stanford Achievement test in which both groups were tested in t.o., the i.t.a. classes showed superiority (after intelligence was held constant) on all the sub-tests, i.e. word reading, paragraph reading, word study and spelling. (No information is given about how many children had made the transition.) The t.o. group had a superior vocabulary according to the Stanford Achievement test after adjustment for differences in reading readiness and I.Q. In the ERC test, in which both groups were tested in their own medium of instruction, the i.t.a. groups were significantly superior, although it must be remembered that this test is in some ways particularly vital to children instructed in the sound syllable system of i.t.a., as it uses more difficult words to spell and requires fine auditory and visual discrimination. The effect of adjusting the mean scores in order to hold intelligence and reading readiness constant was to raise the differences between the groups very considerably.

I. *Evaluation*

This research is important for its demonstration that the use of analysis of covariance may be fruitful, since it increased the differences between the mean scores of the experimental groups, and revealed that the i.t.a. group was superior when differences in intelligence and reading readiness were held constant. Unfortunately, experimental controls are almost completely non-existent as far as can be ascertained from the report.

14 STEWART, M. R. (1966)

Two years with i.t.a. An Interim Report of the Bethlehem-Lehigh Research Project. In A. J. Mazurkiewicz (ed.), *i.t.a. and the World of English*. Hempstead, N.Y.: i.t.a. Foundation.

A. *Basic plan*

The media investigated were t.o. and i.t.a. The length of the research was two years and the criteria of success were the California Reading test and the Stanford Spelling test, administered at the end of the year in t.o. Both teachers and helpers appear to have carried out the testing.

B. *Scope*

The entire first-grade population of one school district (about 1,350 children) was considered part of the project. One-third of these, located in 15 classrooms in 12 schools, of differing socio-economic status, were taught to read in i.t.a.

Over 40% of these i.t.a. children were in schools in areas of low economic status, in many cases coming from Spanish-speaking families. Altogether 410 i.t.a. and 875 t.o. children took part in the experiment.

C. *Allocation of media*

No information is given as to whether the teachers using i.t.a. were volunteers, or how the classes were selected. The teachers were 'considered comparable in age, training and experience'. 114 t.o. children were matched with 114 i.t.a. children for sex, chronological age, socio-economic level and I.Q. (within two points). The entire population was given the California Mental Maturity test at the beginning of the experiment, and no significant differences appeared between the general levels of the i.t.a. and the t.o. groups.

D. *Classroom practice*

Texts and materials used, teaching methods, classroom approaches and time allocations are not mentioned in the report.

E. *Supervision*

There is no mention of any supervision of teaching.

F. *Relations with public*

In the first two years there were 'floods of visitors', hundreds of letters and much interference by mass-media operators.

G. *Statistical techniques*

't' scores.

H. *Results*

At the end of nine months when not all the children had made the transition 5·6% of the i.t.a. population achieved a 3·5 grade or better, a standard reached by only 2·4% of the t.o. population. The corresponding figures after 12 months (following the summer hiatus) were 11·8% and 5·4%. The i.t.a. group scored significantly higher in t.o. spelling after 21 months. The claim is made that the i.t.a. group was also superior in independent learning, motivation, perseverance, the ability to observe and the ability to write.

I. *Evaluation*

The research report gives insufficient evidence regarding volunteering, matching,

221

methods, materials, teachers and supervision. The results, as they stand, despite the size of the sample, can therefore be regarded as little more than suggestive.

15 SWALES, T. D. (1966)

The attainments in reading and spelling of children who learned to read through the initial teaching alphabet. M.Ed. Thesis, Department of Education, University of Manchester, England

A. *Basic plan*

Children taught with i.t.a. and children taught with t.o. were given the NFER Sentence Reading test I and the Daniels and Diack Graded Spelling test at the end of their third school year, and their achievement scores in t.o. were compared and analysed. The testing was carried out by the experimenter.

B. *Scope*

Ninety-nine third-year children from six schools in Staffordshire, where reading had been taught with i.t.a., were compared with 99 children from six other schools in Staffordshire.

C. *Allocation of media*

The six i.t.a. schools investigated were those 'willing and able' to co-operate. All were already using the new alphabet independently of this investigation. The six t.o. schools used as controls were selected as similar to the i.t.a. schools in size, type and catchment area. Children were matched in 99 pairs of sex, chronological age, length of schooling (nine terms) social status and intelligence (NFER Picture Test I). (The i.t.a. and t.o. groups were also each divided into three sub-groups of high, medium and low intelligence.) No information is given concerning teachers.

D. *Classroom practice*

The i.t.a. classes used *Janet and John* (transliterated) and supplementary readers. Four t.o. classes used *Janet and John*, and two *Happy Venture* also with supplementary readers. On teaching methods the writer reports that he was 'forced to the conclusion that medium, method and materials were inextricably mixed'.

E. *Supervision*

There was no supervision. 'Neither group knew at the start that it was to be the subject of a future experiment.' In this way it was hoped as far as possible to avoid any Hawthorne effect.

F. *Relations with public*

No intrusion by the public or contact with the parents is reported.

G. *Statistical techniques*

Analysis of variance was used, controlling sex and I.Q. in the one case and schools in the other. Differences in intelligence were held constant by analysis of covariance.

H. *Results*

It was found that children taught by i.t.a. were neither superior nor inferior in reading or spelling standards to children taught by t.o., taking intelligence into account.

The same number of backward readers were found in each group. The significant variation found between schools suggested the importance of some such factor as teaching quality. There was some indication that i.t.a. is easier to read and spell than t.o. It is possible that the Hawthorne effect was much reduced since the i.t.a. group was accustomed to reading in i.t.a., and that this fact accounts for the closeness in performance of the two groups.

I. *Evaluation*

There are so many important influences in the classroom that were not taken in⁺o account in this small experiment that it cannot be said to contribute any definitive evidence on the problem.

16 TANYZER, H. J. and ALPERT, H. (1965)

Effectiveness of three different basal reading systems on first grade reading achievement. Hempstead, N.Y.: Hofstra University Office of Education Co-operative Research Project No. 2720

A. *Basic plan*

The media studied were i.t.a., the Lippincott phonic approach (t.o.) and the Scott, Foresman eclectic approach (t.o.). The investigation lasted 140 days. The criteria of success were the Stanford Achievement test, administered to the whole sample, and the Gilmore Oral Reading test, the Karlsen Phonemic Word test, the Gates Word Pronunciation test and the Phonetically Regular Word Oral Reading test, administered to a very small sub-sample. All these tests were given in t.o. after 140 days. The tests were administered by research staff, research supervisors, and members of the guidance and psychological departments of schools, and sub-sample tests by research staff, the teachers acting as proctors.

B. *Scope*

653 first grade, predominantly white, pupils constituting 36 first grade classes from 26 public schools in three school areas took part in the experiment. The school areas were 'unincorporated suburban' districts with populations of about 2,500, 20,000 and 50,000 respectively. The teachers differed in age and teaching experience, the i.t.a. group being considerably younger. The children were not all at the first stages of learning to read.

C. *Allocation of media*

Each of the three school districts used only one of the three media. The schools were volunteers, except in the case of the smallest district, where all the schools took part. Classes were randomly selected from the volunteers available (again with the exception of those in the smallest district, where every first-grade teacher took part). The children had attended kindergarten classes before entering first grade, but had received no formal reading instruction. The i.t.a. teachers were, in the course of the experiment, rated better for 'class structure' and 'class overall teaching competence'. They were also younger than the teachers in the other media. The pupils were matched according to the Murphy-Durrell Reading Readiness test, the Metropolitan Reading test, Thurstone's PMA (Identical Forms and Pattern Copying), the Pitner-Cunningham I.Q. test and the Detroit Word Recognition test. Some significant differences were found in I.Q. reading readiness and in Thurstone scores.

D. Classroom practice

The materials used were the *Early-to-Read* Readers (i.t.a.), the Lippincott Readers (t.o.) and the Scott, Foresman Readers (t.o.). Teaching methods varied. 2½ hours per day were allocated in each case to reading instruction and supportive activities, but some significant differences were found in the time actually given.

E. Supervision

Teachers in each medium attended three-day workshops and a research officer (the District Reading Supervisor) paid bi-weekly visits to each class. Teachers were asked to keep a log prepared for them. Time allocations were checked by the 't' test. No significant differences were found on the total time spent on reading, but adherence to the programme was rather more erratic in the autumn (1964) than in spring (1965).

F. Relations with public

Visitors were forbidden.

G. Statistical techniques

The statistical treatment of the data was very thorough including S.D.'s, 't' tests of significance and three-way analysis of variance, interaction diagrams being provided. Partial correlations (holding I.Q. constant) and canonical correlations (with and without I.Q. respectively) were also calculated.

H. Results

When tested in t.o. after 140 days, the i.t.a. group and the Lippincott (phonic) groups (about 70% of the children having wholly or partially made the transition to t.o.) scored significantly higher than the Scott, Foresman (eclectic) group on a composite score of the word reading, paragraph meaning, word study skills and spelling on the Stanford Achievement test. These two latter groups had both made a more analytic approach to reading instruction, with emphasis on word structure and phonetic characteristics. There was no interaction with intelligence, i.e. similar differences were found at all levels of intelligence. The Lippincott group were superior in vocabulary and spelling, and the i.t.a. group in accuracy on an oral test.

I. Evaluation

As a study of basal reading systems this large-scale research is extremely thorough and well designed. The statistical techniques are sound and thorough and the results are highly suggestive and give valuable information on general approaches to reading, but since the two media are invariably associated with different methods and materials, no answer can possibly be obtained regarding their relative efficiency considered *per se*, however many pupils are studied. The authors were, of course, concerned with the broader problem of basal reading systems.

17   TANYZER, H. J., ALPERT, H. and SANDEL, L. (1965)
Beginning reading: effectiveness of different media. Mineola, N.Y.: Nassau School Development Council.

A. Basic plan

The media used were i.t.a. and t.o. This is a two-year experiment reported on at the end of the first year. The criteria of success was a composite score obtained from the Stanford Achievement test, administered at the end of the first year of study in t.o., by which time only half of the i.t.a. children had transferred to t.o. The Detroit Word Recognition tests were also used (transliterated for the i.t.a. group) as an intermediate test administered after six months' instruction. Testing was carried out by research officers appointed in each school district, and given a special course of instruction. The teachers acted as supervisors.

B. *Scope*

1,946 children were used – 1,105 from the kindergarten and 841 from first grade classes. There were 78 classes (44 kindergarten and 34 first grade) and 78 teachers – 44 kindergarten teachers (23 teaching with t.o. and 21 with i.t.a.) and 34 first grade teachers (17 t.o. and 17 i.t.a.). These classes were drawn from 11 school areas where parents had rather more education and were rather more affluent than the average. The school areas were urban, suburban or incorporated villages on Long Island. The teachers, who were all volunteers, were divided into two groups matched (by principals) for teaching experience, level of training and competence. Some of the children had previous reading experience.

C. *Allocation of media*

The school areas were approached and agreed to co-operate. Media were allocated randomly to the schools. Teachers volunteered for the experiment but not for the medium; those who actually took part were selected from the volunteers on grounds of competence. The children were randomly assigned to classes, and since the sample was large, were assumed to be representative for the population of the areas. The children were matched according to socio-economic status, intelligence (Pitner-Cunningham) and reading (Metropolitan).

D. *Classroom practice*

The materials used were the *Early-to-Read* readers for the i.t.a. classes and various readers for the others. In each case 50 library books were provided. There were very large differences in the reading programme. For example, in the i.t.a. sample one class was taught as a single group, three had two groups, eight had three groups, and five had four or more. Furthermore, changes were made as the experiment progressed. The time spent on reading was recorded in minutes. Theoretically 60 minutes each day was devoted to reading instruction and 90 minutes to related activities. In practice there were considerable divergencies in the time-table.

E. *Supervision*

A three-day workshop was held for all teachers in both media. Bi-weekly visits were made to all classes by research officers and local administrators. Regular meetings for teachers were held and a questionnaire was issued to teachers. The teachers kept logs of activities, skills and materials used, from which the time spent in instruction and supportive work was calculated. Visits by the public were not permitted. Parents were asked to reply to a 12-item questionnaire.

F. *Relations with public*

Only research personnel and local school administrators were allowed to visit the classes. The 400 parents of the i.t.a. classes were sent a short questionnaire at the end of the experiment. Nearly all of them answered this (three parents had withdrawn their children at the beginning of the session).

225

G. Statistical techniques

The statistical treatment of the data was thorough, including means, S.D.'s, 't' tests and three-way analysis of variance, holding sex, I.Q. and treatment constant. The unit used is not the individual child; it is the mean of all pupils in each I.Q. group in each class.

H. Results

At the end of the first year of the experiment when about 70% of the children had made the transition to t.o. no significant differences were found between the achievement of the i.t.a. class and the t.o. class in the Stanford Achievement test (administered in t.o.). However, the i.t.a. group showed significant superiority in the Detroit Word Recognition test (60% of these children being placed above the t.o. median) which was administered in the medium of instruction. The t.o. group obtained significantly higher results for t.o. spelling as measured by the Stanford Primary Reading test. Considerable variation was found between classes. Parents reported general satisfaction with the progress made by their children using i.t.a., and the teachers expressed highly favourable views, although they made certain reservations.

I. Evaluation

This is a well-conducted large-scale research into general approaches to reading, but despite the value of the investigation in other respects differences between the materials and the classroom procedures used in the two groups necessarily make the results concerning the media themselves inconclusive, despite the huge sample.

CHAPTER 18

Summary of Research Results

The main task in summarising the researches is to determine whether they show i.t.a. or t.o. (or neither) to be more efficient as a means of teaching children to read. The results are summarised in Section II of the present chapter.

The second main task is to evaluate the results in order to determine whether the observed differences between the two media are likely to be due to factors other than the media themselves. This will be attempted in Chapter 19.

I Scope of researches

A. THE MAIN PREDICTORS—MEDIA USED

Question:

What media were investigated? (A1)*

This report is concerned only with the evaluation of i.t.a. in relation to traditional orthography, not with other forms of simplified spelling such as Wijk's Regularized Inglish, although the results of a few such studies have been included when they have formed part of an investigation into i.t.a. (in Chapter 20, however, on supplementary researches, it is suggested that several media should be investigated in order to separate out the specific effect of particular alphabets from the general influence of coded writing systems).

B. THE CRITERIA OF SUCCESS

Questions:

(*a*) What were the criteria of success? (A2)
(*b*) Who administered the tests? (C6)

(*a*) *What were the criteria of success?* (A2)

The criteria of success must be objectively defined in any crucial research, otherwise it is impossible to compare the results of different investigations adequately. For example, the criterion 'primer reached by the children' depends not only on the pupils' ability to read, but also on the individual judgement of the teacher as to whether they have reached a level of attainment at which it is advisable to proceed to another book. For a given child, on a given occasion, all teachers will not make the same judgement. The ability, personality and attitudes of the teacher as well as the child help to determine these subjective assessments, and introduce an additional disturbing element into the results. The fact that the child is judged fit to make the transition

* These refer to the questions used earlier in Chapter 17.

to traditional orthography has not usually been determined by entirely objective methods.

The criteria used in the literature on the subject can be classified as:

(i) tests of comprehension, which many writers regard as the most important criterion of a child's ability to read;

(ii) other direct criteria of reading, such as accuracy, speed and word-recognition;

(iii) accomplishments allied to reading, such as vocabulary, pronunciation, spelling, creative writing and fluent writing;

(iv) attitudes to reading, such as the range and amount of reading, the degree of enthusiasm displayed;

(v) wider 'whole man' characteristics, such as confidence, independence, maturity, steadfastness of application.

Adequate measures can be obtained of criteria in the first three categories, and the results can be expressed in terms that can be confirmed or rejected in later researches, but satisfactory attitude scales are more difficult to construct, particularly for young children; and the measurement of personal qualities is in its infancy and not understood in this country. The findings in the last two categories are best regarded as anecdotal; they are not necessarily true or false, and they may or may not tell us more about the teacher than the pupils.

In the United States, a very wide range of criterion tests (14 in the contributions under review) has been employed, chiefly the Stanford Achievement tests, followed in frequency by the Gilmore Reading tests and the Gates Word test. In Britain, the tests most commonly used have been the Schonell Graded Word Reading test, the Neale test of reading ability and the Standish N.S.45 test.

Several criticisms have been made of the criterion tests used. In Downing and Jones's (1966) research and Downing's previous research (1967), the tests proved too difficult for many of the children, with the result that the distributions were positively skewed and it was considered necessary to apply logarithmic transformations to the raw scores.

Many criticisms have been made of the use of the Schonell test in experiments into i.t.a. For example, Pitman (1967) has criticised the use of the Schonell test on the ground that no more than 17% of the words are regularly spelled. He has calculated that of the 1000 most frequently occurring words, some 26·5% of connected English may be expected to be regular 34·25% to be irregular, and 39·25% to be 'misleadingly' spelled. He says, 'It will be noted that the incidence of regularly spelled words in Schonell is high (50%) in the first ten words (Nos. 1–10) and that this would flatter the transition at that lowest level where success is least relevant. It will be noted that the incidence is low (4%) in the next fifty words (Nos. 11–60) and nil in the 30 words (Nos. 21–50) which is the most important section of the test because it covers just those standards most relevant to the comparison.' He points out that in the Neale accuracy test, a period of only four seconds is allowed for the solution of each word even though 'misleadingly' spelled and presented out of context. It might be added that accurate and consistent timing between one tester and another is difficult to ensure with so short a time interval. Consequently it is important that the tests should be administered only by trained teachers.

Williams (1965) has expressed some unease about the value of the Schonell test in this context, although he considers the Neale and Southgate tests appropriate. He points out that the Schonell test is based on a standardisation which is decades old, and British reading standards have risen considerably over the past twenty years. Nicholson (1965) also points out that the first three books of the *Janet and John* reading series used for Downing's (1967) experiment, contain only four of the first twenty words on the Schonell test, and the maximum reading age that the control group (who are probably taught by look-and-say) can achieve in these early stages is therefore limited. It should also be remembered that the Neale test does not give fully independent or objective scores. As Downing (1967) has pointed out,

> this is a comprehensive reading test consisting of six passages of English narrative prose. The test provides measures of accuracy, speed and comprehension. It should be noted, however, that these measures are not independent. For example, the accuracy level sets an upper limit to the comprehension score. It is also important to recognise the nature of the comprehension measure. The comprehension score is obtained by scoring children's answers to the passages they have read orally. It should be noted, too, that the administrator is permitted to supply words which the child has not been able to read for himself.

The last condition means that this test is not completely objective.

There is an urgent need for improved tests of reading for young children if this area of research is to be adequately explored. However, this does not mean that the tests in current use are seriously misleading, i.e. that their correlations would be low with tests constructed in the future. In fact, a new test would be validated in part according to the magnitude of its correlation with previously existing tests. It would be surprising if the general trends already found in investigation into i.t.a. were radically different with new criteria of reading attainment.

(b) *Who administered the tests?* (C6)

It is clear that in the interests of objectivity the tests should not be administered by the teachers participating in the experiment, particularly to children of their own classes. Ideally, psychologists specialising in mental testing should give the tests, although educational experts, including external teachers, could do so satisfactorily after following a course of training.

Much more attention appears to have been given to this requirement in the United States than in Britain. For example, in the U.S.A., Tanyzer and Alpert's (1965) tests were administered under strictly standardised conditions by the research staff, research supervisors, and members of the guidance and psychological departments of schools, and the sub-sample tests by the research staff, with the teachers acting as proctors. The scoring was carried out by trained people, supervised by the research co-ordinator.

Tanyzer, Alpert and Sandel (1965) used the teachers as proctors, but not as test administrators. Testing and scoring were carried out by research officers appointed in each school district and given a special course of instruction. Hahn's (1965) teachers carried out no testing, a course of training being provided for members of the project director's staff and a number of local school district supervisors.

McCracken (1966) employed 11 examiners, who were presumably not participating teachers.

In Hayes and Nemeth's (1965) research, the field director undertook the individual testing, but the group tests were carried out by teachers with neutral observers present. All the tests were scored by 'competent third parties'.

Fry (1966) gives no explicit information on this point, but as the 'results were communicated to the teachers', they presumably didn't administer the tests.

Stewart (1966) talks of 'both teachers and helpers in the standardised testing situation'.

In Mazurkiewicz's (1965) experiment all the group tests were administered by specially trained classroom teachers under the supervision of school district administrators and research personnel, but the sub-sample tests were given by research staff. The tests were also scored and re-checked by research staff, following an initial check by the teachers.

In Britain, Swales (1966) carried out his own testing. Harrison's (1964) tests were administered by an expert in the testing of reading.

Milne's (1966) tests were carried out by the local principal psychologist and trained teachers from Colleges of Education.

Downing (1967) used teachers, but not the children's own teachers.

C. LENGTH OF INVESTIGATION

Question:

How long did the investigation take? (A3)

The researches are mainly of either one, two or three years' duration. Ideally all children should be followed up until they make the transition to t.o. In fact, most of the current research reports should be regarded as interim accounts since few experimental groups completed the transition. On the whole, it would appear that at least three years should elapse before an investigation can be soundly based on the performance of the whole experimental system. There is a growing tendency to increase the length of time that children spend on i.t.a.

II The findings

A. READING IN THE MEDIUM OF INSTRUCTION

Question:

(*a*) What were the results of the investigations? (F5)

The investigations included in this report can be divided into two main categories in respect of the value of the information obtained about the relative effects of the two media. First there are those researches in which each medium is used with the same set of reading materials so that at least we know that the children in the two groups were provided with a similar sequence of experiences in learning to read (although as far as we know, other reading materials in the classrooms may have been different). These researches are those of Downing (1967), Downing and Jones (1966), Harrison (1964), Milne (1966) and Robinson (1966). Secondly, there are the remaining researches in which every child who uses i.t.a. is provided with one set of reading materials and every child who uses t.o. is provided with a different set. This does not mean, of course, that the trends evident in a large body of research can be regarded as meaningless because of this restriction but they can be no more than suggestive; they cannot carry full conviction.

The findings are reported briefly in the interests of clarity. It must be remembered, however, that they are based on a great deal of experimentation, involving several thousands of children.

In the most controlled research in the literature, Downing and Jones (1966) found that the i.t.a. group was superior in the Schonell and Neale tests for comprehension, speed and accuracy. Within individual schools 16 out of 17 significant differences were in favour of i.t.a.

In Downing's (1967) experiment (Table 18(a)) after $2\frac{1}{3}$ years' instruction twice as many i.t.a. children had completed the reading scheme as t.o. children and 83% of the i.t.a. group were placed above the t.o. median in respect of progress through the basic series, i.e. more than four-fifths of the 'superior' pupils were from i.t.a. groups.

TABLE 18(a)

Approximate percentage of i.t.a. children reaching t.o.
quartile groups in the basic reader series after $2\frac{1}{3}$ years
(derived from Table E1, Downing (1967))
(tested in the medium of instruction)

	top quarter	2nd quarter	3rd quarter	bottom quarter	top half	bottom half
t.o. pupils	25%	25%	25%	25%	50%	50%
i.t.a. pupils	52%	31%	7%	10%	83%	17%

At Oldham (Harrison (1964)) the corresponding percentage was 92% after six terms and after three years more than twice as many children taught by i.t.a. had completed the reading series (approximately 80% compared with 40%). In the researches in which the reading media had been confounded with the materials, and in which the indications are consequently less convincing, Mazurkiewicz (1965) found that 72·6% of the i.t.a. group had progressed above the t.o. median readers (according to the Botel Inventory) after five months. By this time 5·75% of the i.t.a. children and 2·9% of the t.o. group had completed the reading scheme.

In Tanyzer, Alpert and Sandel's research (1965), 68% of the sample were placed above the t.o. median according to the Detroit Word Recognition test, administered after six months' instruction.

Shapiro (1966) found his i.t.a. groups significantly superior in the ERC test. He points out that this test is in some ways particularly suitable to children instructed in the sound syllable system of i.t.a., as it uses words more difficult to spell and requires fine auditory and visual discrimination in both everyday words and nonsense syllables. The effect of adjusting the mean scores for differences in intelligence and reading readiness was to raise the differences between the groups very considerably.

In Dell's (1967) research the i.t.a. group was about eighteen months ahead of the t.o. group after four terms.

Standard deviations are so rarely quoted in the literature that it is difficult to guess at the extent of the difference in terms of S.D.'s. In Downing's (1967) research differences between the two groups in favour of i.t.a. when tested in the medium of instruction probably vary from about $\frac{1}{3}$ S.D. to 1 S.D., which is a considerable difference between mean scores. In Dell's (1967) investigation the difference is well over 1 S.D.

231

As Burt (1967) has pointed out, perhaps the best way to express these differences is in terms of mean reading book reached by the two groups.

In Downing's (1967) research the i.t.a. group was about two books ahead after $2\frac{1}{2}$ years; in Harrison's (1964) investigation four books ahead after 6 terms, and in Mazurkiewicz (1965) two books ahead after 5 months.

B. READING IN TRADITIONAL ORTHOGRAPHY

As noted in the previous section, in the most closely controlled investigation in the literature (Downing and Jones (1966)), the i.t.a. group was significantly superior in all the Neale tests when tested in the medium of instruction after 18 months. Within individual schools, 16 out of 17 significant differences were in favour of i.t.a. However, when all the tests were given in t.o. it was found that the t.o. group was slightly (but not significantly) superior and that three out of the four significant differences within schools were in favour of t.o., although it must be remembered that only 17% of the i.t.a. pupils had by this time made the transition to t.o. Later results, after 3 years' instruction (with a population a little over 400) when about three-quarters of the children had transferred, showed little change in this position. According to Cartwright and Jones (1967) only one of the five significant differences within schools obtained at this time was in favour of i.t.a., and the later results in Milne's (1966) research show that after 3 years there was no significant difference between t.o. and i.t.a. groups in respect of reading in t.o. (Burt-Vernon and Southgate Tests). By this time almost all of the children had made the transition, suggesting that the t.o. children eventually catch up.

In Downing's (1967) research the i.t.a. classes were significantly superior in word recognition, accuracy and speed of reading after three years' instruction when the medium of testing was t.o. In comprehension the i.t.a. group was significantly superior according to the Neale test, but not by the Standish N.S.45 test. An important finding in this research was that, except for speed, reading scores fell off immediately after the transition to t.o., by weeks according to the Neale test, and by months according to the Schonell test, but the i.t.a. group remained slightly and significantly ahead, according to the test used by Downing.

Swales (1966) found that after three years children taught by i.t.a. were neither superior nor inferior in reading standards to children taught by t.o. There was no clear cut superiority in overall achievement, although there were some significant differences. It is possible that the Hawthorne effect was much reduced in this experiment since the i.t.a. group was accustomed to reading in i.t.a. before the experiment began. This fact may account for the closeness in performance of the two groups.

In Milne's (1966) research the i.t.a. children are shown, after two years when only 60% of them had made the transition, to have done better than t.o. children by about $\frac{1}{4}$ S.D. in t.o. in the N.F. E.R. N.S.45 Group Reading test, and by about $\frac{1}{3}$ S.D. in Burt-Vernon Word Recognition test. (However, after three years when nearly all the children had made the transition there were no significant differences between the two groups, suggesting that the t.o. children catch up by this time.)

Harrison (1964) found that the i.t.a. classes were one year ahead of the t.o. classes in reading age after 18 months' teaching, although less than half of the children had made the transition to t.o. by this time. After three years, the results confirmed the strong superiority of i.t.a., when more than twice as many children (80% compared with 40%) had completed the reading scheme.

In the remaining researches (in which the evidence is less compelling as the reading materials were different in the two groups), Mazurkiewicz (1965) showed that the i.t.a. matched pairs sample was superior in word meaning (for those above average socio-economic level) and word study at the end of the first grade when about two-thirds of the children had made the transition to t.o. At the end of the second year, when nearly all the children (97%) had transferred, a matched sample of 68 pairs showed significant differences in favour of i.t.a. in language skills on the Stanford Achievement test, and random samples of 33 showed the i.t.a. children to be significantly superior in word recognition according to the Fry phonetically regular words test.

Fry (1966) found no difference in reading achievement as measured by the Stanford Achievement test, even after two years when the large majority of children had made the transition, but the i.t.a. children were significantly superior in the Fry phonetically regular words oral reading test.

Tanyzer and Alpert (1965) found that the i.t.a. group was superior in accuracy in oral tests after 140 days when about 70% of the children had either partly or wholly made the transition.

Hahn's (1965) t.o. group was superior in paragraph meaning taking differences in intelligence into account, the i.t.a. group scoring higher on word lists but not on contextual material after 140 days, when about 80% of the children had made the transition to t.o.

At the end of the first grade in the experiment conducted by Tanyzer, Alpert and Sandel (1965), when about half the children had made the transition, no significant differences were found between achievement of the i.t.a. class and the t.o. class in the Stanford Achievement test, but the i.t.a. group were significantly superior in an oral reading test.

Bosma (1965) found that after nine months her i.t.a. group was significantly superior to the t.o. group in reading skills even without the benefit of writing experience.

In Stewart's (1966) research, 5·6% of the i.t.a. population achieved a 3·5 grade or better after nine months, a standard reached by only 2·4% of the t.o. population. The corresponding figures after the summer holidays were 11·8 and 5·4%. 'Not all' the i.t.a. group had made the transition by this time.

Shapiro (1966) found that after eight months the i.t.a. classes were superior on all the sub-tests of the Stanford Achievement test, i.e. word reading, paragraph reading and word study, after adjustments had been made in regard to differences between groups in I.Q. and reading readiness.

In McCracken's (1966) research the i.t.a. class showed a clear-cut superiority in word recognition at the end of one year, but not in overall achievement.

The reluctance of investigators to report standard deviations makes it difficult to evaluate the magnitude of the observed differences. However, they appear after transition to t.o. to be roughly in the range $\frac{1}{4}$ to $\frac{1}{2}$ S.D. (Downing (1967), Milne (1966), Hahn (1965)), something like half the size of those found before transition. Over half of the differences reported in the literature have been non-significant, but it is noteworthy that in no investigation have *overall significant differences for complete samples* been found in favour of t.o. as a medium for learning to read in t.o., although Hahn (1965) found that the t.o. group was superior in paragraph meaning (when differences were adjusted for intelligence) and Mazurkiewicz (1967) found in his matched pairs the t.o. group significantly superior in word study skills, and t.o. is frequently found to be the superior medium in certain schools.

With regard to differences between the various aspects of reading, the general finding is that i.t.a. is relatively less effective in teaching children to read with comprehension, the most important of reading skills. In Downing's (1967) research differences in mean scores in the Schonell test, administered in the middle of the third year, are about 7 points in favour of i.t.a. for rate and accuracy, but only 2 points for comprehension.

Hahn (1965) found the i.t.a. group superior on word lists, but not on contextual material. The i.t.a. children had learned to sound through a word one element at a time and they employed a broader range of word attack skills.

Hayes and Nemeth's (1965) findings were of little value as regards the relative merits of i.t.a. and t.o., as the media were not balanced between the methods, materials and procedures. There was, however, some evidence that the more analytic approaches, viz. Lippincott (phonic) and i.t.a., were superior in word recognition.

Burt (1967b) points out that in Downing's tables:

'the largest of the differences in favour of pupils taught and tested in i.t.a. are to be seen in the marks for *accuracy*, particularly accuracy in pronouncing single words. In *comprehension*, as Dr Downing admits, "the result is less clear": here he is referring to the outcome of the first experiment; in the second experiment the control groups which used t.o. were actually better at comprehension than those taught by the i.t.a. in 8 schools out of 13. In *speed* the control groups in every school except two were faster; the analytical method, as might be expected, tends to slow down the child's rate of reading.'

In fact, according to Cartwright and Jones (1967) in the second experiment after three years the control groups which used t.o. were superior in 4 out of the 13 schools for rate, in 5 for comprehension, in 7 for accuracy and in 7 for word reading.

However, the only instances of significant differences in favour of t.o. in a full experimental sample were for 'paragraph meaning' (Hahn (1965) and 'word study' Mazurkiewicz (1965)), again emphasising that i.t.a. is relatively weak with meaningful material. It would also appear to tend to slow reading, possibly because i.t.a. emphasises structure, accuracy and caution.

In summarising the results, it is important to remember that in many cases the differences observed were in favour of neither i.t.a. nor t.o. Before the transition all the significant differences reported were in favour of i.t.a., but after the transition i.t.a. was the superior medium in about 50% of the cases, t.o. in 5% of cases, and in the remaining 45% no significant differences were found. Thus although the balance of evidence in the above researches is very markedly in favour of i.t.a., it must be remembered that nearly half of the cases show no significant differences after the transition.

Nevertheless, the magnitude of the differences found in favour of i.t.a. are often high, and although the results are not invariably in its favour, they are rarely in the opposite direction. As yet we lack conclusive evidence, but there is a strong presumption that even under rigorous control the results so far obtained for reading before the transition are unlikely to be reversed.

There is no evidence whatsoever for the belief that the best way to learn to read in traditional orthography is to learn to read in traditional orthography. It would appear rather that the best way to learn to read in traditional orthography is to learn to read in the initial teaching alphabet. On the other hand, the evidence is not convincing that i.t.a. is the superior medium *after the transition to t.o.* The results obtained when the children are pursued into the third year suggest that the t.o. groups catch up. We must await the findings of other researches, particularly Downing and Jones (1966), to obtain more conclusive evidence.

C. SPELLING IN TRADITIONAL ORTHOGRAPHY

Downing (1967) found that the i.t.a. groups were slightly superior in spelling, non-significantly in the mid-third year but significantly in the mid-fourth. Similarly in Mazurkiewicz's (1965) research, in both the full sample and in the matched pairs, the t.o. groups were significantly superior in spelling after one year, but the i.t.a. groups were superior after two and three years. Downing suggests that this is a generalised transfer effect of the i.t.a. pupils' early experience of regular grapheme-phoneme relations in i.t.a.

In Stewart's (1966) research the i.t.a. group scored significantly higher than the t.o. group after 21 months.

Shapiro (1966) found his i.t.a. group superior in spelling at the end of the first grade, according to the Stanford Achievement test, after adjustments had been made in regard to differences between groups in I.Q. and reading readiness.

In McCracken's (1966) experiment the spelling achievement of the i.t.a. group at the end of the first grade was equal to that of pupils taught by t.o.

On the other hand Swales (1966) found that after as long as three years, children taught by i.t.a. were neither superior nor inferior to children taught by t.o. Similarly, after three years, in the Downing and Jones (1966) research, the t.o. group remained superior in spelling, although 96% of the children had by this time made the transition.

Hahn (1965) found that after one year his t.o. group were better in spelling than the i.t.a. group, but only about 20% of the children had made the transition at this time.

Fry (1966) found after one year that in spelling the t.o. children were significantly superior, by which time a large proportion of the children had made the transition to t.o.

Tanyzer, Alpert and Sandel (1965) found a significant difference between their two experimental groups in spelling achievement after one year as measured by the Stanford Primary Reading test, with the t.o. group obtaining significantly higher scores (only half the children had made the transition).

Milne (1966) found no significant differences in spelling after three years. He considers that there was sufficient evidence to suggest that the i.t.a. script does cause some interference after the transfer stage to t.o., and that the transition to spelling is a considerably more difficult process than had been realised when i.t.a. was first introduced as an aid to reading in the early stages of primary school. The particular interference that seems to be caused is an over-adherence to phonic spelling influenced by the i.t.a. script. This is consistent with the general i.t.a. superiority in the area of the test which contains a very high proportion of phonic words, i.e. whereas a thorough grounding in a regularised spelling system is an advantage where words are phonic in nature, it would appear to be a disadvantage where words are non-phonic.

Thus the evidence in regard to spelling is completely mixed.

Downing (1967) found that his i.t.a. group had a larger and more extensive written vocabulary, although school differences were considerable.

Harrison (1964) claims that the i.t.a. group had the larger vocabulary.

Hahn (1965) states that the i.t.a. group had a 'more enriched and extensive vocabulary'.

Shapiro (1966) found his t.o. group had a superior vocabulary according to the Stanford Achievement test, after adjustments had been made in regard to differences in reading readiness and I.Q.

Mazurkiewicz (1965), using matched groups, found the i.t.a. children significantly superior in vocabulary at the end of the second grade.

Thus the superior facility in reading gained by the use of i.t.a. certainly does not detract from the volume or quality of children's vocabulary and would appear, on the whole, to lead to an improvement.

E. CREATIVE WRITING

Milne (1966) established by objective measures that after two years the i.t.a. group was very markedly more fluent in writing as regards both the number of words used and the number of different words used. However, the earlier superiority of the i.t.a. child in the first two years of the experiment was lost after three years. He considers that this was because in the first case few of the i.t.a. children had made the transition and therefore the majority were writing in a script which was more conducive to uninhibited output than the one in which the great majority were writing when the sample of composition was taken in their third school year.

In Downing's (1967) research the i.t.a. groups show somewhat superior results in written composition, but unfortunately the theme was not under full experimental control.

Harrison (1964) reported that in the view of their teachers the i.t.a. group showed very considerable superiority in creative writing.

In the researches in which different materials were used for the two media, Stewart (1966) claimed that the i.t.a. group showed a superior ability to write.

However, Dell's (1966) i.t.a. group did not show any marked superiority in written expression, possibly because the vocabulary level of the two groups was too low to allow fluency to manifest itself at that stage.

Fry (1966) found that i.t.a. children wrote longer stories, but with a greater percentage of errors. However, writing was not a carefully controlled factor in this study, and the i.t.a. children were encouraged not to worry about spelling.

Mazurkiewicz (1965) found the i.t.a. group superior in writing, in respect of the number of running words and polysyllabic words.

Thus the balance of this rather flimsy evidence is that i.t.a. classes learn to write more fluently and creatively than t.o. classes.

F. PERSONAL QUALITIES

Hahn (1965), using an objective measure, the San Diego Reading Inventory, found no significant differences between i.t.a. and t.o. groups in attitudes to reading.

Harrison's (1964) sample of teachers claimed that the i.t.a. group were superior in confidence, enthusiasm, independence, steadfastness of application and maturity.

Dell (1966) states that i.t.a. has a good effect on morale, particularly with the slower children.

Stewart (1966) claimed that the i.t.a. group are superior in independent learning, motivation, perseverance and ability to observe.

Thus the only objective test used shows no difference between the children's attitude to reading. The remaining evidence is impressionistic and should be disregarded until objective measures can be devised of these highly important changes in children's behaviour.

CHAPTER 19

Evaluation of Researches

I Experimental balance in respect of various factors

THE evidence presented in Part Three of this report suggests that i.t.a. is a more efficient medium in teaching children to read English *when the reading books are in i.t.a.* On the other hand, the evidence that i.t.a. leads to superior reading *after the transition to t.o.* is indefinite, and the balance of evidence in those researches in which the reading materials were the same in both experimental groups appears to be that i.t.a. loses its superiority after the transition. The next problem that arises is whether these results are due to the reading medium itself, or to extraneous factors. For example, if i.t.a. teachers devote more time to reading activities than t.o. teachers do, then this fact alone might account for the superiority of i.t.a.

Table 16(b) in Chapter 16 gives a list of such extraneous factors. These form the basis of the eight questions below. Answers to these questions should indicate whether the superiority of i.t.a. can reasonably be accepted at its face value or should be attributed to other factors, although no scientific evidence can be obtained about this unless analyses of variance are carried out.

(Answers to the thirty-nine more general questions about individual researches asked in Chapter 17 have also been reclassified in the present chapter.)

The eight questions are as follows:

Do the i.t.a. groups tend to gain significantly higher mean scores in reading because:

1 i.t.a. groups are superior to t.o. groups in relevant personal characteristics such as intelligence and attainment, or in socio-economic background?

2 i.t.a. groups are taught by more efficient teachers?

3 i.t.a. classes are taught in better equipped and more efficient schools?

4 the Hawthorne effect, i.e. the novelty of the medium, makes i.t.a. teachers and children more 'experiment conscious' than t.o. teachers and children?

5 i.t.a. leads teachers to adopt more efficient teaching procedures?

6 i.t.a. teachers give more time to reading activities?

7 the reading materials used in teaching i.t.a. are more appropriate?

8 i.t.a. facilitates phonic methods more readily than t.o. does?

A. PUPILS' ATTRIBUTES

Do the i.t.a. groups tend to gain significantly higher mean scores in reading because they are superior to t.o. groups in relevant personal characteristics such as intelligence and attainment, or in socio-economic background?

238

Questions:

(*a*) Were the pupils matched? (B5c)

(*b*) What contacts were made with the parents of the children taking part in the experiment? (E2)

(*a*) *Were the pupils matched?* (B5c)

On the whole, pupils were very adequately matched, i.e.

(i) for I.Q.

by Bosma (1965), Downing (1967), Downing and Jones (1966), Hahn (1965), Mazurkiewicz (1965), Fry (1966), Robinson (1966), Shapiro (1966), Stewart (1966), Swales (1966), Tanyzer and Alpert (1965) and Tanyzer, Alpert and Sandel (1965). (Robinson (1966) also matched for mental maturity)

(ii) for reading achievement

by Hayes and Nemeth (1965), Tanyzer and Alpert (1965) and Tanyzer, Alpert and Sandel (1965)

(iii) for reading readiness

by Bosma (1965), Hahn (1965), Hayes and Nemeth (1965), Robinson (1966), Shapiro (1966), and Tanyzer and Alpert (1965)

(iv) for vocabulary scores

by Downing (1966) and Milne (1966)

(v) for age

by Bosma (1965), Downing (1967), Stewart (1966) and Swales (1966)

(vi) for sex

by Bosma (1965), Downing (1967), Mazurkiewicz (1965), Shapiro (1966), Stewart (1966), and Swales (1966)

(vii) for socio-economic status

by Bosma (1965), Downing (1967), Hayes and Nemeth (1965), Mazurkiewicz (1965), Milne (1966), Stewart (1966), Swales (1966), and Tanyzer, Alpert and Sandel (1965).

Many investigators match classes rather than individual pupils, i.e. they require that the experimental groups shall not differ significantly from one another in respect of the matched variables, although some investigators such as Mazurkiewicz (1965) have used the technique of matched pairs in which each child in the i.t.a. group has a corresponding 'twin' in the t.o. group. Another important variable that enters the results is, of course, personality, but the assessment of such qualities is difficult to make at as early an age as five. Nevertheless, Mazurkiewicz (1965) has used the California Test of Personality for this purpose. Hayes and Nemeth (1965) equated children for attitude to reading. The intelligence tests which are most frequently used for purposes of matching in Britain include Raven's Matrices and the Moray House Pictorial test, together with the Crichton Vocabulary test. In the U.S.A. there is a wider variety, but there is some stress on the Kuhlman-Anderson and the Lorge-Thorndike I.Q. tests, together with Thurstone's Identical Forms and Pattern Copying. The most commonly used reading readiness tests are the Durrell-Murphy and the Metropolitan tests.

In the U.S.A. children are also frequently matched for reading readiness, and some investigators have, rather importantly, given tests of initial knowledge of the alphabet.

However, these tests are not used in Britain. The usual practice is for the teacher of the reception class to judge on an intuitive basis when the children are ready to begin formal reading, which may include paying regard to such factors as speed, fluency, interest in books and the ability to recognise some of the words displayed around the classroom. In any case, ability in tests of reading readiness is probably highly correlated with intelligence.

Fry (1966) found, in fact, that reading readiness has much lower correlations than I.Q. has with reading achievement.

Mazurkiewicz's (1965) sample appears to be rather extraordinary in so far as the mean I.Q. of the groups of pupils studied is 110, a population which would be regarded in Britain as borderline grammar-school level.

Attempts to match are nearly always claimed to be successful, as the null hypothesis is used the wrong way round. Thus the means for two matched groups are said to be the same unless the odds against this hypothesis reach 19 to 1. Odds of 18 to 1 that they are not the same are taken to prove that they are the same.

On the whole pupils have been very adequately matched for personal characteristics. The superiority of i.t.a. does not appear to be due to any imbalance between the two groups in this respect.

(b) *What contacts were made with the parents of the children taking part in the experiment?* (E2)

Only a few researches overcame the practical difficulties of establishing contacts with parents, despite the importance of the home in providing opportunities for reading. Downing (1967) issued a pamphlet entitled *How your children are being taught to read with i.t.a.* which described the purpose of the experiment and encouraged parents to accept the new writing system as part of the normal educational scene.

It contained a description of the alphabet so that the parents could use it if they wished to write for their children. This pamphlet was distributed to parents with a covering letter from the l.e.a. Some headteachers held parents' meetings at which the Head of the Reading Research Unit gave a talk to explain the experiment. The large majority of parents accepted the experiment although many showed signs of misgiving. Only two or three cases are known of parents withdrawing their children from the experimental school.

Robinson (1966) reports that:

'concurrent with the pre-school workshop, an evening meeting is planned with parents of children who will be in the i.t.a. and control classrooms. The film will be shown and i.t.a. explained. At this meeting, parents will be informed that their children will be enrolled in an i.t.a. class. If any parents raise strong objections, their child will be withdrawn from the experimental group and replaced by another selected at random from children not presently involved in the study. Previous experience with the i.t.a. classroom in the suburban school systems suggests strongly that no objections will be forthcoming. Throughout the year, records will be collected on the titles and number of books read at home and at school by pupils in each group. This information, analysed for quantity and possibly quality of reading, will be reported as part of the study.'

In Hayes' (1965) research:

'the first grade teacher visited each pupil's home during the afternoons. During these visits, the teacher gathered data concerning the educational level of the father, kindergarten experience, the number of books and magazines in the home.

'At the conclusion of the 140 days of instruction, each pupil was asked by the teacher how many times per week an adult read to him at home. Data was collected concerning the total number of independently read books by the pupils. The pupil was encouraged to fill out a record.'

Parental encouragement is clearly an important factor in learning to read, but for practical reasons it has not been possible to match children in this variable. However, matching for socio-economic status has frequently been adopted, i.e. Bosma (1965), Downing (1967), Hayes and Nemeth (1965), Mazurkiewicz (1965), Milne (1966), Stewart (1966), Swales (1966), and Tanyzer, Alpert and Sandel (1965). This must have exerted some incidental control over the influence of the parents' attitude to reading, so that it would not appear that the superiority of i.t.a. can be attributed to the influence of the home.

B. EFFICIENCY OF TEACHERS

Do the i.t.a. groups tend to gain significantly higher mean scores in reading because they are taught by a more efficient teacher?

Questions:

(*a*) Were the teachers matched? (B3d)
(*b*) What types of teacher took part in the investigation? (B3b)
(*c*) How were the media allocated to the teachers? (B3e)
(*d*) How were the media allocated to the classes? (B4c)

(*a*) *Were the teachers matched?* (B3d)

In the Downing and Jones (1966) experiment the same teacher taught both i.t.a. and t.o. classes. In the Robinson (1966) experiment teachers were switched from the i.t.a. class in the first year to the t.o. class in the second year or vice-versa. Teachers were matched for:

(i) age
by Mazurkiewicz (1965) (i.e. they were 'all about 40') and 'considered comparable' by Stewart (1966)

(ii) for experience
by Mazurkiewicz (1965), Tanyzer, Alpert and Sandel (1965), and here again 'considered comparable' by Stewart (1966)

(iii) for level of training
by Tanyzer, Alpert and Sandel (1965), and 'considered comparable' by Stewart (1966) and

(iv) for competence
by Tanyzer, Alpert and Sandel (1965). All Hahn's teachers were 'judged competent'.

It is evident that the number of teachers included in an experiment will be very much less than the number of children (say 3%) with the result that an investigation involving 600 children may require only 20 teachers. The largest number of teachers to take part in any experiment is 80, in Downing's (1967) investigation. If the same teacher takes classes in both media, the number might be as low as eight, even in a fairly large experiment. Thus, although matching is perfect in this design, care should be taken to include teachers with different types of background. The matching of teachers is essential, as randomisation is almost certain to be inefficient with such small numbers.

(b) What types of teacher took part in the investigation? (B3b)

The teachers have been mostly those with satisfactory records in respect of (i) teaching experience, (ii) academic qualifications, (iii) length of training and (iv) competence as judged by the principal or administrator.

Fry (1966) found low positive correlations between reading achievement, age of teacher and length of teaching experience.

In some investigations, such as Dell (1967), differences between teachers are admitted to be present, and in others teachers are 'judged', e.g. Bosma (1965), to be comparable in training and experience. Thus, Hahn (1965) says that:

> 'among the teachers who expressed an interest in this study, local school administrators were asked to select those who had done superior work in teaching the previous group of children during the previous year. This was necessarily a subjective appraisal. However, it was anticipated that many highly competent and interested teachers would be among those chosen. There was no reason to be disappointed with this procedure.'

No doubt considerable differences between teachers sometimes exist. On investigation Tanyzer and Alpert (1965) found differences in age, experience and marital status, but not qualifications. The i.t.a. teachers were rated better for class structure, class participation and attention to individual needs, i.e. overall individual competence. However, Tanyzer, Alpert and Sandel (1965) found only slight differences in age, experience and qualifications.

(c) How were the media allocated to the teachers? (B3e)

The best method of control used so far would appear to be that adopted in the Downing and Jones (1966) and Robinson (1966) experiments, in which the same teacher takes both groups. This is the most stringent form of control possible, since each teacher is matched with herself rather than with another teacher. The matched groups technique in which the two 'twins' in each pair are presumed to resemble each other is very unsatisfactory when used for matching teachers, since they are taken, rather absurdly, to be closely similar in a number of highly important complex characteristics such as professional and academic attitudes, temperament and ability. It must be remembered that two people differ much more between themselves than the same person does in two different settings, i.e. we resemble ourselves more closely than we resemble others, however closely we are matched. The use of the same teacher to teach both alphabets has the advantage of equating a very wide variety of professional and personal characteristics. Another advantage of the same teacher taking both groups is that he is able to equate his teaching techniques and schedules and may therefore be allowed to use his preferred approach. But perhaps the most power-ful argument in favour of this procedure is that it avoids the difficulty of allocating the media to schools and teachers at random, which would otherwise be necessary if the findings are to be generalised to a wider population. Nevertheless, it must be admitted that this one-teacher two-media design has a Jekyll and Hyde quality; it is not ideal that they should both know where the other is up to. The same person might perform differently according to whether she is using i.t.a., which she considers progressive (or cranky), or t.o., which she regards as unimaginative (or sensible).

As Downing and Jones (1966) say:

> 'In an effort to counteract such expected preferences, teachers were reminded often of the need to give the two classes equal treatment, and they may have succeeded in keeping their preferences covert. In considering this problem one should also take into account the possibility that any increase in motivation en-gendered by the i.t.a. teaching situation might spill over to the other in t.o. This seems to be true also of any improvement in teaching due, for example, to improved knowledge of the structure of English through experience with i.t.a.'

They also point out that when the same teacher takes both the experimental i.t.a. classes and the control classes, she is able to make immediate comparisons of the progress of the two classes she is teaching. If i.t.a. does permit an easier beginning, a 'spiral' motivational effect may occur. Quicker progress in the i.t.a. class may produce positive attitudes in the teacher which enhance her work with i.t.a. Furthermore, she may become pessimistic about t.o. with a possible negative influence on her work in the control class.

On the whole Downing and Jones's (1966) prescription of 'one teacher, two media' appears to be the best overall method for purposes of research. In the investigations reported in the present research, the two media are nearly always taught by different teachers. An interesting variation has been proposed by Robinson (1966) i.e. that each teacher swops after one year, thus acting as her own control. The difficulty here would seem to be that cyclic effects may be introduced, due to changes of personnel at yearly intervals. In ordinary school life such changes are very common, but for research purposes it would be preferable for the same teacher to take the same children along for several years.

Usually, the allocation of media appears to have been random, e.g. Hayes and Nemeth (1965), McCracken (1966), Milne (1966), Fry (1966), Robinson (1966) and Tanyzer, Alpert and Sandel (1965), but sometimes it is done by personal preference, e.g. Downing (1967), Hahn (1965) and Tanyzer and Alpert (1965). A method by which classes are taught solely by teachers who are in favour of the medium used is appealing, but it would almost certainly introduce an element of competition which would detract from the objectivity of research.

(d) How were the media allocated to the classes? (B4c)

The media should clearly be allocated to classes at random. This is not necessarily the same thing as allocating the media to teachers, but these two separate steps seem to be confused in the literature, as they are rarely mentioned separately. In practice there is, no doubt, a tendency for teachers to stick to their own classes for the experiment.

The matching of teachers appears to have been carried out much less satisfactorily than the matching of pupils, despite its importance in view of the relatively small number of teachers taking part in an experiment. However, in the most thoroughly designed and hence most convincing experiments, matching has been perfect as each teacher has taught in each medium.

The teachers participating in the experiment have been mostly those with satisfactory records for teaching experience, academic qualifications and length of training. This appears to be a wise precaution in the early stages of research into new methods of classroom teaching. On the other hand, it is important to remember that any future expansion in the use of i.t.a. will probably lead to its use by a wider and more representative sample of teachers, and possibly to somewhat different results concerning the efficiency of i.t.a. in contemporary schools.

(This does not mean that i.t.a. would necessarily be less efficient than t.o. when used by less efficient teachers; it might be less efficient, more efficient, or no different in such circumstances. But now that the initial researches have been completed it would perhaps be advisable to include teachers with widely different qualifications in future investigations.)

C. EFFICIENCY OF SCHOOLS

Do the i.t.a. groups tend to gain significantly higher mean scores in reading because they are taught in better equipped and more efficient schools?

Questions:

(*a*) Were the school areas matched? (B1d)
(*b*) How were the media allocated to the school areas? (B1e)
(*c*) Were the schools matched? (B2d)
(*d*) How were the media allocated to the schools? (B2e)

(*a*) *Were the school areas matched?* (B1d)

The most throughgoing attempts to match schools appear to have been carried out by Downing (1967) and Downing and Jones (1966), who took into account size of school, pupil-teacher ratio, urban-rural location, minimum age of entry, socio-economic level of area and school building amenities (Morris Scale) despite the large size of their sample; Mazurkiewicz (1966) matched schools for urban-rural location and socio-economic status and Swales (1966) for size and type of organisation. Some of the American researches, e.g. Hahn (1965), Tanyzer and Alpert (1965), have apparently relied solely upon weight of numbers and the randomisation process to provide adequate sampling. In other researches no attempt has been made to match schools even when the sample is tiny, e.g. in Bosma's (1965) investigation i.t.a. was taught in a University campus school constituted partly to assist in education research, but t.o. was taught in an ordinary school (though they drew on similar socio-economic strata in the. community). If the experiment is confined to one school district, however, all-schools can sometimes be included (Stewart (1966)), and some researches, such as Dell's (1967) have been conducted in a single school, a design which draws attention to the fact that in a definitive research a broad representation of schools is an essential requirement.

(*b*) *How were the media allocated to the school areas?* (B1e)

There is little information about the allocation of media to school areas, as it is usually assumed that each district will investigate teaching in both media. In Tanyzer and

Alpert's (1965) research the media appear to be confounded with the area, different districts working different media, although this was not the case in Tanyzer, Alpert and Sandel's (1965) experiment, in which the media were allocated at random. In Downing's (1967) first experiment schools chose their own media. The most effective method of controlling school differences is undoubtedly for all schools to teach in both media (Downing and Jones (1966), Robinson (1966)).

(c) Were the schools matched? (B2d)

Apart from the researches of Downing (1967) and Downing and Jones (1966), schools do not appear to have been very adequately matched, and there have been difficulties with matching in Downing's research. In some investigations there may well have been a tendency for the more enterprising and efficient schools to opt for i.t.a. rather than t.o. If all the teachers in the experiment take both i.t.a. and t.o. groups, however, we have perfect matching of schools as well as teachers (although it must be remembered that the sample of schools might not be representative of the full range of schools).

(d) How were the media allocated to the schools? (B2e)

Research reports are not always explicit on this point, but as Hahn (1967) points out personal factors have to be considered, including the interests of principals and class teachers. The allocation of media to schools usually has to be a 'hedged expedient' (Holmes (1967)). There certainly seems to be a wide diversity of practice, e.g. in Bosma's (1965) investigation, i.t.a. was taught in a University experimental school and t.o. in a public school. In Tanyzer, Alpert and Sandel's (1965) experiment media were allocated at random, and in Downing's (1967) first experiment schools chose their own media. The most effective method of controlling school differences is undoubtedly for all schools to teach in both media (Downing and Jones (1966), Robinson (1966)).

On the whole schools do not appear to have been very satisfactorily matched except in those investigations in which the same teacher taught both classes. There is no evidence, however, that the i.t.a. classes were taught in more efficient schools than the t.o. classes.

D. THE HAWTHORNE EFFECT

Do the i.t.a. groups tend to gain significantly higher mean scores in reading because the Hawthorne effect, i.e. the novelty of the medium, makes the teachers and children more 'experiment-conscious' than t.o. teachers and children?

Questions:

(a) What courses of pre-experimental training for teachers were held? (D1)
(b) To what extent was the experiment supervised by research staff? (D2)
(c) Were the public allowed to visit the experimental classes? (E1)

(a) What courses of pre-experimental training for teachers were held? (D1)

Cook (1962), summarising publication of the Hawthorne effect, defines it as follows:

'The Hawthorne effect is a phenomenon characterised by an awareness on the part of the subjects of special treatment created by artificial experimental conditions. This awareness becomes confounded with the independent variable under study, with a subsequent facilitating effect on the dependent variable, thus leading to ambiguous results.'

Thus the Hawthorne effect is most commonly regarded as *awareness that an experiment is being carried out*. Cook (1962) illustrates this by the following story:

'Herzog tells of the little old lady who did her courting in the 'nineties and who liked to tell about her grandmother's efficient chaperoning. Grandmother would just move into the living room where the two young people were sitting on the sofa. She would say, "Now, you two young people go right ahead and visit and don't pay any attention to me. Just act as if I weren't here". As Herzog points out, there was some difference of opinion in the family about whether Grandmother thought they were acting as if she weren't there, but there was no doubt in anyone's mind about whether they were really acting that way. It takes a wary eye to be sure the research project is not playing a role like Grandmother's.'

The Hawthorne effect springs partly from the fact that workshops have to be set up in i.t.a. before the investigation begins, in order to train teachers in the use of the new characters in i.t.a., the spelling system, reading materials, methods of approach and teaching schedules. Similar workshops are usually held for teachers working in other media, but this does not resolve the difficulty that an i.t.a. programme necessarily means greater novelty.

As Downing (1967) has pointed out, the novelty of i.t.a. and the publicity it attracts are not necessarily an advantage, since both the teacher and the pupils are likely to be put off by being a continual centre of attention. In fact, Mazurkiewicz (1965) encouraged special instruction and supervision for the i.t.a. group alone, taking the view that the effect on this group would be deleterious and that any superiority shown in reading by these children would be achieved despite, rather than because of, this factor. Harrison (1964) says that the i.t.a. group 'were facing possibly more than the usual vicissitudes that can affect school work. They were certainly not in any way privileged or cosseted, rather is the reverse true.'

Swales (1966) who worked with classes *in being* hoped to avoid the Hawthorne effect altogether. He held no classes for teachers.

It is common practice to attempt to control the Hawthorne effect by running workshop courses before the experiment begins, varying from about $1\frac{1}{2}$ to 5 days in length, e.g. Downing (1967), Downing and Jones (1966), Hahn (1965), Hayes (1966), Milne (1966), Robinson (1966), Tanyzer and Alpert (1965), and Tanyzer, Alpert and Sandel (1965). Downing and Jones (1966) say:

'In the design of this initial experiment it was recognised that while these meetings would be essential for the teachers using i.t.a., at the same time they might increase the Hawthorne effect in this group although, of course, the importance of the Hawthorne effect has yet to be demonstrated in educational research. Therefore it was proposed that meetings of the control school teachers should also be held in an attempt to induce a similar increase in Hawthorne effect (if any) in this group. It seems probable that these meetings of control group teachers have not been wholly matched in quality with those of the teachers using i.t.a. The purpose was obviously different. We tried, however, to show our concern for the teaching of reading in the control schools where t.o. was being used as usual. Each year a training college lecturer seconded to the Unit was given responsibility to meet this need to show special interest in the teachers in the control schools. Sometimes an outside speaker well-known as an expert in infants' school teaching method was engaged to give an address followed by discussion. Sometimes the secondary training college lecturer conducted the meeting alone. For example, one series of control group meetings included an exhibition of the latest t.o. books and apparatus for reading at the infants' school level, a lecture from the seconded training college lecturer and a discussion of children's books with the control group teachers.

'These control group meetings were sometimes held in the afternoon and in some cases lasted longer than the experimental group meeting. It seems inappropriate to attempt to compare these meetings of the two groups in terms of hours and minutes, but for the record we note that control meetings were held by the seconded training college lecturer on average twice each year, although these arrangements have not been uniformly successful. It seems fair, however, to suggest that although the experimental group leaders met rather more frequently, a reasonable demonstration of our interest in the work of the teachers in the control group was in fact provided.'

'In the case of the second experimental unit (Downing and Jones (1966)) a Hawthorne effect was encouraged by emphasising the experimental nature of the new procedures, by suggesting competition, though not openly inviting competition, and by scheduling visitors to examine the new procedure. The Hawthorne effect was found to be operating in that teachers reported, "I am in competition", "I am not competing but having seen the achievement of the i.t.a. classes I am trying to help my children do as well", etc.

'The children at the same time were aware of the experiment in that t.o. children teased i.t.a.-taught children about their funny writing. They also seemed aware of their status as judged by their positive reaction to visitors.'

Robinson (1966) says:

'A pre-school workshop has been scheduled for all participating teachers. Common sessions will be held for all teachers to develop an understanding of i.t.a. The British i.t.a. film will be shown at this time. Separate sessions will then be held for both experimental and control teachers. For experimental teachers, the sessions will consist of instruction in writing i.t.a. and in the use of the transliterated books. The sessions will be under the direction of a skilled i.t.a. consultant. A consultant with the Scott, Foresman Company will conduct sessions for the control group teachers on the use of the basal reader programme. Services of the consultants, as well as services of a research team from the University, will be available as the need arises. At all times equivalent amounts of time will be spent in giving aid to both groups.'

Burt (1967) has suggested that:

'the control group should itself be converted into an alternative experimental group: e.g. while the material used should still be printed in the traditional style, there should be some novel change in the teaching methods; the teachers in charge should be enthusiastic for some special teaching technique—phonic, look-and-say, or an ingenious mixture; or the reading material, though preserving the usual spelling, might embody some of the supplementary devices which many teachers would favour–e.g. the use of differently coloured letters or of diacritical signs.'

(b) *To what extent was the experiment supervised by research staff?* (D2)

Most researches in the U.S.A. appear to have been supervised. Tanyzer and Alpert (1965) and Tanyzer, Alpert and Sandel (1965) arranged for bi-weekly visits by research officers and local administrators and regular meetings were held for participating teachers. In Hayes' (1966) research one visit per month was paid for seven months by a consultant. There were also 11 visits by the research director and one by the project director, making 19 in the year. McCracken (1966) carried out 30 time studies in each group by observers who arrived about every two weeks 'without warning'. In Mazurkiewicz's (1965) research, visits were made by instructional supervisors at least once a week, and monthly group meetings were held.

In Downing's (1967) research:

'The policy of the experimenter was to equalise the number of visits to experimental and control schools, but it seems likely that this policy has not been effective in several of the control schools in this initial experiment. In the early part of the experiment crisis over materials especially often led to additional visits to experimental schools in order to help teachers to improvise materials or even to deliver books urgently needed for children who were making more rapid progress. Without these visits it seems certain that some experimental schools would have withdrawn from the research project because of these early problems.'

Milne (1966) arranged for one meeting per term for discussion.

(c) *Were the public allowed to visit the experimental classes?* (E1)

The influence of visits by the public had not been foreseen in the early days of experimentation. In Downing's (1967) initial experiment:

'the public interest in the i.t.a. research which began to be aroused mainly after the second year had not been foreseen. It had not been agreed to exclude visitors because the demand had not been anticipated, and as a result some of the experimental schools had considerably more visitors. This does not apply to all the schools using i.t.a., for some schools had relatively few outside visitors, but one may generalise with some certainty that some of the experimental schools had considerably more visitors than any of the control schools. Again, this probably was to be expected because visiting educators are interested in seeing the new experimental approach rather than the traditional approach, but it is a factor which must be borne in mind in weighing the evidence in this first i.t.a. experiment. It will be difficult to assess the influence of these additional outside visitors to the experimental schools because there are likely to be *both negative and positive* effects arising from such visits.'

This factor was controlled rigorously in the second experiment by Downing and Jones (1966):

'Steps were taken to reduce the differential operation of possible sources of motivation. When it was necessary to hold meetings for parents of experimental pupils to explain i.t.a. to them, parallel meetings were held for parents of control pupils. Head teachers were requested to close the doors to visitors as far as

248

possible and to make sure that those who could not be avoided were made to visit control as well as experimental classes. It is recognised that this does not guarantee that equal interest, approval, etc. was shown by visitors in both cases, any more than our meetings for parents ensure comparable attitudes on their part.'

Harrison (1964) reports that:

'during the two years more than 4,000 visitors have gone there and the dislocation of normal working can be imagined. The headmistress and class teachers bore this very cheerfully and accepted the role of "exhibition centre". The children became so accustomed to visitors in their classroom that they took intrusion as a normal part of the school day. Nevertheless, because of this impact their normal routine was affected and their school life was anything but peaceful and orderly.'

Harrison clearly looks upon visits as detrimental to learning.

Stewart (1966) talks of 'floods of visitors', and Mazurkiewicz (1965) claims that the questioning of teachers by authorities on reading had a dampening effect.

There is no doubt that from the point of view of experimental design, the public should not be allowed to intrude into the experimental classes. In fact, in the researches by Tanyzer and Alpert (1965) and Tanyzer, Alpert and Sandel (1965) visitors were forbidden, and Milne (1966) managed to shunt them into other i.t.a. schools.

Statistical estimates of the Hawthorne effect

Various methods of studying the Hawthorne effect have been put forward as follows:

(i) the comparison of the t.o. groups with sub-control groups in which the medium of instruction is t.o. but neither the teachers nor the pupils are aware that an experiment is taking place. The sub-control group pursues a similar course, however, and unexpectedly takes the same criterion tests on its completion.

(ii) the comparison of performance in the experimental t.o. group with t.o. performance in the same school before the experiment was contemplated.

(iii) the comparison of successive i.t.a. intakes in the same school, e.g. successive groups of school entrants in the years 1965, 1966 and 1967, in order to see whether reading performance falls off in successive calendar groups, as the effects of novelty begin to wear off.

The use of a sub-control group is illustrated in the work of:

(i) McCracken (1966) who says:

'Three first-grade classes were chosen randomly from the remaining ten first grades in the Mukilteo School District 6 to serve as a second control group. This group is referred to in this report as the sub-control group. These classes received only initial readiness testing and final reading achievement testing. It was felt that a Hawthorne effect might be present in both the i.t.a. and control groups in the Rose Hill school since the children would be tested individually, and classes observed regularly, throughout the year.'

He found that both the experimental groups (i.t.a. and t.o.) were significantly superior to the sub-control group on all six tests of the Stanford Achievement test. It

249

is difficult to estimate the extent of the Hawthorne effect from the results presented, but the magnitude of the differences between the three groups suggests that they account for some two-thirds of the superiority in mean scores shown by the i.t.a. group over the sub-control group.

(ii) Downing (1967) checked the effectiveness of his attempt to stimulate the Hawthorne effect in his t.o. groups by assessing the reading standards in these schools before and after the commencement of the experiment.

'The Standish N.S. 45 test of silent reading comprehension was administered at the end of the final year of the infants school. Two groups of children were compared, (a) those pupils who had been in the school before the research project began and whose teachers had not participated in the procedures designed to enhance Hawthorne effect, (b) the pupils of the control groups proper in the research project whose teachers had participated in special procedures designed to enhance Hawthorne effect. All entrants were included in this test. In the large majority of cases, there was no significant difference between the results for the pre-research pupils and the results for the pupils whose teachers participated in the research project with the special attempts to enhance the factors believed to cause the Hawthorne effect. In four schools the results deteriorated after the period when Hawthorne effects should have been operating, and in only three schools did standards improve. These results indicated that in most of the schools standards did not change significantly and therefore there is no evidence of Hawthorne effect in the control group. It should be recognised, however, that the measures used may have been inadequate to detect any such effect.'

(iii) The best indication of the extent of the Hawthorne effect is perhaps given by longitudinal studies comparing groups of children setting out on i.t.a. courses in successive school years, i.e. in successive intakes, the assumption being that the effect of novelty will be greatest in the first intake and gradually diminish, e.g. the 1961–2, 1963–4 and 1964–5 intakes will show increasingly poorer performance in i.t.a. Eventually it will be possible to see whether i.t.a. pupils remain more efficient when the Hawthorne effect has vanished, i.e. when reading performance is no longer in decline.

The only detailed evidence is provided by a follow-up of Harrison's (1964) groups beginning i.t.a. at successive dates, as follows:

The argument put forward in the present report is that the Hawthorne effect will become less in each successive intake into a school as the effects of novelty begin to wear off, i.e. it is expected that the excitement that met children when the experiment began in 1961 would have died down by the time the 1965 intake entered the school. Eventually the proportion of i.t.a. children reaching various stages in reading will become more or less constant in successive school intakes, and we may then claim that the Hawthorne effect is no longer present, the new alphabet having been accepted as a normal means of learning to read by both teachers and children. In Oldham (Table 19(a)), after one year (three terms), the percentages of children completing the reading programme in successive annual intakes are approximately 7, 7, 4, 5 and 4. After two years (six terms), the percentages are 66, 44, 37 and 41, and after three years (nine terms), they are 88, 72 and 82. These figures suggest that the Hawthorne

TABLE 19(a)

Percentage of children who completed the reading scheme

| After term | Intake | | | | | | |
	i.t.a. Sept 1961	i.t.a. Sept 1962	i.t.a. Sept 1963	i.t.a. Sept 1964	i.t.a. Sept 1965	t.o. Sept 1961	t.o. Sept 1962
1	0.0	0.0	0.0	0.0	0.0	0.0	0.0
2	0.6	0.2	0.2	2.7	0.5	0.0	0.0
3	7.3	6.7	4.0	4.8	4.2	0.0	0.0
4	27.4	14.3	14.0	13.6	11.0	0.0	0.0
5	57.6	28.2	26.4	25.2		0.8	3.1
6	65.9	43.8	36.5	40.6		5.0	6.6
7	76.3	50.2	56.0	51.1		8.6	13.6
8	81.8	64.3	71.8			17.5	30.8
9	87.9	72.3	81.5			31.5	37.6

FIGURE 19(i)

Intake

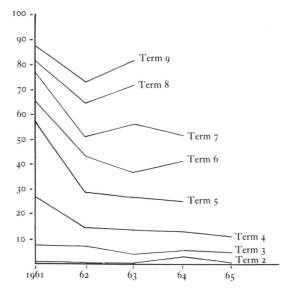

% of i.t.a. children who completed the reading scheme

Term 9
Term 8
Term 7
Term 6
Term 5
Term 4
Term 3
Term 2

1961   62   63   64   65

effect has worked its way out of the system in the later intakes, since these children were performing better (not worse) than their immediate predecessors.

Similarly Figure 19(i) shows that in Term 4 the five successive intakes tend to be less successful than their predecessors, i.e. according to our (rather tenuous) argument some Hawthorne effect is still present. By Terms 8 and 9, however, this is no longer the case and the 1963 intake is actually more successful than the previous one that entered the school in 1962. Looking at Figure 19(i) as a whole there would appear to be a marked tendency for the superiority of the earlier intakes to have worn off by the end of the third year. Concentrating our attention on Term 9 we could claim that the percentage of i.t.a. children in the 1961 intake who had completed the reading scheme was inflated by the Hawthorne effect, but that this was not so in the 1962 intake.

If we assume no Hawthorne effect in the t.o. groups (and both research results and the teachers' evidence suggest that it was very small) we may make an attempt to estimate its extent by calculating (i) the superiority of the 1961 i.t.a. over the 1961 t.o. intake with (ii) the superiority of the 1962 i.t.a. intake over the 1962 t.o. intake. From the last row of Table 19(a) we find *after three years* the superiority of the 1961 i.t.a. intake was $87 \cdot 9 - 31 \cdot 5 = 56 \cdot 4\%$ and for the 1962 intake was $72 \cdot 3 - 37 \cdot 6 = 34 \cdot 7\%$, suggesting that (assuming no Hawthorne effect in the t.o. group) some 40% of the original superiority in 1961 of i.t.a. was due to the Hawthorne effect, i.e. $(56 \cdot 4 - 34 \cdot 7)/56 \cdot 4 = 38 \cdot 5\%$.

It is very important to remember, however, that the decrease in efficiency between the first and second i.t.a. intakes at Oldham may not be due to the Hawthorne effect but to any of a large number of temporary influences, such as a deliberate policy undertaken by the teachers, i.e. a reduction in drive (as defined by Southgate (1965)).

Moreover, the criterion that a child 'completed' a book is a subjective impression of his progress. It is not based on objective test scores. Some teachers will be more lenient than others. Nevertheless, although not all the difference between the two groups can be attributed to the Hawthorne effect, the results do suggest that the early results were very probably a considerable overestimate of the superiority of i.t.a.

Downing and Jones (1966) also found that the results obtained in the second London experiment were:

'by no means identical with previously analysed results from the original i.t.a. experiment which began in 1961. They found that in general the differences between the experimental and control groups of the second experiment were smaller than those between the experimental and control groups of the original experiment. Preliminary analysis suggested that the same was true, though to a smaller extent, of the comparison between the two control groups.'

We are thus restricted to a small amount of contradictory and rather obscure evidence concerning the magnitude of the Hawthorne effect. To take a plunge we could say that the results suggest that the Hawthorne effect has little influence on the t.o. classes, but that it appears to account for pretty well half of the considerable superiority shown by the i.t.a. group. To play safer, we could say that there is a suggestion that extraneous factors associated with the introduction of the new medium exert a strong but not decisive influence on the children's performance in i.t.a.

Do the i.t.a. groups tend to gain significantly higher mean scores in reading because i.t.a. leads teachers to adopt more efficient teaching procedures?

Question:

What general classroom procedures were adopted in teaching reading? (C3)

Classroom procedures covering such matters as the degree of emphasis on group and individual instruction, opportunities provided for writing, etc., must be differentiated from the media, methods and materials employed, despite the conclusion reached by Swales (1966) that 'medium, methods and materials are inextricably mixed'. As Hemming (1967) has pointed out.

'wide variation exists in i t a . . . one can find schools where the children themselves make their first reading books; schools that concentrate work around a course of infant readers; schools that minimise the use of a course, depending for development of skill upon the mixed stimulus provided by a graded class library; schools including more or less phonic practice, and so on.'

Typical of the wide differences between procedures is Downing's (1967) experiment, in which the teaching procedures were matched only in the general sense that in both groups the traditional freedom of the teacher to use the procedure she found most appropriate for her class has been maintained. He says that:

'The weakness of this aspect of the initial experiment is that a number of variables known to be of importance in reading are not under deliberate and direct control. On the other hand, this matching of the liberal approach of reading methods in both groups is a strength of its fulfilment of the 'Field Experiment' aim to produce as far as possible the real-life school situation in this country, for it is probable that variations in emphasis in teaching methods may be balanced out in the quite large samples used.'

However, in the second experiment by Downing and Jones (1966), a somewhat more rigorous attempt has been made to control classroom procedures, teachers in both i.t.a. and control groups being asked to preserve their normal practice in all other respects, e.g. reading-readiness, classroom organisation, formal-informal approach, and proportion of time given to reading. Even then, five out of the twelve teachers said they did phonic work earlier with the i.t.a. class than with the t.o. class, but this was not seen as a change of method, because it was said to be a response to the children's interest and development. As such, it was regarded as an essential part of the method used with both classes.

In Tanyzer, Alpert and Sandel's (1965) research the groups learning to read in t.o. were taught by varying methods, depending upon the classroom teachers' preference. The teachers were allowed to utilise procedures of teaching that are generally approved by language arts specialists. Thus, teachers instructing in t.o. could use a basal or multi-basal approach, or could use an experience approach utilising library books as the core of their instructional programme. The type of classroom organisation used by a teacher was a matter of individual preference as long as the type of organisation was designed to differentiate instruction within the class. Since teachers were chosen on the basis of their competence, as long as proper differentiation of instruction occurred, all materials printed in t.o. which the teacher believed increased teaching effectiveness were approved. The i.t.a. classes, however, were taught to read using a series of graded material printed in i.t.a. entitled the *Early-to-Read* i.t.a. series. Bosma (1965) actually deleted those portions of the i.t.a. reading programme that involved writing. However, extensive provisions were made for teachers' preferences. She made extensive provision for language development through conversation, discussion, listening activities, dramatic play, experience stories recorded by the teacher and oral reading. In addition to supplementary oral language experiences, a continuous art programme specifically designed to prepare the children for writing was undertaken. Stick drawing, involving vertical, horizontal and diagonal lines, as well as circles and arcs, was stressed in these art activities.

There is little objective evidence about differences in classroom procedure. Hahn (1965) found wide differences between some classroom procedures, e.g. in three different groups 67%, 33% and 90% respectively of the teachers decided to allocate the children to four or more teaching groups, and the i.t.a. teachers were ranked top in class participation, awareness of the needs of their pupils and overall teaching competence.

Record keeping was extremely thorough in some of the investigations. For example, the teachers in Tanyzer and Alpert's (1965) experiment kept a complex log of reading instruction and supportive activities relating to the course as a whole, including particulars of (i) *supportive activities*–building experimental background (pictures, discussing trips), oral reading, choral speaking or reading, concept development (language enrichment), experience stories (work type or language charts), drama, puppetry, poetry, spelling, creative writing, book reporting, free play (construction activities, puzzles), oral language development (retelling stories), art expression, recreational reading, supplementary readers, library facilities, handwriting, reading in context areas (social studies, science, maths), transition activities; (ii) *skills*–new words, silent reading, oral reading, comprehension, interpretation; (iii) *word analysis*–phonic, structural, contextual, dictionary, vocabulary development, resource and reference reading, skills-reinforcement, word recognition, listening, following directions, motor co-ordination, visual discrimination, auditory discrimination, picture interpretation; and (iv) *materials*–basal, workbooks, teacher-made materials, (exercises, vocabulary pictures, illustrations), commercial (flash cards, sound symbol cards), films, film strips, recordings (tapes, phonograph), newspapers, magazines, trade books, art and craft supplies, play equipment, hand bound texts, pamphlets.

On the whole, we may say that although there is no evidence that the procedures adopted have been specially favourable to i.t.a., a considerable proportion of the variance attributed to differences between media must, in fact, be due to differences in teaching procedures. Some degree of control, as in Downing's research (1967), is essential if the results concerning the relative efficiency of different media are to be unambiguous.

F. TIME ALLOWANCE

Do the i.t.a. groups tend to gain significantly higher mean scores in reading because i.t.a. teachers give more time to reading activities?

Question:

Was the number of minutes spent in reading activities controlled? (C4)

254

The teaching schedule (as distinct from the teaching method) is concerned chiefly with the total time spent learning to read and on supplementary activities, and the keeping of records of group and individual tuition, as in the work of Hayes and Nemeth (1965). Obviously the control of time is very important since any method which is used twice as many hours (say) as another is obviously more likely to be successful. Robinson (1966), for example, recognises the importance of this by requiring that:

'Instructional time is to be equated in all three groups. Regular and frequent observations of the control and both of the experimental groups are to be scheduled for purposes of checking on time allotment and of determining whether teachers are following the sequence of skills in the manual. Observers will also collect behavioural data on children in experimental classrooms and aid in maintaining the case study records.'

McCracken (1966) conducted a time study of pupil activity throughout the year in the experimental and control groups. Thirteen observers took part in the time study. The observers were asked to record in minutes the amount of time a child spent during the day in reading, in writing, in phonics, in arithmetic, and in miscellaneous activities. They were asked to divide each category into pupil work or teacher work. Observations were started 20 minutes before school officially began with the expectation that some children arriving early might choose to participate in individual reading or writing activities. Observations took place approximately every two weeks. Sixty time-studies were made, 30 in each class, without knowledge beforehand of the teachers or principals.

In Tanyzer and Alpert's (1965) research, all teachers were requested to spend approximately two-and-a-half hours per day in direct reading instruction and supportive activities. Direct reading instruction was defined as time spent in teaching of reading other than the basal reader. The teachers kept time logs of activities, skills and materials used in instruction. Validation of the logs was determined by observation of the research staff who compared their logs, kept when visiting the classroom, with the teachers' logs.

Strict time schedules are not often laid down in Britain, although Downing and Jones (1966) asked teachers to equate their procedures as closely as possible. In the United States some investigators have imposed exact time allowances, e.g. 560 minutes weekly (Hayes and Nemeth (1965)), 510 minutes for language instruction and 655 minutes for all language activities (Mazurkiewicz, (1965)), $2\frac{1}{2}$ hours daily for reading and supportive activities (Tanyzer and Alpert (1965)), 60 minutes per day reading and 90 minutes per day related activities (Tanyzer, Alpert and Sandel (1965)).

The laying down of limits does not guarantee that they will be kept. Tanyzer and Alpert (1965) found no significant difference in the total time spent by different groups, but time schedules were kept much better in the earlier than in the later part of the experiment.

McCracken (1966) found that the i.t.a. group spent significantly more time on independent writing, and the t.o. group more time on reading. When the reading and writing times were combined, there was no significant difference between the two groups. These time differences seem to reflect differences in the two procedures, since the *Early-to-Read* i.t.a. series uses writing as a basic part of its method of teaching reading. There were no significant differences noted in the time teachers spent in teaching, or in the time pupils spent in working independently.

Fry (1966) found surprisingly enough a negative correlation between instruction time and reading. He thinks that this might be because the poorest teachers tend to spend the most time on reading. This is supported by finding that good teachers get better results. It seems possible that the poorer teachers cannot make up their inadequacies by harder work.

On the whole, insufficient consideration has been given to equalising the time devoted to reading activities by i.t.a. and t.o. groups. This is particularly true in Britain. Although there is no detailed evidence that more time has been given to reading in i.t.a. than in t.o., some of the difference found between the efficiency of the two may be due to this highly important factor, although we do not know in which direction the advantage lies.

G. READING MATERIALS

Do the i.t.a. groups tend to gain significantly higher mean scores in reading because the reading materials used in teaching i.t.a. are more appropriate?

Question:

What materials were used? (C1)

In Tanyzer, Alpert and Sandel's (1965) research, the teachers (selected for their competence) chose their own t.o. readers. The i.t.a. classes, however, were taught to read using a series of graded material printed in i.t.a. entitled the *Early-to-Read i.t.a. Series.* Bosma (1965) actually deleted those portions of the i.t.a. reading programme that involved writing.

In Great Britain the *Janet and John* series appears to have been most frequently used for research on the ground that it is the most popular. In the U.S.A. there is a considerable variation, the Scott, Foresman series being the commonest.

Some researchers used the same materials for both media, e.g. Downing (1967), Downing and Jones (1966), Harrison (1964) and Milne (1966) confined their material to the *Janet and John* readers, and Robinson (1966) is using the Scott, Foresman Multi-Ethnic test for both groups. It must be remembered, however, that we also have to take into account published and unpublished workbooks, teachers' manuals, diaries, vocabulary lists and phrase cards, dictionaries and boxes, etc. Several research workers, such as Downing and Jones (1966) have pointed out that it is extremely hard to equate the children's reading opportunities even if the readers are identical, if only because all children meet traditional orthography at home, in comics, on T.V. and in many other ways. They say:

> 'Essentially then, the difference between the experimental group and the control group was not of a pure contrast between the former using i.t.a. materials and the latter using t.o. materials. Actually the situation was that the experimental group had experience of both i.t.a. and t.o. while the control groups' experience was limited to t.o.'

In some researches each medium is used with a different set of reading materials, although the title of the research and the framing of hypotheses suggest that a comparison between i.t.a. and t.o. is nevertheless possible. Examples abound in the

256

literature of the confounding of materials and media. For instance, Hayes and Nemeth (1965), compare (i) a whole word eclectic method (Scott, Foresman), (ii) a phonic method (Lippincott), (iii) a combined method, and (iv) a language arts approach, using i.t.a. Tanyzer and Alpert (1965) and Tanyzer, Alpert and Sandel (1965) make similar distinctions. Hahn's (1965) investigation teachers chose one of the suggested basal readers, which were not the same in all the groups. Fry (1966) used the *Sheldon Basal Readers* for t.o. and d.m.s. groups, but not for i.t.a. Swales (1966) used *Janet and John* for i.t.a. and either *Janet and John* or *Happy Venture* for t.o., Dell (1967) used *Janet and John* for i.t.a. and the *Downing Readers* for t.o., McCracken (1966) used *Early-to-Read* for i.t.a. and the *Ginn Basal Readers* for t.o., Mazurkiewicz (1965) used *Early-to-Read* readers for the more able i.t.a. students and *Downing* for the less able; in the t.o. groups he used *Alice and Jerry* for the more able and *AB Language Arts* for the less able children. He entitles his report 'Comparison of i t a and t.o. achievement when methodology is controlled'. Yet the children in the two groups used different books. His methodology is not controlled at all; in respect of differences in the efficiency of the two media his researches simply show, (i) that i.t.a. might be a better medium than t.o.; or (ii) that *Early-to-Read* and *Downing Readers* might be better texts than the *Alice and Jerry* and *AB Language Arts* readers, or (iii) that both statements might be true.

No proper comparison can be made between children learning to read in different media if the books and materials are different, i.e. if the word-experience, difficulty level, frequency or repetitions, etc. of two sets of readers are different. For example, Tanyzer and Alpert (1965) report that in their own experiment the vocabulary count was considerably higher in the i.t.a. and Lippincott series than in the Scott, Foresman series. Scott, Foresman uses a total of 323 words in its first-grade programme, while Lippincott reports a total of over 2,000 words and the *Early-to-Read* i.t.a. approximately 1,500. All the words appearing in the Scott, Foresman and i.t.a. readers are woven into the printed context, while Lippincott introduces a number of words in lists. Each list contains words illustrating a specific phoneme-grapheme relationship. There is less control over the introduction of new words and significantly fewer repetitions in the i.t.a. and Lippincott series than in the Scott, Foresman programme with its carefully controlled vocabulary and high frequency of repetitions.

It is clearly illogical for i.t.a. invariably to be used with one set of reading materials and t.o. invariably to be used with another set, if we wish to isolate the separate effects of the two media. The size of the sample is irrelevant and offers no solution to the problem. We are not hoping, as with error variables, that the influence of the reading material will cancel out as it will be presented an approximately equal number of times in each medium. On the contrary, in the experiments mentioned above, each medium is invariably used with its own material, whether we test a tiny sample or the entire population of the globe. It is obvious that if an i.t.a. class, having been taught by means of, say, *Royal Road Readers*, is more successful than a t.o. class taught by *Key Words*, then we have the finding that *Royal Road* in i.t.a. is a more successful combination of material and medium than *Key Words* in t.o., and it is logically impossible to draw any valid conclusion whatever about the relative merits of i.t.a. or t.o. (or of *Royal Road* versus *Key Words*). In fact, the superiority of the first group might not be dependent on the use of i.t.a. at all, but might have been obtained despite its use. To adopt an adequate experimental design is to apply logical principles to a problem. To use different materials for different media is as absurd as comparing tomato soup with mulligatawny and always drowning one with ginger and the other with garlic.

Thus researches in which i.t.a. is tied to one s t of materials and t.o. to another cannot be taken as seriously as those of Downing (1967), Downing and Jones (1966), Harrison (1964), in which the materials were the same. For this reason the findings in Chapter 18 have been summarised under two categories, those in which the same materials were used in both media and those (alas) in which the materials were different. A distinction has to be drawn between the bias which arises from inadequate matching and the bias which comes from using different reading materials in the two experimental groups. Investigations in which experimental samples and conditions are not adequately matched *probably* suffer from the limitation that the i.t.a. and t.o. groups differ in important characteristics which are *likely to bias* the results; but an experimental design in which the i.t.a. pupils always use one set of materials and the t.o. pupils always use another set *ensures bias*, and it is logically impossible to come to any firm conclusion about the relative effectiveness of the two alphabets, just as we cannot determine whether A is greater than B by comparing A+Y with B+Z. However, the main question whether the i.t.a. groups have been favoured by the materials used cannot be examined until the relation between reading materials and teaching methods has been considered (in the next section).

H. TEACHING METHODS

Do the i.t.a. groups tend to gain significantly higher mean scores in reading because i.t.a. facilitates phonic methods more readily than t.o. does?

Question:

What methods of teaching reading were used? (C2)

A distinction has first to be drawn between the methods and the procedures of teaching reading. In the literature on i.t.a. the term 'method' is commonly used for what might perhaps be more appropriately described as technique, i.e. a phonic or look-and-say or combined method. In other educational fields the term 'method' usually has a much broader connotation, similar to 'procedure' or 'programme' since it covers such matters as the degree of emphasis on group and individual instruction, the use of library books, opportunities provided for writing, and so on.

In the present report the word 'method' means phonic or look-and-say or a combination of the two, and 'procedure' the more general classroom and lesson organisation.

Within a research, differences are often considerable, and can be illustrated from the work of Tanyzer and Alpert (1965) who say:

'In the Scott, Foresman programme a sight vocabulary is developed initially before any phonics is introduced. Beginning with pre-primer reading, each new word is taught by methods which emphasise recognising the word as a whole. A phonic element is taught to children after several words containing it have been learned as sight words. Children are helped to discover for themselves the relationship between a letter and its corresponding sound value. Word analysis is gradually developed through an eclectic approach which stresses a combination of phonic, structural and context clues.

'The Lippincott Series does not develop an initial sight vocabulary, instead it teaches letter sounds by relating individual sounds in spoken words which are selected on the basis of the phonic elements they contain. New words are not introduced until their component letter sounds have been taught. Some phonetically irregular words are taught as they are used in the stories. Their number is held to a minimum.'

'The i.t.a. series emphasises a combined experience story and phonics approach. Children are taught to associate each of the forty-four characters of Pitman's alphabet with the phoneme it represents. The primary method of identifying an unfamiliar word involves analysing and synthesising the sound elements of the word. A number of new words appearing in the beginning readers and experience stories are taught as sight words if they contain characters not previously introduced. The order of presentation of the i.t.a. characters is primarily based on a study of the frequency of usage of a sound in the speech and writing of children.'

In Downing's (1967) research, five out of the twelve teachers said that with the i.t.a. class they used phonic methods earlier than with the t.o. class, but this was not considered to be a change of method, because it was said to be in response to the children's interest and an essential part of the method used with both classes.

The criticism is sometimes made that the superiority of i.t.a. does not arise from the nature of the alphabet used but from the fact that it facilitates a *phonic method* of teaching. It is said that any procedure which confines itself in the early stages to the phonic regularities that are found in English, whether written in an old or new alphabet, will almost certainly produce better results than conventional teaching in t.o. script, and that in fact children will learn to read more efficiently in t.o. script if efficient methods are used without the superfluity, as in i.t.a. groups, of having to transliterate textbooks into another writing system or of children being compelled to learn to read in two alphabets instead of one. Cartwright and Jones (1967), for example, point out that teaching method may interact with the medium. They say that:

'the early introduction of phonic methods may have a higher "pay-off" in terms of the acquisition of decoding skills (as measured by Schonell's Graded Word Reading Test and Neale Accuracy scores) in conjunction with the use of i.t.a. than with t.o.'

Diack (1967) says:

'If we accept the most favourable statistics put forward by Downing, the most we can say is that children taught to read by means of an i.t.a. version of the *Janet and John* readers made better progress than comparable children taught by the *Janet and John* readers in the normal t.o. version. That is to say, children taught by means of a series of readers which does recognise the alphabetic principle at the earlier stages of reading do not progress so well as comparable children taught by the same records transcribed in such a way that nowhere are they remote from the alphabetical principle.'

Stott (1965) makes the same point, saying that:

'Far from equalising both sides of the experiment, the use of the *Janet and John* scheme, so popular in Britain, grossly unequalises it. These readers are planned on a sight method, and this applies even to the so-called phonic series, since it is only the lists of words at the back and not the texts which are phonically

259

arranged. By transcribing them into i.t.a., however, they become phonic readers and will naturally be used as such by sensible teachers and children. On the other hand, the *Janet and John* books in the traditional spelling do not provide a good introduction to phonics. Several of the letters of the alphabet for example do not occur at all as initials in the early books and those which do are not repeated often enough to give the child phonic practice. Consequently they do not teach children to read in any general sense, but only to recognise a certain number of words. To choose this method as representative of all teaching in the traditional spelling is to load the dice heavily in favour of i.t.a.'

And Reid (1967) has pointed out that as early as Book 1 nine different sounds for the letter 'o' are introduced.

These seem to be valid criticisms. There is little doubt that the t.o. children grew in inferior phonic soil. It is clear that reading materials should not only be the same for both groups of children, they should also be representative of the full range used by schools, including books suitable for teaching by phonic and look-and-say (or mixed) methods respectively.

The problem is an experimental one. By means of analysis of variance we can examine the separate effects of the two media and two types of reader such as *Key Words* (look-and-say) and *Royal Road* (phonic). The table of scores would be as follows:

Medium	Material	
	Key Words (look-and-say)	Royal Road (phonic)
i.t.a.	x	x
t.o.	x	x

with supporters of i.t.a. predicting larger differences between rows (in favour of i.t.a.) than between columns, and their opponents larger differences between columns (in favour of 'phonic') than between rows.

However, despite the phonic limitations of the *Janet and John* readers, it must be remembered that Downing chose them as the most representative of educational practice in Britain at the time when he began his experiment, i.e. he was conducting an educational as well as a psychological experiment, and that as Keir (1967) says, 'if the irregularity of English is a deterrent to progress it is as well to know about it'.

Moreover, the argument put forward by Stott (1965) and Diack (1967) that t.o. children are handicapped because the *Janet and John* series is not suitable for teaching by the phonic method, appears to concede the case for i.t.a., since one of the advantages of this medium is that it extends the phonetic principle to the whole of the English language.

It must be remembered too that Pitman designed i.t.a. to give a new opportunity of raising the standards of literacy through both look-and-say and phonic methods of teaching reading. In his view look-and-say teaching should be helped by i.t.a. because it removes the variations in the visual patterns of words.

Looking at the researches as a whole, there is no conclusive evidence that the use of different materials and methods in the two groups has favoured either i.t.a. or t.o. But the criticism that Stott (1965) and Diack (1967) have raised of the books used in

the important researches by Downing (1967) and Downing and Jones (1966) points
to the necessity for drawing up experimental designs in which the relevant factors
are not only balanced but are also representative of teaching practice.

II Other influences

A. RESEARCH REPORTING

Question:

How were the results interpreted? (F4)

Most researchers state their findings unambiguously, but others are inclined to
insert their argument into their statement of results.

The main argument put forward is usually that i.t.a. is superior as a teaching
medium because it is based on more regular phoneme-grapheme relationships. It
cannot, however, be assumed that a hypothesis is correct simply because the deductions derived from it are verified. For i.t.a. might be more efficient, not because of any
superiority in helping to form visual-auditory associations, but for some other reason,
such as that it is novel, or that both teacher and children give it more attention. These
difficulties can be largely met by employing a suitable experimental design, but complete inductive proof is never possible. We can never exhaust all alternative hypotheses.

For example, Mazurkiewicz's (1965) general conclusion is that 'the use of an identical
methodology with traditional orthography is unable completely to overcome the
inhibiting effects of the phoneme-grapheme correspondence on early reading achievement'. This is an inference that cannot be logically drawn from the fact that in certain
tests the i.t.a. group scored higher than the t.o. group, although phoneme-grapheme
relations can reasonably be advanced as one of the most convincing of a number of
possible explanations in a discussion on the implications of the results. And in the
design adopted by Mazurkiewicz differences in the criterion scores could almost as
easily be due to the nature of the reading material.

Downing (1967) similarly couches some of his hypotheses in a form which suggests
that experimental verification of the deductions drawn from the hypotheses proves
the hypotheses, e.g.

Hypothesis 1 'Because of the reduction in the volume of learning in i.t.a. as
compared with t.o., children in i.t.a. classes should make significantly more rapid progress through their basic reader series.'

Hypothesis 2 'Because of the greater regularity of grapheme-phoneme relations
in i.t.a. as compared with t.o., pupils learning to read with i.t.a.
should achieve significantly higher scores on reading in which
lower-order decoding skills have an especially important role to
play.'

Hypothesis 3 'Because of the i.t.a.'s design as a traditional alphabet, in i.t.a.
classes reading achievement in t.o. should not be inferior to
previous achievements in i.t.a. once fluency in i.t.a. has been
established.'

Hypothesis 4 'Through positive transfer from i.t.a. learning to t.o. learning,
pupils who have first learned to read with i.t.a. and then made

the transition to t.o. should read the latter with significantly greater accuracy, speed and comprehension than pupils who have not used i.t.a. in the beginning.'

Hypothesis 5 'Because i.t.a. also simplifies and regularises the encoded operation, the written compositions of i.t.a. pupils should be longer than those of children who begin reading in t.o.'

Downing (1967) sometimes claims that the superior rate of progress in the experimental groups was achieved in spite of a degree of bias in the conditions favourable to the control groups. It does not necessarily follow, however, that apparently detrimental circumstances are a handicap. Sometimes teachers overcompensate for difficulties, transforming disadvantages into opportunities. It is better to equate conditions than bias them in favour of an opposing hypothesis.

B. TIME OF TRANSFER

Question:

When did the pupils make the transition from i.t.a. to t.o.? (C5)

There has been a great deal of variation from research to research in the time of transition; for example, after 140 school days 70% of the i.t.a. pupils had made the transition in the research of Tanyzer, Alpert and Sandel (1965). Corresponding figures were 72% (Hayes and Nemeth (1965)) and 80% (Hahn (1965)).

During the first year Harrison's (1964) schools had transferred about 7% and Stewart (1966) 88% of the children.

After 18 months (four terms) Downing and Jones (1966) had transferred 17% and Downing (1967) 34%, and after about two years the figures were roughly 50% (Downing (1967)), 60% (Milne (1966)), 66% (Harrison (1964)), 94% (Mazurkiewicz (1965)) and 94% (Stewart (1966)).

After $2\frac{1}{3}$ years (7 terms) Downing and Jones (1966) had transferred 60% and Downing (1967) 78% of the children.

Even after three years only about three-quarters of Downing and Jones's (1966) pupils had made the transition, although 88% of Harrison's (1964) and 94% of Milne's (1966) had done so.

The general tendency in recent work in Britain is to regard at least three years' teaching as necessary before transition is complete.

Downing (1967) has pointed out that in his second experiment only 17% of the i.t.a. group had made the transition at the time of the first test in t.o., whereas the corresponding proportion was 40% in the first experiment. He says, 'We have noticed an increasingly relaxed attitude towards the transfer stage as the use of i.t.a. has spread and teachers have become more familiar with the transfer of reading from i.t.a. to t.o.'

In Britain the tendency has been for very few children to transfer in the first year, a half or two-thirds during the second year and most of the remainder during the third year with a fifth or sixth of the children still remaining on i.t.a. In the United States, on the other hand, transfer has been much more rapid, some three-quarters of the children frequently transferring after one year and almost all of them having changed by the end of the second year.

Certainly a great deal of subjectivity enters into an experiment when decisions are made about the optimum time for transition. Southgate (1963) has made the comment that the transition problem occurs in the mind of the adult and not the child. Downing says (1967):

'It was indicated that transfer from i.t.a. to t.o. should not be dramatic, but that the child should be allowed to move over smoothly when he was ready. For this reason it seems best not to emphasise the difference between i.t.a. and t.o. but to rely chiefly on the similarity of configurations, as had been proposed by Pitman. Precise instructions for transition materials were not given, but a number of alternatives were suggested. These alternatives were necessary in order to allow for differences in the overall "philosophies" of the teachers. Some teachers gave the children the same book in t.o. as they had just read in i.t.a.; some went further back in the t.o. series, others preferred to move to a different series in t.o. or to more individualised reading of t.o. books.'

From the research point of view, the time for the transition should be objectively determined by the child's reading age assessed by standard tests administered by trained testers, despite the practical difficulties that would arise from this experimental procedure. The best time for transition is a problem in cognitive learning that cannot be decided by opinion, as it is too complex a matter to solve simply by taking thought. No doubt wide limits will be permissible in different circumstances, but teachers who transfer children outside these experimentally determined limits will be inefficient and handicapping their pupils unnecessarily.

The timing of the transition is one of the most crucial problems in evaluating the efficiency of i.t.a. since too early transition would obviously not give a new medium sufficient time for its advantages (if any) to become apparent, whereas too late transition might mean that the child's phonetic skills had outrun his vocabulary and understanding and he was simply 'barking at print' (Morgan and Proctor (1967)). In fact, a proper comparison between the effectiveness of the two media obviously cannot be made until all the children have made the transition to t.o.

It is clearly unfair to the i.t.a. group if the whole sample is tested in t.o. including those children who have never been taught in this medium. However, Cartwright and Jones (1967) point out that in certain contexts this argument may not be valid, 'since the varying proportions of children transferred indicate discrepancies between the results of the two experiments; and although the results of the test do not enable performances after transfer to be compared, they provide a general basis of comparison', i.e. the proportion of children who have made the transition is itself a consequence of the success of i.t.a., and is sometimes taken as a criterion of success. When a research has reached a fairly advanced stage, the statement that 'only x% of the children had transferred by this time' is misleading since it assumes that the results will in future be more in favour of i.t.a., whereas the possibility is that the superiority of i.t.a. will decrease (instead of increase) in the future, particularly as the brighter pupils will be transferred first and the duller last. If an attempt is made to allow for this difficulty by comparing those children who have made the transition with the same proportion drawn from the top of the t.o. group, an overestimate of the superiority of i.t.a. is likely to be made since these i.t.a. and t.o. samples will tend to be confined to the brighter children for whom we know that i.t.a. is particularly effective. This procedure has not been adopted in the researches under review except in Downing's second experiment (Cartwright and Jones (1967)) when a comparison of two 'top-third' groups made no dramatic difference to the results.

Although it is true that most of the research findings must underestimate the superiority of i.t.a. when the criterion tests are given in t.o., the extent of the handicap suffered by the i.t.a. children appears to have been somewhat exaggerated. (Although tests in t.o. have often been given to i.t.a. classes, even when a large proportion of the children have never used that medium in school, no one appears to have tested t.o. children in i.t.a. for purposes of comparison.)

C. SPREAD IN PUPILS' PERFORMANCE

The amount of overlap between pupils in i.t.a. and t.o. groups is very considerable. If we look upon researches as a sort of greyhound race between a large number of i.t.a. and t.o. pupils and plot the position of the percentage of runners on the course after a given period of time, e.g. in Downing (1967) (Table E1) after $2\frac{1}{3}$ years (Figure 19(ii), we see at a glance that the i.t.a. group are superior on the whole to the t.o. group, but that the two groups nevertheless string themselves out over the whole field, a considerable number of t.o. children remaining superior to a considerable number of i.t.a. children.

FIGURE 19(ii)

Progress of i.t.a. and t.o. groups through the basic reading series after $2\frac{1}{3}$ years
(derived from Table E1, Downing (1967))
(tested in the medium of instruction)

	i.t.a.	t.o.
Non-starters	/	
Book 1 or 2	/////////	********** ********** *****
Book 3	/////	********** *********
Book 4	////	********** *
Book 5	////	*****
Beyond Book 5	////////// ////////// ////////// ////////// ////////// ////////// ////////// ////////	********** ********** ********** ********

If we divide the t.o. group into quarters we can calculate the percentage of i.t.a. children reaching t.o. quartile groups at the end of the third year, as follows (Downing 1967) additional cyclostyled notes, Tables 27, 28, 29 and 32):

TABLE 19(b)
Percentage of i.t.a. children reaching t.o. quartile groups at the end of the third year
(Tested in t.o.)

	Top quarter	Second quarter	Third quarter	Bottom quarter	Top half	Bottom half
t.o. pupils	25%	25%	25%	25%	50%	50%
i.t.a. Neale test B (accuracy after 3 years)	39%	25%	21%	15%	64%	36%
i.t.a. Neale test B (speed after 3 years)	34%	30%	20%	16%	64%	36%
i.t.a. Neale test B (comprehension after 3 yrs)	33%	33%	20%	14%	66%	34%
i.t.a. Standish N.S.45 test (after 3 years)	21%	33%	28%	18%	54%	46%

In the Neale test roughly two-thirds of the i.t.a. group would be placed in the top half of the t.o. group, or looking at the matter another way, in a group of three superior (top half) pupils two of them would have been taught by i.t.a. and one by t.o. The differences between the effectiveness of the two media are thus strongly marked, but by no means overwhelming. Differences are much smaller according to the Standish N.S. 45 test. However, these figures include the drop in relative attainment following the transition to t.o. after only two years.

D. THE INFLUENCE OF INTELLIGENCE LEVEL

As would be expected, differences between the mean scores for children of different intelligence levels vary considerably, since no medium is likely to influence attainment more strongly than measured ability in so basic a cognitive skill as reading, i.e. in forming sight-sound associations, e.g. Swales (1966), Tanyzer and Alpert (1965), Tanyzer, Alpert and Sandel (1965) and Fry (1966).

Nevertheless, i.t.a. seems to stand up as an independent factor in learning to read. For example, in Tanyzer and Alpert (1965) the prediction of success for boys and girls did not improve significantly by including I.Q. as one of the predicting variables. In Hahn (1965) i.t.a. groups were superior in paragraph meaning, taking intelligence and reading-readiness constant by the method of covariance analysis. The adjustment mean scores were even more in favour of i.t.a. than the unadjusted means.

The important point is whether there is any significant interaction between media and intelligence, i.e. whether either medium is particularly effective at certain levels of intelligence. Downing (1967) compared three sub-groups, (i) high achievers–comprising the top 30% of the i.t.a. group and the top 30% of the t.o. group, (ii) middle achievers–comprising the middle 40%, and (iii) low achievers–comprising the bottom 30%. He found:

'(a) that the high achievers in the i.t.a. group were superior to the high achievers in the t.o. group on most tests. Generally among the high achievers the i.t.a. group demonstrated a greater degree of superiority over t.o. pupils than was found among the middle and low achievers;

(b) that middle achievers taught by i.t.a., though not as markedly superior to t.o. pupils as high achievers, nevertheless showed an important degree of superiority over the t.o. pupils of the same level in the control group;

(c) that among the low achievers on the earliest tests, little or no measurable differences existed between the scores of the i.t.a. and t.o. groups. However, later tests (at the end of the third year) indicated that the i.t.a. low achievers became superior to their t.o. counterparts, but that this was not true of the poorest students of all, represented by the lowest ten per cent of the samples.'

Dell (1967) found that the superiority of the i.t.a. group was not confined to the 'best readers', but was maintained at least two-thirds of the way down each class. Nevertheless, both groups included some virtual non-starters. Reading and Matrices scores are considerably more highly correlated in the i.t.a. than in the t.o. group. He concludes that there may be a closer association between learning to read and general ability in the i.t.a. group.

McCracken (1966) found that when reading from i.t.a. script i.t.a. pupils were markedly superior to the t.o. pupils reading from t.o. script, although this tended to be limited to above-average achievers, with the less able third of the class continuing to be in difficulties.

Swales (1966) found the same number of backward readers in each I.Q. group. There was no significant interaction between medium and intelligence level.

Milne (1966) says that i.t.a. script appeared to have helped the lowest I.Q. group most, a result contrary to that found in most investigations. But his diagrams of reading attainment plotted against I.Q. show little evidence of interaction, either for reading or word recognition scores. Tanyzer and Alpert (1965) found no tendency for i.t.a. groups to be better at any I.Q. range than any other. Tanyzer, Alpert and Sandel (1965) found no significant interactions between media and intelligence. Nor do there appear to be significant interactions in the work of Milne (1966).

No significant interactions have been found between the reading medium and other factors, although as might be expected, the girls often show better performance than the boys (Swales (1966)), (Hahn (1965)), (Tanyzer and Alpert (1965)), (Fry (1966)), (Hayes and Nemeth (1965)).

The weight of definite evidence thus suggests that i.t.a. is more effective for bright than for dull children. This might have been expected on the ground of the structured analytic properties of i.t.a. On the other hand, this tendency is not very marked.

E. VARIATION IN THE RESULTS FOR DIFFERENT SCHOOLS AND CLASSES

As might be expected, there are wide differences between the results for different schools. Cartwright and Jones (1967), commenting on the results for the important 'second experiment' (Downing and Jones (1966)) after as long as three years, say:

'These generalisations overlook the large differences which exist between the results from individual schools. While the results from a few schools are consistently, if not often significantly, in favour of their experimental groups, at the other extreme one school shows larger and equally consistent differences in favour of the control groups.'

Downing and Jones (1966) gave five criterion tests in the medium of instruction in 13 schools, which thus furnished a total of 65 differences between the i.t.a. and t.o. groups. For the combined sample, the i.t.a. group was very significantly superior in all five tests. Within schools, 16 out of 17 significant differences were in favour of i.t.a. Nevertheless, 48, i.e. three-quarters, of the differences were non-significant. (This may be partly due to the fact that the number of children in each school was not very large. On the other hand, it was not very small either, averaging 85 pupils per school.) If we regard the results from the 13 schools as 13 separate experiments, the overall statistical verdict is: i.t.a. significantly superior in 7 schools, t.o. significantly superior in 1 school, and non-proven in 5 schools. From the practical point of view of making a decision concerning the desirability of introducing i.t.a. into schools, it is perhaps rather inconclusive to adopt statistical criteria of significance as these are made extremely rigorous in the interests of scientific caution and often lead to a high proportion of non-proven cases. In brute fact, i.t.a. is superior in 10 schools and t.o. superior in 3 schools.

Is there any significant *interaction* between school (or class) and media, i.e. is either media particularly effective in certain schools? Hahn (1965) found a significant interaction between reading approach and *school districts*. The analysis of variance presented by Tanyzer, Alpert and Sandel (1965) shows that although class differences are more than twice as great as differences between media in terms of mean squares, there are no significant interaction effects between class media. But we shall have little clear evidence of this extremely important point until more researches employing analyses of variance have been undertaken, including 'classes' and 'media' as main effects, and 'classes × media' as an interaction term. Some slighter evidence can be obtained, however, by seeing whether the superiority shown by i.t.a. is consistent in magnitude and direction throughout all schools.

The overall results thus suggest that *even before the transition* the superiority of i.t.a. cannot be generalised to all schools, although such a claim can be made for most of them unless very rigorous statistical criteria of significance are demanded.

F. REPRESENTATIVENESS OF SAMPLES

Questions:

(*a*) How many school areas took part in the investigation? (B1a)
(*b*) How many schools took part in the investigation? (B2a)
(*c*) How many teachers took part in the investigation? (B3a)
(*d*) How many classes took part in the investigation? (B4a)
(*e*) How many pupils took part in the investigation? (B5a)
(*f*) What types of class took part in the investigation? (B4b)
(*g*) What types of school area took part in the investigation? (B1b)
(*h*) What types of school took part in the investigation? (B2b)
(*i*) What types of pupil took part in the investigation? (B5b)

(*a*) *How many school areas took part in the investigation?* (B1a)

267

Many of the researches were carried out in a single l.e.a. or school district, but some were quite extensive. Downing (1967), for example, appears to have worked in two dozen or more local education authorities and Hahn (1965), Tanyzer, Alpert and Sandel (1965) and Shapiro (1966) in about a dozen.

(b) How many schools took part in the investigation? (B2a)

In general, the number of schools studied has been very adequate, and the range is wide, from 1 in the study by Dell (1967) to 158 in Downing's (1967) investigation. Hahn (1965) worked in 36 schools, Mazurkiewicz (1965) in 26, Tanyzer and Alpert (1965) in 26 and Fry (1966) in 21, although it is common practice to exclude some of the experimental schools from the final analysis of results, as in Downing's (1967) ultimate restriction to a (very adequate) sample of 66 schools and 16 sub-control classes.

(c) How many teachers took part in the investigation? (B3a)

The number of teachers varies a great deal from experiment to experiment. In the researches cited in this report the range is from 2 in Bosma (1965) and Dell (1967) to over 80 in Downing's (1967) first experiment.

(d) How many classes took part in the investigation? (B4a)

The number of classes included in researches is often quite considerable. Downing (1967) has more than 80. Samples of over 30 classes are fairly often found in the literature, especially in the preliminary stages of the experiment. On the other hand, Bosma (1965) has only 2 classes.

(e) How many pupils took part in the investigation? (B5a)

Samples of pupils vary in size from the order of a thousand or more in the researches of Downing (1967), Hahn (1965) and Shapiro (1966), down to Bosma's (1965) two classes of 22 pupils each.

(f) What types of class took part in the investigation? (B4b)

An important consideration is that classes should be confined to children beginning to learn to read. If they are not, an attempt has to be made either to assess gains on a wide variety of reading tests, or to use analysis of covariance in order to hold initial reading attainment constant; both these methods are statistically unsatisfactory. It is particularly difficult to ensure that all pupils are beginners in the case of children from middle-class homes, in which some informal instruction in reading might well have been given before the children come to school. In the United States, the difficulty of first-grade children who have previously attended kindergarten is fairly common. This factor is perhaps best controlled by the administration of a pre-experimental reading test and the exclusion from the experiment itself (but not necessarily from the experimental classes) of children who are not starting at the beginning.

Swales (1966) studied children in their third year of schooling with an average age of 7·9 years and Hahn (1965) included a class in which there were as many as 17 pupils with some reading experience. Tanyzer and Alpert's (1965) sample included some children who had received pre-first grade training of up to 200 half-days, and there were some non-beginners among Tanyzer, Alpert and Sandel's (1965) pupils. In Britain it is apparently rare for school entrants to be able to read with any fluency.

(g) What types of school area took part in the investigation? (B1b)

The social background of the school areas is not always stated in the description of researches. Most have been urban working-class districts and Stewart (1966) included some subjects in his lower socio-economic groups, from predominantly Spanish speaking homes. Some of Tanyzer, Alpert and Sandel's (1965) sample came from more affluent districts, and urban, suburban and village districts were included. Milne (1966) also included urban and rural schools in his sample. On the whole, the range has been narrow. Any important investigation which hopes to influence national policy or gain a consensus of opinion in the profession should obviously be spread over a wide area.

(h) What types of school took part in the investigation? (B2b)

Most of the schools investigated have been urban working-class, although Milne (1966), Hahn (1965) and Tanyzer, Alpert and Sandel (1965) have included rural and Robinson (1966) and Tanyzer, Alpert and Sandel (1965) some pupils of higher socio-economic status. Considerable differences are often found, however, within these general categories: Harrison (1964) for example, reports that in Oldham two of the experimental schools were on housing estates, one of these temporarily organised as part of a junior school but soon to start a separate existence; three others were very old denominational schools, two were due for closure under the schools development plan and only one had modern buildings.

(i) What types of pupil took part in the investigation? (B5b)

This question is answered in the sections dealing with the types of school and school area included in the investigations. There is some concentration on urban working-class children, but many rural and higher socio-economic grade pupils have also taken part.

On the whole, investigations have covered an adequate and representative range of schools in respect of such variables as sex, socio-economic status and geographical background, although–as with teachers–the schools taking part in an experiment may well be of above-average efficiency, so that the superiority of i.t.a. might not be maintained if it became more widely used.

G. VOLUNTEERING

It is difficult to describe volunteering procedures under separate headings such as school areas, schools, teachers, classes and pupils although an attempt has been made to do so in the present section. Volunteering should perhaps be regarded as a single topic.

Questions:

(*a*) Did the school areas volunteer? (B1c)
(*b*) Did the schools volunteer? (B2c)
(*c*) Did the teachers volunteer? (B3c)

(a) Did the school areas volunteer? (B1c)

It is not easy to say exactly why an investigation into i.t.a. is set up in some school areas and not others. Government departments or educational bodies sometimes invite certain local educational authorities to co-operate. For example, in Downing's (1967) first experiment:

'recruitment to the experimental and control groups was made by approaching Directors of Education. The selected areas were chosen in consultation with the then Ministry of Education, the aim being to provide a cross-section of the school population in areas reasonably accessible to the experimenter and his assistants. When the areas had been chosen, the Directors of Education concerned were approached personally by the experimenter.'

But even in such cases it seems likely that choice will often be restricted to areas that have shown an interest in such problems in the past, i.e. there will be a tendency for investigations to be carried out where they are most welcome (and will be carried out most efficiently). For example, much of the pioneer work in Britain has been carried out in Oldham and some of the earliest and most extensive researches have been conducted in schools in this town, partly because of the interest that Mr Harrison, the Director of Education, and some of the local teachers have taken in the use of the initial teaching alphabet. The 13 areas included in Hahn's (1965) research volunteered for the project, but information on this point is often missing altogether from research reports or is ambiguous, e.g. in Tanyzer and Alpert's (1964) research, school districts volunteered 'except when requested'.

(b) *Did the schools volunteer?* (B2c)

Stewart (1966) included all schools in the area, an excellent procedure when it can be arranged; Hahn's (1965) schools are said to have been selected by the experimenter and Swales (1966) studied classes in being. Otherwise, volunteering, at least nominally, would appear to be the common rule, although this is sometimes implied rather than explicitly stated in the reports. The degree of enthusiasm shown by the volunteers cannot, of course, be ascertained from these research reports. It probably varies a great deal from school to school, which is a highly desirable situation from the point of view of research design.

(c) *Did the teachers volunteer?* (B3c)

Harrison (1964) is certainly in favour of volunteers and says in his book, 'I would like to put on record the names of the headteachers and the class teachers who volunteered. Theirs was no easy task with so much to be done and so many things to be improvised in the early days. With their colleagues in other areas they merit the gratitude of educationists everywhere for entering upon this experiment in the interests of educational research and in the face of much scepticism about the outcome.' The same considerations apply, of course, to teachers as to schools; volunteering is, at least nominally, the common rule.

We are on the horns of a dilemma in deciding whether or not to confine the experimental sample to volunteers. This is a crucial issue in studies whose main purpose is to examine the efficiency of i.t.a. in the contemporary school system and to predict its efficiency in the future, since although, on the one hand, education authorities, schools and teachers who volunteer to take part in an experiment will probably be over-enthusiastic, on the other hand, non-volunteers may be too apathetic. The important point is that the future population of schools to which the findings are to be generalised will, at least in Britain, also be volunteers. The tradition in British education is that schools decide for themselves what teaching methods to adopt, and they will not take up i.t.a. unless they feel the urge to do so. It is true, of course, that the later converts will be less enthusiastic than the earlier ones were. This is a weakness in Downing's (1967) research, but it must also be borne in mind that not all of his very large sample were zealots, and that, on the whole, they probably did not differ a great deal from those who were going to take up i.t.a. in the future. The basic issue is whether more accurate prediction of the efficiency of i.t.a. would be gained by introducing compulsion. Although on first consideration it would perhaps seem best to include school districts, schools and teachers who did not volunteer, it is doubtful whether such a sample would in fact throw as much light on the viability of the new alphabet as would volunteers. It is the non-volunteers, not the volunteers, who are atypical of the future.

H. STATISTICAL TESTS OF SIGNIFICANCE

Questions:
(*a*) What statistical techniques were used in the analysis of results? (F1)
(*b*) What statistical matching techniques were used? (F2)
(*c*) What variables other than the media were included in the main statistical results? (F3)

(*a*) *What statistical techniques were used in the analysis of results?* (F1)

The statistical techniques used in the various researches are chiefly mainstream. Hahn (1965), McCracken (1966), Tanyzer and Alpert (1965), Tanyzer, Alpert and Sandel (1965), Swales (1966) and Shapiro (1966), all used analysis of variance, the latter two with supplementary analysis of covariance. McCracken (1966) also used the Wilcoxon two-sample test, chi-square and a sign test.

Some of the reports represented in the literature, however, are statistically naive. For example, mean scores are frequently quoted without the standard deviations, which makes it impossible to interpret them satisfactorily. The techniques used in Downing's (1967) research, for instance, seem superfluously complicated and involve unnecessarily complex corrections for skewness, such as Hald's logarithmic transformations, and non-parametric techniques such as the one-tailed Kolmogorov-Smirnov test which is sensitive to several types of differences between groups as well as means, e.g. it can yield a significant difference between two groups with identical means, if the two distributions are sufficiently dissimilar. Moreover, the one-tailed version of the test is used, whereas the two-tailed test would seem more appropriate in view of the fact that the differences observed in this experiment sometimes favour one group and sometimes the other.

The writer of the present report was unable to trace the use of either the Kolmogorov-Smirnov test or Hald's procedure in any article published in the *British Journal of Educational Psychology*. These techniques are rarely used in research, e.g. in educational psychology, and need special justification.

Marsh (1966) contends that:

'the Kolmogorov-Smirnov test is primarily intended for use with small samples (i.e. samples of less than 50). At best, even then, it has only 95% of the power-efficiency of the standard error technique for small samples (the "t" test) and there is a tendency for this level of power-efficiency to decline as the sample size increases (Siegel (1956)); so that with sample sizes as great as the ones in the London i.t.a. study, the standard error technique gives a much more reliable result when both are applied in the proper way to the same data. However, in order to approach its maximum level of power-efficiency, the Kolmogorov-Smirnov test requires the data to be grouped over as many intervals as possible. In the reference that Downing gives for this test (Siegel (1956)), the author warns about this requirement when he is discussing an example with 8 categories for only 11 cases. Downing uses from 5 to 10 categories on different occasions for an aggregate of nearly 1,000 cases. While the use of such a large number of cases would offset to some extent the need for an almost one-to-one ratio of categories to cases for examples such as Siegel presents, it in no way compensates for a reduction in this ratio by between 100 and 150 to 1.

Downing would have achieved much more accurate results had he grouped his data at every unit in his various measurement scales instead of grouping over several of them. For these two reasons, the tendency of the power-efficiency of the test to decline with an increase in the sample size, and the insensitivity of the test through the grossness with which the data is grouped, we may disregard the results of applying the Kolmogorov-Smirnov test to the data in this report.'

However, Siegel (1956) merely states that as the sample size increases the power-efficiency would tend to decrease *slightly*. And Downing (1967) takes the view that the significance of a difference is likely to be underestimated if the number of categories (into which test scores are grouped) is small, so that it imposes a more stringent criterion.

Several more general objections can be raised to the use of non-parametric statistics, such as the Kolmogorov-Smirnov test, despite the fact that they make fewer statistical assumptions about the nature of the distributions. Although non-parametric statistics can be used with advantage in restricted circumstances, they are in general less satisfactory than orthodox tests of statistical significance which have the considerable advantage of being based on the two major statistical properties of any set of observations, namely (i) central tendency (mean) and (ii) dispersion (variance); i.e. (i) the general level of a set of measurements, and (ii) the amount of variation around that level. These two measures take into account the observed values instead of the cruder measures such as ranks, medians, runs, signs and ties used in non-parametric methods. Educational research would become chaotic if individual investigators started using special statistical methods for every particular purpose. There is no justification (in the opinion of the writer) for the belief that we should apply crude statistical techniques simply because our data are fallible. We do not use a blunt carving knife because the joint is tough. The final test of the value of the analytic methods used is their practical not their theoretical appropriateness; it is the cogency and the consistency of the results obtained and their fecundity in suggesting further hypotheses that ultimately justify our procedures. No doubt we sometimes violate basic theoretical assumptions, but most of the standard techniques are robust enough to survive (Lewis (1967), Boneau (1960)). The non-parametric cure is worse than the parametric disease.

Lastly, even if non-parametric methods were justifiable it would be advisable to use orthodox methods on transformed scores *as well*, if only for the purpose of checking the findings and drawing comparisons with other studies in the field.

It is also highly important to present standard deviations (which are not always given when non-parametric techniques are used) in order to gain some insight into the non-statistical significance of the observed differences, since the fact that differences are significant in the statistical sense does not necessarily mean that they are important, i.e. significant, in the practical sense (or that they are large). There is little doubt, for example, that a significant difference would be found, perhaps of a few hundredths of an inch, between the mean heights of the inhabitants of North and South London, the significance arising not from a large difference in inches, but from the fact that the samples are so large. Significance simply means that we have confidence in the results, i.e. we can feel sure that some difference, *however small*, exists between the two populations. Confidence is a more meaningful term than significance in this context. The establishment of statistical significance merely permits us to proceed to the next stage, and ask ourselves whether differences are large or small in terms of standard deviations. From the statistical point of view the most striking feature of research into i.t.a. is the failure to apply analysis of variance more extensively. As Burt (1946) has pointed out:

'An analysis of variance has at least five advantages, compared with the ordinary comparison between means. (i) It is more economical; with a separate research (instead of an analysis of variance research) for each of four factors, we should require four times the number of cases. (ii) It is more precise; with a planned and randomised arrangement we at once refine and reduce our estimates of error. (iii) It is more comprehensive; by allowing subsidiary factors to vary, we increase the breadth of our induction. (iv) The conditions are more natural; and experimental control or elimination of subsidiary variables would introduce artificial restrictions. (v) By allowing several factors to vary concurrently, we can study the *mutual interaction* of factors, for their joint effect may be quite different from the sum of their effects in isolation.'

Certainly the method has some limitations, such as that (i) the experimenter assumes he knows the important factors to compare, (ii) all variables (except the crucial variable) are made orthogonal (uncorrelated) to one other in the experiment, whatever they may be in nature, (iii) it does not assess the degree of association, but only the probability of association, (iv) few variables can be studied in one inquiry: six is too many, whereas in other methods, such as factor analysis, a hundred variables may be included.

In some of the larger experiments into i.t.a. such as those by Downing (1967), Downing and Jones (1966), Hahn (1965), Harrison (1964), Mazurkiewicz (1965), Milne (1966), Robinson (1966), Shapiro (1966), Stewart (1966), Tanyzer and Alpert (1965) and Tanyzer, Alpert and Sandel (1965) in which the number of subjects is several hundreds or more, analysis of variance including at least sex, socio-economic status, and intelligence, could easily be set up, and other variables could be studied either in conjunction with or separately from them, such as size of school, size of class, urban-rural area, home influence and teacher characteristics. Several of the researches did, in fact, use analysis of variance in limited degree.

(b) *What statistical matching techniques were used?* (F2)

Most investigations used orthodox statistical tests of the efficiency of matching methods, i.e. whether there was a significant difference between matched groups in respect of the variable they were matched on. Bosma (1965) and Mazurkiewicz (1966) used 't' scores or 'z' scores and Tanyzer and Alpert (1965) the more approximate critical ratio. Fry (1966) used Wilcoxon's two-sample techniques for frequencies, times, etc. and otherwise chi-square. Shapiro (1966) merely reports that the mean scores were 'close'. Fry (1966) applied no matching techniques, although the pre-experimental reading-readiness scores for his three groups differed considerably, standing at the 45th, 35th and 33rd percentiles respectively. McCracken (1966) used the Wilcoxon two-sample test, and analysis of variance, and Downing (1967) chiefly the Kolmogorov-Smirnov one-tailed test and chi-square.

A fundamental objection can be raised to using tests of statistical significance in interpreting the similarity of matched groups, namely that they claim that *the means for the matched groups are the same unless they are significantly different*. This places the burden of proof the wrong way round and capitalises on the heavy odds conventionally laid down in the interests of scientific caution against investigators who are trying to establish the separateness of mean scores. Thus, the means for two matched groups are said to be the same unless the odds against the hypothesis reach 19 to 1. Odds of 18 to 1 that they are *different*, i.e. not the same, are taken to prove that they are the *same*. The group-matcher can scarcely lose on this, particularly if he takes care to keep the sample as small as possible. It is contrary to normal scientific usage for a hypothesis to be easy rather than difficult to prove, and for small samples to yield more conclusive results than large ones.

(*c*) *What variables other than the media were included in the main statistical results?* (F3)

The results presented in most reports are confined to the comparison of groups working in i.t.a. or t.o. However, the interaction of these two alphabets with other factors, such as socio-economic level (Hahn (1966), Robinson (1966)); sex (Hahn (1965), Shapiro (1966), Tanyzer and Alpert (1965), Swales (1966)); and I.Q. (Tanyzer and Alpert (1965), Swales (1966)), are sometimes discussed.

A considerable tightening up of these investigations would follow from the use of analysis of variance taking into account age, sex, socio-economic level, I.Q. and school and teacher differences as well as reading media. The interaction terms in such an analysis give valuable indications of the relative effectiveness of the two media with different types of children, in different sorts of environment, without–it is important to note–increasing the number of children or groups it is necessary to test. In fact, a sample of 200 children classified according to the requirements of analysis of variance might very well give more valuable results than a haphazard sample of 1,000.

CHAPTER 20

Conclusions drawn from the Research Evidence

I The validity of the findings

THE general conclusion drawn from these various researches is that i.t.a. is a superior medium to t.o. in teaching young children to read, and that this advantage may be lost after the transition. Is it possible that the differences are illusory and depend on less obvious but more powerful extraneous factors? The answer appears to be that, although the findings have to be qualified in many important respects, there is no reason to believe that they are misleading so far as the relative effectiveness of the two media are concerned.

The pupils were adequately matched for personal characteristics and background. The superiority of i.t.a. does not seem due to any imbalance between the two reading groups in this respect. Nor is there any evidence that it is due to the influence of the home. The matching of teachers and schools was less satisfactory than the matching of pupils. Nevertheless, in the most thoroughly designed, and hence the most convincing, experiments it was almost perfect, since each teacher taught in each medium.

The teachers participating in the experiment had for the most part good academic qualifications and experience. Any future expansion in the use of i.t.a. will probably lead to its use by a wider and more representative set of teachers, and possibly to somewhat different results as regards efficiency. However, the fact that most of the participating teachers were volunteers does not necessarily detract from the educational significance of the results. It is doubtful whether non-volunteers would throw as much light on the efficiency of the new alphabet as volunteers would. It is the non-volunteers, not the volunteers, who are likely to be atypical of the future.

There is only a small amount of contradictory and rather obscure evidence concerning the Hawthorne effect, which seems to have had little influence in the t.o. classes, but may account for nearly half of the initial superiority shown by the i.t.a. classes. The teaching procedures (including the amount of time spent on reading activities) do not appear to have favoured i.t.a. However, a proportion of the variance attributed to differences between media must be due to these factors, as they have not always been kept under rigorous control.

Nor is there any evidence that the use of different materials and methods in the two groups has usually been in favour of either i.t.a. or t.o., but criticism raised by Stott (1966) and Diack (1967) point to the need to use books and materials that are representative of the full range used by teachers. There is also a strong need for improved tests of reading attainment in young children.

The amount of overlap between pupils in i.t.a. and t.o. groups is considerable. After the transition a fair proportion of the above-average pupils came from the t.o. groups.

The results also suggest that even before the transition, the superiority of i.t.a.

275

cannot be generalised to all schools, although it can be extended to most of them. On the other hand, the practice of testing all children in t.o., including those who have never read in that medium, must underestimate the superiority of i.t.a., at least in the early stages, when very few children had made the transition. i.t.a. is not a universal panacea such that every child taught in this medium will learn more rapidly than every child taught in t.o. The exceptions may be partly due to the influence of intelligence, as there is some evidence that i.t.a. is less effective with the dull child. Nor is there any indication that i.t.a. will prove superior to t.o. in every school in the country; differences in the efficiency and attitudes of the teachers and the lesson procedures and materials they adopt may be the deciding factors.

In summary, the research evidence obtained in the United States strongly suggests that i.t.a. reading programmes (i.e. the use of i.t.a. together with its associated materials and methods) are more efficient than t.o. programmes, even after the transition. However, the experimental design of these American investigations is usually such that it is logically impossible to be certain that the superiority of the i.t.a. group is due to the alphabet itself and not to the reading materials. This criticism cannot be made of most researches into i.t.a. carried out in Britain, since the same materials were usually used in both groups. In these investigations, the indications are that i.t.a. is the superior medium in learning to read, but that after transition to t.o. this advantage is lost. Since the purpose of this section of the report is to examine the relative advantages of the i.t.a. and t.o. *alphabets*, not *reading programmes*, the evidence from Britain, particularly the researches of Downing and Jones (1966) and Milne (1966) become paramount. Certain criticisms can be made of these two investigations; Milne (1966) used different teachers to take the two groups, and in Downing and Jones's (1966) investigation the samples in the later stages were relatively small (400 pupils) and the methods of testing statistical significance were unorthodox, but none of these limitations is sufficiently severe to invalidate the results. *In evaluating almost any field of educational research* the problem arises whether, for practical purposes, the results obtained in a large number of fallible investigations can *in toto* be regarded as having established certain findings, particularly if the results are almost invariably in the same direction. In the researches summarised in the present report only Swales (1966) finds that i.t.a. does not have the overall advantage. If there were no real trend running through all the researches we would expect the results to be less one-sided, sometimes favouring i.t.a. and sometimes t.o. On this ground our final recommendation is in favour of the use of i.t.a. (albeit with many qualifications). The chief doubt is whether the consistent superiority of i.t.a. is due to the Hawthorne effect and other environmental influences. Here again there is no completely convincing evidence, but the figures in Oldham, where the full school population has demonstrably used i.t.a. long enough for the effect of novelty to wear off, are still markedly in favour of i.t.a. The main limitations are that the superiority of i.t.a. cannot be generalised to all pupils and schools, and that it may not survive the transition to t.o., however long delayed.

The evidence suggests that, for most children in most schools, the use of i.t.a. as an *initial* teaching alphabet would considerably raise the children's standard of reading and their rate of scholastic progress, although it seems likely that this advantage will be lost after the transition.

Although this section of the report is not concerned with the broad educational implications of the results, it must be emphasised that the general findings do not necessarily imply that i.t.a. has failed. The educational and intellectual advantages of a child learning to read fluently at a very early age are very considerable and may affect his whole confidence and future progress. The interpretations placed on the findings will vary from one person to another according to the views they hold on the importance of reading in the infant and primary school.

Postscript

A recent (November 1967) report by Cartwright and Jones (briefly referred to in an earlier section of this book) gives some results for the research of Downing and Jones (1966) at the end of the third year, when about 80% of the children had made the transition. The findings indicate a continuation of the trends established earlier.

'(i) When the experimental group was being tested with transliterated versions of the tests, its performance was, on the whole, superior to that of the control group.

(ii) As soon as the testing of both groups in t.o. began, the experimental group lost its superiority, and did not regain the lead. Indeed, although the difference between the groups reached statistical significance only in the N.S.45 test, the general trend favours the control group. Of the eight measures of reading ability, seven of the z-scores are in this direction.

Within individual schools one out of the five significant differences which met the experimental criteria were in favour of t.o.

However, even at the time of the latest test, approximately 20% of the experimental children had not transferred to t.o. reading, and so a final assessment cannot be made.'

Thus a decision is still to be made. But the findings in other researches suggest that the transfer of the last 20% is not likely to make much change in the overall trend.

II   The need for further research

There are several reasons why research into the use of i.t.a. in schools is highly desirable.

(i) Pitman has put forward a strong case for the probability that children will find it easier to read in i.t.a. than in t.o. His arguments are based on the inherent simplicity of his alphabet (in which each symbol represents a single sound and each sound is represented by a single symbol) and on the economy of the demands it makes on the reader.

(ii) The experimental results so far obtained suggest very strongly that i.t.a. is, in fact, a more efficient medium for teaching reading to beginners than traditional orthography. The magnitude of the differences found in its favour in many different researches is unusually high. And although results are not invariably in favour of i.t.a. they are rarely in the opposite direction. As yet we lack conclusive evidence, but there is a strong presumption that, even under rigorous control, the results so far obtained for reading before the transition are unlikely to be reversed.

(iii) i.t.a. has been extremely well received by practising teachers, to a degree which suggests that avant-garde enthusiasm and the novelty of the medium are not the sole explanation of its success.

(iv) It is also clear that there are considerable educational advantages in learning to read quickly, since early acquaintance with books should lead to an invaluable enrichment of experience at an early age and to a more rapid and comprehensive development of interest and appreciation during the most formative and impressionable period of a child's life.

(v) i.t.a. is already a thriving business. Some of its promoters will set up their own investigation willy-nilly. It is therefore highly desirable that research work of good standard should be carried out.

We should have a great deal more insight into needs for research if the data of the Downing and Jones (1966) experiment, which was the most closely-controlled and hence the most important that we have in Britain, were analysed by the method of analysis of variance. The influence and interaction of important factors, such as intelligence, sex, socio-economic status, teaching procedures and school attitudes to reading could then be systematically examined. Tests of statistical significance could be applied to the data and the standard errors of the observed differences scrutinised in order to gain some insight into their magnitude and significance in educational terms. Although this research suffers from certain limitations, it is difficult to see how it could have been much more closely controlled without destroying the educational reality of the situation and it would be extremely difficult to launch another investigation of this scope in Britain.

Burt (1967) makes a similar point saying:

> 'It is now just six years since the first large batches of children started their reading with the new medium. Would it not be possible, before the Research Unit is finally disbanded, to obtain results with pairs of well-matched samples drawn from these original experimental groups and their controls, in order to see what differences, if any, are now discernible?'

With regard to further researches that might be carried out we would suggest that:

(i) The main need is to study the effect of transition in more detail by using objective tests instead of teachers' estimates to determine the best time for the transfer. This might prove to be after a longer period of time than was previously envisaged, e.g. after five years rather than three.

(ii) An investigation into the best age for beginning to read in the two alphabets might be included.

(iii) Certain anomalies remain in i.t.a. and it is by no means certain that the most efficient new alphabet would bear any close resemblance to i.t.a. The construction of such an alphabet based on extensive research and intended for use in schools is scarcely practicable in the next few years, but some improvements could no doubt be made in i.t.a. It would be difficult, however, to satisfy simultaneously the two opposing criteria put forward by Pitman, viz. (i) that a new alphabet should simplify grapheme-phoneme relations, but (ii) should not differ too markedly from traditional orthography. This research could include an examination of several media such as Wijk's Regularized Inglish and other coding systems such as *Words in Colour* in order to study the general effect of using coded instead of orthodox systems.

(iv) Researches should be set up into the effects (if any) of i.t.a. on (*a*) school subjects other than English, and (*b*) reading habits outside school.

(v) Psychological studies should be carried out in which the precise behaviour of individual children learning to read is recorded, leading to interpretations in (*a*) psychological terms, e.g. perceptual sets, and (*b*) educational terms, e.g. transfer of training, knowledge of results.

(vi) The influence of the type of imagery used by the child, visual, audile or motile, as suggested by Burt (1967) could also be investigated.

(vii) There is an urgent need for the construction of suitable tests of reading for children aged 5 to 11.

III Final comment

It is clear that in Britain, we are mainly indebted to the work of Downing. All in all, the writer of this section of the report agrees warmly with Holmes (1967):

> 'It would be a relatively simple matter to set an ideal but unrealistically high *post hoc* standard for the experiment, and from such a position just as unrealistically proceed to cut the study to ribbons. However, this reviewer prefers to temper the tone of his critical remarks by his considered judgement of the difficulties Downing faced.'

Even from the depths of an armchair it has been an arduous and hazardous task to write the present brief evaluation. But it is comforting to agree with the Director of the University of London Institute of Education (Elvin (1967)), that if educational research confines itself to what is safe, it will fail in its duty to the country at the present time.

FINAL CONCLUSIONS

CHAPTER 21

Conclusions drawn from the Total Evidence

I Three kinds of evidence

IT is important to note that although the three main sections of this research project (Parts One, Two and Three) were planned to form a comprehensive evaluation, yet each part was carried out relatively independently of the other two parts, and on quite different lines. Moreover, the conclusions drawn from each section were not compared until the final stages of preparing the written report. In these circumstances it is particularly interesting to observe that the conclusions obtained from the three different kinds of evidence lead broadly in the same direction–that is towards a favourable impression of i.t.a. as a means of beginning reading with infants.

In Part One–'A brief enquiry into the extent of the use of i.t.a. in England and Wales', the collection of factual evidence from local education authorities indicated that, by 1966, 9% of all schools in England and Wales containing infant pupils were to some extent experimenting with i.t.a. Verbal evidence given during the evaluation suggested that this quite rapid spread in the use of i.t.a. had occurred, not as a result of pressure by local education authority officials, but rather in response to personal recommendations by teachers in schools using i.t.a. to their colleagues in t.o. schools.

In Part Two–'i.t.a. in practice: evidence from interviews', the views of teachers, parents and educationists closely connected with practical aspects of infants using i.t.a. were found to be mainly favourable and quite often extremely favourable.

In Part Three–'i.t.a. in practice: evidence from research', the balance of evidence favoured i.t.a. as an *initial* teaching alphabet.

The evidence from research and the verbal evidence are clearly complementary. The criteria of reading achievements, in so far as they are merely scores on attainment tests or records of books read, provide both interesting and useful information, but tell us little of the actual process of learning to read. The reactions of teachers and others, who have had first-hand experience of i.t.a., augmented by observations of children using this new medium filled in the framework of test results.

Thus, the report as a whole, comprising three kinds of evidence, collected and evaluated by means of different techniques, and by two people whose backgrounds, interests and beliefs are by no means identical, proved to be consistent and to lead to common conclusions.

II Unequivocal conclusions

1 *Reading progress*
Both the verbal evidence and the research evidence indicate that in the majority of schools, although not in all, infants using i.t.a. have learned to read earlier, more

easily and at a faster rate than similar children using t.o. Both kinds of evidence also indicate that after about three years of schooling, the reading attainments of most children taught initially by t.o. are approximately equal to those of children whose initial medium of instruction was i.t.a.

2 The complexity of any reading situation

Visits to schools, discussions with teachers and other educationists, consideration of numerous publications relating to i.t.a. and to other means of learning t.o., as well as detailed evaluation of 17 researches concerned with i.t.a., all emphasise the multitude of factors which affect children's reading progress and the difficulty, if not impossibility, of separating them.

3 The need for further research

Both verbal evidence and research evidence point to the need for further research into the early stages of learning to read. It should include fundamental research into how children learn to read and the production of more useful assessments of early reading ability, as well as investigations into the value of different media, materials, methods and teaching procedures.

In particular, the most urgent need, from the viewpoint of the practising teacher, is the setting up of a large-scale experiment in which a number of different approaches to beginning reading are compared. These approaches should include different ways of working with t.o., as well as the use of a variety of simplified spelling systems and signalling systems, including colour codes and systems of diacritical marks. In this experiment, many more of the classroom variables should be controlled than has usually been done in former experiments. The results of such an experiment would prove of real practical value to teachers, by providing them with reliable information about the effects of using many of the current approaches to reading.

III Divergent conclusions

1 The transition in reading

The verbal evidence, especially from teachers experienced in helping children to transfer from i.t.a. to t.o., almost invariably indicated that children found no difficulty in transferring from one medium to the other, as far as reading was concerned. On the other hand, evidence from research was not so uniform; some, but not all, researches noted a setback in reading attainment immediately after the transition.

2 i.t.a. related to children's intelligence

There was a certain divergence between the conclusions drawn from the verbal evidence and the research evidence concerning the relative performances of children of high, average and low intelligence. The verbal evidence suggested that i.t.a. had proved beneficial to children of all levels of intelligence. The research evidence suggested that i.t.a. was more effective for bright than for dull children.

3 Factors affecting reading progress

Although the authors of this report agree on the multiplicity of the variables affecting reading progress, their separate evaluations of the two sorts of evidence, in Parts Two and Three, sometimes led them to form different conclusions regarding the relative importance of the various factors, as noted in these two parts of the report.

IV The final word

It would be unfortunate if the mainly favourable tone of this report was taken to imply that the use of i.t.a. for beginning reading with infants was the final and only solution. The experiments of the past six years have demonstrated that in many cases the usual ways in which children have been taught to read can be improved. We should continue to investigate how children learn to read and the most effective media, methods, materials and procedures for helping them.

REFERENCES

AND

APPENDICES

References

ASHLEY, E. (1932). *The John and Mary Readers*. Huddersfield: Schofield & Sims Ltd

ASHLEY, E. (1938). *The Mac and Tosh Readers*. Huddersfield: Schofield & Sims Ltd

BONEAU, C. A. (1960). The effects of violations of assumptions underlying the 't' test. *Psych. Bull.*, 575, 49-64

BOSMA, R. L. (1965). Teaching reading with i.t.a. *Reading Horizon*, 6, 6-19

BOYCE, E. R. (1959). *The Gay Way Series*. London: Macmillan & Co. Ltd

BURT, C. L. (1946). Teaching backward readers. *Brit. J. Educ. Psychol.*, 16, 116-132

BURT, C. L. (1967a). Evaluations 2. In: DOWNING, J. A. (ed.), *The i.t.a. symposium*. London: National Foundation for Educational Research in England and Wales

BURT, C. L. (1967b). The initial teaching alphabet. *Association of Educational Psychologists News Letter*, 9, 2-6

CARTWRIGHT, D. and JONES, B. (1967). Further evidence relative to assessment of i.t.a. *Educ. Res.*, 8, 65-71

CHALL, J. S. (1967). Approaches to beginning reading: what is new in America? In: JENKINSON, M. D. (ed.), *Reading Instruction: An International Forum*. Newark, Delaware, U.S.A.: International Reading Association

COOK, D. L. (1962). The Hawthorne effect in educational research. *Phi Delta Kappan*, 116-122

DANIELS, J. C. and DIACK, H. (1957). *The Royal Road Readers*. London: Chatto & Windus

DAVENPORT, P. (1953). *Pilot Reading Scheme*. Leeds: E. J. Arnold & Son Ltd

DELL, G. A. (1967). *The i.t.a. Approach to Reading*. Glasgow: The Corporation of Glasgow Education Department

DIACK, H. (1967). Evaluations 3. In: DOWNING, J. A. (ed.), *The i.t.a. Symposium*. London: National Foundation for Educational Research in England and Wales

DOWNING, J. A. (1962). *To Be Or Not To Be*. London: Cassell

DOWNING, J. A. (1963). *The Downing Reading Scheme*. London: Initial Teaching Publishing Co

DOWNING, J. A. (1964a). *The Initial Teaching Alphabet*. London: Cassell

DOWNING, J. A. (1964b). *The i.t.a. Reading Experiment*. University of London Institute of Education, Studies in Education

DOWNING, J. A. (1967). Research report on the British experiment with i.t.a. In: *The i.t.a. Symposium*, Chap. I. London: National Foundation for Educational Research in England and Wales

DOWNING, J. A. and JONES, B. (1966). Some problems of evaluating i.t.a.: a second experiment. *Educ. Res.* 8, No. 2, 100-14

ELKONIN, D. B. (1963). The psychology of mastering the elements of reading. In: SIMON, B. &. J. (eds.), *Educational Psychology in the U.S.S.R.* London: Routledge and Kegan Paul

FREIS, C. C., WILSON, R. G. and RUDOLPH, M. K. (1966). *Merrill Linguistic Readers*. Columbus, Ohio: Charles E. Merrill Books Inc.

FRY, E. (1964). A diacritical marking system to aid beginning reading instruction. *Elementary English*, May 1964

FRY, E. (1966). Comparison of three methods of reading instruction. Results at the end of second grade. Office of Education Co-operative Research Project No. 3050. New Brunswick, New Jersey: Rutgers University

GATTEGNO, C. (1962). *Words In Colour*. Reading: Educational Explorers

GRASSAM, E. H. (1922, revised 1957). *The Beacon Readers*. London: Ginn

GRAY, W. S. (1956). The teaching of reading and writing—an international survey. *UNESCO Monographs on Fundamental Education*, X, London: Evans Bros

GRAY, W. S., MONROE, M., ARTLEY, A. S. and ARBUTHNOT, M. H. (1956). *The Happy Trio Reading Scheme*. Exeter: Wheaton

GULLIFORD, R. Evaluations 4. In: DOWNING, J. A. (ed.), *The i.t.a. Symposium*. London: National Foundation for Educational Research in England and Wales

HAHN, H. T. (1965). Relative effectiveness of three methods of teaching reading in grade one. Lansing, Michigan: Michigan Department of Public Instruction, Office of Education, Co-operative Research Project No. 2687

HARRISON, M. (1964). *Instant Reading*. London: Pitman and Sons Ltd

HAYES, R. B. and NEMETH, J. S. (1965). Factors affecting learning to read. Harrisburg, Pennsylvania: Department of Public Instruction, Office of Education, Co-operative Research Project No. 2697

HAYES, R. B. and NEMETH, J. S. (1966). The New Castle beginning to read study–a preliminary report. In: MAZURKIEWICZ, A. J. (ed.), *i.t.a. and the World of English*. Hempstead, New York: i.t.a. Foundation

HAYES, R. B. (1966). i.t.a. and three other approaches to reading first grade. *The Reading Teacher*, **19**, 8, 627–631

HEMMING, J. (1967). Evaluations 5. In: DOWNING, J. A. (ed.), *The i.t.a. Symposium*. London: The National Foundation for Educational Research in England and Wales

HOLMES, J. A. (1967). Evaluations 6. In: DOWNING, J. A. (ed.), *The i.t.a. Symposium*. London: The National Foundation for Educational Research in England and Wales

JOHN, Sister (1964). Private communication. In: DOWNING, J. A. (ed.), *The i.t.a. Reading Experiment*. London: Evans Bros

JONES, J. K. (1967). *Colour Story Reading*. London: Thomas Nelson & Sons Ltd

KEIR, G. (1967). (review). The i.t.a. symposium. *Brit. J. Educ. Psychol.*, **37**, 408–413

KETTLES, P. and MACDONALD, R. A. D. (1949, revised 1963). *Vanguard Readers*. Edinburgh: Holmes McDougall

LEWIS, D. G. (1967). A critical examination of the design of the first i.t.a. research. *Educ. Res.* (to be published).

MARSH, R. W. (1966). Some cautionary notes on the results of the London i.t.a. experiment. *Reading Research Quart.* 119–126

MAZURKIEWICZ, A. J. (1965). First grade reading using modified co-basal versus the initial teaching alphabet. Bethlehem, Pa.: Lehigh University Office of Education Co-operative Research Project No. 2676

MAZURKIEWICZ, A. J. (1966a). A comparison of i.t.a. and t.o. reading achievement when methodology is controlled. In: MAZURKIEWICZ, A. J. (ed.), *i.t.a. and the World of English*. Hempstead, New York: i.t.a. Foundation

MAZURKIEWICZ, A. J. (1966b). i.t.a. and t.o. reading when methodology is controlled. *The Reading Teacher*, **19**, 8, 606–611

MAZURKIEWICZ, A. J. (1967). The initial teaching alphabet in reading instruction. Comprehensive Final Report. Lehigh University and the Bethlehem Area Schools

MCCRACKEN, R. A. (1966). A two year longitudinal study to determine the ability of first grade children to learn to read using the *Early-to-Read* i.t.a. program. (An interim report of the first year). In: MAZURKIEWICZ, A. J. (ed.), *i.t.a. and the World of English*. Hempstead, New York: i.t.a. Foundation

MCKEE, P., HARRISON, M. L., MCCOWEN, A. and LEHR, E. (1956). *The McKee Readers*. London: Nelson

MILNE, A. (1966). The Scottish i.t.a. research. Paper read at the Third International i.t.a. Conference, Cambridge University

MORGAN, A. H. and PROCTER, M. (1967). Evaluations 8. In: DOWNING, J. A. (ed.), *The i.t.a. Symposium*. London: National Foundation for Educational Research in England and Wales

MORRIS, J. M. (1959). *Reading in the Primary School*. London: Newnes

MURRAY, W. (1964). *Key Words Reading Scheme*. Loughborough: Wills & Hepworth

NEALE, M. D. (1967). Evaluations 9. In: DOWNING, J. A. (ed.), *The i.t.a. Symposium*. London: National Foundation for Educational Research in England and Wales

NICHOLSON, C. (1965). i.t.a. *The Guardian*, **23**, 2, p.8

O'DONNELL, M. and MUNRO, R. (1951). *Janet and John*. Edinburgh: Oliver & Boyd

PITMAN, J. (1959). *The Ehrhardt Augmented* (40-*sound* 42-*character*) *Lower-Case Roman Alphabet.* (The reasons & intentions underlying its design together with a specimen.) London: Pitman

PITMAN, J. (1961). Learning to read: an experiment. *Journal of the Royal Society of Arts*, Feb. 1961 and reprinted London: Pitman (Fourth printing Oct. 1965)

PITMAN, J. (1967). A note on the i.t.a. symposium. Privately circulated document

REID, J. D. (1967). Evaluations 10. In: DOWNING, J. A. (ed.), *The i.t.a. Symposium.* London: National Foundation for Educational Research in England and Wales

ROBINSON, H. M. (1966). Effectiveness of i.t.a. as a medium for reading instruction. In: MAZURKIEWICZ, A. J. (ed.), *i.t.a. and the World of English.* Hempstead, New York: i.t.a. Foundation

SCEATS, J. (1967). *i.t.a. and the Teaching of Literacy.* London: Bodley Head

SCHONELL, F. J. (1958). *The Happy Venture Readers.* Edinburgh: Oliver & Boyd

SIEGEL, S. S. (1956). *Non parametric Statistics for the Behavioural Sciences.* London: Evans Bros

SHAPIRO, B. J. (1966). A comparison of the reading achievement of i.t.a. and t.o. groups in first grade. Cleveland, Ohio: Educational Research Council of Greater Cleveland

SOUTHGATE, V. (1963). Augmented Roman Alphabet experiment: an outsider's report. *Educ. Rev.*, 16, 1, 32–47

SOUTHGATE, V. (1965). Approaching i.t.a. results with caution. *Educ. Res.*, 7, 83–96

STEWART, M. R. (1966). Two years with i.t.a.–an interim report on the Bethlehem-Lehigh research project. In: MAZURKIEWICZ, A. J. (ed.), *i.t.a. and the World of English.* Hempstead, New York: i.t.a. Foundation

STOTT, D. H. (1962). *Programmed Reading Kit.* Glasgow: Holmes

STOTT, D. H. (1965). Anti-i.t.a. *The Teacher*, January 22

SWALES, T. D. (1966). The attainment in reading and spelling of children who learned to read through the initial teaching alphabet. M.Ed. Thesis, Department of Education, University of Manchester

TANYZER, H. J. and ALPERT, H. (1965). Effectiveness of three different basal reading systems on first grade reading achievement. Hempstead, New York: Hofstra University Co-operative Research Project No. 2720

TANYZER, H. J. and ALPERT, H. (1966). Effectiveness of three different basal reading systems on first grade reading achievement. In: MAZURKIEWICZ, A. J. (ed.), *i.t.a. and the World of English.* Hempstead, New York: i.t.a. Foundation

TANYZER, H. J. and ALPERT, H. (1967). Three different basal reading systems and first grade reading achievement. *The Reading Teacher*, 19, 8, 636–643

TANYZER, H. J., ALPERT, H. and SANDEL, L. (1965). Beginning reading: effectiveness of different media. Mineola, New York: Nassau School Development Council

TENSUAN, E. and DAVIS, F. S. (1963). The phonic method v. the combination method in teaching beginning reading. Paper presented at the Conference on Perceptual and Linguistic Aspects of the Reading Process. Stanford, California: Center for Advanced Study in Behavioral Studies

THE SCHOOLS COUNCIL. (1965). *Change and Response.* London: Her Majesty's Stationery Office

VERNON, M. D. (1967). Evaluations 11. In: DOWNING, J. A. (ed.), *The i.t.a. Symposium.* London: National Foundation for Educational Research in England and Wales

WIJK, A. (1959). *Regularized Inglish.* Stockholm: Almqvist & Wiksell

WILLIAMS, P. (1965). Initial teaching alphabet. *The Winnower*, 1. University of Wisconsin

Appendix A: Terminology

The following terms, referring to the early stages of learning to read, are used throughout this report according to the definitions and descriptions given.

1 Medium

The word *medium* is taken to mean the form of written and printed symbols which represents the spoken language. Examples of certain *media* which might be employed for early reading instruction are given in Appendix B. Media which are currently being used and discussed may be conveniently divided into three broad categories, although in certain cases there is some overlap.

(*a*) *t.o.*

't.o.' is the accepted abbreviation for 'traditional orthography' which refers to the usage of our 26-letter alphabet, employed according to the accepted rules of the English spelling system.

(*b*) *Signalling systems*

'Signalling system' is the term employed in this report for any written or printed code which, while employing the 26-letter alphabet and the traditional spelling rules of 't.o.', superimposes certain signals on the written letters. The originators of such systems, while being willing to accept our alphabet and the irregularities of our spelling system as they stand, are attempting to simplify them in the initial stages for the beginning reader. The signals are intended only as temporary props, to be discarded as reading fluency is achieved. There are two main types of signals: one consists of the printing in different colours of some, or all, of the letters; while the other adds differentiating marks (usually called 'diacritical marks') to certain of the letters. The purpose of both the colours and the marks is to act as signals regarding the pronunciation of letters and digraphs in different circumstances. Gattegno's *Words in Colour* and Fry's *Diacritical Marking System* represent two examples of these contrasting types of signalling systems. A third system, Jones's *Colour Story Reading*, employs, as signals, both colours and shapes superimposed on certain letters.

(*c*) *Simplified spelling systems*

Media described as 'simplified spelling systems' can incorporate changes in, or additions to, the traditional alphabet or changes in the spelling rules or both. Examples of four different forms of simplified spelling systems, not all of which were designed for the specific purpose of teaching beginning reading, are as follows:

(i) A simplified spelling system can, while retaining the 26-letter alphabet and the regular rules of English spelling, attempt to abolish or reduce the irregularities. The Simplified Spelling Society's 'New Spelling' and Wijk's 'Regularized Inglish' are two examples of such a system.

(ii) A simplified spelling system can retain all or most of the letters of the traditional alphabet while augmenting them with additional characters, in order that one character represents solely one sound and vice-versa. In such circumstances, only one spelling rule is necessary, namely that there is a one-to-one relationship between spoken sound and symbol. The International Phonetic Alphabet, in so far as it is concerned with the written form of standard English, is an example of such a system, which employs a total of 38 characters, 22 of which are letters used in t.o.

(iii) A simplified spelling system can be a compromise between absolute regularity of sound-symbol relationship and the traditional spelling system. One example of such a system is Pitman's 'Initial Teaching Alphabet', usually abbreviated to 'i.t.a.'. i.t.a. retains 24 letters of the traditional alphabet and augments them with 20 new characters, so that the main spelling rule employed is a one-to-one relationship between sound and written symbol.

Yet, at the same time, with an eye to easing the transition, it retains certain examples of the same sound being represented by two written characters, as well as examples of one written symbol representing two sounds.

(iv) A simplified spelling system can employ an entirely new alphabet in which the sound-symbol relationship is absolutely invariable. The Shaw Alphabet is an example of such a system.

2 Materials

The medium chosen to represent the written form of the spoken language is utilised in the preparation of all kinds of materials designed to help the child to learn to read. The term 'reading materials' is used in this report to mean basic reading schemes with all their supporting supplementary books, apparatus, games, pictures and so on; other printed books and publications of all kinds; as well as handwritten cards, labels, lists, charts, stories and every other form of written letters or words.

3 Method

In the literature on the teaching of reading, and likewise in practice, the word 'method' has tended to be employed in a rather narrow sense, to represent two different ways of commencing reading instruction. On the one hand are what Gray (1956) describes as 'global methods', in which whole words or sentences are considered as the initial basic units. In the everyday phraseology of teachers and most educators, global methods are mostly referred to as 'look-and-say word method' or 'look-and-say sentence method', as the case might be. On the other hand, there are 'phonic methods', in which the initial emphasis is on the establishment of sound-symbol relationships within regular words.

In practice, the irregularity of English spelling has been partially responsible for leading the majority of teachers to employ both methods, in what is usually termed an 'eclectic approach' to reading. The main variations are generally represented by the selection of one of these methods for use in the initial stages, and the timing of the introduction of the other method in the reading programme. Accordingly, although the word 'method' has a wider connotation in everyday language, it is used throughout this report in the narrower, but accepted, sense to refer mainly to 'look-and-say methods', 'phonic methods' and a combination of both. In practice, the 'method' used for beginning reading tuition is usually closely linked with 'procedure' as described in the following definition.

4 Procedure

The word 'procedure' is being adopted throughout this report to include and extend what is meant in ordinary usage by the word 'method', that is 'method of procedure'. The term 'procedure' is being taken to include, among others, the following factors:

(a) The grouping of children for the purpose of learning to read – the range of which can extend from a whole class being considered as a homogeneous unit, through two or three large reading groups or eight or ten small groups, to the acceptance of each child as an individual learning unit;

(b) the varying roles of the teacher and the pupil, as exemplified in the ratio of teacher-instruction to pupil-participation in, and initiation of, the learning process;

(c) the formality or informality of the working relationships between teacher and pupil – which is closely related to points (a) and (b) above;

(d) the emphasis given to pre-reading activities;

(e) the timing of the introduction of the more formal beginnings of reading;

(f) the emphasis on other linguistic skills, such as speech and writing, in relation to learning to read;

(g) the rigidity or otherwise of the time spent on reading and literacy training, that is the extent to which it is confined to definite lesson periods or spread throughout the day;

(h) the use made of various reading materials, exemplified in a dependence on a basic reading scheme, the use of a variety of books and printed materials or an emphasis on words springing from the children and written by the teacher or pupils.

Appendix B: Examples of Different Media

Example B/1   t.o.

An extract from *Children and their Primary Schools*, (1967), a report of the Central Advisory Council for Education (England), (generally referred to as 'The Plowden Report'), Volume 1, paragraph 583. Her Majesty's Stationery Office.

Traditionally one of the first tasks of the infant school was to teach children to read. It is still, quite rightly, a major preoccupation, since reading is a key to much of the learning that will come later and to the possibility of independent study. In many infant schools, reading and writing are treated as extensions of spoken language. Those children who have not had the opportunity at home to grasp the part that they play are introduced to them by the everyday events and environment of the classroom. Messages to go home, letters to sick children, labels to ensure that materials and tools are returned to their proper place; all call for reading and writing. Many children first glimpse the pleasures of reading from listening to stories read to them at school . . . Books made by teachers and children about the doings of the class or of individuals in it figure prominently among the books which children enjoy. They help children to see meaning in reading and to appreciate the purpose of written records.

Traditionally one of the first tasks of the infant school was to teach children to read. It is still, quite rightly, a major preoccupation, since reading is a key to much of the learning that will come later and to the possibility of independent study. In many infant schools, reading and writing are treated as extensions of spoken language. Those children who have not had the opportunity at home to grasp the part that they play are introduced to them by the everyday events and environment of the classroom. Messages to go home, letters to sick children, labels to ensure that materials and tools are returned to their proper place; all call for reading and writing. Many children first glimpse the pleasures of reading from listening to stories read to them at school .... Books made by teachers and children about the doings of the class or of individuals in it figure prominently among

294

Example B/3   Gattegno's 'Words in Colour'

fan fun fist fit
if of fat uff fuss
send sent dad I
sad mad fed and
send mend sand
mud fund stand end
dust did that this
them then the
thin yes yet fifty

hate same late
male more fatal
home bone woke he
me we date egg
use unite fuse
girl first go got
get leg globe make
made nose any like
fire nine ninety

mat tim met tom
mum must mum s
miss mist mess
map am stamps
a mops pump sum
sam pam not nut
net ten men man
an sun in on
tent u on sent

her his has ha
him hot bat but
brick promise flat
simple impossible
suddenly horror worry
word work world
there burden back
black sorry brother
son from little

pat pit pet
pot at it u
tap tip top
pep pup pop tot
as us is
sat sit set
stop step toss
stops steps spat
sap sips test pest

pant wins thus rat
ran red fur strip
my sister wild mind
rest kid kit kill
neck milk skill silk
kiss pile mile
skip sick line fine
truck track struck
run rust strike

o o aa aaa
u u uu uuu
au ua uau aua
i i ii iii
e e ee eee
aei eua eaii
o o oo ooo
aaeeoo ieoii
oaa aoie oou

let lad sell tell
lots small smell slap
list slit doll dull
mill ill until till
lend lent land less
unless filthy funny
wet wit with
swim was will
sunset slept

18th story

All the ▲ friends go to ● Ink's party.

The ▲ party is in a ▲ tent.

Orange ● said,

"What was the ▲ green cloud like ● ?"

Up jumps the ▲ square green cloud.

All the ▲ friends saw it.

They did like ● the ▲ square green cloud.

29

Traditionally wun ov the first taasks ov the infant scoole woz to teach children to read. It iz still, quite rightly, a major preoccupation, since reading iz a kee to much ov the lerning that will cum later and to the possibility ov independent studdy. In meny infant scooles, reading and writing ar treated az extensions ov spoken language. Thoze children hoo hav not had the opportunity at home to graasp the part that they play ar introduced to them by the everyday events and environment ov the claasroome. Messages to go home, letters to sick children, labels to enshure that materials and tooles ar returnd to their proper place; aul caul for reading and writing. Meny children first glimpse the plezures ov reading from lissening to stories red to them at scoole .... Books made by teachers and children about the dooings ov the claas or ov individuals in it figur prominently amung the books which children enjoy. They help children to see meaning in reading and to appreciate the purpos ov written records.

* Professor Wijk has suggested that, if this particular form of simplified spelling system were used as an initial medium of reading instruction with English-speaking children, certain additional simplifications could be made.

trədiʃənəli wʌn əv ðə fəːst taːsks əv ði infənt skuːl
woz tu tiːtʃ tʃildrən tu riːd. it iz stil, kwait raitli, ə
meidʒe priokjupeiʃn, sins riːdiŋ iz ə kiː tu mʌtʃ əv
ðə ləːiniŋ ðət wil kʌm leitə ənd tu ðə posibiliti əv
indipendənt stʌdi. in meni infənt skuːlz, riːdiŋ ənd
raitiŋ aː triːtid əz ekstenʃnz əv spoukən laŋgwidʒ.
ðouz tʃildrən huː həv not had ði opoːtʃuːniti ət houm
tu graːsp ðe paːt ðət ðei plei aːr introudjuːst tu ðəm
bai ði evridei ivents ənd envaiərənmənt əv ðə
klaːsruːm. mesidʒiz tu gou houm, letəz tu sik tʃildrən,
leiblz tu enʃuə ðət mətiəriəlz ənd tuːlz aː ritəːnd tə
ðeə propə pleis; oːl koːl fə riːdiŋ ənd raitiŋ. meni
tʃildrən fəːst glimps ðə pleʒə əv riːdiŋ frəm lisniŋ tu
stoːriz red tu ðəm ət skuːl. . . . buks meid bai tiːtʃəz
ənd tʃildrən əbaut ðə duːiŋz əv ðə klaːs oːr əv
individjuəlz in it figə prominentli əmʌŋ ðə buks witʃ
tʃildrən endʒoi. ðei help tʃildrən tə siː ðə miːniŋ in
riːdiŋ ənd tu əpriːʃieit ðə pəːpəs əv ritən rekoːdz.

* This example employs Daniel Jones's Simplified Transcription. There are ways in which it could be
simplified if it were used as a medium for initial reading instruction with English-speaking children.

tradiſhonally wun ov ſhe first tasks ov ſhe infant scꙍl woꭗ tꙍ teeʧh ʧhildren tꙍ reed. it iꭗ still, kwiet rietly, a mæjor pre-occuepæſhon, sins reediŋ iꭗ a kee tꙍ muʧh ov ſhe lerniŋ ſhat will cum læter and tꙍ ſhe possibility ov independent study. in meny infant scꙍlꭗ, reediŋ and rietiŋ ar treeted aꭗ ekstenſhonꭗ ov spꙍken laŋgwæj. ſhꙍꭗ ʧhildren hꙍ hav not had ſhe opportuenity at ·hꙍem tꙍ grasp ſhe part ſhat ſhæ plæ ar introduest tꙍ ſhem bie ſhe everydæ events and envieronment ov ſhe classrꙍm. messæjeꭗ tꙍ gꙍ hꙍem, lettersꭗ tꙍ sick ʧhildren, læbelꭗ tꙍ enſhuer ſhat mateerialꭗ and tꙍlꭗ ar returnd tꙍ ſhær proper plæꭗ; aull caull for reediŋ and rietiŋ. meny ʧhildren first glimps ſhe pleʒuerꭗ ov reediŋ from liseniŋ tꙍ storiꭗ red tꙍ ſhem at scꙍl. . . . bꙍks mæd bie teeʧherꭗ and ʧhildren about ſhe dꙍiŋꭗ ov ſhe class or ov individuealꭗ in it figuer prominently amuŋ ſhe bꙍks whiʧh ʧhildren enjoi. ſhæ help ʧhildren tꙍ see meeniŋ in reediŋ and tꙍ appreeſhiæt ſhe purpos ov ritten recordꭗ.

Appendix C: Information from l.e.a.s

TABLE C/1
Sample of questionnaire sent to l.e.a.s

PRELIMINARY EVALUATION OF i.t.a.

(A research project sponsored by the Schools Council)

Questionnaire to all Directors of Education in England and Wales

1 Total number of schools within the l.e.a. which contain infant pupils.   . . . .

2 The total number of the *above* schools which are using i.t.a. with any *infant* class.   . . . .

3 (*a*) The number of schools (if any) containing infant pupils, who began to use i.t.a. but who have discontinued its use.   . . . .

   (*b*) If any school comes within the category of 3(*a*), would you be willing to supply us with the address of the school and the name of the head-teacher, in case we should require further information?   . . . .

   (yes or no)

4 The number of schools using i.t.a. with older backward readers (other than as a continuation of i.t.a. teaching begun in infant class)

   (*a*) Junior schools   . . . .

   (*b*) Secondary schools   . . . .

5 Is i.t.a. being used in circumstances other than those mentioned above? (e.g. Special Schools, Child Guidance Clinics, classes for immigrant children or adult illiterates)

   Please give details. . . . .
   . . . .
   . . . .
   . . . .

Appendix D: People who gave Verbal Evidence

TABLE D/1
Details of l.e.a. officials who gave evidence

Directors of Education	2
Advisers and Inspectors of Primary Education	28
Educational Psychologists	2
Others	3
Total:	35

TABLE D/2

Details of situations in which l.e.a. officials gave evidence

	No. of officials	No. of l.e.a.s represented
A *Individual Discussions*		
(1) In l.e.a.s in which schools were visited	12	9
(2) From l.e.a.s in which schools were not visited	8	5
Totals:	20	14
B *Group Discussion*	15	14
Grand Totals:	35	28

TABLE D/3

Schools visited

Reading Research Unit's first experiment

	Commencing date			Total
	1961	1962	1963	
Experimental schools	11	12	2	25
Control schools	7	2	—	9
Junior schools fed by experimental schools				5

Total = 39 schools

Reading Research Unit's second experiment	2
Schools with their own experiments	7
Schools using i.t.a. outside experiments	7
t.o. schools other than control schools	7
Grand total:	62*

* N.B.   The total number of schools actually visited was 46. The number tabled is greater owing to the fact that some schools fell into two categories, e.g. a school which began as a control school in 1961 and then used i.t.a. later, either as an experimental school or independently.

Teachers interviewed

A. IN SCHOOLS

Reading Research Unit's first experiment

Experimental schools	Commencing date			Total	Grand total
	1961	1962	1963		
Headteachers	10	13	4	27	
Experimental class teachers	29	27	7	63	
Other teachers	5	10	—	15	105

Control schools

	1961	1962	1963	Total	Grand total
Headteachers	8	3	—	11	
Control class teachers	10	5	—	15	26

Junior schools fed by experimental schools

	1961	1962	1963	Total	Grand total
Headteachers	4	2	—	6	
Class teachers	8	1	—	9	15

Total = 146 teachers

Reading Research Unit's second experiment

Headteachers	2	
Teachers	5	7

Schools with their own experiments

Headteachers	7	
Teachers	14	21

Schools using i.t.a. outside experiments

Headteachers	7	
Teachers	23	30

t.o. schools – other than control schools

Headteachers	7	
Teachers	15	22

B. OUTSIDE SCHOOLS   Total: 226

Approximate number of additional teachers interviewed, other than in their schools, from all over Great Britain and abroad and falling into most of the above categories.   +50

Grand total in all categories: 276

N.B. The actual number of teachers was 196 in schools and 50 outside schools, making a total of 246. The above total of teachers, in various categories, is greater than the actual total because of teachers who were able to give evidence in two categories, e.g. a teacher who was originally in charge of a control class and later in charge of an i.t.a. class.

TABLE D/5

Details of schools in those l.e.a.s from which officials gave evidence

COUNTIES

	l.e.a.	*(1)	*(2)	*(3)	*(4)	*(5)
Individual Discussions	C. 1	347	69	19.9	–	S.V.
	C. 2	208	50	24.0	–	S.V.
	C. 3	414	—	0	–	
	C. 4	820	12	1.5	–	
	C. 5	998	172	17.3	5	
Group Discussions	C. 6	377	35	9.3	–	
	C. 7	229	30	13.1	–	
	C. 8	287	16	5.6	–	
	C. 9	132	10	7.5	1	
	C.10	215	10	4.7	1	
	C.11	326	5	1.5	–	
	C.12	97	5	5.2	–	
	C.13	147	4	2.7	–	
Totals:		4,597	418		7	

COUNTY BOROUGHS (including London Boroughs)

	l.e.a.	*(1)	*(2)	*(3)	*(4)	*(5)
Individual Discussions	B. 1	36	36	100	–	S.V.
	B. 2	25	11	44	–	S.V.
	B. 3	52	14	26.9	–	S.V.
	B. 4	91	12	13.2	–	S.V.
	B. 5	24	23	95.8	–	S.V.
	B. 6	54	4	7.4	1	S.V.
	B. 7	183	12	6.6	1	S.V.
	B. 8	18	6	33.3	–	
	B. 9	166	41	24.7	–	
Group Discussions	B.10	24	12	50.0	–	
	B.11	49	12	24.5	–	
	B.12	42	9	21.4	–	
	B.13	24	8	33.3	–	
	B.14	37	7	18.9	–	
	B.15	26	4	15.4	–	
Totals:		851	211		2	
Grand Totals:	28	5,448	629		9	9

(1) The total number of schools within the l.e.a. containing infant pupils.
(2) The total number of the above schools using i.t.a. with any infant class (Summer Term 1966).
(3) The percentage of schools containing infant pupils using i.t.a. with any infant class (Summer Term 1966).
(4) The number of schools containing infant pupils who began to use i.t.a. but discontinued its use.
(5) S.V. indicates the schools in the l.e.a. were visited and discussions took place with head-teachers and members of their staff.

TABLE D/6

Lectures and conferences at which verbal evidence was obtained

Date	Venue	Details of the course or conference	Approx. No. present*
Oct–Dec 1965	University of Manchester	Course of nine lectures entitled *New Approaches to the Teaching of Reading.* Nine lecturers who were authors or supporters of different approaches to reading, including i.t.a.	250
April 1966	University of Swansea	*Annual Conference of the British Psychological Society.* Two papers on i.t.a. by John Downing and Donald Labon	560
July 1966	University of Cambridge	*Third Annual Conference of the United Kingdom Reading Association.* Papers read by John Downing and others	120
July 1966	University of Cambridge	*Third International i.t.a. Workshop and Conference.* Some 36 lectures on various aspects of i.t.a. by Block, Daffon, Downing, Gardner, Mazurkiewicz, Milne, Pitman, Tanyzer and others	200
Aug. 1966	Paris (Unesco Palace)	*First World Conference on Reading.* Lecturers of international repute representing 18 countries. Delegates from 24 countries	500
April 1967	University of London	*i.t.a. Research Evaluated.* A conference arranged by the National Foundation for Educational Research, following their publication of *The i.t.a. Symposium* (Downing, 1967). Speakers included Brimer, Diack, Downing, Elvin, Gulliford, Hemming, Merritt, Nisbet and Wall	140

* N.B.   These figures are given as an indication of the opportunities presented at these conferences for discussions about i.t.a. with teachers and other educationists.

People with whom discussions took place

SUMMARY

		Total No.
Teachers		246
l.e.a. officials		
Directors of Education	2	
Advisers and Inspectors of Primary Education	28	
Educational psychologists	2	
Others	3	35
Other visitors to schools		
Her Majesty's Inspectors	3	
University staff	6	
College of Education lecturers	10	
Remedial teachers	7	
Others	2	28
Other knowledgeable or interested people		
From the i.t.a. Foundation	2	
From the Reading Research Unit	4	
Professors and educationists from abroad	15	
Educational psychologists	6	
Linguists	6	
Publishers	8	
Others	5	46
Parents		41
	Grand total:	396

N.B.   Included in the above total were three group discussions, as follows:

(1) Advisers and Inspectors	15
(2) College of Education lecturers	8
(3) Parents	34
Total:	57

Accordingly, the number of people with whom individual discussions took place was 339.

Appendix E: Interviewing Procedures

Examples of extension questions

I   *To headteachers and class teachers in i.t.a. schools and advisers and Inspectors who had observed i.t.a. in use*

(1)   How does i.t.a. work with dull, with average and with bright children?

II *To l.e.a. advisers and inspectors*

(1) What were the characteristics of the schools which first used i.t.a. in your area?
(2) Are schools with different characteristics now using i.t.a?
(3) Which type of school has done best with i.t.a?
(4) Which type of school has done least well with i.t.a?

III *To headteachers of original i.t.a. schools*

(1) What made you decide to experiment with i.t.a?
(2) What were parents' reactions at first and now?
(3) Did changes of staff create problems?
(4) Now that you have used i.t.a. for three or four years, do you perceive any differences between the first year you used it and now?
(5) Have you any comment to make on the experiment itself?

IV *To headteachers of original control schools*

(1) What made you decide to become a control school?
(2) Have you any comment to make on the experiment itself?

V *To headteachers and class teachers of original control schools*

(1) Did you visit any i.t.a. schools?
(2) If so, what were your reactions?

VI *To headteachers of original control schools who are now using i.t.a.*

(1) What made you decide to begin to use i.t.a?

TABLE E/2

Examples of factual background questions

I *To l.e.a. officials*

(1) When did schools in this local education authority begin to use i.t.a?
(2) If the local education authority took part in a particular experiment, how many schools were original experimental schools and how many were control schools?
(3) How many of the original experimental schools are still using i.t.a?
(4) Have any of the original experimental schools ceased to use i.t.a? If so, what are the reasons?
(5) How many of the original control schools later began to use i.t.a?
(6) What is the total number of schools now using i.t.a?

II *Other visitors to schools*

(1) How many schools have you visited in which i.t.a. was being used with infants?
(2) Had you observed the reading in these same schools when they used t.o?

III *Headteachers of all schools*

(1) How old is the school?
(2) What are the occupations of the children's parents?
(3) How many children are in the school?
(4) How many teachers are there on the staff?
(5) How are the classes organised?

IV   *Headteachers of i.t.a. schools*

(1) When did you begin to use i.t.a?
(2) How many classes were using it at first?
(3) How many classes are using it now?
(4) Which reading schemes and books are used?
(5) When you used t.o. what proportion of children had completed an infant reading scheme before they were promoted to junior classes?
(6) What proportion of children who have used i.t.a. have now completed a reading scheme before they go to junior classes?
(7) What proportion of children have transferred to t.o. before they leave infant classes?

V   *Headteachers of i.t.a. experimental schools*

(1) How many visitors did you have?
(2) How often did meetings take place?
(3) Who did the testing?

VI   *Headteachers of control schools*

(1) How many visitors did you have?
(2) How many lectures and meetings were arranged for you?
(3) Who did the testing?

VII   *Headteachers of junior schools*

(1) Did you formerly test children's reading ability in t.o. as they entered your school?
(2) Do you now test children's reading ability as they enter the school? If so, how do these two sets of results compare?
(3) If the school is fed by both i.t.a. and t.o. children how do the results of the two groups of children compare?
(4) What proportion of children taught by i.t.a. are still using i.t.a. as the medium of reading when they enter the school?

VIII   *Teachers of i.t.a. classes*

(1) How long have you been using i.t.a?
(2) With what ages of children?
(3) How much experience did you have with using t.o. with the same age of children?
(4) Which t.o. reading schemes have you used?

IX   *Teachers of junior classes*

(1) Have you had previous experience of teaching this particular class at the time when the children had been taught to read by t.o?

TABLE E/3

Examples of concluding questions

I   *To headteachers and class teachers in i.t.a. schools, advisers, Inspectors and all visitors to i.t.a. schools*

(1) Can you sum up, in a few words, your general impressions of i.t.a?
(2) What do you consider to be the main advantages of i.t.a?
(3) What disadvantages have you noticed?

II   *To headteachers of i.t.a. schools*

Key Question: Do you intend to continue to use i.t.a. or will you return to t.o?

III *To class teachers in i.t.a. schools*

Key Question: If you were appointed as headteacher of a new infant school, before you could order all the necessary books you would need to reach a decision as to whether you would use i.t.a. or t.o. Which would you use?

IV *To headteachers and class teachers of the first two years in junior schools fed by i.t.a. infant schools*

Key Question: If you could decide whether the infant schools that feed your school should use i.t.a. or t.o., which would you choose?

TABLE E/4

Topics for discussion introduced at a group meeting of fifteen l.e.a. officials

I *Details of schools using i.t.a.*

(1) The type of school–all-age primary or infant, its socio-economic level and the level of intelligence of the children.

(2) The internal organisation of the schools–whether the children were grouped in age-groups or family groups, streamed or unstreamed and whether formal or informal approaches were used.

(3) The attitude of the schools to reading–an emphasis on reading or not, a belief in an early or a delayed start.

(4) The methods of reading, the materials and the procedures used.

(5) Reading standards before the use of i.t.a.

(6) The quality of the headteachers and staff.

(7) Differences, if any, between schools which first used i.t.a. and those which began to use it more recently.

(8) The reasons why schools had discarded i.t.a., if any had done so.

II *The observed results of using i.t.a.*

(1) Reading.

(2) Writing.

(3) Spelling.

(4) Other subjects or other aspects of the school life.

III *The observed advantages and disadvantages of i.t.a.*

Appendix F: Details of Certain Schools involved in Experiments

1 Details of junior schools fed by experimental schools

JUNIOR SCHOOL 1

A *Details of the school*

In this two-form entry school, in a rather poor socio-economic area, the children were in streamed classes. The headmaster stated that the school had always had a reading problem.

One class of 1961 i.t.a. experimental children were in their second junior year, while two classes of 1962 experimental children were in the first year.

B *Main points raised by the headmaster*

1 The first experimental class to enter the junior school had made 'phenomenal progress in

reading and writing'. (N.B. It was later learned that this class had been in the charge of the same teacher for three years in the infant school and that she was an 'exceptionally good teacher'.)

2   The results from the second intake of i.t.a. children were rather disappointing: 26% of the children had not transferred to t.o., as opposed to only 7% of the first intake.

3   Consequently, although the first group of children put up 'a fantastic performance', the headmaster felt he must temper this with his observations of the following year.

4   However, most children were now reading when they came into the junior school, even if it was in i.t.a.

5   The last two children from the original 1961 experimental group transferred to t.o. at Easter 1966. The dullest one of these children came from a family of whom none had previously learned to read. This child would still have another two years in the junior school and so should be a fluent reader in t.o. before he left.

6   i.t.a. does help these slower children, as well as the children of average and above average ability.

7   One advantage of i.t.a. to the junior school concerns the fact that most teachers in junior schools just do not know how to teach the beginnings of reading. Formerly, with t.o., those children who were promoted from the infant to junior school having barely made a start at reading were the teachers' biggest bugbear. With i.t.a. there are far more children, in fact nearly all, reading something. The junior teacher is then able to carry on.

8   If the headteacher had any choice in the matter, he would like to see the infant school which feeds his junior school continue with i.t.a.

JUNIOR SCHOOL 2

A   *Details of the school*
This two-form entry school, in which the children were in streamed classes, was in the charge of a headmaster. It stood in the centre of a council house estate in a poor socio-economic area. One 1961 experimental class was in the second junior year, and one 1962 experimental class in the first junior year.

B   *Main points raised by the headmaster*
1   Despite the poor area, the reading standards of children coming into the school had always been good because the infant headmistress had always been concerned about reading and was the sort of person who achieved success with any method.

2   There were rather different circumstances in the two intakes of i.t.a. children which made comparisons difficult. The 1962 children came from poorer backgrounds than the 1961 children, due to an influx of poorer families into the council house estate. Furthermore they had been taught in a much larger class in the infant school than the 1961 experimental class.

3   For many years the headmaster had tested each intake of children on Schonell's Graded Word Reading Test and so he had an objective standard of comparison of reading attainments.

4   *Conclusions regarding the 1961 children*
    (a) In the A stream, of whom about half had been i.t.a. children and half t.o., the results of Schonell's Graded Word Reading Test in t.o. were good, but no better than in previous years.
    (b) In the B stream there were fewer non-readers than ever before. Knowing the families of some of the children who were reading, the headmaster would not have expected these children to be doing so if it had not been for i.t.a. Only two children had not transferred.

(c) There were some vastly superior compositions from i.t.a. children–mainly in the A stream–compositions such as he had never seen before.

(d) He thought that the whole intake was poorer in arithmetic than formerly, in both streams. He wondered whether arithmetic time had been devoted to reading.

5 *Conclusions regarding the 1962 children*

(a) This was a disappointing year, probably because of the two features mentioned already (point B2).

(b) The A stream children had Reading Ages similar to the previous year's results.

(c) In the B stream the children's Reading Ages were not as good as in the preceding year. The results were similar to the years prior to the use of i.t.a. Nine children had not transferred. Some of the non-readers, however, were of very low intelligence and had only moved into the area less than a year before the children were transferred from the infant to the junior school.

6 The problems which he and the staff had feared, for instance the transition in spelling, had just not proved to be problems, even for B stream children.

7 It was difficult for him to judge between t.o. and i.t.a. because of the recent changes in circumstances in the area. On balance, if he could choose whether the infant school feeding his junior school should use i.t.a. or t.o., he would decide on i.t.a. because it would be easier for the children.

C *Class teachers' comments*

1 The teacher of the second-year A stream, consisting of some 1961 i.t.a. children as well as t.o. children, said that this was an exceptionally good class but that she had been particularly delighted by the reading of those children who had learned to read by means of i.t.a. The children had 'not gone off reading at all', as some people had predicted would happen. The top reading group, in the class comprising five children, had all been taught by i.t.a., and they were among the youngest children in the age-group. Their spelling was also excellent and they were interested in, and good at, all sorts of subjects.

2 The teacher of the first-year A stream, containing some 1962 i.t.a. children, had something to add to the headteacher's remarks concerning test results. She had noted that, 'Although the test scores of i.t.a. children were similar to those of the t.o. children on Schonell's Graded Word Reading Test, the i.t.a. children had more general interest in books, used the library a lot more and were really reading books and not just looking at pictures'.

JUNIOR SCHOOL 3

A *Details of the school*

This large junior school, with a four or five form entry every year, arranged the children in streamed classes. The school was built on a good council house estate. The headmistress stated that the children were of average intelligence and that most parents were interested in their children's reading progress. This junior school drew children from its own infant department (which until recently was a separate infant school using t.o.), and another infant school in an identical area, which was one of the original 1961 i.t.a. schools.

B *Main points raised by the headmistress*

1 Not only do the i.t.a. children and the t.o. children come from the same backgrounds but the teacher in the top infant class in each case is excellent. Furthermore, the junior headmistress had always been delighted with the children who were promoted from the i.t.a. school, both in the days of t.o. and now with i.t.a. The children's work was always good and they were lively and interested in everything. The children from these two schools merge in the junior classes 'as though they had always been brought up together'.

2 The results of Burt's (Rearranged) Word Reading Test for the four streams of children revealed no differences between i.t.a. and t.o. children, who were scattered about equally between the four streams.

3 The headmistress was equally satisfied with i.t.a. and t.o. children. The reading standards were the same. Neither was there any real difference in the quality or quantity of their free written work.

4 The i.t.a. children had more difficulty with spelling than the t.o. children in their first year in the junior school. In the top half of the A stream, the i.t.a. and t.o. children were equally good spellers but in the lower half of this class and in lower streams the i.t.a. children were poorer spellers.

5 The very dullest children find reading difficult whether it is with i.t.a. or with t.o. Originally, when i.t.a. children who had made practically no progress with reading entered the junior school, the teachers tried to continue with i.t.a., without much success. Now they use t.o. with this group of children on the following grounds. If children have not started to learn to read by the time they enter the junior school, they are going to be so slow at learning anyway that, in four years in the junior school they will not have time to learn i.t.a., unlearn it, and then learn t.o. Consequently they may as well learn t.o. 'and the bits that do go in and stick will be useful to them'.

6 She had not thought of changing the infant department to i.t.a. because they obtain such excellent results with t.o.

7 The original 1961 i.t.a. children are still being tested by the Reading Research Unit. The higher up the school these children go, the less point she can see in this testing. By the end of the second year, and probably even before that, the junior school has either built on to whatever was done in the infant school or rectified it. Hence, the later in the junior school the testing is carried on, the more are the results attributable to the work of the junior school than to the alphabet which the children used in the early stages of the infant school. Spelling tests afford one example: this junior school actually sets about teaching spelling and thus the results of spelling tests are the results of what the junior school has done about spelling, rather than the results of conditions in the infant school.

8 She thinks that from the infants' point of view i.t.a. probably provides a more enjoyable start to reading.

JUNIOR SCHOOL 4

A *Details of the school*

This was an old school in which children and staff were working in very poor conditions. It was a four form entry school, the children being in unstreamed classes. The school served an area of mixed socio-economic backgrounds: some children came from owner-occupied houses, but the majority were from a council house estate and a few were from extremely poor families. The headmaster thought that the children were of average intelligence. The school was fed by infant schools which used t.o. and by schools which had joined the Reading Research Unit's first experiment in 1961 and 1962.

B *Main points raised by the headmaster*

1 The first small group of 1961 i.t.a. children entered the school in September 1964. They were split up among the four unstreamed classes, made up mainly of t.o. children. The headmaster now thinks that this was a mistake.

2 The 1962 i.t.a. children numbered 27 out of a total intake of 180 children. Thirteen of the 27 i.t.a. children had not transferred to t.o. These 27 children were all placed in the same class, together with a group of t.o. children.

3 A few parents of those i.t.a. children who had not transferred, had expressed their uneasi-

ness to him on the grounds that they had expected their children to have finished with i.t.a. before they left the infant school.

4 He did not feel that he had yet had sufficient experience of i.t.a. to be able to make a judgement, but he was certainly not against it. He looked forward to the following year when the whole intake of children would have used i.t.a.

C *Additional points raised by a teacher*

1 The teacher of the first-year Junior Class, in which 27 i.t.a. children had been placed alongside t.o. children, had been faced with an extremely difficult task. In this unstreamed class, with its wide range of intelligence and attainments she had the extra problem of two alphabets. In addition, there was a group of non-readers among the t.o. children.

2 She did not find it possible to judge whether the i.t.a. children in her class were better or worse than the t.o. children.

3 There was a book problem in this class because they only had a small proportion of i.t.a. books.

4 Basically she approved of the idea of i.t.a. and would have welcomed the opportunity of trying it in the initial stages with a group of children. Having seen the complications in her current class she was not quite as enthusiastic at the end of the year as she had been at the beginning.

JUNIOR SCHOOL 5

A *Details of the school*

The children in this two-stream entry school mostly came from a council house estate, although there were a few middle-class families. The headmaster considered the level of intelligence to be just below average. The school was fed by both t.o. and i.t.a. children; the latter were from the 1962 experimental group and so were in their first junior year.

B *Main comments of headmaster*

1 Of the non-readers who entered this junior school, those most receptive to teaching were the children who had come from the i.t.a. group. They were more ready to learn to read than the children coming from the t.o. school.

2 i.t.a. children, even when they had not got very far, had better attitudes to reading than the t.o. children.

3 Only a few teachers in the school could teach i.t.a. sympathetically and it was important that the i.t.a. children should be put with them.

2 **Details of junior classes in all-age primary schools**

PRIMARY SCHOOLS 6 AND 7

These two schools were similar in that they were both situated in very poor socio-economic areas, where 'reading had always been a struggle'. Comments from the headmistress of one school and the first-year junior teacher in the other school are listed.

A *Main points raised by one headmistress*

1 They always had backward readers in this school, in every class, even non-readers at 11 +. The headmistress was always having groups of older backward readers in her room to give them some phonic training.

2 After using i.t.a. not one non-reader left the infant classes to go into the first junior class. Even the poorest child was able to read in i.t.a.

3 She would never go back to t.o. now.

B *Comments of a first-year junior teacher*

1   A much smaller number of non-readers was now coming up from the infant classes. When she received her current class, all but two had transferred to t.o. She had always tested children every year on Schonell's Graded Word Reading Test. Formerly many children could not even attempt the test. Now they could all do some of it in t.o.

2   There was an improvement in the free writing. The teacher could read what the children had written and the children could read their own work.

3   Even E.S.N. children made some progress in reading and writing because i.t.a. was so logical.

4   Children were becoming more independent, even the slowest of them.

5   She was 'sold on i.t.a.–hook, line and sinker'.

PRIMARY SCHOOL 8

The headmaster of this all-age primary school, who had five years' experience of i.t.a., expressed his opinion that children who had learned to read using i.t.a. were neither better nor worse at spelling than children who had learned to read using t.o. He said:

'I am surprised that the spelling in the junior classes isn't better. I would have thought that i.t.a. would have made children into better spellers. Not that i.t.a. children are worse spellers; they are the same standard as children used to be when they were taught by t.o.–the spelling tests which I have always given as children came up to the junior classes show this.'

PRIMARY SCHOOLS 9 AND 10

Although in these two schools children from the 1962 experimental infant classes had reached first-year junior classes, the only two definite comments made regarding the effects of i.t.a. noted in junior children, were as follows:

'The transition in writing is a problem. In the infant classes the children have gone on and on writing. It is difficult for the junior class teacher when order has to be brought into it– sentences, capital letters and so on.'

'Children who have ability are working at no higher level than in the days of t.o. but slower children have gained.'

Nevertheless, despite the remarks quoted in the foregoing three schools, the headmasters intended to go on using i.t.a., the reasons they gave referring to its advantages for infants.

3   **Details of schools with their own experiments**

SCHOOL E.I

This school had been one of the experimental schools in the Reading Research Unit's first experiment in 1961. During the first year the children's reading had gone ahead, the reading standards being better than previous reading standards when t.o. had been used. By 1964, however, the headmistress had reached the following conclusions:

(*a*) i.t.a. was of most value for bright children.

(*b*) It was not necessarily the answer for the slowest group of children, although, when they did really grasp it, they went ahead.

(*c*) Some of the middle group of children, having started quite well, then seemed to 'get bogged down' before they made the transfer. The headmistress commented, 'Something didn't seem to be working properly, although I couldn't quite put my finger on it'.

Consequently, she started her own experiment by forming two vertically grouped classes of five- and six-year-olds, both using the *Janet and John* reading scheme, but one in t.o. and the other in i.t.a. During the year, the i.t.a. children began to read earlier than the t.o. children and got through the reading scheme more quickly. Yet the headmistress still had her doubts about the slower and middle groups of children as outlined above. When seen by the interviewer, she had finally decided that, in the next school year, she would adopt the following procedure:

(*a*) All children entering the school would begin with i.t.a. and at the end of a year she would review each child's progress.

(*b*) Children who were fluent in i.t.a. would continue with it.

(*c*) Children who had not really made a start with i.t.a. would then be started on t.o.

(*d*) The middle group of children could go on with i.t.a. until they became bogged down and lost their fluency, as for instance when they began to read the later books in the *Janet and John* scheme, then they would be transferred to t.o.

Regarding this fourth point, the headmistress indicated that she had previously tried this procedure successfully. When the children had begun to lose their fluency in i.t.a. because the content of the books was too hard for them, she had given them very simple t.o. books which they had read fluently. She had also taken a few children who had reached the top of the infant school, 'having got nowhere on i.t.a.', turned them over to t.o. and they had gone ahead. Now she sees that every child has been transferred to t.o. before he leaves the school.

This headteacher's views were of particular interest in that she had five years' experience of i.t.a., of which the last two were concerned with her own experiments. Her points about the transfer give food for thought. She described the advantages of i.t.a. as follows:

(*a*) The children read fluently as soon as they get over the initial difficulties.

(*b*) They read 'sense', not just words.

(*c*) They really read library books, not just look at the pictures.

(*d*) The creative writing is better.

She saw two main disadvantages:

(1) It is no good for the slow readers – the really backward ones.

(2) It is time-wasting for the teacher of the transfer class who has to write everything in two alphabets.

Her summing up was: 'I think that it's worth starting with i.t.a. to see how far children will go. I'm also keen on it because of the free writing which comes with it.'

Details of the discussions with two of the teachers in this school round out the headteacher's comments. One was a teacher experienced in both t.o. and i.t.a. She had used i.t.a. for three years, then taken the school's own t.o. experimental class for one year and was currently in charge of the school's own i.t.a. experimental class. She was extremely interested in reading and talked in a carefully considered manner about t.o. and i.t.a. She was certainly not a dogmatic person and stressed that she had used i.t.a. with an open mind. When asked which group she had most enjoyed teaching, she replied that she had been interested in both. Having had experience of these two experimental classes, her conclusions were that her t.o. children last year were as good at reading as the i.t.a. children this year. On the other hand, the children found writing stories and news easier in i.t.a., and did so with greater fluency. The main disadvantage about i.t.a. was that the teacher is slowed up when some of her children begin to transfer. She also stated that she was somewhat disillusioned because i.t.a. did not help the slowest children. This teacher was one who replied 't.o.' to the key question of what she would use if she became headmistress of an infant school.

The second teacher was also an experienced teacher, who had used i.t.a. for five years. She thought i.t.a. was much easier for children and she was pleased by their keenness to read and by their abundant free writing. She stated that she was 'very enthusiastic about i.t.a.', although as she pointed out, she had only used it with five-year-olds and so had no experience of the transition. When she was asked the 'key question', the result was surprising. She did not say 'i.t.a.', as one would have expected but replied that she was not sure: perhaps she would use both i.t.a. and t.o., as in the current experiment in the school.

SCHOOL E.2

This school had been an original control school in the Reading Research Unit's experiment in 1961. In 1962, the headmistress had wanted to start i.t.a. but only one member of the staff was keen so the idea was left for a year. Then in 1963 they began their own experiment with one i.t.a. class and one t.o. class of reception children. The children came from an exceptionally poor area and were in classes of 40. Both classes used the *Janet and John* reading scheme. The system of allocating the new children alternately to i.t.a. and t.o. classes had been continued in succeeding years.

In this school the headmistress stated that there was no pressure on making children read, whether in t.o. or i.t.a., for as she said, there are many other things in the school besides reading. Yet the children did read and write well, in fact, exceptionally well for children coming from such poor home backgrounds. This was true in t.o. and i.t.a. classes alike, as the interviewer observed when she visited all nine classes in the school. In every class the standards of reading and writing were good and all the children were obviously enjoying reading. It was one of those schools in which the whole ethos was so delightful that it was a pleasure to visit it. There was a calm, happy atmosphere everywhere and both the headteacher and the staff were clearly much more concerned about the individual children, their needs and all-round development, than in being partisan about i.t.a. and t.o.

The headteacher confirmed what the four teachers who had used i.t.a. said, that all but one of them had been rather reluctant to try i.t.a. at first but that all now approved of it. It was also stated that the children were keen on i.t.a. although, as already noted, both t.o. and i.t.a. children appeared to be doing well in this school. Of the 132 children who were due to be promoted to the Junior School at the end of the term, only five had not got very far with reading. They could recognise some words on a look-and-say basis but could not yet do any word-building. Four of the five were from the t.o. class and one from the i.t.a. class. Three of the five were going to an E.S.N. school.

When asked whether she had thought of using i.t.a. for all children, the headmistress replied that she thought their experience of i.t.a. was still too short to make a decision. Also, they had a school full of t.o. books. She would like to carry on using both alphabets for a few years until she had what she took to be conclusive evidence, although she was then satisfied that i.t.a. was best.

When the four teachers who had used i.t.a. were asked whether, if they became heads of infant schools, they would use i.t.a. or t.o., three replied that they would use i.t.a., on the grounds that children enjoy reading so much more and that they don't get stuck. The fourth teacher, who was the original keen one, said that if it were a one-form entry school she would use i.t.a. If it were a larger school, she would use both i.t.a. and t.o. because this was so stimulating for the teachers.

SCHOOLS E.3 AND E.4

These two schools were similar in that the classes in both were vertically grouped. In addition, each headmistress stressed that she believed in a delayed start to reading and, accordingly, did not feel ready to sum up her conclusions regarding the experiment after just over two years. When a school believes in delaying the beginning of reading, it naturally follows that appraisals of reading approaches must be postponed until the very end of the infant school.

In discussions with the three teachers who had used i.t.a. in these schools, all indicated that they would use i.t.a. if they became heads of infant schools.

In the remaining three schools, which had been running their experiments for a little over two years, the headteachers had already made up their minds about i.t.a., and in each case the result was approval. One headmistress had already started another reception class on i.t.a. and thought that eventually she would turn the whole school over to it. A second headmistress spoke on these lines:

> 'From a reading point of view, I have no hesitation in approving of i.t.a. There are fewer children who are not reading when they leave the admission class. All the children have read more books and their attack on words is better. i.t.a. also helps free written work. I should not like to think of dropping i.t.a., although at present it is useful to have a t.o. class so that if parents really don't want a child to do i.t.a. he can go into this class.'

The third headmistress began by stating that she thoroughly approved of i.t.a. and that at the beginning of the next school year she would start all children on i.t.a. The reasons for her approval were as follows:

(*a*) It is easier for children.

(*b*) Teachers get an earlier response from children.

(*c*) The reading and writing certainly go ahead much earlier.

(*d*) The children become more self-reliant.

(*e*) There is a marked difference between the t.o. and i.t.a. classes in their general attitudes; it is this general effect on the children which is most important.

The teachers who had used i.t.a. in these three schools would all choose to use i.t.a., in preference to t.o., if they became heads of infant schools.

Appendix G: A Selected Bibliography 1967-9

BLOCK, J. R. (1968). Criticisms of i.t.a. In BLOCK, J. R. (ed.), *i.t.a. as a Language Arts Medium*. Toronto: Pitman

DOWNING, J. (1967). E.S.N. school teachers assess i.t.a. *Special Education*, **56**, 12–16

DOWNING, J. (1967). The effects of the Initial Teaching Alphabet on Educationally Sub-Normal pupils–A survey of teachers' reports. *The Slow Learning Child*, **13**, 164–75

DOWNING, J. (1967). The effects of the Initial Teaching Alphabet (i.t.a.) on young children's written composition. *Educational Research*, **9**, 137–144

DOWNING, J. (1967). Can i.t.a. be improved? *Elementary English*, **44**, 849–855

DOWNING, J. (1967). *Evaluating the Initial Teaching Alphabet*. London: Cassell

DOWNING, J. (1968). Conclusions and recommendations from the British i.t.a. research. *Reading Teacher*, **21**, 640–46

DOWNING, J. (1968). Seven years of i.t.a. in Britain: results, conclusions and implications. *The Peabody Reflector*, **41**, 85–88

DOWNING, J. (1968). Some difficulties in transfer of learning from i.t.a. to t.o. In FIGUREL, J. A. (ed.), *Forging Ahead in Reading*. Newark, Delaware: International Reading Association

DOWNING, J. (1969). Initial Teaching Alphabet: results after six years. *Elementary School Journal*, **69**, No. 5

DOWNING, J. (1969). An educational theory for i.t.a. *New University*, April 1969

DOWNING, J., CARTWRIGHT, D., JONES, B. and LATHAM, W. (1967). Methodological problems in the British i.t.a. research. *Reading Research Quarterly*, **3**, 85–100

DUNN, L. M. (1968). The efficacy of the Initial Teaching Alphabet and the Peabody Language Development Kits with southern disadvantaged children in the Primary Grades: A final report after three years. In BLOCK, J. R. (ed.), *i.t.a. as a Language Arts Medium*. Toronto: Pitman

FRY, E. (1967). The diacritical marking system and a preliminary comparison with i.t.a. In DOWNING, J. and BROWN, A. L. (eds.), *The Second International Reading Symposium*. London: Cassell

FRY, E. (1967). First grade reading instruction using diacritical marking system, initial teaching alphabet and basal reading system–Extended to second grade. *The Reading Teacher*, **20**, No. 8, 687–93

FRY, E. (1969). Comparison of beginning reading with i.t.a., D.M.S. and t.o. after three years. *The Reading Teacher*, **22**, No. 4, 357–62

HARRISON, M. (1967). *Teaching Reading–an i.t.a. Approach*. London: Initial Teaching Publishing Co.

HARRISON, M. (1968). *Seven Years of i.t.a. in Oldham*. London: i.t.a. Foundation

HAYES, T. B. and WUEST, R. C. (1968). A three year look at i.t.a. In BLOCK, J. R. (ed.), *i.t.a. as a Language Arts Medium*. Toronto: Pitman

LEIGH, T. (1967). *i.t.a. in the Classroom*. Edinburgh: Chambers

MAZURKIEWICZ, A. J. (1968). Fourth year results–Bethlehem i.t.a. study. In BLOCK, J. R. (ed.), *i.t.a. as a Language Arts Medium*. Toronto: Pitman

MAZURKIEWICZ, A. J., MCNERNEY, R. E. and STEWART, R. W. (1969). *A Fifth Year Report of the i.t.a. Language Arts 1967–8 Study*. Bethlehem Area School District

MILNE, A. and FYFE, T. W. (1969). An attempt to control and assess the teacher variable in reading research. *Reading*, **3**, No. 1, 22–7

O'DONNELL, M. and SMITH, S. (1968). St Bonaventure's Infant School and St Bonaventure's Junior School. *i.t.a. Journal*, No. 12. London: i.t.a. Foundation

PITMAN, J. (1969). *Alphabets and Reading*. London: Pitman

RIEMER, G. (1968). The Great Grade School Scandal. In BLOCK, J. R. (ed.), *i.t.a. as a Language Arts Medium*. Toronto: Pitman

RIEMER, G. (1969). *How they Murdered the Second R*. New York: Norton

SHAPIRO, B. J. and WILLFORD, R. E. (1968). i.t.a.–kindergarten or first grade? In BLOCK, J. R. (ed.), *i.t.a. as a Language Arts Medium*. Toronto: Pitman

SHAPIRO, B. J. and WILLFORD, R. E. (1968). The effects of three different methods of transition on tested reading achievement. In BLOCK, J. R. (ed.), *i.t.a. as a Language Arts Medium*. Toronto: Pitman

STEWART, J. R. (1968). The Language Arts Curriculum–after i.t.a. In BLOCK, J. R. (ed.), *i.t.a. as a Language Arts Medium*. Toronto: Pitman

TANYZER, H. J., ALPERT, H. and SANDEL, L. (1968). The effect of i.t.a. and t.o. when beginning reading instruction in the kindergarten. In BLOCK, J. R. (ed.), *i.t.a. as a Language Arts Medium*. Toronto: Pitman

TANYZER, H. J., ALPERT, H. and SANDEL, L. (1968). The effects of transition from i.t.a. to t.o. on reading and spelling achievement. In BLOCK, J. R. (ed.), *i.t.a. as a Language Arts Medium*. Toronto: Pitman

TANYZER, H. J. ALPERT, H. and SANDEL, L. (1968). A comparison between the oral and written responses of first grade children in i.t.a. and t.o. classes. In BLOCK, J. R. (ed.), *i.t.a. as a Language Arts Medium*. Toronto: Pitman

INDEX

Index